MORMON MISSIONARIES
ENTER EASTERN EUROPE

Studies in Latter-day Saint History

An imprint of BYU Studies and the
Joseph Fielding Smith Institute for Latter-day Saint History

Brigham Young University
Provo, Utah

MORMON MISSIONARIES
ENTER EASTERN EUROPE

Kahlile B. Mehr

with excerpts from Mischa Markow's Missionary Journals,
edited by Matthew K. Heiss

Brigham Young University Press, Provo, Utah, and
Deseret Book, Salt Lake City, Utah

This volume is part of the Smith Institute and BYU Studies series
Studies in Latter-day Saint History.

Also in this series
Nearly Everything Imaginable: The Everyday Life of Utah's Mormon Pioneers

Voyages of Faith: Explorations in Mormon Pacific History

Trial Furnace: Southern Utah's Iron Mission

To contact BYU Studies, write to
403 CB, Brigham Young University, PO Box 24098, Provo, Utah 84602.
To contact the Joseph Fielding Smith Institute for Latter-day Saint History, write to 121 KMB, Brigham Young University, Provo, Utah 84602.

Library of Congress Cataloging-in-Publication Data
Mehr, Kahlile B.
Mormon missionaries enter Eastern Europe / Kahlile Mehr ; with excerpts from Mischa Markow's missionary journals, edited by Matthew K. Heiss.
p. cm. — (Studies in Latter-day Saint history)
Includes bibliographical references and index.
ISBN 0-8425-2482-7 — ISBN 0-8425-2508-4 (pbk.)
1. Mormon missionaries—Europe, Eastern—History—20th century. 2. Church of Jesus Christ of Latter-day Saints—Missions—Europe, Eastern—History—20th century. I. Markow, Mischa, b. 1854. II. Heiss, Matthew K. (Matthew Kevin), b. 1957. III. Title. IV. Series.
BX8661 .M44 2002
266'.9343—dc21
2002071120

Printed in the United States of America
10 9 8 7 6 5 4 3 2 1

Contents

Illustrations

Preface

Over twenty years ago, I became fascinated with the possibility of the Church being established in the Communist world. At that time, this dream was only a distant hope. Over the years, I have conducted numerous interviews and published various articles on central and eastern European Latter-day Saint history in journals and magazines. Those articles constitute about a third of the present volume. Even so, I have reworked this material considerably and expanded my research to provide readers with a single, comprehensive volume on the subject.

This book opens new windows of understanding, even though much of the documentation for these recent developments is nonexistent or currently unavailable. The introduction of the gospel into Communist-dominated Europe was not publicized as it occurred. In fact, Church officials scrupulously avoided publicity, which could have become an uncontrolled factor operating against its initiatives; this concern is not entirely gone. News of significant events was generally preserved, but many sensitive communications and developments will not be made public for years. Writing the story of those dramatic, recent events also runs the risk of publicly portraying the acts of people who are still living. I have sought to preserve confidentiality and avoid embarrassment to the living while still providing an objective presentation of the events.

I greatly benefitted from the oral histories, conducted by Matthew Heiss and others, that are part of the James H. Moyle Oral History Collection at the archives of The Church of Jesus Christ of Latter-day Saints. Several people read various drafts of the manuscript and provided helpful suggestions. Stanley B. Kimball, professor emeritus of history at the University of Illinois at Urbana–Champaign, read and ruthlessly marked the manuscript. Edwin B. Morrell, professor emeritus of political science at Brigham Young University, also offered recommendations.

Elder Spencer J. Condie read many of the chapters and added valuable perspective and comments. I appreciate the efforts of David Stewart, who compiled and distributed information on events as they occurred in central and eastern Europe. Many unsung and unknown editors have improved the previously published material that is now included in this volume—I thank them as well. Likewise, I appreciate the editorial staff of BYU Studies, primarily Heather Seferovich, Marny Parkin, Amy Felix, and Emilee Wood. Finally, I express thanks to my wife, Marolyn, who supports me in all my endeavors.

Introduction

In the nineteenth century, leaders of The Church of Jesus Christ of Latter-day Saints anticipated the day when they could take the gospel to all nations, including those in central and eastern Europe. But given the Church's small membership (less than 285,000 in 1900) and the meager financial resources of the Saints, missionaries tended to concentrate their labors in North America, the South Pacific, and northern Europe—all sites of early conversion successes. The members' limited foreign language skills, combined with the obstacles of cultural differences and entrenched religious traditions in unfamiliar countries, also delayed missionary work in places such as central and eastern Europe.

Undaunted by such challenges, a few elders ventured eastward in Europe. By the late 1880s, Elder Jacob Spori, president of the Turkish Mission, taught a Hungarian named Mischa Markow, who soon asked for baptism. This new member essentially laid the foundation for proselytizing in central and eastern Europe. Because of his knowledge of several European languages and his zeal for sharing his religion, Brother Markow served multiple missions to various central and eastern European countries. A few dozen missionaries followed him into these countries in the ensuing decades. Entering these new areas did not translate immediately into large numbers of conversions; to the contrary, it typically ensured persecution, arrest, and often banishment. The Church's only success during the first half of the twentieth century was a small enclave of faithful Church members in Czechoslovakia.

As the century progressed, the powerful influence of entrenched religious orthodoxy was succeeded by the stranglehold of Communist atheism. Together, they precluded the populace from considering a new faith from the West. Under Communism, couple missionaries—who were less visible and less threatening to the political authorities—typically represented the Church. These couples quietly sustained the handful of Church members, responded to questions from the public, and baptized a few people in diverse locations. Soon small congregations came into being. Both members and missionaries who pioneered the Church in Communist countries had to base their belief in the Church on testimony alone because the fellowship of believers living gospel principles and worshipping together did not exist. Rather, these pioneers had to overcome daunting obstacles to create the ambiance of a faithful community. The faithful enclave survived quietly in Czechoslovakia under a Communist regime.

In 1978 young missionaries entered Yugoslavia, breaching the Iron Curtain that isolated central and eastern Europe politically, economically, and socially from the West. As Communist power abated, young missionaries also entered Hungary (1987), Poland (1988), Estonia (1989), Russia, Czechoslovakia, Ukraine, Bulgaria, Romania (1990), Latvia, Lithuania, Albania (1992), Belarus (1993), Armenia (1994),[1] and Moldova (1997). Concurrently, Church leaders mounted an impressive welfare effort, addressing the temporal needs of countries set adrift by the demise of an established system with nothing to replace it. The volunteer time of humanitarian service workers and welfare donations from the Church helped many Saints and others through the perilous economic turmoil that continued to pervade that region as the twentieth century closed.

The year 1999 was a significant anniversary for the Church in central and eastern Europe for three reasons. First, it marked the centennial of Mischa Markow's service there as a missionary, the first to be so assigned. He labored in Serbia, Hungary, Romania, and Bulgaria and succeeded in establishing a temporary branch at Temesvár, Hungary (now Timişoara, Romania). Second, 1999 commemorated the seventieth anniversary of Elder John A. Widtsoe's 1929 dedication of Czechoslovakia for preaching the gospel and the establishment of the Czechoslovak Mission, the Church's first Slavic mission. Third, 1999 signaled the end of a decade since the Berlin Wall fell in 1989.

This book focuses on the Church's formative years in Communist-dominated Europe before its missions took root in the 1990s and the Church's regular programs were formally established. Church leaders often took active roles in these countries before receiving government recognition as a religion. Lack of official recognition did not preclude the Church's presence, but it did limit its ability to own property, proselytize publicly, and operate normally. When political recognition came, Church leaders proceeded to increase the missionary force, establish congregations, and strengthen the members.

East Germany is omitted from this volume. The large number of Church members there as compared to elsewhere in the former Soviet bloc is not typical of the Mormon experience in the rest of the Communist world. Furthermore, East German members could meet openly, though with circumspection, while members in the other countries covered by this volume were isolated and worshipped primarily as individuals.[2]

Missionaries serving in the new missions of central and eastern Europe experienced a recurring pattern: they typically had high numbers of baptisms at first, but the numbers soon diminished and then leveled off. Early converts seem to have been as interested in the fact that the missionaries represented the unknown West as much as an unknown religion. They were eager to learn about that which they had been denied for seventy years. In time, the commitment needed to remain faithful in the Church winnowed the membership. Missionaries who taught constantly at first had to resort to more traditional efforts, such as visiting door-to-door and trying to interest new contacts in their message. Still, the progress has been exciting. At the end of 2001, approximately thirty-two thousand members live in countries where there were only hundreds prior to 1989.

Notes

1. Armenia is included, although it is geographically separated from the other countries covered in this volume, because it was part of the Church's eastward push.

2. For a brief overview of the Church in East Germany, see Douglas F. Tobler, "Before the Wall Fell: Mormons in the German Democratic Republic, 1945–89," *Dialogue* 25 (winter 1992): 11–30. Two recently published books also document Church history in East Germany: Garold N. Davis and Norma S. Davis, *Behind the Iron Curtain: Recollections of Latter-day Saints in East Germany, 1945–1989* (Provo, Utah: BYU Studies, 1996); and Thomas S. Monson, *Faith Rewarded: A Personal Account of Prophetic Promises to the East German Saints* (Salt Lake City: Deseret Book, 1996).

1

Empires of the East

1865–1917

T he efforts of leaders in The Church of Jesus Christ of Latter-day Saints to move eastward in Europe before World War I were diffuse and the barriers overwhelming. The native religious establishment was embedded in both the culture and its government. Religious leaders showed little tolerance for creeds that threatened their hegemony, and civil leaders supported their battle against heretical intrusions with imprisonment, fines, and deportation. At the same time, the population was largely uneducated and agrarian. Citizens were not generally disposed to question authority, either ecclesiastical or civil. These barriers stemmed the meager missionary effort. A few congregations were organized but did not survive. As was common in the nineteenth century, some converts emigrated to Utah, while a few scattered members remained faithful, though isolated, from the main body of the Church. In brief, the initial Church emissaries to central and eastern Europe confronted the powerful and ingrained traditions of the Austro-Hungarian and Russian Empires.

Religious Creeds of Imperial Austro-Hungary

The Hapsburg dynasty dominated central Europe from the thirteenth to the twentieth centuries—a total of nearly seven hundred years—from the middle ages to the Ottoman invasion, to the Napoleonic wars, and dissolved only in the catastrophe of World War I. Between 1806 and 1815, the Hapsburg emperors were forced to retreat in the face of Napoleonic armies. But with Napoleon's defeat, the Hapsburg emperor, ruling from Vienna, controlled the territory of the modern day Czech Republic, Slovakia, Hungary, Slovenia, Croatia, and parts of Poland, Ukraine, and Romania (illus. 1-1). Hungarians sought independence throughout the nineteenth century and eventually achieved co-equal power in 1867.

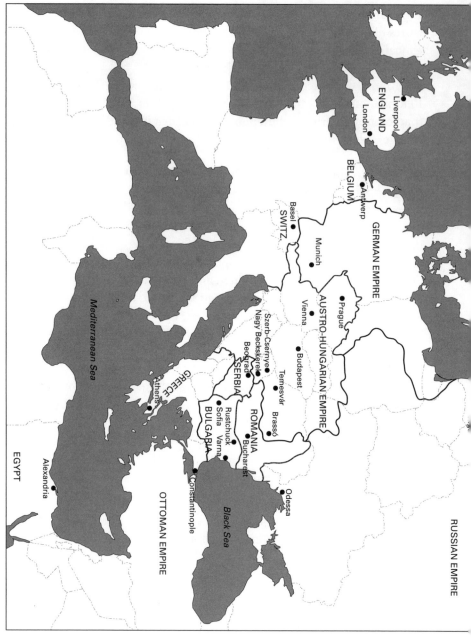

Illus. 1-1. Map of nineteenth-century Europe.

Renamed Austro-Hungary, the Empire "effectively became two states joined in personal union through a common monarch (the Hapsburg emperor of Austria and king of Hungary)." The empire shared "ministries of foreign affairs, war, and finance." And both nation-states held annual conventions of "delegates from the separate parliaments in Vienna and Budapest" that resolved mutual concerns (illus. 1-2).[1]

Roman Catholicism prevailed for many years prior to the Protestant Reformation in the early 1500s. However, reformer Jan Hus in Bohemia (part of the modern Czech Republic) succeeded in creating a climate for change early in the 1400s. His movement, and the United Brethren who broke from the Hussites in 1467, preceded the general Reformation that engulfed Europe during the years 1520–60. Lutherans and Reformed Protestants made some in-roads into the Empire, but the Catholic Counter-Reformation, on the heels of the Reformation, succeeded in returning much of the Empire to Catholicism. Many Protestants fled, but the religion maintained a toehold in Hungary despite the Empire's Catholic status.

Extending southeast from this empire is the Balkan peninsula. During the fifteenth century, the Ottomans, ruling from Istanbul (formerly Constantinople), enslaved the inhabitants of this area. Four centuries later, various nations began to emerge and achieve their autonomy. The first such nation was Serbia, which gained a measure of self-government

Courtesy Kahlile B. Mehr

Illus. 1-2. The Imperial Palace of the Austro-Hungarian Empire, Vienna, Austria.

in 1817. With the Ottoman defeat in the Russo-Turkish War of 1828–29, Greece gained independence, Serbian autonomy was strengthened, and two provinces west of the Black Sea, Walachia and Moldavia, gained their autonomy. These two provinces joined to form Romania in 1862. After another Ottoman defeat in the Russo-Turkish War of 1877–78, Bulgaria, Serbia, and Romania became fully independent.[2]

Eastern Orthodoxy was the dominant religion in southeast Europe. Orthodoxy derived from the form of Christianity that arose in the eastern half of the Roman Empire. Its center was Constantinople, founded in the fourth century by Constantine, who accepted Christianity and the religion of the Roman Empire. Unlike Roman Catholicism, Orthodox churches were roughly coterminal with the nations where they existed and not subject to a single central authority, such as the pope in Rome.

Mormon Missionaries Enter Austro-Hungary

Political authority and religious tradition, entrenched for centuries in Austro-Hungary and the Balkans, boded poorly for any messenger from America, much less the unknown territory of Utah. The entities of state and church sustained each other to maintain a status quo that ensured the privileges of those in power.

In 1865, Elders Orson Pratt and William W. Riter attempted to preach in Vienna, capital of the Austrian Empire renamed Austro-Hungary just two years later. But they had little success because, as Elder Pratt wrote home to Juliaet, his wife, "No one is permitted to teach any religion but the Catholic, either publicly or privately, under heavy penalties."[3] Austro-Hungary survived for another half century as a vast expanse of territory where civil and ecclesiastical authorities opposed the preaching of new ideas that threatened the existing social order and their hegemony.

William Maxwell Evarts, U.S. Secretary of State in 1879, predisposed Austro-Hungary against the Church when he published a circular to U.S. diplomatic officers in Europe requesting that they encourage foreign officials to thwart Latter-day Saints from converting foreign nationals to the Mormon "system of Polygamy." The Austro-Hungarian minister of foreign affairs, Count Gyula Andrássy, forwarded this advice to all governors in the Empire.[4] The letter undoubtedly remained on the books and lingered in the minds of the magistrates.

In 1883 the next set of Mormon missionaries entered Vienna. Thomas Biesinger[5] of Lehi, Utah, and Paul E. B. Hammer[6] of Salt Lake

City proselytized in Vienna from November 1883 to March 1884, baptizing three. Chance of further success was suddenly curtailed when the government, suspecting a socialist uprising, put Vienna under martial law. This meant arrest and deportation of all foreigners. Consequently, the missionaries separated to increase their chances of evasion. Elder Biesinger journeyed northward to Prague, capital of Bohemia and a major center of the western Slavs, while Elder Hammer stayed briefly in Vienna and then went to Silesia in East Germany.[7]

Elder Biesinger did not preach openly in Prague. Instead, he approached people in casual conversation, testing their interest in learning about a new religion. He remained incognito for only a month before getting arrested. He languished in jail for thirty-eight days before being brought to court and questioned. He later wrote, "In answering their questions, I had a tolerable good chance to explain the principles of the gospel and bear my testimony." The court convicted him of a misdemeanor for teaching a religion that conflicted with the laws of the land and the prevailing moral code, an obvious allusion to polygamy. The prosecution cited Evart's circular letter of 1879 to bolster the state's case.

After his conviction, Biesinger remained in jail for another thirty days. Released but not banished, he chose to continue preaching. On the day of Biesinger's departure, June 21, 1884, he baptized Antonín Just. Ironically, Just had been one of those whose accusation had sent him to jail. The historical records make no further mention of this first convert in Slavic Europe.

Elder Biesinger preached in Switzerland for several months and then, in February 1885, headed east again, this time to Budapest, Hungary, where he was joined by Elder James E. Jennings. To avoid confrontation with the authorities, they used the same tactics Biesinger had used in Prague: engaging passers-by in casual conversation with the hope of digressing into a religious discussion. Although they avoided notice by officials, they were unable to interest anyone in their message. After a little more than a month's effort, the two missionaries despaired and departed— Biesinger to Bavaria and Jennings to Vienna.[8] Nevertheless, Elder Biesinger's voice would be heard again, in the next century, in Prague under circumstances reversed from those of the nineteenth century.

Mischa Markow Hears an "Angel"

While the fate of Antonín Just is unknown, the second convert in eastern Europe made a lasting mark. Mischa Markow, a barber from

Szerb-Csernye, Hungary (today Srpska Crnja, Serbia), joined the Church in 1887 and subsequently began preaching in many areas of eastern Europe (see chapter 10). Exhibiting tenacity and faith, he baptized new members in Hungary, Romania, and Bulgaria.

As an adult, Markow had been religiously inclined (illus. 1-3). In 1886, at age thirty-two, he traveled to Jerusalem as a Serbian Orthodox pilgrim. He then continued to Alexandria, Egypt, to ply his trade while pursuing a study of the Bible. After eight months, Markow decided against continuing in the Orthodox church and began praying to find the true church. He decided to search for such a church in the cosmopolitan Ottoman capital city of Constantinople (today Istanbul, Turkey), situated astride the conjunction of Asia and Europe between the Black and Mediterranean seas.[9]

Jacob Spori[10] had proselytized in Constantinople, Jerusalem, and the seaports of Haifa and Jaffa in Palestine for two years when he had a dream of preaching to a man in Alexandria, Egypt. He sailed there in January 1887 and searched fruitlessly for three days. Having booked passage to Constantinople, he was standing on the steamer's deck when he saw

Markow coming up the gangplank and felt he had found the man from his dream. Spori introduced himself and told Markow of his vision. The Serbian pilgrim recorded: "He start[ed] to Preach the Gospel to me and I [th]ought he was an Angel so did [he] appear to me." When the two arrived in Constantinople, they were joined by Elders Ferdinand F. Hintze[11] and Joseph M. Tanner. Hintze baptized Markow in the Black Sea, and Tanner confirmed him on February 1, 1887. Though not yet called as a missionary, Markow returned home to Hungary to share the gospel message with his family. When some of them responded positively, the elated Markow telegraphed Elder Hintze to come at once.[12]

Courtesy Church Archives

Illus. 1-3. Mischa Markow (1854–1934), a native of Hungary, joined the Church in 1887. Between 1899 and 1905, he served two missions covering central and eastern Europe including Russia.

Ferdinand Hintze Visits the Markow Family

Iron wheels clanked on ties, wind scratched past windows, a swaying passenger wagon groaned, and a steamer engine chugged rhythmically. The train headed west, traversing the massive gorge known as the Iron Gate, a slit in the Carpathians through which the Danube flows on its course to the Black Sea. Markow's hometown was still a day's journey ahead, even after six days of travel. Hintze's March 1888 visit was the first of several sporadic preaching ventures in eastern Europe before World War I that spawned numerous short-lived outposts. The missionaries encountered barriers that bent little and ultimately hardened against them. Of the handful of converts who accepted baptism, most emigrated to America to join the body of the Church.

Elder Hintze (illus. 1-4) entered Hungary three years after Biesinger and Jennings. Taking a steamer from Constantinople to the Bulgarian port of Varna on the Black Sea, he then journeyed by rail to Rustchuck (today Ruse, Bulgaria), crossed the frozen Danube, and finally boarded a train to Bucharest, Romania. From there, Hintze journeyed to the Hungarian border, through the Iron Gate. Detraining in Hatzfeld (now Jimbolia, Romania) just west of the larger metropolis of Temesvár (now Timişoara, Romania), he headed south, traversing the final five miles on foot.[13]

After the week-long journey, Elder Hintze entered Markow's Hungarian village. To his astonishment, Brother Markow reported that his family's desire to be baptized had cooled.[14] Elder Hintze salvaged some benefit from the journey, however, by ordaining Markow to the priesthood. With Markow interpreting, Hintze also preached to Markow's curious neighbors who began to pour in from the countryside the day after his arrival. Local priests soon informed the police of the unwanted visitor. Appearing before the local

Courtesy Church Archives

Illus. 1-4. Ferdinand F. Hintze (c. 1885) visited the Hungarian home of Mischa Markow in 1888 and ordained him to the priesthood.

magistrate, Hintze was ordered to depart. Whereas Biesinger and Jennings had failed because of public apathy, Hintze was foiled by the authorities. As Hintze recorded, "No Elder can go there yet, the priests govern to [sic] much." Yet he harbored the hope that "if the Lord opens the way, saints may yet be found in those places."[15]

Soon after Hintze returned to Constantinople, Markow also left Hungary. He proselytized in Belgium for a year before immigrating to Utah. There Markow married, fathered two children, and grew in his new faith. He returned to Europe in 1899 as an official missionary and as a U.S. citizen, a status that offered some protection as he dealt with foreign authorities.[16]

Mischa Markow's First Mission

When Elder Markow returned to Hungary, the missionaries in western Europe were enjoying unprecedented success. In 1898 a new German Mission had been created from the former Swiss-German Mission. It covered not only Germany but all countries further east in Europe. A handful of missionaries encountered a season of success, particularly as they probed eastward. They arrived at Königsberg, Prussia (now Kaliningrad, Russia), in March 1899. Within fourteen months, the missionaries had baptized 29 people.[17] Baptisms throughout the mission increased from 158 in 1899, to 301 in 1900, to 514 in 1901.[18] Most of these occurred in Germany, but a few resulted from Markow's work in Austro-Hungary and the Balkans.

Markow reported to the German Mission president, Arnold Schulthess, and labored in Serbia for three months. Then he was summoned before the Serbian supreme court for preaching: its verdict was banishment. The police took him to the train station and bought him a train ticket to go across the border to Hungary. Markow ended up in Nagy Becskerek (today Zrenjanin, Serbia), situated approximately thirty miles south of his hometown of Szerb-Csernye. [19]

Markow spent forty days preaching in Nagy Becskerek. Then one day the mayor appeared at his door with two policemen who apprehended him on the charge of anarchy. The mayor motioned to hit Markow with his cane but was stayed when the missionary claimed American citizenship. Markow was searched, deprived of his possessions, and marched with a policeman on each side down the city's main street. Adding to the spectacle, an accuser tagged along yelling, "Anarchist! Anarchist!"[20]

Elder Markow waited in a dimly lit cell while the authorities sought to decipher the English on his passport and missionary certificate. A local merchant who could speak English provided the translation. Having confirmed his citizenship, the authorities puzzled over a way to charge him with a crime sufficient to silence him. They dispatched a cell-mate who offered Markow liquor and tried to engage him in a political discussion. Elder Markow simply preached to his new acquaintance. The court, failing to find charges that would stick, still banished Markow.

Having been expelled by Serbia and Hungary, Elder Markow went to Constantinople to confer with Hintze, who was serving a second mission in Turkey. He then headed to Bucharest, capital of Romania, accompanied by a Bulgarian investigator, Argir Dimitrov. On July 30, 1899, Elder Markow baptized Dimitrov in the Black Sea. The two preached in Bucharest for six months, baptizing only one man, John Rulea, on September 14, 1899. Then, in answer to a prayer, Markow dreamed that a crowd of people tried to prevent him from visiting a family he apparently knew. He was able to push them away and enter a room to find an older lady leaning on her elbow at a table and a younger lady standing by the door. In the dream, he asked the older lady if she had a Bible. The three read it together and rejoiced. After the dream, he went to the women's residence, and everything from the vision was fulfilled. On February 16, 1900, Johanna and Karolina Hinz were baptized. Six more were baptized before Markow was arrested, tried by the courts, and banished—as had happened in Serbia and Hungary. The fate of the Romanian members remains unknown.[21]

Next, Elder Markow traveled south to Sofia, capital of Bulgaria. A Protestant pastor vowed to stop him and led a media campaign to deter potential listeners. Despite the negative publicity, Markow preached to large audiences. When he happened to meet the pastor on the street, he thanked him for the publicity. But arrest soon followed, and Bulgaria became the fourth country to banish him.

In late August 1900, the dauntless missionary headed west, traveling by boat up the Danube River and praying to know where he might labor next. During this trip, he dreamed that he was preaching in the city of Temesvár, Hungary (now Timişoara, Romania), not far from the other Hungarian cities where he had previously labored. This city would be the site of his greatest success. In Temesvár he encountered a group of Catholics anxiously seeking new spiritual guidance. He wrote to President Schulthess for assistance, and Hyrum M. Lau arrived on October 4, 1900.[22]

The missionary activity soon stirred the opposition of the local Catholic bishop, who informed the court about it. The week after Lau's arrival, the court duly summoned the pair for a hearing. Unsure how to rule, the judge gave the missionaries a reprieve to continue their work without restriction until the supreme court ruled on the case.[23] The missionaries baptized nine people on January 24, 1901, the Church's first conclave in Hungary. The nine new members included an elderly couple, six middle-aged women, and thirty-five-year-old Franz Kortje, who was later called to be a local leader.[24]

Having established a congregation, Elder Markow requested official permission to hold meetings. The mayor denied permission to meet and informed the local court, which then prohibited any further proselytizing. Markow, determined to continue work in Temesvár on the "sly," sent Lau to Budapest to argue their cause and seek the assistance of the American consulate. Meanwhile, Markow initiated a schedule of unofficial meetings after dark thrice weekly and at ever-changing locations. Ten more persons, mostly young adults in their middle twenties, joined the Church in early March 1901.[25]

The Hungarian supreme court ruled against the missionaries in late March, and the local court ordered them to leave in three days. On the evening of Saturday, March 30, a dozen prospective members were baptized after dark. The branch now consisted of thirty-one members. After bidding farewell at a Sabbath meeting, the missionaries departed Monday, April 1, leaving local leaders Franz Kortje and Matthaus Sadorf in charge of the branch.[26]

The banished missionaries reported to President Schulthess in Oderberg, Austria. President Schulthess immediately made plans to send another missionary, Henry Mathis, to sustain the fledgling branch and ensure that the work proceeded cautiously, avoiding further confrontations with the authorities.[27] The president then assigned Elder Markow to labor in Munich for five months before returning home to the United States.[28]

The Rise of the Hungarian Conference

The arrival of Henry Mathis at Temesvár on May 10, 1901, temporarily restored the momentum of previous success. For four months, he taught earnest investigators; two accepted baptism, and others were preparing to receive the ordinance. Just after the start of an evening Bible class on August 22, a stranger appeared and requested that Mathis step outside. The stranger, a policeman in plain clothes, summarily arrested him. The court sentenced Mathis to a fine of thirty krone and banishment, which Mathis calmly accepted. Apparently impressed by his demeanor, the judge reconsidered the fine and remitted it. Most of the branch came to the railroad station to send off the banished missionary.[29] Mathis's absence left the Hungarian members separated from the rest of the Church for two years, except for those who decided to emigrate: Matthaus Sadorf, Jacob Pfeiffer, Johann Schweburger, and Leopold Koszka, leaving by August 1901.[30]

A local elder, Franz Kortje, performed baptisms in late 1901 and early 1902. However, these additions were not a sign of things to come. Like a lighted match, the flame eventually died out as it consumed the match stick. Even though missionaries returned in 1903 and revived the effort, numerical success never equaled the Temesvár conversions. Of the total persons converted in Hungary before World War I, more than a third joined the first year (1901).

In July 1903, Hugh J. Cannon, who had replaced Schulthess as the German Mission president, once again sought legal recognition for the Church in Hungary.[31] In the meantime, Mischa Markow, returning to Europe a second time, reentered the country. Appointed to preach in Russia, he spent some time in Hungary first. On this occasion, he chose to preach in the city of Brassó (now Brasov, Romania), two hundred miles east of Temesvár. He approached the mayor, openly explained his purpose, and obtained permission to preach in the city for five weeks before leaving for Russia.[32] While he did not baptize any converts, Markow ignited interest in Anna Wachsmann, who later joined the Church. His work also laid the foundation for Brassó to become the locus of missionary success in Hungary for the next seven years.

As Elder Markow preached in Brassó, William A. Wetzel and Frank Pingree successfully entered Temesvár and reestablished contact with the branch.[33] President Cannon then created the Austro-Hungarian Conference (conferences were later called districts) of the German Mission in January 1904, which included Vienna, Temesvár, and Brassó. By the end of January, other missionaries went to Brassó and continued the work Markow had begun.[34] The authorities expelled Wetzel and Pingree from Temesvár during 1904, but other missionaries replaced them, and a baptism occurred before the year ended. In September 1904, the Hungarian Minister of the Interior rendered a verdict against the Church, prohibiting further preaching on the grounds that it was "undesirable" to both state and religious interests.[35] President Cannon felt the prospect for missionary work was sufficient to justify a continued missionary presence in the country, even though this presence was technically illegal.[36] The desire to operate openly continued to prompt efforts for recognition, but the religious imperative to proselytize took precedence over legal prohibition.

Missionaries pursued the work cautiously and discretely. In July 1905, Serge Ballif, successor to President Hugh J. Cannon, visited Temesvár, where he noted the police kept close watch, requiring the missionaries to be constantly on guard. During the visit, the missionaries conducted a baptismal service late at night, adding two more members to the branch. Ballif then traveled to Brassó, where he found the missionaries conducting most of their work under the guise of teaching English. At another late-night baptismal meeting, four people joined the Church. This group, plus a member who had been baptized a month earlier, formed a branch of five.[37]

No matter how intimidating the conditions were in Hungary, Ballif found the prospects for missionary work much better there than in Austria. Even though the numbers were modest, 1905 was still the second most productive year in the early history of the mission. Severing Austria from the Austro-Hungarian Conference, he concentrated his efforts in Hungary. At the same time, he continued to seek legal status for the Church in that country. Returning to Germany through Budapest, Ballif consulted an attorney who wisely advised patience and quietude for the present.[38]

While outside circumstances hindered the work, circumstances inside the newly founded congregations of the Church militated the establishment of a firm base in Hungary. Missionaries sought to attract new converts, but those who converted soon left Hungary to gather with the Saints in the United States. Half of the forty-five Temesvár converts who joined before December 1904 had already emigrated by that date. The pattern continued in 1905 as seven of the nineteen persons converted that year left Hungary by August, and six more by 1913.[39]

Several factors contributed to this emigration. The doctrine of the gathering, less emphasized in the twentieth century than in the nineteenth century, still motivated Church members to leave their home countries for Utah. The prospect of a new life in a land of freedom, far from the unstable politics of Europe, which constantly teetered on the edge of armed conflict, appealed to Church members as well as other Hungarian emigrants who streamed to American shores. A total of three hundred thirty-five thousand Hungarians immigrated to America between 1900 and 1910, three times more than in any other decade. In 1911, President Joseph F. Smith reported that seventeen Hungarian families lived in Salt Lake City and that fifteen of them were members.[40]

Back in Hungary, the combination of members emigrating and the lack of new converts dimmed President Ballif's prospects for success. In March 1906, he temporarily closed the Hungarian Conference.[41] A lone missionary, L. Lambert Pack, remained in Brassó until May, when he left after having baptized a family of three. Although the nine members who made up the small branch sustained their faith alone for five months, there was a sense of relief and happiness when Elders Leland Accomb and J. E. Langford arrived in September to resume the work.[42] Again the missionaries succeeded for a season. The nine baptisms for 1906 and 1907 occurred in Brassó as did nine of the sixteen registered in Hungary during 1908.

Though baptismal numbers had risen, internal strife began to take a toll on missionary progress. During July and August 1908, President Ballif toured both Temesvár and Brassó. In Temesvár, he encouraged Franz Kortje to improve his leadership skills. In Brassó, he discovered conditions that reflected "great discredit" upon the missionaries who had worked there.[43] Nevertheless, he buoyed the Brassó members' spirits during the Sabbath meetings. Two days later, a group went to the woods to hold baptismal services for five new converts. Afterward, they celebrated with a barbecue.[44]

While emigration and internal discord weakened the Church, the mission was hampered because the missionaries spoke only German and preached primarily to the German minority. Not until 1909 was an attempt made to remedy this situation. When newly appointed Elder John Ensign Hill arrived at the Swiss-German Mission headquarters in Basel (Swiss and German missions had been reunited in 1904), knowing only English, President Ballif assigned him to Budapest saying, "You go down to Hungary. There is a grand work for you to open up."[45]

Elder John Ensign Hill's "Grand Work"

It was not until he arrived in Budapest that Elder Hill discovered the nature of the grand work before him. Hamilton Gardner and Earl Davenport, already serving in the capital city, met Hill and informed him that he would be the first missionary to preach in the Hungarian language. Hill wrote home that the announcement "almost took my breath." Later, he learned that President Ballif had requested someone to preach in Hungarian and that the prophet himself, Joseph F. Smith, had selected Hill to be that person.[46]

On January 3, 1909, the three missionaries conducted the first public Church meeting ever held in Budapest. Besides them there was one member, George Albert Thies Jr. His parents had been baptized in Brassó the previous August, and George had joined the Church in Budapest only the month prior to the meeting. Since it was fast day, each bore his testimony.[47]

Elder Hill began studying Hungarian at the local Berlitz school on January 5, 1909. The teacher did not speak English, and the other pupil spoke only German. After three hours, Hill departed the class feeling "somewhat blue." Still, he began tracting in Hungarian the week following his first lesson. Using the two words he had learned—one for "Good day!" and one for "Please!"—he went from door to door, handing out tracts. When asked "What is this?" he could offer no explanation, but simply went to another door to repeat the process. Armed with his limited vocabulary, he went to thirty-four places his first day and left twenty-one tracts.[48]

Elder Hill arranged to meet privately with his Hungarian instructor on the condition that he teach the man English while Hill learned Hungarian. The duo walked about pointing at items such as the street, buggies, or people and saying what they were in their respective languages. Elder Hill thought that the Hungarian words all sounded the same and lamented, "It is just like trying to climb a steep, slippery wall where there is nothing to get hold of." Later he consoled himself: "The horses and the dogs seem to understand this language, so there is still hope for me."[49]

The police in Budapest barely reacted to the presence of missionaries in the city. Missionary activity may have seemed less threatening in a large cosmopolitan center than in the provincial cities of Temesvár and Brassó. Summoned to a Budapest police station to report the reason for his presence, Elder Hill charmed the authorities with a jovial disposition. Taking a liking to the grinning missionary, the police permitted him to buy a citizenship for a nominal fee and left him to continue his work. The other missionaries were summoned later, and when it was determined that they knew Hill, the police dismissed them to continue their work without any further questions.[50]

Elder Hill worked as a Hungarian-speaking missionary without a companion for a year and a half. Although Church leaders at that time permitted missionaries to work alone, this was the exception, not the rule. Hill occasionally met with the other elders for meals and visits.

After six months of language study, Elder Hill felt sufficiently skilled in Hungarian to begin attempting translations. He was helped by fourteen-year-old Ottille Franzen, a new member of only one month. Ottille was the stepdaughter of Karl Nemenz and daughter of Anna Nemenz, a

couple who boarded the two German-speaking missionaries in Budapest. Elder Hill, unsatisfied with the translation after several months,
obtained the assistance of his new landlord, Antal Weinzierl. Weinzierl,
an educated man, showed an interest in reading the translated tracts and
offered to help reword them. Because the landlord was not available during the workday, the two translators often began work at 10:00 P.M. and
continued until midnight or later. A bond of genuine affection developed
between them as they labored together on the tracts. In December the
first results of their labors came off the press in a run of ten thousand
tracts—two thousand each of five separate publications (illus. 1-5).[51]

During the time Hill worked on the translations, he also preached the
first sermon in Hungarian. The occasion was a fast and testimony meeting on August 8, 1909. He followed that with the first meeting conducted
entirely in Hungarian on November 28, 1909. Ten members of other
faiths attended, forming the largest service up to that time in Budapest.
Early the following year, he conducted the first baptismal service in Hungarian when he baptized Gustave Franzen, stepson of Karl Nemenz.[52]

On his own initiative, Elder Hill, assisted by Weinzierl, began to
translate the Book of Mormon into Hungarian on November 3, 1910.
Because Weinzierl did not know English, he translated from the German
Book of Mormon while Hill worked from the original English. They
compared notes and produced a single text.[53]

After a week of working on the translation, Elder Hill wrote to
Thomas E. McKay, who had replaced President Ballif in 1909, about the
translation and projected printing costs. The response received later in
November shocked Hill—the Church was not prepared to print a Hungarian Book of Mormon.[54] Available sources do not reveal whether
Church leaders felt Hill had overstepped his bounds by commencing the
project without approval, if the cost was the major consideration, or if
some other factor influenced this decision. Receptiveness to the gospel
message in Hungary had not been encouraging, and perhaps it was
insufficient to merit the further application of resources. In retrospect,
World War I was in the offing, and language reform occurred after the
war. The war eliminated the possibility of proselytizing, at least temporarily, and the subsequent language reform would have made any early
publication obsolete.

Elder Hill pleaded with President McKay to continue the translation,
offering to pay for the printing himself. A second "no" came in the mail
on December 1, 1910. Hill wrote in his journal, "It was a blue day for me.
I felt that half my life had been taken away." He then sent his resignation

Rays of Living Light.

No 6.

___

BY CHARLES W. PENROSE.

___

That there has been a great departure from the doctrines, ordinances and discipline of the Church as it existed in the days of Christ and His Apostles, must be evident to every unbiased enquirer into religious truth. This has been demonstrated to some extent in tracts already presented to the reader. But the full measure of the apostacy that has taken place would take volumes to represent in detail. The proofs are ample that it has been universal.

When Jesus Christ commenced His ministry on earth He found the people who claimed to be the special subjects of divine blessing and approbation, with all their Priests and ministers and learned divines, entirely out of the way of life and salvation. None were acceptable unto God. He denounced the most pious, respectable, devout and educated among them as hypocrites and "whited sepulchres." Their foreign missionary enterprises he declared obnoxious to the Almighty, and informed them that when they compassed sea and land to make one proselyte they made him "two fold more the child of hell." (Matt. XXIII; 15). He pronounced them blind guides who made clean the outside, but within were full of extortion and excess. The spirit of the Lord had departed from those who honored His name with their lips, but who had departed from His ways, and who, in place of the word of God, "taught for doctrine the commandments of men." , They were without authority from God, although they claimed to have it by descent and ordination through a long line of predecessors and prophets. It should not be deemed impossible that a similar universal apostacy could take place after the establishment of the Church of Christ by Him and His Apostles. But whether so considered or not, the facts are too patent to be denied when they confront the honest and enlightened mind.

It has been shown that the Gospel as taught and administered by Christ and His Apostles required first, faith in God and Jesus Christ; second, repentance, which included reform of conduct; third, baptism by immersion for the remission of sins; fourth, the reception of the Holy Ghost by the laying on of the hands of divinely authorized men; and that obedience to these brought the gifts of the spirit, including love, joy, peace, patience, brotherly kindness, charity, healings, tongues, interpretations, discerning of spirits, miracles, prophecy, revelation, and the unity in one body of all who were baptized into

Illus. 1-5. Elder Charles Penrose published this tract in Liverpool, England, in 1898.

Az élő világosság sugarai.

6-ik szám.

Penrose W. Charles-től.

Az igaz hittől való elszakadás.

Hogy az eredeti krisztusi egyház tanaitól, rendeleteitől és berendezéseitől lényegesen elpártoltak, minden pártonkivüli vallás-igazságkutató előtt kétségen kivül álló. Ez már az előbb előadottakban bizonyos fokig be lett bizonyitva. E nagy szakadások minden részletének leirása köteteket tenne ki. A kéznél levő gazdag bizonyitékok mutatják, hogy az elszakadás általános volt.

A zsidók elszakadása.

Midőn az Úristen tanitói hivatását a földön megkezdé, úgy találta, hogy Izrael népe, mely azt állitá, hogy Istennek kiválasztott népe, minden papjaival, tanitóival és irástudóival együtt általánosságban és lényegében letért az élet és üdvösség útjáról. Senki sem volt az Úrnak kedves. A legjámborabbakat, legtiszteletreméltóbbakat és jobban nevelteket közülök képmutatóknak nevezte és kifestett sir-ásókhoz hasonlitotta. Hivatásukat olyannak minősitette, mint amely az Úrnak visszatetsző és azt mondá nekik, hogy »megkerülitek a tengert és földet, hogy egy pogányt zsidóvá tegyetek, és ha azzá lett, őt magatoknál kétszerte erősebben a pokol fiává avatjátok«. (Mátyás 23:15.) Vak vezetőknek nevezé őket, és ismételten kifejezte felettük való sajnálatát. Az Úr szelleme elhagyta őket, azokat, akik nevét ajkaikkal tisztelték, de akik az Ő útjairól eltértek és Isten szavai helyett az emberek tanait parancsok gyanánt hirdették. Nem volt erre Istentől meghatalmazásuk, és noha az elődök és próféták hosszu sora útján továbbszármaztatott rendeltetésük alapján igényt támasztottak erre. Nem vehető képtelenségnek, hogy Krisztus és apostolai által hirdetett érintetlen tiszta evangéliumtól ilyen elszakadás bekövetkezhetett. Ily elszakadás tünetei túltiszták, semhogy helyesen gondolkozó intelligens embert félrevezethessen.

A Krisztus által tanitott alapelvek.

Megmutattatott, hogy az evangélium, amint az Krisztus és apostolai által tanittatott, először az Isten és az Ő fiában, Jézus Krisztusban való hitet, másodszor bűnbánatot, harmadszor bűnbocsánat iránti megkeresztelést és negyedszer istenileg meghatalmazott férfiak kézfeltétele útján a Szentlélek adományát igényli, és hogy ezen tanok követése a Szentlélek adományait: a szeretetet, örömet, békét, türelmet, testvéri jóságot, irgalmasságot és egyetértést, betegek gyógyitását, nyelvek ismeretét, a szellemek megkülönböztetését, csodatéveseket, kinyilatkozásokat és a jóslásokat magában foglalja. Megmutattatott továbbá, hogy az evangélium rendeleteit oly emberek hajtották végre, kik erre ösztönt Isten útján nyertek, kivel összeköttetésben állottak és ki felhatalmazta őket, hogy az Ő nevében hivataloskodjanak, úgy hogy az, amit ők ezen felhatalmazás alapján a földön cselekedtek, az égben elismerhetővé lett. Az iránt is történt intézkedés, hogy Krisztus templomában apostolok, próféták, evangélisták, tanitók, vének és más hivatalnokok legyenek, kiknek kötelességük volt

Illus. 1-5. Elder John Ensign Hill translated Penrose's tract into Hungarian and published it in Budapest in 1928.

as a missionary to the president. Evidently, the depression passed. Within a month, McKay called Hill to serve as the president of Hungarian Conference.[55]

The effort to preach in the Hungarian tongue lasted for five years, but with little effect. Baptismal figures stagnated, then dwindled. After four baptisms in 1909, there were six in 1910, another six in 1911, two in 1912, one in 1913, and one in 1914.

The Fall of the Hungarian Conference

From the beginning, the ban against Latter-day Saint meetings in Hungary severely hampered missionary work. Missionaries skirted the rule by holding public Sunday Bible classes and organizing choirs to learn songs in English on the Sabbath. They met privately with members to partake of the sacrament. In Brassó, some missionaries avoided confrontations with authorities by working in the countryside.[56] Those who continued to preach in town played a game of cat-and-mouse with local officials. On June 30, 1910, the police forbade Elder E. L. Smith to hold public meetings. Later, on August 6, he recorded that his song class was attended by sixteen friends (investigators).[57]

Similarly, members encountered difficulties when their allegiance to the Church was discovered. Young Helene Bammer, already baptized into the Church, was required by local tradition to be confirmed (a Catholic ordinance in which a teenager reaffirms his or her baptismal covenant). While she was attending classes to prepare for confirmation, the priest asked each student to choose a verse from the Bible that he or she would discuss privately with them. When Helene's turn came, the pastor was impressed with her knowledge and asked her to pray at the conclusion of the interview. When the prayer was finished, tears of admiration swelled in the pastor's eyes as he said, "My dear child, I must admit, you are the first among my pupils to be confirmed who really knows how to pray." He asked what the source of her knowledge had been. When she truthfully revealed her religion, his disposition changed dramatically. In Helene's words: "Since that time benevolence on the minister's part towards me was gone."[58]

In January 1911, the missionaries in Brassó unexpectedly received the long-sought-after permission to hold public meetings (illus. 1-6).[59] On behalf of the Church, Elder Hill had cultivated the influence of the American Consul General, Paul Nash, who helped reverse the anti-Mormon disposition of Hungarian officials.[60] Under the auspices of the newly achieved recognition, a missionary conference was held in Brassó on April 22. President McKay and ten missionaries attended. The conference was a festive occasion, and everyone gathered for a group picture. Helene affirms,: "These were days of blessing and joy."[61]

Subsequent to the change in official status, Elder T. R. Jones reported in a letter to the *Improvement Era* that "the police and officers generally are friendly. They know every missionary personally, and are glad when they can help them. One policeman said to the writer: 'We like you Americans, and the gospel of Christ is good for our people.'"[62]

Efforts to receive legal recognition in Hungary also prevailed. Josef Ritter Grieg von Ronse, representing the Church, carried a petition through the negative rulings of two lower courts to appeal to the country's supreme court, which reversed the lower court opinions and granted the desired religious recognition in November 1911.[63]

Yet the official recognition ultimately made little difference. Although the legal opposition of the authorities was now gone, the apathy of the populace remained. On March 5, 1913, a group of Church authorities gathered in Budapest: Elder Rudger Clawson, then European Mission president; Hyrum Valentine, who had succeeded McKay as the Hungarian Mission president; Spencer Felt, Hungarian Conference leader; and missionaries Samuel V. Spry, J. Elmer Johansen, S. Joseph Quinney, and Elmer P. Madsen. During the conference, they decided to cease missionary work among the Hungarian-speaking people for the time being.[64] However, this decision did not preclude leaving a few missionaries to

Courtesy Church Archives

Illus. 1-6. Branch members and missionaries in Brassó, Hungary, c. 1911.

tend to the needs of the members, primarily ethnic Germans. Elder Claw-son reported in the *Millennial Star* that missionaries had labored for four years in Budapest without success, noting that, in one specific instance, an elder had distributed eight hundred tracts a month for nine months and had nothing to show for it.[65]

Only one active Church member, Anna Kaufmann, remained in Budapest. Seven others had been baptized there since 1909, but they had all moved, emigrated, or lost interest. In the country as a whole, of the 107 persons baptized since Markow's arrival in 1888, 59 (55.6 percent) had emigrated to America, 5 (4.7 percent) had moved elsewhere in Europe, and 3 (2.8 percent) had died, leaving 40 members (37.7 percent) on the rolls with only a few of those still active.[66]

In the end, it was not the opposition of the political authorities but the lack of public response that precluded baptismal success in Hungary. The missionary force in Europe was small. Unrewarded effort simply dictated that the energy be expended elsewhere. President Valentine reported to Elder Clawson in October 1913 that the mission in Germany had been favored with many good, solid converts, while "our actions [the Conference closing] in Budapest have proven the right thing and a bur-den has been lifted from the shoulders of this mission and a mill-stone from our elders' necks."[67] If the work would not proceed in Hungary, it surely would elsewhere.

Of the missionaries that remained to tend to the German-speaking members, only two were there at the onslaught of World War I—David Stoddard and Charles Martin. Elder Stoddard found the people there more friendly than any he had previously encountered in Germany. His one concern was that the majority of those attending their meetings were "young ladies" and "the different preachers in town don't love us too much . . . and if they know that several young ladies are coming to our meetings they will have some nice stories to tell."[68] This was either an allusion to polygamy or to potential improprieties as imagined by Church detractors.

After Austria declared war on Serbia for the assassination of Arch-duke Franz Ferdinand, Elder Stoddard wrote, "The farm lads were brought into town and given uniforms very quickly. They were bedded down for two nights in piles of straw that had been brought in and dumped in the streets, . . . were drilled for a short time, outfitted with weapons, and sent to the front." One young man wanted to join the Church before he left for war, so he called the missionaries at 4:00 A.M. and made arrangements to be baptized before his anticipated departure at 10:00 that morning. The plan was thwarted when he had to leave unexpectedly at 6:00 A.M.

On August 10, 1914, the missionaries left Hungary. Helene (Bammer) Bernhardt, a member in Brassó who remained faithful, reported years later, "Long and dreary years now began for us all—isolated, no connection with the Church whatsoever, only dependent on ourselves. But this time also went by. The Lord was with us and did not leave us."[69]

The Lindelöf Family of Imperial Russia

North and east of Austro-Hungary and the Balkans lay the Russian Empire. The princes of Moscovy emerged in the fifteenth century, liberating this area from two centuries of Asian-based Mongol rule. In 1649 the chief prince, or tsar, legalized serfdom. This created a rigid class structure of peasants, 80 percent of the population, bonded to the private estates of privileged nobles or to the state. Peter I (the Great) expanded the Russian domain in the early eighteenth century and, in 1721, founded the Russian Empire. During the century, his successors, particularly Catherine II (the Great), expanded the empire by annexing territory in modern-day Latvia, Lithuania, Poland, Belarus, Ukraine, and the Crimean Peninsula in the Black Sea. In the nineteenth century, successive tsars acquired Finland, Bessarabia (today Moldova), the Caucasus (Georgia, Armenia, Azerbaijan), Siberia, and portions of Central Asia. In 1861, Alexander II dissolved serfdom; however, the serfs remained under heavy financial obligation to their former masters. Internal dissent and external war led to an abortive revolution in 1905 and a successful overthrow of the centuries-old tsarist regime in spring 1917. Russia was dominated by Orthodoxy, and Russians asserted that Moscow was the third Rome, successor to corrupted Christianity in either Rome or Constantinople. Cut off for centuries by Mongol suzerainty, late to implement social freedoms, religiously unreceptive to the West, Russia was not fertile soil for the gospel message or that of various Protestant groups that began operating in Russia during the late nineteenth century.

While in Austro-Hungary the missionary work flickered and then faded, it touched the life of only one family in the Russian Empire. The desire to proselytize in Russia traces back to early Church history when Joseph Smith appointed Orson Hyde and George J. Adams to preach there in 1843.[70] Had they gone, Russia may have become a mission along with French Polynesia, either third or fourth in the history of the Church. But they delayed their departure, and, after Joseph Smith's death, the project was never undertaken. It was another half century before the effort was renewed and missionaries entered the empire of the tsars.

On February 1, 1884, John Bloom stood at the entrance of the state prison in Helsinki, Finland, sentenced to twenty-eight days on bread and water for a "breach of the Sabbath." (In 1878, Elder Bloom had joined the Church in Sweden and three years later had moved his family to Finland for the express purpose of missionary work.) His "breach" had been to baptize two Finnish women, Wendla Lindelöf and Maria God, on a Sunday. Wendla's twenty-six-year-old son, Johan Maurits Lindelöf, witnessed the event.[71] A decade later, Johan and his wife became the first converts to the Church in Russia.

Born in 1857, Johan Lindelöf emigrated to St. Petersburg, Russia, in 1879 at age twenty-two.[72] St. Petersburg, capital of the Russian empire, was a cosmopolitan center with large communities of Germans, Swedes, French, Finns, and other nationalities. By 1887, Johan worked as a journeyman in the gold and silversmith trade. In that year, he returned home to Finland and married Alma Augusta Holmberg.[73] His first child was born in Finland the next year, but the second child and subsequent children were born in St. Petersburg. By 1895, Johan decided to be baptized. He corresponded with President Peter Sundwall of the Scandinavian Mission, and Sundwall sent a lone missionary, August Joel Höglund, to St. Petersburg in June 1895. At the Lindelöf home, they supped on a good meal, then conversed about the gospel until daybreak. After a rest on Monday, they resumed their conversation, and both Johan and Alma asked for baptism.[74]

On Tuesday, June 11, 1895, the three hired a boat and rowed out on St. Petersburg's Neva River, looking for a secluded place where they could perform the ordinances unnoticed. Initially, they searched in vain as strolling pedestrians crowded the banks, sailboats dotted the river, and fishing boats bobbed about. They picked a place, rowed ashore, knelt in prayer for assistance, and soon "as if by sudden command the boats sailed away," and the people departed. After the baptisms and confirmations were performed, the group knelt again in a prayer of thanks. Elder Höglund recorded Sister Lindelöf's words of elation: "Oh, how happy I am! I know God has forgiven my sins!"

Elder Höglund remained with the Lindelöfs for another week and a half, continuing to instruct them in gospel principles and encouraging Brother Lindelöf to visit friends, read the Bible to them, and instruct by inspiration. The day before leaving, he ordained Brother Lindelöf an elder and blessed the three Lindelöf children, Johannes Lenard, Oskar Edvard, and Agnes Irene. Together they partook of the sacrament. When he parted, Elder Höglund noted, "During the short time I was with them I learned to love Brother and Sister Lindelöf, they in turn learned to love me with that love which the Gospel gives, and bound together in the holy covenant we could not part without our feelings being deeply wrought upon."

When Elder Höglund reported to President Sundwall, he explained that the couple already lived consistent with gospel principles. A later visitor noted that Brother Lindelöf was "good at heart" and that there could not be found a "more faithful, patient woman than sister Lindelöf."[75]

With the missionary gone, the Lindelöfs faced the task of living and preaching the gospel while isolated from the body of the Church. Johan was in a position to do much good since he was conversant in Swedish, Russian and Finnish, well acquainted with the Scandinavian community, and prosperous as a gold and silversmith. Yet the task was formidable given the isolation from the body of the Church.

In succeeding years, the spiritual isolation of the Lindelöfs was infrequently punctuated by visits of missionaries from the Scandinavian Mission. In August 1896, Alonzo Irvine spent a week with them and recorded: "He received a hearty welcome by this family of Saints, which constituted the whole membership of the Church in Russia at that time."[76] In May 1897, Carl Ahlquist and Norman Lee arrived and held a public meeting "to which were invited a number of his [Johan's] friends and some Europeans who lived in the same court. . . . Brother Lindelöf had talked the Gospel for weeks to a highly cultured woman who lived next door to them and she applied for baptism."[77] Amalia Josefina Linbohm[78] was baptized in the Neva River, June 2, 1897. Unfortunately, she moved to Helsinki by the end of the month, leaving the Lindelöfs isolated once again. Three years later, Elder Charles Leroy Anderson Jr. went to St. Petersburg and baptized the Lindelöf's first Russian-born son, Oskar Edvard.[79] These contacts brought the family much-needed comfort and encouragement. In 1903 the Lindelöfs were overwhelmed by the visit of Elder Francis Marion Lyman, European Mission president (illus. 1-7), who arrived to dedicate Russia for missionary work.

A Promise of Religious Liberty

Church President Lorenzo Snow counseled President Lyman, prior to his departure for Europe, that he should get into every corner of the European Mission as soon as possible.[80] Lyman's formal commission from the First Presidency conveyed a similar directive:

It will now become your duty . . . to see that the Gospel is preached as far as possible, throughout the nations where the Elders now labor, and, as the Lord shall open the way, to seize any new opportunities which may present themselves for the introduction of the Gospel to regions where it has not yet been preached.[81]

The general counsel had been given, and it was up to Lyman to provide the framework for achieving it.

Courtesy Church Archives

Illus. 1-7. Francis M. Lyman, European mission president (1901–4), dedicated Russia for missionary work in 1903.

The Russian Empire was one of the untouched corners, and thoughts of a mission to Russia began to interest President Lyman shortly after he arrived at European headquarters in Liverpool, England, in 1901. As European Mission president, he directly supervised the missionaries in Great Britain and indirectly supervised those laboring on the continent. Subordinate missions in Scandinavia and several in Europe were each headed by a mission president who reported to Lyman. He frequently called on the missions on the mainland, visiting Scandinavia on one of his first tours. In a 1903 letter to President Joseph F. Smith, who had succeeded Snow, Lyman wrote, "Ever since my trip to Scandinavia in 1901 I have had it in my mind to put Elders into Finland and into Russia."[82]

The event precipitating the actual dedication of Russia appears to have been an unexpected political development. As part of the Tsarist government's movement toward greater religious toleration, Nicholas II issued a proclamation on Friday, March 13, 1903, providing for religious freedom throughout the realm. Thereafter, those of non-Orthodox persuasions were supposed to be able to openly practice their creeds. The

Western press proclaimed the decree as perhaps the most significant act of state since the serfs' emancipation in 1861.[83]

President Lyman felt prepared to take advantage of the opportunity. He wrote to the First Presidency in May 1903 that he intended to test the tsar's professions in favor of religious liberty.[84] The First Presidency was willing to entertain the possibility. In a letter to another Apostle, Heber J. Grant, then in Japan, the First Presidency wrote that Lyman was contemplating moving missionaries into Finland and Russia, and that they would doubtless soon learn what the tsarist manifesto amounted to.[85]

The 1903 Manifesto was the first of several edicts to be issued through 1905 that guaranteed religious freedom. Rather than being an affirmation of the tsar's aspirations, they were, in reality, an aberration. Hopelessly reactionary, Nicholas II had persecuted non-Orthodox religion in Russia before the proclamations. His edicts in the early 1900s appear to have been a sop to appease tensions in the empire—an unsuccessful gesture, as witnessed by the revolutions that convulsed Russia in 1905 and 1917.

Without the hindsight of history, President Lyman formulated a proposal for two men, ages twenty to twenty-five and of "superior intelligence," to go to Russia for four years. Their main purpose would be to learn the language and "in a modest way advocate the Gospel and feel their way gently and wisely till they master the situation and can recommend to us the next best step to be taken." Lyman felt their work, if successful, could later be carried on by native members. He wanted the First Presidency to have the elders called and on their way by July or August, when he intended to bless Russia for the preaching of the gospel.[86]

President Lyman's plan was a novel departure from the traditional Mormon missionary pattern of preaching at the first opportunity. It reflects a cautious attitude toward a society perceived as radically different from others in western Europe—stock from which the early Church members derived their cultural bias. This alien perception was reinforced by the gulf between the Catholic and Protestant religious tradition of the West and the Orthodox tradition of the East. Few if any in the Church had any acquaintance with Russian customs, the Russian language, or Russian religion. Lyman's plan attempted to reverse the dearth of knowledge that hindered the possibilities of converting Russian souls.

The response of the First Presidency, which was sent to President Lyman in May 1903, shows hesitation to commit themselves to such a venture. They wrote: "The promised liberty of worship in Russia, we fear, will take some time before it will be enjoyed."[87] Their caution probably stemmed from the reports, then filtering into the West, of pogroms being renewed against Russia's Jews. Not long after the 1903 Manifesto was issued, anti-Jewish pogroms erupted in Kishinev, a major city in southern Russia, and in other localities of the Russian empire with Jewish populations. The incidents received enough attention in the West that U.S. President Theodore Roosevelt petitioned Russia to halt the massacres.

President Lyman remained hopeful in spite of the pogroms. Having received the hesitant response of the First Presidency, he replied in June 1903. Lyman agreed with their dismal estimate, but he still promoted the attempt, arguing:

> I have thought as feelers, prospectors or fore-runners we could afford to place two able young men as students in St. Petersburg for three years to master the language, and become thoroughly acquainted with the people and the laws, and in that way get a foothold that we could ever after maintain. . . . If it was found in one two or three years it was necessary to increase the number, all well, and if not . . . we could withdraw for a time, and would have men ready for the work when the way should open. This suggestion is I think in harmony with the modesty we are compelled to observe at home and abroad while the elements are so disturbed.[88]

While the political turmoil of the period dictated caution, in Lyman's view, it did not obliterate his plan.

Political Upheavals Confront President Lyman

The "disturbed" elements referred to by President Lyman included not only the persecution of Jews in Russia, but also the disruption of Mormon missionary efforts in Germanic Europe. Since Lyman's arrival in Europe, the threat of banishment had hedged missionary work in many quarters. As previously noted, Henry Mathis, laboring in Hungary, was deported in 1901. The following year, the threat of expulsion began to loom in Germany, the heart of continental Europe. President Lyman noted in a letter to the First Presidency in May 1902 that there appeared to be a scheme contrived by the clergy to remove all missionaries from Prussia, a major component of the German Empire.[89]

As the furor grew, President Lyman became concerned that should Prussia expel all missionaries, other countries might be soon to follow.[90] He sought the assistance of the First Presidency to elicit U.S. government support, but the U.S. ambassador to Germany opposed the Latter-day Saint cause. President Lyman lamented in a letter to Elder Heber J. Grant that the prospects for converts were better in Germany than any other section of the continent, and he presumed the devil had likewise discovered this.[91]

The turmoil climaxed in April 1903 when Prussia and Mecklenberg, two kingdoms of the German Empire (a confederation of various kingdoms and principalities) formally banished the missionaries. The denial of religious liberty in Germany would naturally have tinged Lyman's fear of the same occurring in Russia, a land where religious liberty was yet but a promise.

President Lyman's response to opposition was moderation. In 1902 he had directed the missionaries to avoid confronting the ministers.[92] Following Germany's expulsion order, Lyman discussed his plans in a letter to Lofter Bjarnson, a missionary in Iceland:

> We must study moderati[o]n in presenting our cause for the consideration of the world. We may well avoid debate and every kind of contention. If we meet those who do not want our doctrines we may turn quietly to others till we find those who do. All that we do should be done pleasantly. We can't hope to convert many people, only a few such as the Lord can draw by His Spirit to the fold.[93]

This disposition to moderation later tempered his enthusiasm to pursue missionary work in Russia.

Banishment from Germany was not the Church's only challenge that had an impact on the Russian venture. Elder Reed Smoot, a member of the Quorum of the Twelve Apostles, had been elected as a U.S. senator from Utah in January 1903. Protesters feared that his loyalty to the Church would influence his political decision-making. This opposition resulted in a senatorial investigation. The political battle brought many of the Church's activities under scrutiny during 1903, absorbing the attention of the First Presidency and precluding them from attending to other matters, such as preaching the gospel in Russia.

The pogroms in Russia, the banishment of the Church in Germany, and the Smoot hearings in the U.S. all had a negative influence on the denouement of missionary work in Russia. Yet President Lyman countered these problems with optimism. His attitude is characterized by his bold, even flamboyant, words to Brigham Young Jr., president of the Quorum of Twelve Apostles in January 1902: "We are planning to break over into Austria from Switzerland and into Finland from Sweden."[94] In spring 1902, missionaries arrived in Austria for the first time in many years. During a summer tour of the Mediterranean, Lyman dedicated Italy, Greece, Turkey, and Egypt for missionary work. Later that year, he encouraged Hugh J. Cannon, German Mission president, to send missionaries to Prague and test the situation there.[95] When the First Presidency proposed reopening the South African Mission in winter 1902, Lyman responded ebulliently that such a mission had his unhesitating approval.[96] Before the year ended, he had submitted a proposal to the First Presidency that he perform a world tour, before leaving Europe, in which he would visit the Eastern hemisphere and pronounce apostolic blessings on India, China, Japan, the Philippines, Australia, New Zealand, Samoa, and the Sandwich Islands.[97] The proposal was not approved. Yet Lyman remained ever positive, explaining to the First Presidency that their decision had removed a great burden from him, and he rejoiced that he now would be able to turn to other responsibilities.[98]

President Lyman Dedicates Russia for Missionary Work

At the end of June 1903, President Lyman left for Scandinavia on the first leg of his trip to Russia. Before departing, he reaffirmed his purpose in a letter to a fellow Apostle, Matthias Cowley:

> If I can take the pulse of those peoples and turn the key for the introduction and preaching of the Gospel I shall feel that we have another foothold in an important and extensive section of the whole world where we must yet preach the Gospel of the Kingdom as a witness before the end shall come.[99]

After touring through Norway, Sweden, and Finland, Lyman and his traveling companion, Joseph J. Cannon, arrived in St. Petersburg on August 5, 1903. They might have been stranded at the station indefinitely, had it not been for the propitious encounter with an Englishman who was fluent in Russian and able to get some response from the scores of cabbies who merely shook their heads when addressed in English. At the hotel, Lyman and Cannon were surprised to find Elder John P. Horne in the room to one side and Elder Kenneth Crismon in the room to the other. Both were missionaries serving in Germany who had been in Christiania, Norway, for Lyman's dedication of the Oslo chapel in July and had preceded Lyman and Cannon to St. Petersburg to be present for Russia's dedication.[100]

In St. Petersburg, Lyman and Cannon were delighted to visit the Lindelöfs. President Lyman viewed this family as a refuge for any future missionaries to Russia. Even though the First Presidency had not endorsed his plan, he seems to have felt that they would support him eventually. The family was likewise delighted to hear of Lyman's proposal to send missionaries there on a permanent basis.[101] Elder Cannon recorded: "They would be glad indeed for Elders to come, for now they are shut off from communion with the Saints, except when an Elder visits St. Petersburg, and that is seldom."[102] Several months after the visit, Brother Lindelöf wrote to the *Millennial Star* in Liverpool, saying that his family still felt comfort from Lyman's visit and that they awaited "with much yearning the arrival of a missionary." He anticipated that his family would "help as much as possible in the spreading of the Gospel."[103]

The prayer of dedication was offered on August 6. According to the Russians' dating (they had not yet abandoned the Julian calendar) it was July 24, a day commemorating the 1847 pioneers who entered the Salt Lake Valley in Utah. They chose for the dedication site the wooded privacy of the Summer Garden, situated at the junction of the Neva River and the Fontanka Canal, just to the east of downtown St. Petersburg (illus. 1-8).

The group seated themselves on a park bench, shaded from the blue sky by a canopy of stilled leaves on the overhead tree branches. The four men bowed their heads while President Lyman prayed. Spreading out in all directions from the park, St. Petersburg, the two-hundred-year-old city built to bring Russia out of its oriental isolation, rested tranquilly during the half-hour prayer of its occidental visitor. Joseph Cannon explained:

Courtesy Kahlile B. Mehr

Illus. 1-8. Elder Francis M. Lyman (in 1903) and Elder Russell M. Nelson (in 1990) dedicated Russia for missionary work at the Summer Garden in St. Petersburg.

It was a fervent petition for the Lord to open this great land that His servants may preach the Gospel here. . . . He called upon the Lord to bless this great empire, in many respects the greatest in the world, and endow its rulers with wisdom and virtue, that there may be peace and progress here, that darkness may flee and the voices of His servants may sound the glad tidings to the uttermost parts of this great land.[104]

Lyman described his feelings in the following words: "The very peace of heaven was upon us. A more perfect spirit or occasion could not be conceived. Our hearts were melted within us for joy. . . . It was as glorious a quiet and peaceful moment as I remember ever to have experienced."[105]

This event sharply contrasted with the rest of their experiences in St. Petersburg. Elder Cannon described a scene they witnessed at the Kazan Cathedral:

Russian churches have no seats, and there is room for the devotee to kneel or prostrate himself if he wishes. People of all classes were there. Beggars in their rags (their purpose being to obtain charity), the lame, the halt, the blind, laboring people, richly clad men and women, officers of the army, all kissed the same icons, made the cross and bowed before the images, and in some cases kneeled and touched their foreheads to the floor. One poor fellow, evidently with a heavy weight on his conscience, we noticed when we entered, making the cross, kneeling, bowing to the floor and rising again only to repeat the movements. During the whole time we were there he continued.[106]

One detects that the incident was disconcerting to the visitors accustomed to the more staid atmosphere of congregational worship practiced by the Latter-day Saints. President Lyman later wrote to the First Presidency: "We shall need much help from the Lord to open up the Gospel in this church-ridden country. Idolatry is brazen at every sight. I have seen people in many countries who were slaves to it, but never anything like what is met here every day and all the time."[107]

Departing from St. Petersburg, Lyman and Cannon traveled to Moscow and visited the Kremlin. Standing next to the wall at the Alexander Garden, President Lyman prayed a second time for the emergence of religious freedom and "petitioned the Lord to send servants full of wisdom and faith to declare the Gospel to the Russians in their own language."[108] He prayed that missionary work might begin, that religious liberty would take hold, and that peace and progress would prevail. It was the culmination of a president's counsel and of an Apostle's hopes to take advantage of a Russian tsar's unprecedented declaration. The spiritual experience was overshadowed by Lyman's feeling that they "were besieging Satan's stronghold," a "center of spiritual darkness and diabolical priest-craft."[109] In spite of these premonitions, Lyman and Cannon continued on their mission, passing through Warsaw on their way back across Europe and walking to a grove of trees in Lazienski Park to dedicate Poland, then part of the Russian Empire, for the preaching of the gospel.[110]

Unlikely Prospects

"Poor, ignorant, oppressed Russia; freedom will come some day. May that time approach steadily without the horrors of bloodshed and revolution."[111] So wrote Elder Cannon after he and President Lyman had returned to England from Russia. Was the prospect of religious freedom more than just a hope in that era?

Several Christian denominations penetrated Russia during the latter half of the nineteenth century. The Baptists enjoyed the most success, with some twelve thousand adherents by 1886.[112] Seventh-Day Adventists grew from forty to four hundred in the four years from 1887 to 1890.[113] In 1903 the number of Baptists approached eighty thousand.[114] Baptist missionaries often endured incarceration or banishment for proselytizing illegally.[115] Criticizing the Orthodox Church was punishable by two years of exile in Siberia, and converting anyone from Orthodoxy carried a sentence of twelve years. Whatever the sentence, few were known to have returned from Siberia.[116] While dissenters from Russian Orthodoxy were dealt with harshly by civil and religious authorities, the Baptists showed that the obstacle could be overcome.

The Church might have enjoyed similar success if it had mounted a sustained effort. To accomplish this, it would have had to have done several things. The first would have been to make a commitment of manpower. In contrast to mass meetings and conversions, the Church's proselytizing paradigm has always focused on a missionary companionship teaching a single person or a single family at a time. This is probably why President Lyman, with between five hundred and six hundred missionaries at any given time in the various missions of the British Isles and Europe,[117] felt pitifully deficient to deal with the millions living there. He wrote to Elder Heber J. Grant in June 1902: "We are generally in need of more men, and if we had them we could open up fields in France, Italy, Austria, Russia and Greece. . . . We are doing so little among the millions of the Father's family, that at our present pace we are not gaining on the world."[118]

But at the turn of the twentieth century, the Church was still small—only three hundred thousand members—and did not have sufficient young men to meet the need. In addition to overall numbers, there were financial issues. The Church was heavily in debt in the early 1900s. Likewise, many did not have the wealth to sustain family members on missions. To deal with this situation, leaders conducted an experiment in some United States missions: elders were permitted to work during the day to earn money to support themselves so they could do missionary work at night.[119] A few men could probably have been spared for Russia to carry out the plan conceived by Lyman, but availability of manpower for an extended effort may have seemed too imposing either to him or the First Presidency.

Another obstacle was the language barrier. Few in the Church could speak the languages of the countries east of Germany and south of Switzerland. When missionaries ventured into these countries, it was normally to work with groups speaking German or some other language known by the missionaries. Language was not an insurmountable barrier, as proved by the success of both Alma O. Taylor in Japan (1901–10 during the first decade of the mission there)[120] and John Ensign Hill in Hungary (as previously related). Other people like Taylor and Hill might have made some headway in Russia, but the investment was never made.

A more serious obstacle was the perception that the Church was a heretical sect that siphoned converts off to Utah and enslaved them under a dictatorial theocracy where they were forced to live polygamy. Mormon missionaries would most likely have been opposed by the Russian Orthodox Church, not to mention by the Christian minorities already in Russia.

Latter-day Saints were also less disposed to confronting political power when compared to other denominations, such as the Baptists. Church leaders hesitated to have missionaries preach in countries where it was not a legally recognized religion. Its doctrine encouraged submissiveness to civil government, even when that government opposed its work. Such opposition was overcome in Austro-Hungary as seen in the legal recognition achieved in 1911. Even if this obstacle had been removed in Russia, the general attitude Lyman and Cannon observed in St. Petersburg would not have augured missionary success. Missionaries would have likely received the same response from Russian citizens as they did from Austro-Hungarian—indifference and apathy.

Mischa Markow Travels to Russia

When he returned to Liverpool in August 1903, President Lyman found Mischa Markow newly arrived for his second mission to Europe. Elder Markow must have seemed the answer to Lyman's hopes for the land he had just dedicated—he commissioned Markow to go to Russia.[121] Even though President Lyman had received no commitment from the First Presidency to pursue the Russia venture, he sent Markow, cautioning him to "be wise as a serpent and harmless as a dove."[122] He did not want Markow to be banished or imprisoned, nor did he want anything to occur that might hinder future efforts in Russia. Consistent with his earlier response to trouble in Germany, he counseled moderation. Lyman explicitly told Markow that if he encountered any danger he must flee.[123]

Soon after Markow departed, Lyman received a letter from the First Presidency written August 21, 1903, before they had received details of Russia's dedication. (The correspondence lag of the period was significant. A month or two might pass before a reply arrived.) In the letter, the First Presidency expressed their hope that conditions for missionary work in Russia were more favorable than anticipated.[124] They had not yet vetoed Lyman's proposal to send missionaries into Russia, so he took the opportunity to write back and express to them his plan to begin missionary work in Russia. He explained that he was favorably impressed with the people, if not with their superstition and idolatry. Lyman advocated pursuing the project, but he added, "I would not urge this matter upon your attention, and whatever the Spirit indicates to you is just what will please me."[125] Whatever his hope for success in Russia, he expressed his willingness to defer to the First Presidency's decision.

The response came in a letter written September 23, 1903. The First Presidency had not been persuaded. They explained that the matter of the Russian mission required more careful consideration than they had time to give it then.[126] Preoccupied with the pending Smoot hearings, stunned by the banishment from Germany, and unconvinced that religious liberty would prevail in Russia, they sidestepped the issue for the time being.

As this letter was traveling through the post, Elder Markow was en route to Russia after a short episode of preaching in Brassó, Hungary. Arriving in Riga on October 9, 1903, he registered with the district court. Markow was well aware that many Russians perceived Latter-day Saints as a fanatical sect in central and eastern Europe and that the name carried a negative connotation. Markow avoided certain banishment by registering as a preacher of The Church of Jesus Christ of Latter-day Saints rather than as a Mormon. The registrar shortened it to Church of Christ to fit into the space provided in his register.[127]

Markow's missionary approach was not at all like what Lyman had proposed to the First Presidency. He began placing some of his 150 German tracts in the city's German enclave. He explained that the priests did not have authority from God because of the Apostasy, but that authority had been restored. Within a short while, three families requested baptism. Had Markow baptized them, Church history in Russia may have been different. Success may have encouraged Lyman and persuaded the First Presidency to reconsider. As it was, Elder Markow began to encounter opposition and deferred performing the baptisms. Apparently informed on by a Baptist pastor, Markow was summoned to court. The court advised him to get a lawyer and petition the governor for permission to continue preaching. The lawyer he consulted seemed unwilling to help.[128] Markow's German contacts pleaded with him to stay, saying he would not be endangered if he preached only to the Protestants and Catholics. Yet Markow *felt* endangered, and, remembering Lyman's counsel, he prepared to leave. He departed on November 5,[129] and traveled to Liverpool, England, where he met with Lyman, who had recently received the First Presidency's counsel to desist in Russia. President Lyman subsequently reassigned Markow to the Turkish Mission. In late November 1903, Elder J. A. Hedrikson visited St. Petersburg,[130] making him and Markow the only two recorded missionaries to follow up Elder Lyman's dedicatory visit.

Failure to Establish the Church in Russia

What might have happened had congregations been established in Russia in the early twentieth century? If missionary work had been restricted to foreign minorities, the Russian authorities might have ignored it. A small foundation may have flourished in the wake of events fast transpiring to bring real religious freedom to Russia, if only temporarily. The Russian religious manifestos issued from 1903 to 1905 and an abortive revolution of 1905 engendered a dramatic increase in missionary activity by Baptists, Adventists, and Methodists from the West.[131] In 1905 the persecution of Christian denominations in Russia relaxed, and proselytizing became legal. Within the next six years, the Baptists obtained twenty-five thousand converts, nearly one-fourth of their total strength. Other Christian denominations experienced similar success.[132] For instance, the number of Adventists rose from two thousand in 1905 to almost five thousand in 1912.[133]

In September 1905, Peter Matson, the first president of the Church's newly formed Swedish Mission, visited the Lindelöf family in St. Petersburg. Responding to their warm reception, Matson considered sending missionaries to Russia.[134] However, no action was taken, and there is no indication that Elder Heber J. Grant, who succeeded Lyman as president of the European Mission, ever responded to the opportunity.

The Lindelöfs confided in President Matson their desire to leave Russia and go where there were more Church members.[135] They had lived isolated from the Church for a decade. But in the end they remained, and there is no record of further visits until seven years later. In September 1912, Swedish Mission President Andreas Peterson, accompanied by A. Theodore Johnson, found the family still faithful. To keep them better informed of Church events, President Peterson sent them the *Nordstjarnan,* a Church periodical published by the Scandinavian Mission. His successor, Theodore Tobiason, visited the family in August 1914 just as World War I engulfed Europe.[136]

Beginning in the 1910s, the aggressive foreign missionary campaigns provoked a combined backlash of civil and church authorities in Russia. In 1912 the tsarist government ordered the Adventists to close their publishing house in Riga. By early 1914 practically all Protestant religions were suffering under a strong political reaction and religious repression. With the outbreak of World War I, the government adopted a new law "prohibit[ing] sectarian ministers from preaching at any place except their approved home church, and in subsequent months police officials . . . arrested and jailed many preachers."[137]

The Lindelöfs endured the privations of war and revolution, which in their case ended tragically in 1918. As related by Brother Lindelöf many years later, it was 3:00 A.M. when the sleeping family was suddenly roused by several armed trespassers who announced the family was under arrest because of "their wealth." The parents were released because of old age, but their possessions were confiscated and their children sentenced to hard labor, some never to return alive. It was not because of their religion but rather their possessions, which Russian revolutionaries coveted and sought to redistribute. An incipient Church organization may have fared no better than the Lindelöfs during Russia's revolution.

The oldest surviving Lindelöf son moved his parents back to Finland in 1928. In May 1929, Swedish Mission president Gideon Hulterstrom visited the Lindelöf's Helsinki residence and recorded, "They had endured much for 'Mormonism' [and] were willing to endure more if necessary."[138] They did endure more, because the Church was not established in Finland, and for the rest of their lives they were the only members in Helsinki. Alma Lindelöf passed away in 1939 on the eve of World War II and Johan on February 23, 1944. Before Johan's death, he received one last visit from a Church representative, Carl Fritz Johansson, the acting mission president in Sweden. In May 1941, Johansson recorded that the aging Saint was being cared for by a daughter, who spoke bitterly of the family experiences.[139]

For seventy-five years, the Church waited for another opportunity to reestablish missionary work in Russia. When the time came, the Church was more prepared than it had been formerly in terms of manpower, willingness to commit that manpower, and the ability to field language skills. This second entrance occurred in a fluid cultural and political environment reversed from that of tradition-encrusted imperial Russia.

End of the Empires

In the late nineteenth century, Elders Ferdinand Hintze, Mischa Markow, John Ensign Hill, August Joel Höglund, and a handful of others preached in central and eastern Europe but met with little success because of deeply ingrained cultural, religious, and political traditions. While opportunities may have existed, Church leaders did not devote sufficient resources to the effort. Those who joined emigrated to Utah or fell back into obscurity caused by their isolation. Meanwhile, the empires of the past disappeared as the victors of World War I redrew the political map of Europe and the Bolsheviks replaced the Romanovs in Russia. A decade passed before a Slavic mission was established, which occurred not because of Church initiative, but rather at the insistence of a widowed sister, isolated from her faith by distance but not by testimony. However, political upheavals leading up to World War I and the Bolshevik Revolution of 1918 transformed the political map of Europe and temporarily stalled all missionary efforts.

Notes

1. Paul Robert Magocsi, *Historical Atlas of East Central Europe* (Seattle: University of Washington, 1993), 80.

2. Magocsi, *Historical Atlas,* 83–84.

3. Breck England, *The Life and Thought of Orson Pratt* (Salt Lake City: University of Utah Press, 1985), 227.

4. Stanley B. Kimball, "The Mormons in the Habsburg Lands, 1841–1914," *Austrian History Yearbook* 9–10 (1973–74): 147–49.

5. Thomas Biesinger was thirty-nine years old, born in Wiesenstetten, Württemberg, Germany, convert to the Latter-day Saint faith and emigrant to Utah in 1865. He had two wives and five children at the time of his mission.

6. Paul Hammer was forty-four years old, a native of Denmark and had driven an ox team across the plains to Salt Lake City in 1861. He had served previously as a missionary in Denmark.

7. Kimball, "Mormons in Habsburg Lands," 150–55; William G. Hartley, "A Missionary's Two Months in Jail," *New Era* 12 (November 1982): 10. Source for next two paragraphs as well.

8. Kimball, "Mormons in Habsburg Lands," 156–57.

9. Mischa Markow, "Life and History of Mischa Markow," 50–51, Church Archives, The Church of Jesus Christ of Latter-day Saints, Salt Lake City. Source for next paragraph as well. This source is published herein.

10. Jacob Spori was native Swiss. When he joined the Church in the late 1870s he lost his job and was separated from his family of a wife and four children by his vengeful father-in-law. He emigrated to Logan, Utah, where he lived until called to serve a mission to Turkey in 1884. After his mission he was reunited with his family and became the founding father of Ricks College, now BYU–Idaho.

11. A native of Denmark, Ferdinand Hintze had emigrated with his family to Utah at the age of ten. Raised in the American west, he was a veteran missionary, having served two missions for a total of four years in the northwest portion of the United States. Espoused to two living women, he was assiduously hunted, along with his polygamous contemporaries, and incarcerated by federal officials in Utah. His service in the Middle East placed him far from their grasp.

12. Markow, "Life and History," 52.

13. Ferdinand Hintze, Journal commencing November 1, 1886, entry dated March 10, 1888, 175–76; Ferdinand Friis Hintze, papers, 1882–1916, Church Archives.

14. Hintze, Journal, 176, and Markow, "Life and History," 52.

15. Hintze, Journal, 177.

16. William Hale Kehr, "Missionary to the Balkans: Mischa Markow," *Ensign* 10 (June 1980): 31–32.

17. James L. McMurrin to Francis M. Lyman, April 11, 1901, cited in *Millennial Star* 63 (April 25, 1901): 268.

18. Arnold Schulthess, Autobiography, 38, Arnold Henry Schulthess papers, 1866–1924, Church Archives.

19. Kehr, "Missionary to the Balkans," 31–32.

20. Markow, "Life and History," 60–61. Source for the next paragraph as well.

21. Markow, "Life and History," 62–64, 175–76.

22. Markow, "Life and History," 77–78.

23. Markow, "Life and History," 78–79.

24. Hungarian District Manuscript History, December 31, 1904, Church Archives; Hungarian Conference Record of Members, 1901–14, Family History Library, The Church of Jesus Christ of Latter-day Saints, Salt Lake City (hereafter cited as Family History Library). Except as otherwise noted, source for next paragraph as well.

25. Markow, "Life and History," 78; Hungarian District Manuscript History, December 31, 1904; Hungarian Conference Record of Members, 1901–14.

26. Markow, "Life and History," 79.

27. James L. McMurrin to Francis M. Lyman, April 4, 1901, cited in *Millennial Star* 63, no. 16 (April 18, 1901): 253.

28. Kehr, "Missionary to the Balkans," 31–32.

29. H. G. Mathis, "Experience in Hungary," *Deseret Evening News,* October 12, 1901, 22; Francis M. Lyman to George F. Gibbs, September 10, 1901, Francis M. Lyman letterpress copybooks, 1901–3, Church Archives.

30. John Schweburger, "Autobiography of John Schweburger 1931–32," copy in possession of author.

31. "Notes from the Mission Field," *Millennial Star* 66 (October 6, 1904): 636.

32. Markow, "Life and History," 80.

33. Kimball, "Mormons in Habsburg Lands," 160. The Kimball source conflicts with Markow's journal, which is cited above.

34. Helene Bernhardt, "History of the Saints in Roumania," 1, Church Archives.

35. "Events of the Month," *Improvement Era* 8 (November 1904): 80.

36. "Notes from the Mission Field," 636.

37. Serge F. Ballif, Journals, 1905–9, entries from July 31 to August 7, 1905, Church Archives.

38. Ballif, Journal, August 7, 1905.

39. Hungarian District Manuscript History; Hungarian Conference Record of Members, 1901–14.

40. "What a Hungarian Gentleman Writes," *Improvement Era* 14 (July 1911): 815. Of the Hungarian converts in Utah, Jacob Pfeiffer became a prominent metalworker. He founded the Utah Ornamental Iron and Bronze Works. Some of his work included the balustrades at the Utah State Capitol Building and the vault of Zion's Bank in downtown Salt Lake City. See Jacob Pfeiffer, "Ornamental Metal Work Done in Utah," Church Archives. Johann Schweburger, whose father was a shoemaker, became a leather merchant.

41. Ballif, Journal, March 30, 1906.

42. Bernhardt, "Saints in Roumania," 2.

43. Ballif, Journal, July 30 and August 2, 1908.

44. Ballif, Journal, August 4, 1908.

45. Ivy Hooper Blood Hill, ed. and comp., *John Ensign Hill: Diaries and Biographical Material* (Logan: J. P. Smith, 1962), 28.

46. Hill, *John Ensign Hill,* 29, 32.

47. Hill, *John Ensign Hill,* 30. This is an assumption based on the fact he was the first person ever baptized in Budapest and it happened only a month earlier. See Hungarian District Manuscript History and Hungarian Conference Record of Members, 1901–14.

48. Hill, *John Ensign Hill,* 30–32.

49. Hill, *John Ensign Hill,* 32, 37.

50. Hill, *John Ensign Hill,* 34–35, 41.

51. Hill, *John Ensign Hill,* 41–44, 55. Although this particular source says her last name was Nemenz, the Record of Members gives her proper surname as Franzen, and page 40 of the Hill book explains that her mother was previously married to a Frazen.

52. Hill, *John Ensign Hill,* 47–48, 54–55, 57–58.

53. Hill, *John Ensign Hill,* 75.

54. Hill, *John Ensign Hill,* 76.

55. Hill, *John Ensign Hill,* 78.

56. Bernhardt, "Saints in Roumania," 3.

57. Edmund LeRoy Smith, Record book, 1908–11, entries for the dates noted in text.

58. Helene Bernhardt to Oliver Budge, November 7, 1933, accompanies Bernhardt, "Saints in Roumania."

59. Bernhardt, "Saints in Roumania," 3.

60. Hill, *John Ensign Hill,* 76.

61. Bernhardt, "Saints in Roumania," 3.

62. "Editor's Table," *Improvement Era* 14 (October 1911): 1,116.

63. "Says Church Is Recognized: Thos. E. McKay So Writes from Swiss and German Mission," *Deseret News,* November 18, 1911, 2.

64. Hungarian District Manuscript History, March 5, 1913.

65. "President Clawson on the Continent," *Millennial Star* 75 (March 13, 1913): 174.

66. Hungarian Conference Record of Members, 1901–14.

67. Hyrum Valentine to Rudger Clawson, October 20, 1913, Hyrum Washington Valentine, papers, 1911–40, Church Archives.

68. Mary Ellen Stoddard Smith, *Wheatfields and Meadowlarks* (Bountiful, Utah: M. E. S. Smith, 1992), 40–43. Source for next paragraph as well.

69. Bernhardt, "Saints in Roumania," 5.

70. Gary Browning, *Russia and the Restored Gospel* (Salt Lake City: Deseret Book, 1997), 3–5.

71. John Bloom to Historian's Office, April 29, 1925, transcribed in Finnish Mission, Manuscript History, April 29, 1925, 24, Church Archives. The name Lindelöf can be spelled as Lindelov, Lindlof, or Lindlov. His age comes from "Johan Maurits Lindlöf" family group sheet, Family Group Record Archive, Joseph Smith Memorial Building, Salt Lake City.

72. August Höglund to President A. H. Lund, June 18, 1895, in *Millennial Star* 57 (June 27, 1895): 413–15.

73. Pohja, Finland, births and marriages, Family History Library.

74. Höglund to Lund. Source for next four paragraphs as well.

75. Stockholm Conference Historical Record Book D, 1901–18, 187, Church Archives.

76. Andrew Jenson, *History of the Scandinavian Mission* (Salt Lake: Deseret News Press, 1927), 350.

77. William L. Knecht, *From Brigham City to St. Petersburg: Sketch of the Life of S. Norman Lee* (Moraga, Calif.: Knecht Family Association, [1980?]), 25.

78. The spelling of the surname may have been Lindbohm or Lindholm.

79. Stockholm District Record of Members, early to 1930, Family History Library.

80. Francis M. Lyman to First Presidency, May 5, 1902, Lyman letterpress copybooks.

81. "Apostle Francis M. Lyman's Address," *Millennial Star* 63 (June 6, 1901): 369.

82. Francis M. Lyman to First Presidency, May 1, 1903, Church Archives.

83. "Czar Decrees Reforms," *New York Times,* March 13, 1903, p. 1, col. 1.

84. Lyman to First Presidency, May 1, 1903.

85. First Presidency to Heber J. Grant, May 16, 1903, Japan Mission letterpress copybooks, Church Archives.

86. Lyman to Smith, May 1, 1903.

87. "Letter from the First Presidency," *Millennial Star* 65 (June 11, 1903): 380.

88. Francis M. Lyman to First Presidency, June 5, 1903, Church Archives.

89. Francis M. Lyman to First Presidency, May 30, 1902, Church Archives.

90. Francis M. Lyman to First Presidency, September 6, 1902, Church Archives.

91. Francis M. Lyman to Heber J. Grant, March 5, 1903, Church Archives.

92. Francis M. Lyman to Joseph F. Smith, June 19, 1902, Church Archives.

93. Francis M. Lyman to Lofter Bjarnson, June 17, 1903, Church Archives.

94. Francis M. Lyman to Brigham Young Jr., January 21, 1902, Church Archives.

95. Francis M. Lyman to Hugh J. Cannon, September 13, 1902, Church Archives.

96. Francis M. Lyman to George Reynolds, November 12, 1902, Church Archives.

97. Francis M. Lyman to Joseph F. Smith, December 19, 1902, Church Archives.

98. Francis M. Lyman to Joseph F. Smith, February 27, 1903, Church Archives.

99. Francis M. Lyman to Matthias Cowley, June 29, 1903, Church Archives.

100. Joseph J. Cannon, "Praying in St. Petersburg for the Land of Russia," *Millennial Star* 65 (August 20, 1903): 530.

101. Francis M. Lyman to Joseph F. Smith, August 9, 1903, Church Archives; this letter is filed at the beginning of October, v. 2, 79–80.

102. Cannon, "Praying in St. Petersburg," 531.

103. *Millennial Star* 65 (November 26, 1903): 761.

104. Cannon, "Praying in St. Petersburg," 531–32.

105. Lyman to Smith, August 9, 1903.

106. Cannon, "Praying in St. Petersburg," 530.

107. Lyman to Smith, August 9, 1903.

108. Cannon, "Visit to Moscow," 548.

109. Albert R. Lyman, *Biography of Francis Marion Lyman, 1849–1916* (Delta, Utah: Melvin Lyman, 1958), 160.

110. Joseph J. Cannon, "President Lyman's Travels and Ministry," *Millennial Star* 65 (September 3, 1903): 565.

111. Joseph J. Cannon, "The Visit to Moscow, the City of Churches," *Millennial Star* 65 (August 27, 1903): 546.

112. Thomas Armitage, *A History of the Baptists* (New York: Bryan, Taylor, 1887), 830.

113. David S. Fogelsong, "Redeeming Russia? American Missionaries and Tsarist Russia, 1886–1917," *Religion, State, and Society* 25, no. 4 (1997): 355.

114. A. I. Klibanov, *The History of Religious Sectarianism in Russia, 1860–1917* (New York: Pergamon Press, 1982), 276.

115. Armitage, *History of the Baptists*, 830.

116. Markow, "Life and History," 82–83, 85–86.

117. "To the Ministry and Saints of the European Mission," *Millennial Star* 61 (January 7, 1904): 1.

118. Francis M. Lyman to Heber J. Grant, June 10, 1902, Church Archives.

119. Thomas G. Alexander, *Mormonism in Transition: History of the Latter-day Saints, 1890–1930* (Urbana: University of Illinois Press, 1986), 216–17.

120. R. Lanier Britsch, *From the East: A History of the Latter-day Saints in Asia, 1851–1996* (Salt Lake City: Deseret Book, 1998), 51–58; Reid L. Neilson, *The Japanese Missionary Journals of Elder Alma O. Taylor, 1901–10* (Provo: BYU Studies and the Joseph Fielding Smith Institute for Latter-day Saint History, 2001).

121. Markow, "Life and History," 80.

122. Francis M. Lyman to Joseph F. Smith, August 25, 1903, Church Archives.

123. Markow, "Life and History," 80.

124. "Letter from the First Presidency," *Millennial Star* 65 (September 10, 1903): 580.

125. Francis M. Lyman to Joseph F. Smith, September 7, 1903, Church Archives.

126. "Letter from the First Presidency," *Millennial Star* 65 (October 8, 1903): 652.

127. Markow, "Life and History," 80–81. Also source for the next paragraph.

128. Markow, "Life and History," 82–83.

129. Markow, "Life and History," 82–83.

130. *Millennial Star* 65 (December 17, 1903): 810.

131. Fogelsong, "Redeeming Russia," 356.

132. Klibanov, *History of Religious Sectarianism*, 276.

133. Fogelsong, "Redeeming Russia," 357.

134. Stockholm Conference, Historical Record Book D, 187.

135. *Nordstjarnan* (October 15, 1905): 319.

136. Stockholm Conference, Historical Record Book D, 187, 221.

137. Fogelsong, "Redeeming Russia," 359.

138. Hugo M. Erickson, "President Hulterstrom Visits Finland," *Millennial Star* 91 (August 22, 1929): 538–39.

139. Carl Fritz Johansson, interviewed by Carl-Erik Johansson, Salt Lake City, 1973, typescript, 41, James Moyle Oral History Program, Church Archives.

2

Slavic Mission

1929–1939

The opposing basketball teams faced each other across center court in Prague, Czechoslovakia, in 1929. The Czech YMCA team had been undefeated for three years. Their opponents wore red uniforms highlighted by jerseys emblazoned with four large block letters, "UTAH." The dark-horse Utah team consisted of six Americans newly arrived in Czechoslovakia, not necessarily to compete in athletics but rather to preach religion. The Czech captain stepped forward and, in English, presented his nation's flag to the Utah team. The Utah captain, speaking Czech, responded with an American flag. The crowd roared in applause, showing approval of the exchanges. When the final basket was made, the score stood: Mormon Utes 32, Prague YMCA 18. At the after-game dance, the missionaries, wearing suits and ties, only watched the dancing but entertained the crowd during intermission with English songs and repeated encores. This was not a standard format for preaching the gospel, but it was consistent with the Czechoslovak mission motto, "Join in and be one with them."[1]

For two decades, the Czechoslovak Mission was a lone salient of the Church in Slavic Europe, which besides Czechoslovakia included Poland, Bulgaria, and the states of the Soviet Union and Yugoslavia. Missionaries served in Czechoslovakia for fourteen years, from 1929 to 1939 and 1946 to 1950. A total of 286 people were baptized (137 before, 10 during, and 139 after World War II). Several branches were organized, the strongest in Prague and Brno. In 1950 a Communist regime installed after World War II destroyed the Church organization in Czechoslovakia but not the gospel testimony in its members' hearts. For the next forty years, until the demise of Communism in 1989, the Czech membership was isolated but resilient, stilled outwardly but silently believing, acting as an enduring outpost of their faith. In 1990 a small group that endured—

grandchildren of the generation that first accepted the gospel in a Slavic land—welcomed the return of the missionaries.

In the 1930s when Latter-day Saint missionaries began entering the country, Czechoslovakia was a young republic created from the Austro-Hungarian provinces of Bohemia, Moravia, and Slovakia by the 1919 Treaty of Versailles. Because U.S. President Woodrow Wilson had been instrumental in negotiating that treaty, Czechs thought well of Americans and were favorably disposed to learn something of these young men from overseas. A country of approximately fifteen million people, it stretched six hundred miles from the southeastern corner of Germany, past Austria, Hungary, and Romania on the south and Poland on the north, to the western borders of the Ukraine. Under the leadership of President Thomas Masaryk, the country enjoyed political stability and economic vibrancy. As for religion, Czechoslovakia, which was two-thirds Roman Catholic, had a tradition of religious dissent dating back to Jan Hus, who was burned at the stake in 1415 for denouncing Roman Catholicism. Thus the country was fertile ground for the LDS Church's first Slavic mission.

Mormon Missionaries Enter Czechoslovakia

The Church's presence in Czechoslovakia in 1929 was preceded by the efforts of a persevering missionary and a lone family. In 1902, Thomas Biesinger and his former mission president, then Apostle John Henry Smith, met on a street in Salt Lake City. Elder Smith asked if Biesinger would like to return to Europe. After Biesinger expressed his willingness, he promised, "You shall have the privilege."[2] That year the European Mission president, Elder Francis M. Lyman, gave permission for the German Mission president, Hugh J. Cannon, to "experiment by sending two wise elders into Prague, in Bohemia but I would not hurry out any others, till we feel quite sure that our feet are secure in Germany."[3] But in 1903 two German kingdoms, Prussia and Mecklenburg, banished Mormon missionaries, cooling plans to proselytize in Bohemia and delaying the possibility of Biesinger's return. Missionaries threatened the religious hegemony of state religions in early twentieth-century Europe. Several decades passed before this obstacle began to recede in the face of an increasingly cosmopolitan world.

The beginnings of the Church's lasting presence in Czechoslovakia was an indirect result of the wrenching dislocations caused by World War I. In 1919, Františka Brodilová, her nonmember husband, and their two daughters were jobless and penniless Czechs in Vienna, the Austrian capital. Františka, born in southern Bohemia in 1881, had moved to Vienna at age eighteen to live with an older sister and married there in 1904 (illus. 2-1). She read the Bible assiduously and regularly attended mass, even when she began questioning her faith. She continued to pray after she stopped attending mass and felt her prayers were answered when the missionaries knocked on her door.[4] Františka joined the Church in 1913 on the eve of World War I. The family nearly starved during the last two years of war, and in 1919 they returned to Czechoslovakia where Sister Brodilová's husband died. She and her two daughters, fourteen-year-old Františka and thirteen-year-old Jana (they later adopted the English names of Frances and Jane), eked out a meager living with the assistance of Františka's brother who lived in South America. Although isolated

Courtesy Ruth Pratt

Illus. 2-1. Františka Brodilová, a native of southern Bohemia, joined the Church in 1913 in Vienna. She and her two daughters lived in Czechoslovakia—isolated from the Church and other members but faithful to their religion—for more than a decade before the mission was established in that country in 1929.

from the Church, they continued to live according to its teachings. Serge F. Ballif, president of the Swiss-Austrian Mission, and Brother Niederhauser, of the Vienna branch, visited them and on June 3, 1921, baptized the two daughters in the Vltava River—the first baptisms in Czechoslovakia since Antonín Just in 1884.[5] Though visited only from time to time, Sister Brodilová prayed for missionaries, faithfully sent her tithing to the Church in Vienna every six months, and endured a decade of disappointment that the Church was still absent from her homeland.

The Church refrained from acting in Czechoslovakia for the same reasons that limited its expansion elsewhere in Slavic Europe. The sparse missionary force was concentrated where successes had already occurred—Scandinavia, the British Isles, western Europe, and Germany. Slavic languages were not easily learned since they had a totally different structure from the Romance and Germanic languages of Europe. Limited success in Hungary may have convinced Church authorities that it was not yet time to pursue other efforts in Slavic Europe. Furthermore, Czech authorities were still leery of the Latter-day Saints. A Czech consul in Hamburg informed Elder John A. Widtsoe in the early 1920s that "no Mormons are going to take Czech girls away."[6]

In far-off Salt Lake City, eighty-four-year-old Thomas Biesinger had not forgotten his Czech experience. He fully remembered the words of John Henry Smith, spoken twenty-six years earlier, that he would have the privilege of returning to Czechoslovakia. He confided his hopes of renewing missionary work in Czechoslovakia to President Charles Nibley, second counselor in the Church's First Presidency, whom he visited as a block teacher (precursor of the home teacher). At Nibley's suggestion, Brother Biesinger took his case to President Heber J. Grant of the First Presidency and was soon called to open the Czechoslovak Mission. Arriving alone in Prague in February 1928, he was lovingly welcomed by the Brodil[7] family. He immediately contacted police and government officials, requesting "permission to preach the gospel of Jesus Christ." To his satisfaction, none of the officials opposed his proposition. He reported to the German-Austrian Mission president, Hyrum Valentine, that the way was open.[8] Sister Brodilová's hopes soared with Biesinger's news. But the aging Biesinger was released after two and a half months, and no one replaced him. Františka, knowing that missionaries could but did not come, despairingly announced to her daughters: "Children, I'm going to write to the President of the Church, and then I'll give up because Satan is after me."[9]

It must have seemed a bold move to the humble sister in Prague to address the leader of the Church, President Heber J. Grant. But her act of desperation turned the key, and a locked door now creaked open. The First Presidency instructed newly appointed European Mission president, John A. Widtsoe, to investigate. He corresponded with Františka to obtain information on conditions in the country and then selected the messenger, Arthur Gaeth.[10]

The Church's First Slavic Mission

On May 19, 1929, Elder Gaeth, a tall and gangly twenty-four year old, was enjoying the last day of his three-year mission at a German-Austrian Mission gathering in Leipzig. President Widtsoe's request that he serve a special mission in Czechoslovakia was welcome, though somewhat unexpected. Elder Gaeth's mother was a Czech, and her patriarchal blessing had promised that her posterity would take the gospel to her native land.[11] Elder Gaeth departed for his new assignment, not expecting that it would last seven years. He entered Prague alone early on the morning of June 8, 1929.

He detrained at Wilson Station, auspiciously named after U.S. President Woodrow Wilson, and found himself walking along Hoover Street, named after the War Relief Commissioner who aided thousands of Czechs in the postwar period. Within a half hour, he had located the Brodil home, rousing them from bed at his knock. Sister Brodilová's long-suffering faith that had endured since her baptism sixteen years earlier was finally rewarded. The family eagerly assisted the missionary and helped him get acquainted with his new field of labor.

Imposingly tall, energetic, and engaging, Elder Gaeth unhesitatingly and incessantly announced the arrival of the Church to the media, government officials, and prominent citizens. Unlike the suspicion and opposition missionaries had experienced throughout Europe in the early part of the twentieth century, the reaction Elder Gaeth encountered was friendly curiosity or, at worst, apathy. Government officials were generally helpful and encouraging. Elder Gaeth wrote:

> It warmed my heart and lighted a flame of gratitude in me. After all, I was a stranger among a strange people. I knew not one word of their language. I represented a religious institution which was anything but popular in Europe. I made no pretense to hide the purpose of my coming and yet, not one of these men [had] been unkind, [but] had only been helpful to me.[12]

He eventually befriended several of Czech President Thomas Masaryk's secretaries, establishing an important presence at high government levels.[13]

Elder Gaeth promptly began learning the Czech language. However, he initially relied on German, which was widely spoken in Czechoslovakia, until he developed facility in the native tongue. With a journalistic bent and a resonant voice, Gaeth was particularly skilled to make good use of the media and to publicly represent the Church. Within ten days he had written an article for a German newspaper, made arrangements for two ten-minute radio talks to be read in Czech, planned an interview on a German radio show, and organized a lecture in German for the Urania (a German adult education institution).[14]

Equally important was Elder Gaeth's association with the Czecho-slovak YMCA, instituted by the Czechoslovak Legionnaires[15] after World War I to promote sports, cultural, and social programs. In Prague it operated a five-story building with three hundred rentable rooms and

Courtesy Kahlile B. Mehr

Illus. 2-2. In 1929, President John A. Widtsoe dedicated Czechoslovakia for missionary work at this site near Karlštejn Castle.

many English-speaking employees. Elder Gaeth lodged there, as did the missionaries who followed; later, they moved into apartments and private residences.[16] The YMCA provided a friendly milieu for missionary work and a forum to reach people through the game of basketball, a newly introduced sport in Czechoslovakia.

Having established his bearings in the capital, Elder Gaeth visited several other cities. Returning from Plzeň, approximately fifty miles southwest of Prague, he saw a magnificent castle upon a hill (illus. 2-2). His guide book told him it was Karlštejn, built six hundred years earlier by Charles IV, revered as the Father of Bohemia and ruler of that country at its cultural and political peak. At the site, Elder Gaeth found a wooded knoll adjacent to the castle and determined it to be a suitable location for Church leaders to dedicate the land for missionary work.

In July 1929, five missionaries from the German-Austrian and Swiss-German missions, President John A. Widtsoe, and others[17] arrived in Prague to dedicate the country. On the morning of July 24, they woke to thunder and rain. Ignoring the inauspicious weather, the group gathered with the Brodil family and headed for Karlštejn. By the time they arrived at the wooded knoll, the sun had broken through to announce a beautiful summer day. They began by singing "The Morning Breaks," a hymn that was fitting both for the occasion and for its message of the restoration.

Frances and Jane sang the "Hus Song," commemorating the Czech religious reformer, a symbol of religious freedom to the nation. Always observant, President Widtsoe noted the ancestral heritage of the six missionaries present: Alvin Carlson, Scandinavian; Wallace Toronto, Italian; Charles Josie, Hungarian and Mongolian; Willis Hayward, Jewish; Joseph Hart, English; Arthur Gaeth, Germanic and Slavic. Nationalities from all points of the globe were represented at the commencement of this new venture.[18]

President Widtsoe announced the establishment of a mission and appointed Gaeth as its president. Elder Widtsoe then prayed, dedicating the land for missionary work. The first mission in a Slavic country was now organized, symbolizing the introduction of the restored gospel to a major new segment of humanity.

Missionaries Teach in the "Modern Way"

With the mission established, the missionaries began their labors. Consistent with the approach used throughout the missions of that period, they sought to make "friends" first and converts later. "Friends" were people who were not interested in investigating the Church, but who were not antagonistic and, thus, potential investigators. No standard discussion format existed yet, so missionaries taught as they thought best, usually waiting for people to ask for baptism rather than challenging them to work toward the ordinance. It was a soft-sell approach that did not rush the baptismal date. The first Czechoslovak converts were baptized a year and a half after the Czechoslovak Mission was organized.

In addition to the basketball games in the Prague YMCA, the missionaries participated in community service. In July 1930, President Gaeth, Elder Ivan Zundel (who arrived in May 1930), and Elder Victor Olson taught leather work and English at YMCA summer camps for boys. Four missionaries assisted in summer camps the following year. At the YMCA, the missionaries also came into contact with the Sokol (meaning "falcon"), a nonpolitical organization founded in Prague in 1871 to promote physical fitness, morality, and good citizenship. In the early 1930s, it boasted six hundred fifty thousand members—both adult and teenage men and women. At its annual Sokol Slet, thousands performed gymnastics in unison at Prague's Sokol Arena. As part of their proselytizing effort, the missionaries organized a basketball league with the Sokols. President Gaeth and Elders Joseph Hart and Paul Tolton (who arrived in April 1930) eventually played on the Czech national team.

President Gaeth also refereed international matches with Estonia, Latvia, Lithuania, Poland, Italy, and France.[19] As Wallace Toronto wrote, these sports activities were preaching the gospel in the "modern way, through channels which reach[ed] the lives of the people."[20]

The missionaries also engaged in more traditional missionary labors: learning the language, publishing newspaper articles, writing tracts, and holding meetings. The Brodil women frequently assisted them. Františka "mothered" the missionaries, her daughters helped translate missionary literature, and all three family members taught in Sunday School and coached the missionaries in speaking Czech.

The missionaries began their study of Czech with several out-of-print English–Czech grammar books from the YMCA library. They also hired a language instructor for six weeks. More informally, the missionaries traded English for Czech lessons with other boarders at the YMCA.[21]

The lack of information about the Latter-day Saints disposed the Czech press to print most anything the missionaries submitted. During the first two years of the mission, two hundred fifty favorable articles authored primarily by the mission leaders and missionaries appeared in Czechoslovak newspapers and journals.[22] The favorable press coincided with the general easing of anti-Mormon tension in Europe as the image of the Church began to improve worldwide.[23] The plural marriage issue had faded with the publication of the 1890 Manifesto, Utah's admission to statehood, and the seating of Reed Smoot in the U.S. Senate. Church leaders successfully convinced some media leaders in Europe that the Church was not a threat. The lack of negative publicity was a welcome change from the unfavorable press that had hampered European missionary work earlier in the twentieth century.

The mission published two Czech language tracts in October 1929 and obtained permission from the police to distribute them, thus presenting the Church's doctrines even when the missionaries could not yet speak the language. These were the first of twenty-five tracts published during the mission's first three years, mostly translations from works authored by Elder Widtsoe.[24]

The missionaries held regular Sunday School and testimony meetings (usually in English) with an average attendance of nine or ten. The first public lecture (also in English) about the Church occurred on September 20, 1929, drawing an audience of just over a hundred. A regular series of public lectures through the end of 1929 averaged fifty-two in attendance.[25] By early 1930, the missionaries spoke Czech confidently enough to begin holding Sunday School in the native tongue, reading prepared scripts that friends had translated into Czech for them.[26] At the same time, the missionaries offered English classes not only to teach their language, but also to interest the students in their faith.[27]

The missionaries reached a milestone in their fluency when they held an all-Czech conference in April 1930, commemorating the centennial of the Church's organization.[28] From 1930 to 1931 they increasingly used Czech in street conversations and home instruction.[29] Late in 1931, some missionaries began to deliver ten-minute unscripted talks in Czech.

A National Sport and Health Exhibition held at Pardubice during summer 1931 provided a major opportunity to publicize the Church. The missionaries' basketball exploits were widely known and helped them gain permission to participate in the exhibit. Their display covered Utah athletes and how they observed the Word of Wisdom. Approximately two hundred thousand people, including Czech President Thomas Masaryk, viewed the exhibit and saw the attendant missionaries.[30]

From the beginning, President Gaeth established himself as a popular lecturer. In fall 1929, he addressed the English clubs in Prague, clubs whose membership included many prominent Czechs. He spoke on Utah and the Book of Mormon, mixing topics of general and religious interest.[31] Gaeth's relationship with the English clubs lasted through the seven years of his presidency and took him to lecture halls throughout the country. In November 1929, he addressed a large public gathering of five hundred in Prague on "Utah and Mormonism." The next month, he lectured at Charles University. Gaeth enriched some of his lectures with slide shows and a singing missionary quartet. In April 1930, he delivered a national radio broadcast in German entitled "One Hundred Years of Mormonism." By the end of 1930, he could also lecture in Czech.[32]

President Gaeth continued to be a public figure throughout his presidency. Unlike most mission presidents who attended exclusively to religious matters, Gaeth was remarkably involved in all aspects of Czech society, living his own motto to be "one with them." During 1932 he pursued an exhausting schedule of public lectures. He continued to represent the Church indirectly by dealing with nonreligious topics in lectures such as "New America," "Utah, Wonderland of America," and "Modern Education."[33] In 1933, Gaeth pursued other public activities such as attending the International Scout Jamboree in Gödöllö, Hungary, and serving as the secretary of the English Club Union, an umbrella organization for clubs in thirty-three communities countrywide.[34]

President Gaeth also kept Church leaders in America well informed of activities in the Czechoslovak Mission. His predilection for journalism resulted in his publishing a large number of articles, as compared to other missions, in the *Church News*—a weekly account of Church events published in Salt Lake City. (After his mission, he pursued a career as a professional correspondent and journalist.)

The missionaries worked only in Prague until early 1930 when two went to Brno in Moravia (central Czechoslovakia), and two others to Hradec Králové, about seventy miles northeast of Prague. New missionaries entered the country in 1930, raising the total missionary force from five to twelve. With increased personnel, President Gaeth could send missionaries to two more cities: Pardubice, seventy miles east of Prague, and Mladá Boleslav, thirty miles north of Prague.

Because of his extended missionary service, thirty-one-year-old President Gaeth had not been able to marry and had no prospects. Elder Widtsoe introduced him to twenty-nine-year-old Martha Králíčková, a Chicago school teacher, in November 1929.[35] The occasion was an address of Widtsoe's wife, Leah Eudora Dunford Widtsoe, to a gathering of the Prague English clubs. Martha's father, a university professor and close associate of President Masaryk, had earlier visited Salt Lake City, met Church officials, and become friends with Elder James Talmage. Martha was in Czechoslovakia to settle her father's estate. At that time she was not a member of the Church, but with President Widtsoe's encouragement, President Gaeth began to court her. Like Gaeth, she was well educated, politically aware, and socially polished. Before she left in summer 1930, he had proposed, and she had accepted.[36]

In January 1931, Arthur Gaeth took a three-month leave of absence to baptize and marry Martha Králíčková in Salt Lake City. After they returned to Czechoslovakia, Sister Gaeth added new dimensions to the mission. She advised the missionaries in matters of personal care and manners, such as wearing hats, as it was improper to go without.[37] More important, Sister Gaeth's social connections allowed the newlyweds to circulate in Prague's best circles. Sister Gaeth became no less prominent than her husband. She joined the Czechoslovak National Council of Women and served as one of eleven delegates from Czechoslovakia to the International Convention of Women's Clubs held in Paris in 1934.[38]

The Church acquired a fashionable villa in a new section of Prague to serve as the mission home. There the Gaeths hosted social gatherings, not only for Church members but also for prominent Czechs such as the members of the Foreign Ministry and professors from Charles University in the spring and fall of 1935 respectively.[39] Social gatherings such as these promoted goodwill and, undoubtedly, left favorable impressions with those who attended.

The Czech Mormon Community Takes Root

Despite considerable missionary effort, conversions were sparse. Although people responded cordially to the amiable young Americans, they were not as interested in their beliefs. Conversion entailed commitment to a different mode of thinking and living. Without functioning congregations or a Czech Book of Mormon, there was little beyond a spiritual witness to persuade friends to investigate.

There were ten members within the mission boundaries when it was first organized. All had moved into Czechoslovakia after being baptized, and they were scattered geographically. Only the Brodil women contributed to the mission's development. Finally, in 1931, four baptisms took place. Ironically, the first one occurred in Romania. Etelka von Haragos had learned about the Church from a Vienna Conference meeting announcement and had written to Gaeth when he was president of the conference. President Gaeth visited relatives in Romania for Christmas 1930 and, on his way back to Prague, baptized Sister von Haragos. Since she was Hungarian, she desired to translate the Book of Mormon into her native tongue and in January 1933 sent Gaeth the manuscript.[40]

Also baptized in 1931 were two more women and a man: nineteen-year-old Bohumila Moracová of Celákovice, about ten miles outside of Prague; seventy-eight year old Emilie Hromatko, a German living in Pardubice; and thirty-one-year-old Jaroslav Kotulan, a well-educated Czech in Brno who had helped translate mission texts and had gone door-to-door with the missionaries.[41]

In April 1931, the persevering Sister Brodilová became the mission's first Relief Society president, responsible for directing the Church's female members in Prague. Her service was cut short by an untimely death seven months later. Still she had lived to see the Church established in her homeland. Her two daughters, Frances and Jane, continued to sustain the Church after her death. They helped translate texts into Czech, taught investigators, and filled leadership positions in Church auxiliary programs. Frances served in the Sunday School and Jane in the Mutual Improvement Association, which provided non-Sunday youth activity.

The Czechoslovak Mission organization continued to develop. In 1932 missionaries labored to establish permanent branches in various cities. Thirteen new converts during the year began to make this a possibility. A second Sunday School began in Brno, and "amusement committees," which provided for organized social activities, were established in Prague and Mladá Boleslav. Martha Gaeth organized a Beehive Group for young teenage girls in Prague.[42] A welfare effort was organized to assist the poverty stricken Šebek family living in Čerčany, south of Prague, by helping them obtain a more suitable cottage, some clothing, and a little money.[43]

The full complement of missionaries gathered annually at each Church branch to hold a conference, build up the faith of the members, and coordinate the missionary work. They preached, sang in quartets, and performed violin and piano solos. Providentially, many of the early missionaries were musically talented.[44]

During the summers, Church activity came to a halt in most branches as members vacated the cities to take weekend excursions. An attempt was made during summer 1932 to compromise with this tradition by holding some branch meetings in the forest.[45]

Because of the lack of members, President Gaeth encouraged those of other religions to participate in Latter-day Saint Church worship services and activities. The Relief Societies and Beehive groups from 1929 to 1932 consisted mainly of members of other faiths, some of whom even held leadership positions. The activity of these girls was encouraged by dealing with subjects other than strictly religious topics. For instance, the Relief Society concerned itself with national as well as religious issues.[46]

The membership was still sparse, and growth lagged severely behind Germany to the north. Conversions there were in the hundreds, and membership rose to the thousands. But in Czechoslovakia, friendship rather than fellowship remained the norm as the people warmed only slowly to this new religion. One had to be a visionary to expect that these small beginnings would have a future, but such was the vision of Elder Widtsoe.

The European Mission Presidents Convene in Prague

In summer 1932, the mission presidents from Europe convened in Prague for an annual conference (illus. 2-3). Newspaper articles, handbills, and large posters advertised the sessions. A banquet held on July 8 included prominent Czechoslovak editors, publishers, and other professionals and leaders, as well as the mission presidents and Czechoslovak missionaries. President Gaeth, feeling the need to address all levels of

Courtesy Nan Beesley

Illus. 2-3. Missionary conference in 1932. Back row *(left to right):* Thurlburn Holt, Sterling Beesley, Martin Ririe, Victor Olson, Spencer Taggart, Dresden Miller, Joseph Toronto, Lynne Pettit, Ivan Zundel, Paul Tolton, and Heber Hansen. Front row *(left to right):* Leah D. Widtsoe, John A. Widtsoe, Arthur Gaeth, Martha Gaeth.

Czechoslovak society, was encouraged that this session permitted the Church to break the "crust of higher society."[47]

The culminating worship service on Sunday, July 10, was in President Gaeth's words "one of the greatest spiritual feasts held by a group of people." During the conference, Elder Widtsoe envisioned the future, predicting that instead of tens, thousands of members would meet in Prague and that the gospel door would be opened to all Slavic peoples: "When Russia has prepared herself for the Gospel, think how great the harvest will be."[48]

Even as the conference was in session, the Czechoslovak nation celebrated Sokol Slet, a festival occurring every six years where thousands of Czechs honored their nation's heritage with a massive display of coordinated calisthenics at the Sokol Stadium in Prague. It was a bright day for the Czechoslovak nation, but distant rumblings were troubling those attuned to the times. On the last day of the conference, a young Jewish woman who had been investigating the Church approached Elder Spencer Taggart and said she had finally decided to be baptized. As the afternoon waned on the second day after the conference, four missionaries, three members, and Elfrieda (Frieda) Glasnerová traveled to a small village on the banks of the Vltava, then ferried to a small island. The baptism was performed as a brilliant sun descended below the western horizon. Elder Taggart confirmed her as, in his words, "The subdued colors of a summer twilight and silhouette of the rolling Bohemian hills pronounced a fitting benediction."[49] One of eight children, Glasnerová was baptized against the will of her father, who felt disgraced that she had abandoned her Jewish heritage.[50] The loss of a Jew by conversion was soon to be dwarfed, however, by a tragedy then in the making as a resurgent Germany listened to Adolf Hitler's ravings.

Adolf Hitler became the chancellor of Germany in January 1933. The next month, the Nazis burned the Reichstag and laid the blame on the Communists. By July, Hitler's Gestapo were systematically hunting down his opponents. Freedom of the press was abolished, and all labor unions and parties except the Nazis were banned. In August, Hitler gave himself the title of Führer and set his nation on a course to conquer Europe. But that was still in the future, and, for the moment, missionary work proceeded in an atmosphere of tranquillity, tinged only occasionally by trouble.

The Missionary Force Diminishes

The year 1933 began auspiciously with the publication of the Book of Mormon in Czech. Edward Havránek, a reporter for a Czechoslovak magazine, translated the work under President Gaeth's direction. The Brodilová sisters reviewed his translation. Their understanding of the gospel provided the basis for correcting mistakes made by a translator who did not fully comprehend the concepts and words.[51] In February 1933, three thousand copies came off the press. The mission sent a hundred to libraries throughout the country and presented others as Christmas gifts to the country's leaders.

Even as the availability of Latter-day Saint scriptures enhanced the opportunity to preach, the number of missionaries began to diminish because of the Great Depression in the United States. The numbers peaked at fourteen in January 1931. The first six missionaries left, and few replacements arrived. The second wave of Czech missionaries began to leave in December 1932. Elders Thurlburn Holt and Ivan Zundel left a half year early because of increasing economic difficulty in their families. Fortunately, three new missionaries arrived the same month.[52] But in 1933 the situation became tight. Three missionaries left early in the year without any arrivals to replace them. At the end of 1933, the missionary force had dropped from the fourteen of early 1931 to eight. While this presented a significant problem for the Czechoslovak Mission, it was not any different in other missions worldwide. The Church had sent out approximately a thousand missionaries each year during the 1920s. In 1932 it sent out only 399.[53]

President Gaeth found various ways to compensate for the shortage. He brought twenty-one-year-old Olga Komárková into the mission office to work half days in November 1933. The Gaeths had befriended her when they requested that she translate James E. Talmage's *Articles of Faith* into Czech, since she had studied English in school and taken private lessons at an English institute. After reading twenty pages, she became enthralled, and, when she finished the manuscript, she asked to be baptized.[54] Sister Komárková continued to assist at the mission home for nearly two years.

Missionary numbers reached their nadir in 1934. Two missionaries arrived in March, but four left in November. The total force then comprised seven, only one more than on the first day of the mission. To remedy the situation, President Gaeth began calling members on local missions. In February 1935, he called twenty-year-old Karel Mueller and twenty-eight-year-old Lidmila Pichová, both of Kosmonosy (close to Mladá Boleslav), and thirty-six-year-old Jaroslav Kotulan of Brno.[55]

Missionary Routines and Diversions

The normal missionary routine consisted of going door-to-door with tracts for two to three hours each day, visiting, teaching English classes, and helping manage branch activities.[56] Summarizing the experiences of a tracting day, Elder Spencer Taggart wrote, "Today I made forty-nine personal contacts, gave away sixty-three tracts, and 12 people shut the door in my face."[57] Visiting those who had become acquainted with the Church or the missionaries might lead to gospel conversations and the opportunity to teach. The missionaries continued teaching English classes, taking advantage of the widespread interest in United States culture. Elder Taggart recorded that the classes led directly to the baptism of a young woman studying law, as well as her sister and her son.[58] As an adjunct to their primary purpose, missionaries carried the load of branch leadership until new converts could follow their model and conduct the Church program on their own.

The missionaries assisted Gaeth during his public lectures and other activities. Some of these were not just placid affairs. During one of Gaeth's lectures in Pardubice, an Adventist preacher in the group became agitated and wanted to argue. After the session, four of his friends waited outside and distributed handbills that invited people to their meetings. Close by, Salvation Army troopers handed out their magazine to the crowd of 180 people exiting the lecture hall.[59]

On one occasion, while speaking at an orphanage, he took along missionaries to perform quartets, double quartets, solos, and comic songs. It was part of his program of being "one with the people" and preaching the gospel in the "modern way" or, as Elder Taggart termed it, in "different ways."[60]

Experienced missionaries indulged in mild teasing of newcomers. Elders Spencer Taggart and Milton Smith posted themselves apart from each other at Wilson Station behind slouched hats and newspapers, awaiting the arrival of Leland Murdock and William South. Two bare-headed youths, loaded with luggage, wandered into view. They saw Taggart and headed in his direction, then "spied [his] companion and changed course." Confused, they stopped to counsel. One remarked, "That fellow over there looks something like a Mormon missionary." They headed toward Taggart, who could not keep a straight face when one asked, "Aren't you a Mormon missionary?"[61] They also enjoyed watching the "greenies" get accustomed to the new culture. William Rigby wrote home, "I surely get a kick out of eating with these new missionaries. They think every thing isn't fit to eat, so particular. About all they need to do is get good and hungry then it tastes good to them. I am so now that I can drink sour milk and eat most any thing they give me."[62]

Despite teasing their greenies, older missionaries fulfilled their duty of teaching the language to newer arrivals. The efforts of the young missionaries to develop speaking skill could lead to mirth. For instance, one of the younger missionaries became confused and started using a tracting speech for a prayer.[63] To assist the seniors in teaching the language, specifically the gospel language needed to proselytize, Elder Sterling Beesley wrote a Czech language study key in 1933.[64]

President Gaeth encouraged the missionaries to become acquainted with the people and the land of Czechoslovakia. He also saw travel as an opportunity for the missionaries to develop their language skills by being in provincial areas where they were forced to rely on Czech rather than English or German. In the summertime, when Church attendance faded, missionary companions headed into different portions of the country.

Hoping to teach them humility, President Gaeth advised them to go without "purse or script," imitating a practice of nineteenth-century missionaries.[65] Sometimes the missionaries used knapsacks to carry their supplies, bought food from local farmers, and slept in the open air or at hotels in the larger communities. They enjoyed the expansive vistas, lush forests, and valleys dotted by humble villages as well as the more frequented tourist sites. Permissible under mission rules of the period, occasional excursions were planned outside mission boundaries. In August 1930, the entire group of missionaries traveled to Bavaria in southern Germany and attended the world famous Oberammergau Passion Play.[66] On one occasion, Elder Sterling Beesley was even permitted to go sightseeing with Elder Robert Toronto from the German-Austrian Mission.[67]

A Secure Foothold amid Trials

Despite these diversions to missionary life, the young elders still performed their work faithfully, establishing a small but firm foothold in Czechoslovakia that endured war, repression, and even internal disruption for sixty years. In terms of numbers, missionary success in Czechoslovakia prior to World War II was modest, but in terms of faith it was enduring, even though it was hindered by a limited missionary force, internal dislocations among the membership, opposition from without, and insufficient facilities and funds. During 1933 and 1934 the greatest baptismal success, and then the greatest mission problems, occurred in the neighboring communities of Mladá Boleslav and Kosmonosy, to the northeast of Prague. There twenty-six of the thirty-six baptisms registered for the two-year period were performed. Twenty-one of the converts were women, and the mission organized a second Relief Society in March 1933. In early 1934, the average attendance at meetings in Mladá Boleslav ranged from 60 to 140 people, and in Kosmonosy, 30 to 60.[68]

Even though these baptisms constituted the first concentrated missionary success in the country, they also engendered the first major mission crisis. In late 1933, the Relief Society president and a counselor, who had jointly purchased a coat, quarreled over sharing it according to a pre-purchase agreement. The counselor was released in January 1934, and Sister Gaeth circulated "Rules of Order" for Relief Societies in the mission. Still, the counselor bitterly denounced the Church, distributed anti-Mormon literature, and attempted to stop people from attending meetings. In October the former counselor was excommunicated, but good feelings in the branch were blighted and further missionary success stymied.

The first major external opposition ensued soon thereafter. Catholic priests in Mladá Boleslav and Kosmonosy filed police complaints against the missionaries in January 1934. Though these were quickly dismissed for insufficient evidence, a new complaint in May accused the missionaries of being "immoral and undesirable" aliens and charged that "Mormons are a sect forbidden in every state outside of Utah because of polygamy." The local Catholic press threatened that those attending Latter-day Saint church meetings would be excommunicated. At the suggestion of his political friends in the office of President Masaryk, President Gaeth sued for libel, hoping to protect the missionaries from legal harassment and squelch the spread of rumors that might hinder the proselytizing effort.[69]

The trial was conducted in three sessions between July and October. The prosecution could provide no witnesses to immorality, though they did muster complaints from parishioners "forced" to take Church literature or angered by the doorbell being rung "severely." At Gaeth's request, J. Reuben Clark of the First Presidency transmitted a statement through his contacts in the U.S. State Department to the Czechoslovak consul in Prague. The statement contradicted the inaccurate information about the status of the Church in the United States. The priests finally signed a retraction.[70]

In 1935 the press mounted its first serious anti-Mormon campaign. A February article entitled "Queer Missionary Activities of Mormon Preachers" appeared in *Lidové Listy* (Peoples' Pages), a Prague Catholic paper. It purported that the missionaries were German espionage agents. Fearing that any connection between the Church and the rising specter of Nazi Germany could have serious repercussions, President Gaeth sued the paper and obtained a favorable judgment. The paper published a retraction, paid court costs, and contributed a small sum to charity.[71]

With limited facilities and funds, circumstances for member activity were not always ideal. Early meetings in Pardubice were held in a hotel, and sometimes in its bar. Elder Spencer Taggart complained, "This evening we were wedged in among a ping pong tournament, a club dinner, a violin concert, and a dancing class. I had spent about thirty hours preparing my talk but I could hardly be heard."[72] In 1935 the Prague Branch had to move to another hall because the building in which they had held their meetings began accommodating prostitutes.[73]

These problems notwithstanding, the mission modestly progressed. Fifteen converts were baptized in 1935 and thirty in 1936—the highest annual total before World War II. The missionary force grew. New arrivals gradually increased the number to its highest prewar total of twenty-four in 1938. President Gaeth sent them to additional cities, including Bakov (north of Prague), Tábor, and Soběslav (both south of Prague) beginning in 1935.[74]

As membership increased so did the opportunity to create branch leadership. In May 1933, the first branch presidency was organized at Prague.[75] Josef Roháček was called as the first male Czech to a leadership position—first counselor in the branch presidency.[76] Anticipating the development of branch programs throughout the mission, President Gaeth published a manual for branch leaders in September 1933.[77] Before World War II, branches were also established in Brno and Mladá Boleslav.

In 1933, Elder Spencer Taggart initiated the Church's genealogical research program by teaching classes in Prague on basic techniques and record keeping. Auxiliary programs within the branches continued to develop through the prewar period. For example, in 1933 the branch Relief Societies began holding annual bazaars, consisting of entertainment and the sale of homemade goods with the proceeds being donated to the poor. The Prague branch held the first "swarm day" in May 1933 for the young women involved in the Beehive program (illus. 2-4); eighteen teenage girls attended and participated in a variety of activities.[78] By 1935 twenty-six young women were consistently involved.[79] There were too few young men to establish a complementary male youth program.

Activities committees functioned in the branches. Beginning in 1933, President Gaeth encouraged each branch to have a monthly social. Activities in early 1934 included a surprise birthday party for Sister Gaeth, a masquerade party, the first mission dance, excursions to the countryside, and a Relief Society party. In February 1936, the mission held a Gold and Green Ball, an event held annually in Church units worldwide.[80]

To further assist the development of branches, President Gaeth began a unique program of "spiritual rejuvenation" in 1935. Meetings with preaching, worshipping, and singing were scheduled daily for an entire week in each branch. Gaeth gave lectures such as "Is Religion a Dead Issue?" and "What Constitutes Evil?" Average attendance ranged from 108 per meeting in Prague to 34 per meeting in Pardubice.[81]

Members living outside the branches were not forgotten. President Gaeth sent letters and mission literature to them. He supplemented this contact with infrequent visits. In June 1933, he visited Adelheid Passinger at Nové Sedlo (at the western edge of the country); Passinger had been baptized in Germany before World War I and was one of the members living in Czechoslovakia before the mission was formed. During summer

Courtesy Nan Beesley

Illus. 2-4. Beehive girls in the Czechoslovak Mission, c. 1935. Martha Gaeth *(center)* is flanked by Frances Brodilova *(left)* and Jane Brodilova *(right)*.

1933, the young people of the Prague Branch visited the Šebeks, who were then living isolated in the village of Nový Vestec.[82]

The paucity of faithful and eligible Czech men left the unmarried sisters open to consider the attention of young American men. The tacit mission rule was that an elder had to wait six months after returning home before pursuing serious relationships.[83] This did not deter the ardor of three missionaries who, after the wait, sent proposals to their mission acquaintances. The first sister to accept, Olga Komárková, left for Provo, Utah, to wed Dresden Miller in September 1935. The other two to accept were the Brodil sisters. Frances had secretly admired missionary Calvin McOmber and mourned his departure in fall 1935. Calvin began to correspond with the Brodil sisters after his return to Idaho. By fall 1936, he proposed to Frances. In April 1937, she arrived in Pocatello and embraced and kissed her future husband for the first time.[84] Jane received a proposal from former missionary William South and departed for Salt Lake City in May 1938. Both sisters realized a blessing promised them in 1932 by the patriarch of the European Mission, James H. Wallis, to be married in the Salt Lake Temple.[85]

These departures aside, the legacy of the Gaeth years was a small but secure foothold in Czechoslovakia. The Church grew slowly but firmly. President Gaeth fomented a wide range of missionary activity that built upon the curiosity of a people little aware of this American faith. Not many passed from curiosity to conversion, but the few who did faced an uncertain future in their isolated situation on the edge of conflagration. The denouement of Elder Widtsoe's prediction that Church numbers would someday reach the thousands was delayed, but not doomed.

Church Enclaves in Yugoslavia and Romania

Czechoslovakia was not the only eastern European country to receive tidings of the Church between the wars. President Gaeth envisioned the gospel going to all Slavic nations, and, for the moment, prospects looked encouraging. As a direct result of publicity from the 1932 mission president's conference, he received several inquiries from Yugoslavia. One came from Eviza Arbicz of Croatian descent, baptized in Budapest, Hungary, in 1914 when she was nineteen years old. She was the only southern Slav (a large ethnic group in the Balkan Peninsula of southeastern Europe) baptized during a decade of missionary work in Austro-Hungary.[86] Another inquiry came from a merchant in Zemun, across the Sava River from Beograd, capital of Yugoslavia.[87]

Sister Eviza Arbicz Vujičić wanted to know about the Church that had orphaned her nearly two decades earlier. She had not lost contact entirely, having received issues of the Church's German publication *Der Stern* and occasional letters from several presidents of the German Mission. Through years of isolation she had remained faithful. As President Gaeth recorded: "My visit brought her the greatest joy she had experienced in years. We talked for hours and she reiterated to me the experiences and trials she had undergone since the war." Indicative of her commitment, she turned over the tithing she had saved since her baptism.

After talking with Sister Vujičić, President Gaeth visited Matej Spaček, the second correspondent. Because of Gaeth's letters, the merchant was anticipating his call and welcomed him and his companion warmly. Tears of joy welled in his eyes as he listened to the gospel message. President Gaeth returned for a second visit the next day. As Gaeth left, Matej said baptism could not come too soon for him. After his departure, Sister Vujičić continued to regularly visit and teach the gospel to Matej. The following year, President Gaeth and Elder Dresden Miller visited Yugoslavia and baptized Brother Spaček. The ceremony, the first ever to take place in Yugoslavia, occurred in the Danube River near Zemun on August 14, 1933.[88]

In spite of these successes, the missionary effort still had hurdles to clear. Most serious was the Yugoslav law against proselytizing of any kind.

It prohibited distributing religious literature and preaching publicly. John D. Prince, the American Consul in Beograd, was still optimistic, suggesting to Gaeth that missionaries might be sent to the country to learn the language and teach English, and through these contacts, teach in homes.

Even less encouraging for President Gaeth was a visit to Zagreb, capital of the Yugoslav state of Croatia. There he met another of his correspondents, a graduate student majoring in languages at Zagreb University. For hours they talked about the gospel, prayed, and discussed the conditions of the country. The student had been sufficiently interested to translate the Articles of Faith into Croatian. Then he proclaimed his readiness to be baptized. Gaeth related:

> We finally set the day for baptism, but on our journey to the river I became moved and disturbed and something told me not to baptise [sic] him, that he was not yet ready for such an important step, inspite [sic] of his earnest talking and apparent conversions. When we arrived at the banks of the Sava, we found the river a roaring torrent, swollen two meters over its banks. We decided to postpone the baptism until my next visit.

Before Gaeth left, the young man confided that he was without work and would like to serve as a missionary and receive remuneration. Gaeth explained that missionary work was performed gratis and advised him to find a job. The student's promise to do his best to promulgate the gospel and to translate tracts ended with a single card, received later, notifying President Gaeth that he had left for another city to find work.[89]

Helene Bernhardt, living in Brassó (Braşov, Romania, after World War I), awaited the return of the missionaries since they had departed just before World War I (see chapter 1). In 1926, Elders Thalman Hasler and Obert Tanner from the German-Austrian Mission visited the branch. Sister Bernhardt wrote later: "Can you realize what it means to be able to partake of the Sacrament and to enjoy the spirit of a meeting after such a long time of twelve years?"

In 1929, President Gaeth made his first visit to Braşov. That same year, Hyrum Valentine, the last mission president to preside over Hungary before World War I, also visited. Sister Bernhardt felt as if "good old times had returned."[90] President Oliver Budge of the German-Austrian Mission and Don Corbett passed through in 1931. President Budge later noted that Sister Bernhardt was holding together "a group of the best women he had ever met." The group operated as a Relief Society. Unfortunately, priesthood leadership had ended with the death of Andreas Bergel in 1923.[91] With priesthood holders present again, the women could once more partake of the sacrament, weeping for joy at the privilege.[92]

In 1933, Sister Bernhardt wrote: "In all these years we have had 48 missionaries here in Kronstadt [the German name for Brassó], and 38 baptisms were performed. Really not many for such a number of years."[93]

In 1934, President Gaeth called on Sister Bernhardt and visited for three days. There he held a fast and testimony meeting at which all the sisters bore staunch testimonies. He also held a public service for friends and contacts of the sisters.[94]

Beginning July 28, 1934, President Gaeth visited Romania, Turkey, Bulgaria, and Yugoslavia. At Zalău, Romania, he visited Etelka von Haragos, one of the first to be baptized after the creation of the Czechoslovak Mission. At Valea Lungă, Romania (also known by the German name of Langenthal), he met Johann Fielker and his wife. Brother Fielker had been baptized over twenty years earlier in Germany, and he had not seen missionaries since then. Gaeth ordained Brother Fielker to the office of deacon. While there, he also preached to sixteen friends of the Fielkers for several hours that evening.

President Gaeth continued on to Turkey and Bulgaria. He gathered information about religious affairs but did not visit any members, since the fate of Markow's converts in Bucharest thirty-five years earlier was apparently unknown. He then returned to Czechoslovakia via Yugoslavia. President Gaeth spent three days in Beograd, visiting two members and teaching others. He held a sacrament meeting with six people in attendance. The group was so enthusiastic about the service that they prevailed upon Gaeth to hold another meeting with them on the following evening.[95]

In August 1935, President Gaeth again visited Etelka von Haragos in Romania for a few days. Her life had taken a tragic turn during 1932 and 1933 when her husband and then her daughter died. Living in isolation from the Church, she felt little purpose or hope. She had not resolved her grief, which, at the time, was making her life miserable.[96]

The reports of the Czechoslovak Mission are silent with regard to the ultimate fate of most members surviving outside the edges of an organized Church congregation.

János Denndörfer: Isolated Yet Stalwart

The decision against proselytizing in Hungary did not change between the world wars. In 1929 the lone member in Budapest since World War I, Anna Kaufmann, passed away.[97] During his 1934 trip to

Romania, President Gaeth learned of a member, János Denndörfer, living in Debrecen, Hungary, located near the eastern border with Romania.[98] Brother Denndörfer had been born in 1894 at Langenthal (today Valea Lungă, Romania), Transylvania, a German enclave in Austro-Hungary. Just prior to World War I, János followed his father and friends to Germany's Ruhr Valley to supplement the family income by working for German industry. He lodged with a Latter-day Saint family, the Webers, and joined the Church in December 1911. Two years later, he was arrested by German police after a church service and was banished from Germany. Deciding to confer with Swiss-German Mission president Hyrum Valentine, nineteen-year-old János fled to the mission headquarters in Basel, Switzerland. He stayed, working and assisting the missionaries for a year. At the beginning of World War I, he returned to Hungary, ended up in the army, and fought on the Russian front in 1915. Returning home injured, Brother Denndörfer convalesced in Budapest for a year. Local Church members Anna Kaufmann and Eviza Arbicz visited him regularly.[99]

Brother Denndörfer, though isolated from the Church for forty years, corresponded with friends in Germany and Switzerland and regularly received copies of *Der Stern* by post. During this time, he studied the scriptures and retained his testimony. Employed as an estate manager, he worked first for a Hungarian count and later for the Catholic Church in Grosswardein. Brother Denndörfer married Luise Lephardt, and together they raised four children. The family moved to Debrecen to obtain a better education for the children. Although Brother Denndörfer taught them the gospel, his family remained Catholic, not willing to accept a Church that existed only in their father's words. Unable to visit him in 1934, President Gaeth wrote and sent some tracts that had been translated into Hungarian before World War I.[100] However, another twenty years passed before a fellow member was able to visit Brother Denndörfer.

These isolated, early members on the fringes of the Church had many unfortunate experiences. The Church was simply too small to exert its influence in all areas where it had members. Those who remained faithful, without the strengthening influence of fellow members, demonstrated a religious commitment equal to any in Church annals.

The Torontos Assume the Helm in Czechoslovakia

In 1936, after three years of service in Germany and seven in Czechoslovakia, Arthur Gaeth was released. Ten years was not an entirely uncommon term of Church service for the period.[101] For example, in

Courtesy Church Archives

Illus. 2-5. Wallace Toronto (c. 1935) was one of the first missionaries to serve in Czechoslovakia. He then served as mission president, with his wife, Martha, from 1936 to 1968.

1934, Samuel Bennion completed twenty-eight years and Charles Callis twenty-six years as presidents over the Central States and Southern States missions respectively. In 1935, Karl Stoof was released after nine years in the South American Mission, and in 1936, Willard Smith was released after serving nine years in Samoa.

President Gaeth was replaced by twenty-eight-year-old Wallace Toronto, one of the first Czechoslovak missionaries (illus. 2-5). Toronto served for an unprecedented thirty-four years. Devoted, sincere, and friendly, President Toronto deeply loved Czechoslovakia and its people. Less flamboyant than Gaeth, he continued only a portion of Gaeth's public activities, serving as secretary for the English Club Union and lecturing frequently.[102] Overall, he spent less time in social activities and more time nurturing a growing membership.

Martha Sharp Toronto, Wallace's wife—who at the time was pregnant with their second child—accompanied him to Czechoslovakia with a year-and-a-half-old toddler. At age twenty-four, Martha was younger than some of the missionaries she "mothered." Wallace taught her a few phrases of Czech, but to really begin learning the language she enrolled at the Berlitz school in Prague. Martha, who had grown up in provincial Utah, was suddenly thrust into an undreamed-of world, new and frightening in its challenges. Within six months of her arrival, she delivered her second child. Because her language skills were still lacking, an interpreter assisted during the childbirth.[103]

Even as President Toronto's family grew, he energetically visited every branch each month. He found turmoil in Mladá Boleslav but was encouraged with the stability in both Brno and Prague. These visits resulted in a revamping of the missionary effort (illus. 2-6). Consequently,

Illus. 2-6. Communities in Czechoslovakia where Mormon missionaries preached, 1929–39.

Mnichovo Hradiště (north of Prague) and Kolín (east of Prague) were opened in 1936. He opened Prostějov (twenty-five miles northeast of Brno), Královo Pole (a suburb of Brno), Olomouc (thirty-five miles northeast of Brno), and Benešov (south of Prague) the following year. Furthermore, he removed missionaries from cities where meetings were poorly attended or where lack of baptisms prohibited the organization of a branch. This revamping closed Pardubice in 1936 and Mladá Boleslav in 1937, and the missionaries were reassigned elsewhere.[104]

Church President Heber J. Grant boosted Toronto's efforts during his July 1937 visit. The eighty-one-year-old prophet pursued a fatiguing schedule without showing signs of weariness, always conversing, mixing humor with his serious guidance and instruction. On July 11, he consoled the missionaries about the slow progress by sharing stories of his mission to Japan, where only three people were baptized while he was there, all of whom were eventually excommunicated. To encourage the missionaries, he related successes in Europe and Hawaii. In the afternoon, he addressed a public audience of two hundred fifty people, only one-fifth of them members. The visit generated forty articles in the local press, giving the Church a much-needed boost of visibility.[105]

By 1938 the number of missionaries had risen to twenty-four, permitting President Toronto to open new cities including Plzeň, its neighbor Rokycany, Kladno (west of Prague), and Přerov (thirty-five miles northeast of Brno). He also reopened Mladá Boleslav, which had been closed the previous year. The branches in Prague and Brno continued to be active. Prague even instituted a Junior Sunday School in 1938 even though the ten children were not members. In May the branch held a play and an evening of song and dance.[106]

In July 1938, the missionaries gathered in Prague for a conference that, unbeknown to them, would be the last for almost a decade. An era of peace was nearing an end. Between conference sessions, they attended the demonstrations of the tenth Sokol Slet, celebrating national unity and being "one with the people." But it was a unity that could not be sustained in the face of brute German force.

On the Eve of War

Omens of war were evident years before that era ended. Elder Spencer Taggart recorded on January 31, 1933, "Tracting was very difficult today. No one cared to listen to my message. Everyone wanted to talk about a man named Hitler who became Chancellor of Germany yesterday. They all seem to be extremely apprehensive of how this may affect Czechoslovakia."[107] As political tension intensified, missionary work suffered. Preoccupied with political developments, people had less time to discuss or ponder religion.

President Toronto witnessed a similar mood soon after his arrival in 1936 when he recorded: "Despite that fact that one of the Olympic runners, carrying the torch of peace and good will from Athens to Berlin, passed through Prague on the evening of July 30th, the war clouds still seem to hover over Europe with mocking uncertainty." The next month, three elders were apprehended for carrying cameras in a restricted military area close to the German border. Fortunately, they were able to prove their innocence.[108] But this was not the last time missionaries would be arrested.

As the portents of conflict increased, baptisms dwindled from a high of thirty in 1936, to seventeen in 1937, to six in both 1938 and 1939. Attendance at meetings diminished, and the payment of both tithing and fast offerings decreased. Missionaries labored under increasingly discouraging circumstances. They could not compete with the traumatic events distracting the nation. The Germans occupied Austria in March 1938, and in September Hitler demanded the Sudetenland in western Czechoslovakia, where a substantial minority of Germans lived. Soon afterward, the First Presidency ordered the missionaries and the Torontos to leave immediately for Switzerland. Concurrently, the Czech government banned all public meetings. The mission temporarily ceased to function.[109]

The Munich Pact, signed at the end of September 1938, was engineered by the British Prime Minister, Neville Chamberlain, to appease German aggression and avoid a war. As Hitler's armies poised on the border of the Sudetenland ready to invade, Chamberlain offered the Sudetenland in exchange for a pledge of peace. The French concurred, and the Russians remained silent, leaving the Czechoslovak government without strong political allies. This loss deprived Czechoslovakia of its western mountains, the major geographical obstacle to German invasion. With the country's future uncertain, eight of the senior missionaries waiting in Switzerland were released, and the eight junior missionaries were reassigned to England.

In November 1938, President Toronto received word in Switzerland that Josef Roháček, a prominent member in Prague for many years, had died. Acting without any certainty of what might befall them, Toronto and Elder Asael Moulton headed back to Czechoslovakia. Their train stopped at the new frontier, and the two men got off and walked an hour to the Czech railhead. They missed the funeral, but found a grateful membership anxiously awaiting their return. The brief experience of separation was but a foretaste of what was to follow.

President Toronto immediately called local leaders to take charge of the branches until the missionaries could return: Jaroslav Kotulan in Brno and Josef Roubíček in Prague. In December 1938, Toronto brought his family and the eight displaced missionaries back to Prague. Reviving a mission tradition, Toronto organized a basketball team and a male quartet to once again attract public attention. Foreseeing the need for gospel study material if the missionaries were no longer present, President Toronto distributed or published several Church texts in 1939, including the Doctrine and Covenants, the Pearl of Great Price, Talmage's *Articles of Faith*, and the Relief Society handbook.[110]

The young country, but two decades old when faced with German aggression, was not yet socially and politically united. Two major Slavic ethnic groups lived in Czechoslovakia, the Czechs and Slovaks. Ethnic diversity was accompanied by political disharmony between these two group, and Germany deftly took advantage of these conditions. In early 1939, Hitler urged the Slovaks and Ruthenians (Ukrainians living in eastern Slovakia) to declare their independence, then proffered German intervention to safeguard against civil war. In March 1939, the German army occupied the country swiftly and without any resistance. President Toronto observed, "Their reception was as cold and hateful as the rain and the sleet which accompanied them."[111]

Within two weeks of the occupation, most missionary activity had ceased. Tracting was not considered advisable. Basketball could not be played because German troops used the gymnasiums as dorms. A ban on public gatherings canceled all engagements for the missionary quartet as well as Toronto's lectures.[112] To further complicate matters, the Torontos' third child had just been born. Responsible for three small children in a land beset by uncertainty was no small strain for the couple to bear. Though nothing came of it, Sister Toronto was appalled one day to see her three-year-old son goose-stepping with some passing soldiers.[113]

Under these circumstances, the Prague Branch met to celebrate Mother's Day in May 1939. The service was drawing to a close when a uniformed German officer came through the back door. Anticipating the worst, the congregation froze in their seats. Hesitating but a moment, the officer smiled and walked down the center aisle. President Toronto left the stand to meet him. They conferred in German, everyone else sitting in stunned silence. The two then walked to the podium. Speaking in Czech, Toronto announced that the officer had something to say. The officer then addressed the group, saying among other things, "You and I have something in common, something which oversteps the boundaries of race, language, and color. . . . Despite the fact that I speak German and you Czech, yet because of the Gospel we still speak in common terms." The congregation all knew enough German to understand. Women wept in relief while men nodded in approval. The officer bore his testimony to the enemies of his country but the friends of his religion.[114]

The Nazi Expulsion

In Nazi-occupied Czechoslovakia, President Toronto successfully confronted a continuing sequence of unusual and unpredictable circumstances threatening him, his family, and the missionaries. In July 1939, the German Gestapo arrested four missionaries. The problem was not as easily resolved as the first arrest of missionaries had been two years earlier. Early the next morning, a Gestapo agent escorted Asael Moulton, one of the detained missionaries, to the mission office and then ordered President Toronto to open the mission's strongbox. Thinking quickly, Elder Moulton distracted the agent, which allowed Toronto the chance to slip a large bundle of bills from the box into a desk drawer. The agent confiscated the rest. The salvaged money proved essential to the missionaries' evacuation a few days later.[115]

The agent informed Toronto that Elder Robert Lee had been caught exchanging money on the black market. It was a practice prohibited by mission policy and a crime under German occupation. The president learned from the agent that while the Gestapo searched Lee and Moulton's apartment, Elders Verdell Bishop and Rulon Payne had walked in and were also arrested. The agent demanded a ransom of $10,000. President Toronto refused and headed to the Gestapo headquarters, where he joined a long line of petitioners. A guard moved down the line dismissing some petitioners, but granted Toronto permission to remain. Once inside, Toronto requested the release of the missionaries. The Gestapo commander blithely told him that his church was rich and could afford the ransom. In a moment of inspiration, President Toronto explained there were still one hundred fifty missionaries in Germany, each pumping $50 to $75 into the German economy every month, and if they did not release the Czech missionaries, he would order the withdrawal of all German missionaries. The ruse worked. For the sum of $1,000 the missionaries were eventually released after forty-four days in confinement.

During this crisis, Elder Joseph Fielding Smith visited Czechoslovakia while he was in Europe appraising the Church's situation there. On Saturday, July 24, the anniversary of the country's dedication for missionary work at Karlštejn, sixty-eight people traveled by bus and taxicab to the wooded knoll where, because of a ban on open air meetings, the group simply bowed their heads in a few moments of silence.[116]

Elder Smith and President Toronto finalized arrangements for the evacuation, which had been ordered by cablegram on August 24. Sister Toronto and her three children left first, traveling to the safe haven of neutral Denmark. Wallace had entrusted $3,000 to his wife to buy boat tickets to send the missionaries home. Martha traveled through hostile territory with three small children and the large sum of money. Although the Gestapo was less likely to search her than a man, the possibility still existed. In Berlin she observed the people screaming, pushing, and crowding aboard the train to assure their own escape. Fortunately, an elder from the East German Mission helped her get seats for Denmark. There Martha waited, trusting that her husband and the missionaries would also escape.[117]

On August 27, President Toronto set apart twenty-one-year-old Josef Roubíček[118] to preside over the Church in his absence. On August 30, he sent the missionaries to Denmark while he remained to negotiate the release of Elder Rulon Payne, arrested again because his name was purportedly the same as that of a British spy. He was soon freed and the two left Czechoslovakia on August 31. Back in Denmark, Elder Joseph Fielding Smith assured Sister Toronto that the war would not start until her husband and the missionaries had escaped. President Toronto and Elder Payne obtained passage on a special train carrying the British Legation out of Berlin, the last train to leave before war engulfed Europe.[119]

An epoch ended abruptly. The achievements of ten years, 1929–39, had been minimal. Fifty-six missionaries had preached in nineteen cities, published 350 articles in the Czechoslovak press, and publicized the Church widely through sports, public displays, lectures, and other activities. There were 141 names on the membership record and only seventeen priesthood holders. Czechoslovakia was much better informed about the Latter-day Saints, but clearly not disposed to accept its teachings in significant numbers. The Church had not shaken its provincial identity as a deviant sect concentrated in the American West, and its universal doctrines were still suffused by its parochial trappings.[120]

Still, the fact that a few joined may be considered significant. Why should a Czech, having a rich Christian heritage, be interested in a faith whose preachers came primarily from another country? And if one joined, it was not a matter of making a casual commitment—the Church required active participation. The main reason a few individuals decided to join was simply because the gospel answered their inner questions about life.

This commitment is illustrated in the life of one member who faced a major trial of faith soon after conversion. Bohdan Tarnavski, a thirty-two-year-old Ukrainian studying for the ministry in the Greek Catholic Church, happened by the Prague Mission home in November 1937. He entered to inquire about the Church and within a few weeks was baptized. However, Bohdan's family did not share his excitement, and they wrote for him to renounce his faith. He sought employment in the Ruthenian portion of Slovakia, a newly declared independent state. When the Hungarian army invaded Ruthenia at the beginning of World War II, they imprisoned him. Judged before a tribunal with nine other Ukrainians, the Hungarian officer questioned each about his or her religion. Bohdan honestly revealed his faith. The officer responded, "I have read of you in the newspapers of Budapest. I hear your people have done some good in this world." Bohdan lived while his compatriots were shot. He later wrote to President Toronto: "The Gospel is the most priceless thing I have in the world. I know that the Lord has preserved my life, that I may be a beacon light to my fellow men."[121]

Unfortunately, not all converts felt this deep commitment nor had such a strong testimony. The mission's first decade ended tragically for the Church when nine members were excommunicated for disaffection. One of them was found guilty of secretly baptizing a number of people, holding unauthorized meetings, and claiming to be an Apostle; he had even gathered a following of two families. Three other members were excommunicated in August, and in October 1939 five more requested that their names be removed from the membership rolls.[122] Only a small nucleus of faithful members remained, and, though severed from the Church, they endured in their belief. Elder Widtsoe's vision of thousands populating the congregations of central and eastern Europe was delayed, but a foundation had been established that survived a war and then forty years of spiritual isolation from the main body of the Church.

Notes

1. Wallace F. Toronto, "Champion 'Mormon Utes,'" *Improvement Era* 33 (March 1930): 325–26.

2. Thomas Biesinger, "Experiences of Missionary Life," typescript, ca. 1929, 5, Church Archives, The Church of Jesus Christ of Latter-day Saints, Salt Lake City.

3. Francis Lyman to Hugh J. Cannon, September 13, 1902, Francis Lyman letterpress copybooks, Church Archives.

4. Frances Brodilová McOmber, "Memories," typescript, 1983, 2–3.

5. Arthur Gaeth, "Praying a Mission into Existence," *Millennial Star* 94 (March 31, 1932): 195–96.

6. Joseph Y. Toronto, interviewed by author, February 19, 1990, Provo, Utah.

7. While the family name was Brodil, naming custom added the suffix *ová* to the family name for the females.

8. Biesinger, "Experiences of Missionary Life," 6–7.

9. McOmber, "Memories," 4.

10. Gaeth, "Praying a Mission into Existence," 196–97.

11. Arthur Gaeth, "Relating Czechoslovak Mission History at the German-Austrian Missionary Reunion, October 2, 1981," typescript, 6, Church Archives. A patriarchal blessing is given to a member upon request typically once in a lifetime. It normally states what a person can accomplish during his or her life if faithful. See William James Mortimer, "Patriarchal Blessings," in *Encyclopedia of Mormonism,* ed. Daniel H. Ludlow, 4 vols. (New York: Macmillan, 1992), 3:1066–67.

12. Arthur Gaeth, "Recalling How the Way Was Cleared for Formal Opening of Czech Mission," *Church News,* published by *Deseret News,* February 29, 1936, 8.

13. Arthur Gaeth, interviewed by Ronald G. Watt, 1976, Denver, Colorado, 5, James Moyle Oral History Program, Church Archives.

14. Gaeth, "Opening of Czech Mission," 8. Except as otherwise noted, source for the next two paragraphs as well.

15. An organization of survivors from the fifty thousand Czech and Slovak soldiers that were taken prisoners or deserted to the Russians during World War I and who were permitted to organize themselves into a fighting force on the side of the

Allies. When the Communists concluded peace with the Germans, the legion was ordered to lay down their arms. The soldiers refused and fought their way across Siberia to Vladivostok. Many returned home by way of the United States and Canada, becoming acquainted with the YMCA and establishing it in their native land. Gaeth, "Opening of Czech Mission," 8.

16. Gaeth, interview, 10.

17. Hyrum W. and Rose Valentine, president and matron of the German-Austrian Mission, Fred Tadje, president of the Swiss-German Mission, and Joseph N. Symans, his secretary.

18. Arthur Gaeth, "What a Day to Open a Mission!" *Church News*, March 7, 1936, 8.

19. Gaeth, "Relating Czechoslovak Mission History," 1; Gaeth, "What a Day to Open a Mission!" 8.

20. Wallace Toronto, "Champion 'Mormon Utes,'" 326.

21. Czechoslovak Mission Manuscript History, June 20–December 20, 1929, Church Archives.

22. Arthur Gaeth, "The Evolution of a Mission," *Church News*, February 17, 1934, 2.

23. Thomas G. Alexander, *Mormonism in Transition* (Urbana: University of Illinois Press, 1986), 234.

24. Gaeth, "Evolution of a Mission," 2.

25. Czechoslovak Mission Manuscript History, December 20, 1929.

26. Sterling Beesley, interviewed by author, February 5, 1990, Bountiful, Utah; Joseph Toronto, interview.

27. Czechoslovak Mission Manuscript History, December 20–March 20, 1930.

28. Czechoslovak Mission Manuscript History, March 20–June 20, 1930.

29. Czechoslovak Mission Manuscript History, March 20–June 20, 1930; March 20, 1931.

30. Arthur Gaeth, "Million Persons Visit Show at Pardubice City," *Church News*, August 8, 1931, 3.

31. Czechoslovak Mission Manuscript History, June 20–December 20, 1929.

32. Czechoslovak Mission Manuscript History, June 20–December 20, 1929; March 20–June 20, 1930.

33. Czechoslovak Mission Manuscript History, March 20, 1932.

34. Czechoslovak Mission Manuscript History, December 20, 1933; Gaeth, "Relating Czechoslovak Mission History," 2–3.

35. Czechoslovak Mission Manuscript History, December 20, 1929–March 20, 1930.

36. Gaeth, "Opening of Czech Mission," 1; Beesley, interview.

37. Spencer Taggart, "Becoming a Missionary, 1931–1934," typescript, 1989, 5, copy in possession of author.

38. Czechoslovak Mission Manuscript History, June 20–December 20, 1934.

39. Czechoslovak Mission Manuscript History, June 20–December 20, 1935.

40. Czechoslovak Mission Manuscript History, March 20, 1931; July 26, 1933. The translation was never published.

41. Czechoslovak Mission Manuscript History, June 20, September 20, and December 20, 1931. Source for the next two paragraphs as well.

42. Czechoslovak Mission Manuscript History, March 20, June 20, September 20–December 20, 1932.

43. Czechoslovak Mission Manuscript History, December 20, 1929; December 20, 1932. The Šebeks were baptized in Germany in 1918. They were very poor, eating one meal daily. The wife had borne twenty-eight children, four of which still lived. Even though she was in her sixties, the wife worked daily in the fields. Taggart, "Becoming a Missionary," 21.

44. Taggart, "Becoming a Missionary," 6.

45. Czechoslovak Mission Manuscript History, September 20, 1932.

46. Gaeth, interview, 18.

47. Czechoslovak Mission Manuscript History, June 20, September 20, 1932.

48. Joseph Y. Toronto to family, July 17, 1932, Church Archives; Czechoslovak Mission Manuscript History, September 20, 1932. Elder Widtsoe is alleged to have made several comments on communism during the conference. These comments cannot be substantiated by contemporary documentation. For a more complete discussion of Widtsoe's statements, see Dennis L. Lythgoe, "Widtsoe 'Prophecy' Makes the Mormon Folklore Circuit," *Sunstone* 14 (February 1990): 54–56.

49. Taggart, "Becoming a Missionary," 16–17.

50. Beesley, interview.

51. Czechoslovak Mission Manuscript History, December 31, 1930; McOmber, "Memories," 4.

52. Czechoslovak Mission Manuscript History, December 20, 1932.

53. Richard O. Cowan, *The Church in the Twentieth Century* (Salt Lake City: Bookcraft, 1980), 163–64.

54. Olga Komárková Miller, interviewed by Bruce Blumell, 1976, Salt Lake City, Utah, 1–2, James Moyle Oral History Program, Church Archives.

55. Czechoslovak Mission Manuscript History, June 20, 1935.

56. Gaeth, interview, 22.

57. Taggart, "Becoming a Missionary," 6.

58. Taggart, "Becoming a Missionary," 40.

59. Taggart, "Becoming a Missionary," 31.

60. Taggart, "Becoming a Missionary," 12.

61. Taggart, "Becoming a Missionary," 39.

62. William Rigby to Crystle Keller, February 20, 1931. "Sour milk" (*kvašne mleko*) is fermented milk.

63. Taggart, "Becoming a Missionary," 10.

64. Czechoslovak Mission Manuscript History, June 20, 1933.

65. Gaeth, interview, 17.

66. Taggart, "Becoming a Missionary," 17–19; Czechoslovak Mission Manuscript History, June 20–September 20, 1930.

67. Beesley, interview.

68. Czechoslovak Mission Manuscript History, June 20, 1934. Also source for the next paragraph.

69. Czechoslovak Mission Manuscript History, June 20, 1934; Gaeth, interview, 5.

70. Czechoslovak Mission Manuscript History, December 20, 1934.

71. Czechoslovak Mission Manuscript History, June 20, December 20, 1935.

72. Taggart, "Becoming a Missionary," 29.

73. Czechoslovak Mission Manuscript History, June 20, 1935.

74. Czechoslovak Mission Manuscript History, June 20, December 20, 1935; December 20, 1938; Czechoslovak Mission, annual genealogical reports (Form E), 1935-36.

75. A branch president supervises the activity of members in a geographic location within a Church mission.

76. Czechoslovak Mission Manuscript History, June 20, 1933.

77. Czechoslovak Mission Manuscript History, December 20, 1933.

78. Czechoslovak Mission Manuscript History, June 20, December 20, 1933.

79. "Bee-Hive Work Grows in Czech Mission," *Church News,* July 27, 1935, 6.

80. Czechoslovak Mission Manuscript History, December 20, 1933; June 20, 1934; June 20, 1936.

81. Czechoslovak Mission Manuscript History, December 20, 1935.

82. Czechoslovak Mission Manuscript History, June 20, December 20, 1933.

83. Beesley, interview.

84. McOmber, "Memories," 5-6.

85. Beesley, interview. See note 11.

86. Hungarian Conference Record of Members, 1901-14, Family History Library, The Church of Jesus Christ of Latter-day Saints, Salt Lake City.

87. Czechoslovak Mission Manuscript History, Special Report to the First Presidency, in Historical Report, December 20, 1932. Also source for next two paragraphs.

88. Eva Vujičić passed away in 1937. Nothing more is known about Matej Spaček. Czechoslovak Mission Manuscript History, December 20, 1933; June 20, 1938. Source for the next two paragraphs as well.

89. Czechoslovak Mission Manuscript History, Special Report to the First Presidency. Also source for next paragraph.

90. Bernhardt, "Saints in Roumania," 5.

91. Czechoslovak Mission Historical Report, December 20, 1934.

92. Note appended by Oliver Budge to Bernhardt, "Saints in Roumania."

93. Helene Bernhardt, "History of the Saints in Roumania," 5, Church Archives.

94. Czechoslovak Mission Manuscript History, December 20, 1934. Source for the next two paragraphs as well.

95. Czechoslovak Mission Manuscript History, December 20, 1934.

96. Czechoslovak Mission Manuscript History, December 20, 1935.

97. *Die Geschichte der Mormonen in Österreich* (Wien: Kirche die Jesus Christi der Heiligen der Letzten Tage, 1965), 16.

98. Czechoslovak Mission Manuscript History, December 20, 1934. Johann Fielker probably told Gaeth about Brother Denndörfer. Johann's brother, Michael Fielker, was baptized at the same service as Denndörfer in Herne, Germany, December 3, 1911.

99. Douglas F. Tobler, "Alone with God," *Ensign* 23 (April 1993): 50–52. Source for the next paragraph as well.

100. Czechoslovak Mission Manuscript History, December 20, 1934.

101. Mission presidents cannot, of course, have occupations during their period of service. The Church provides them a budget and funds their expenses.

102. Czechoslovak Mission Manuscript History, June 20, 1938.

103. Martha Toronto Anderson, *A Cherry Tree behind the Iron Curtain: The Autobiography of Martha Toronto Anderson* (Salt Lake City: by the author, 1977), 13–15.

104. Czechoslovak Mission Manuscript History, June 20, December 20, 1936; September 20, 1937.

105. Czechoslovak Mission Manuscript History, September 20, 1937; June 20, 1938.

106. Czechoslovak Mission Manuscript History, June 20, 1938.

107. Taggart, "Becoming a Missionary," 31.

108. Czechoslovak Mission Manuscript History, December 20, 1936.

109. Czechoslovak Mission Manuscript History, December 20, 1938; June 20, 1939. Unless otherwise cited, sources also for the next three paragraphs.

110. Czechoslovak Mission Manuscript History, June 20, 1939.

111. Czechoslovak Mission Manuscript History, June 20, 1939.

112. Czechoslovak Mission Manuscript History, June 20, 1939.

113. Anderson, *Autobiography*, 18–19.

114. Anderson, *Autobiography*, 19–21; Wallace Toronto, "Love Thy Neighbor Even as Thyself," *Church News*, May 25, 1940, 3.

115. Anderson, *Autobiography*, 21–26. Source for the next paragraph as well.

116. Czechoslovak Mission Manuscript History, December 31, 1939.

117. Anderson, *Autobiography*, 27–29.

118. Joseph Roubíček had been converted through the encouragement of Frances Brodilová, who worked in his office. She introduced him to the missionaries, who later challenged the investigator to deliver a talk at a Church meeting. He gave the talk and was baptized two months later in June 1936. In 1938 he was sustained as the second counselor in the Prague branch presidency, the lone native member in the presidency, consisting otherwise of missionaries. He had been a convert for only three years when set apart as the acting mission president. He had married Marta Teitzová in January 1939. After World War II the family emigrated to Canada and then Utah. Hoyt Palmer, "Young Czech Convert Guides Mission during War Period," *Deseret News*, February 14, 1951, 7, 13.

119. Anderson, *Autobiography*, 27–32. For information on mission evacuation in Europe see David F. Boone, "The Evacuation of the Czechoslovak and German Missions at the Outbreak of World War II," *BYU Studies* 40, (no. 3): 123–54.

120. Alexander, *Mormonism in Transition*, 237–38; Czechoslovak Mission Manuscript History, December 31, 1939.

121. Toronto, "Love Thy Neighbor," 3.

122. Czechoslovak Mission Manuscript History, December 31, 1939.

3

Soviet Empire

1946–1985

Central and eastern Europe succumbed to the temporary onslaught of Hitler only to be repressed by the more lasting juggernaut of Soviet leader Joseph V. Stalin. The trappings of the Soviet Union were new, but the substance was the same as that of the empire it replaced: a dictator controlling a populace that was either apolitical or cowed by governmental authority. The Soviet empire consisted not only of the Soviet Union, but also of satellite states on its western border that were independent in title only. The heavy hand of internal authorities that had hindered the Church's missionary work in the early twentieth century was replaced by iron-fisted, external authorities who effectively abrogated missionary work for the middle part of the century. The Church survived, but only barely, in Czechoslovakia. Members there hoped that some day the Church would return. Quietly, and with little recognition, a few émigrés from the East worked on Book of Mormon translations, anticipating the day when missionaries could use them in their native lands. Ever vigilant for an opportunity, Church officials began to exercise increased influence in the 1970s. They tempered their effort by avoiding the use of clandestine activity to spread the gospel and obeying the dictates of governing authorities, even when they opposed religious freedom. Over time, the power of this new political empire started to wane, and the Church's presence began to filter through the Iron Curtain. Headway occurred first along the western fringe in Czechoslovakia, Hungary, and Poland.

The Report of Roubíček

On October 27, 1945, a tall, gangly man arrived in Prague. On Wenceslaus Square he joined a crowd of four hundred thousand who listened raptly to their newly installed president. Later the country's president, Eduard Beneš, and its foreign minister, Jan Masaryk, received the visitor as an old acquaintance, Arthur Gaeth. Gaeth was in Europe as a correspondent covering the Nürnberg war trials. After visiting governmental authorities, he spent an evening with Church members, learning how they had fared through six years of war.[1] German occupation had brought widespread suffering. More than two hundred fifty thousand Czechoslovaks had died in uprisings, but the country had been spared from extensive destruction since campaigns had not been fought on its territory.

Church membership had been thinned by death, inactivity (it was dangerous to belong to an "American" organization), and the extradition of members of German ancestry to Austria or Germany.[2] Josef Roubíček, the acting mission president during the war, still knew the whereabouts of eighty-six members in the country.[3] "Their testimonies of the truthfulness of the gospel have not wavered," he wrote at war's end, "even in the worst moments of this great conflict."[4]

During the war, Roubíček sustained members' faith and courage despite privation, destruction, and fear. He conducted meetings regularly for most of the war, sent a mimeographed letter to each member every ten days, and led an annual excursion to the wooded knoll by Karlštejn, the site of Elder John A. Widtsoe's dedicatory prayer. In 1944 members

Illus. 3-1. This monument on Priest's Hill memorializes the 1929 dedication of Czechoslovakia by Elder John A. Widtsoe. The plaque is normally removed to protect it from vandalism.

erected a stone monument there, quietly announcing their intention to overcome challenges to the Church's existence (illus. 3-1 and 3-2). The monument consisted of twenty-nine stones, representing the dedication year (1929). It was finally erected after four months of negotiations that had elicited governmental permission for it to be built.[5]

In March 1946, Ezra Taft Benson, representing the Quorum of the Twelve Apostles, arrived in Czechoslovakia, presaging the official return of the Church to that country. He visited Czechoslovakia as well as other European countries to evaluate the members' needs. He was impressed to see people at work, factories operating, and shop windows decorated with displays. He found Church members to be as resilient as the country in serving each other and teaching friends the gospel. Fourteen baptisms had been performed during the course of the war. With President Roubíček and a group of twenty-eight members, Elder Benson held a warm and heartfelt testimony meeting. When he visited government offices to inquire about reopening the mission, he discovered that the Church had an excellent reputation and would be welcomed back.[6]

Courtesy Jiří Šnederfler

Illus. 3-2. Czech members visit the dedication memorial site on Priest's Hill in 1978. Jiří Šnederfler is standing on the far left and his wife, Olga, is seated on the bottom right. The plaque's inscription is translated as "At this site on the 24 July 1929 the Czechoslovak Mission of The Church of Jesus Christ of Latter-day Saints was founded."

The Torontos Resume Leadership

On June 28, 1946, three missionaries reentered Czechoslovakia: Wallace Toronto (as mission president), Victor Bell, and Heber Jacobs. Church members had waited seven years for this reunion. Brother Roubíček turned over $1,160, the excess of the tithing and fast offerings collected but not expended during the war.[7] President Toronto immediately began to reestablish the mission and tend to members' needs, particularly their temporal needs, by distributing aid from America.

Church members in Czechoslovakia had survived every hardship endured by their countrymen. For example, Sister Frieda (Glasnerová) Vaněčková, the 1932 Jewish convert, had spent two years in a concentration camp with her husband and two sons. She was scheduled for execution the day she was freed by the Americans.[8] When President Toronto found her in the hospital recovering from her ordeal, she wept with joy. Frieda's father, mother, and eight siblings had all died at Auschwitz. She was the lone survivor, and now she had been reunited with someone of her faith. After she was released from the hospital, she faithfully saved a tenth of her meager income to pay tithing and had her two sons baptized.[9]

Recovering from the disruption of war was arduous and time-consuming. It took a year for President Toronto to find and rent a suitable mission home, a three-story villa in Prague. It would serve as an office and as a residence for his family, now consisting of five children, ages two to thirteen. Shortly afterward, Toronto's wife and family crossed the ocean, accompanied by four missionaries. Church leaders supplied the mission with a new Ford to help the president assist the members.[10]

Arriving in LeHavre, France, the Toronto family and four missionaries traversed a desolated continent en route to Czechoslovakia. Many skylines had been leveled. Rubble now replaced the once beautiful homes, buildings, and transportation facilities. In Prague, Sister Toronto began setting up a household, no small task as necessities were scarce. Rationing severely limited the available foodstuffs, and the family could not afford to buy on the thriving black market. Each person received two eggs per month, one pound of meat, and a quarter pound of sugar. Sister Toronto shopped daily, going from the butcher to the vegetable market to the baker and then to the dairy for the children's small ration of milk.[11]

Beyond her duties for her own family, Sister Toronto oversaw the Relief Society in each of the large branches. She executed programs as nearly as possible according to outlines in the *Relief Society Magazine.* She supervised the translation of Relief Society lesson materials into

Czech, adding materials specific to the country, such as lessons about Czechoslovak authors.[12] In addition to family and Relief Society duties, Sister Toronto also managed the activities in the mission home. Youth involved with the Mutual Improvement Association (MIA) congregated there. Many of the Church's new converts were young adults. The average age dropped from thirty-six in the prewar period to twenty-nine after the war.[13] Because of a housing shortage, many missionaries stayed at the mission home for several months before being assigned to senior companions. The extended stay at the mission home also afforded them time for concentrated language study.[14]

A steady stream of missionaries began to swell the mission forces. In August 1947, six missionaries joined the four that had come with the Toronto family in June 1947. In October 1948, the proselytizing force totaled thirty-nine, the largest group of U.S. citizens in Czechoslovakia except for the U.S. embassy staff.[15] There was no missionary shortage as had existed in the prewar period.

Communism: A New Tyranny

Free Czechoslovakia survived less than three years. In 1945, Soviet leaders pressured the Czechoslovak government to appoint high-ranking officials of Communist persuasion. After a Communist coup in February 1948, the government began controlling all businesses, industries, churches, and schools. Mormon missionaries came under secret police surveillance. The police ordered publication of the mission magazine, *Nový Hlas* (New Voice), to cease, ending its influence over three thousand readers, mostly members of other faiths.[16] Church sermons and lessons had to be submitted to the authorities six weeks before being delivered. When the materials returned censored, they had to be rewritten. Agents attended meetings to ensure everything was said as written. Police threatened members who came to meetings and ordered some to spy. If they refused, they could lose their jobs or have their rations reduced.[17] In 1949, Brother Otakar Vojkůvka[18] was taken to a forced labor camp at Třinec near the Polish border. His only crime was that he was a successful businessman. He had to serve only six months of the original two-year sentence.[19]

Given the political repression, the Church had little chance to operate openly. What proved to be the final opportunity to publicize the Church echoed an earlier scene in the mission's history—the basketball prowess of the Mormon Utes in 1929. The government permitted the

British Mission's basketball team, national champions in England, to visit Czechoslovakia from February to March 1949. In four weeks, the team played nineteen games in seventeen cities, losing just once. The missionaries in Czechoslovakia passed out tracts during half-time, gave short talks in connection with the game, and held special meetings to explain the players' religion.[20] The visit generated more than a hundred articles in the press.[21]

Nevertheless, the Communist government soon ceased to grant or renew resident permits for the missionaries, making their presence in the country illegal. In May 1949, officials expelled three missionaries, claiming they were a danger to the nation's safety and security. By October 1949, the number of missionaries had been reduced to half that of the previous October, leaving only about twenty. Local authorities ordered expulsions. Processing by the central government initially delayed departure dates, but the authorities became more efficient, and the grace period granted for leaving the country dropped from two weeks to one day. Toronto protested these orders but had no basis on which to reverse them.[22] Though disappointed, the missionaries realized the futility of refusing to leave.

Surprisingly, the duress of government censure was inversely proportional to the rate of conversions. Baptisms rose from twenty-eight in 1948 to seventy in 1949 and thirty-seven in the first three months of 1950. Among the new converts was seventeen-year-old Jiří Šnederfler, who later became a major Church leader. Attendance at Church meetings reached unprecedented levels. Tithes and offerings increased, as a majority of members paid a full tithe. Toronto's lectures typically drew crowds from seventy to nine hundred. At one lecture, two hundred people had to be turned away due to lack of space.[23] Opposition engendered a greater commitment among members and increased interest among those not yet of the faith.

Spiritual considerations aside, an analysis of the convert population in 1949 suggests possible motives for conversion. Two-thirds of the converts were under age thirty. Youth, stirred from the long-accepted traditions and, finding little in Communist doctrine to sustain belief, may have found meaning in the Church's message. Only five converts belonged to the thirty–forty age group and ten in the forty–fifty age group. Middle-aged people, stable in their traditional belief, established in their professions, and worried about supporting families, may have been less disposed to take chances by adopting a new religion. Twelve converts fell into the fifty–seventy age group. One would assume this group might be beyond the age of questioning their beliefs, so the reason for their conversion is unclear. However, more than half of these were single adults, suggesting that the Church provided comfort in their partners' absence.[24]

Anticipating the eventuality of being expelled, President Toronto encouraged a rigorous course of training and study for Czech priesthood holders. He prepared priesthood and auxiliary courses of study to last for the next three and a half years.[25]

The government found a pretext for expulsion in January 1950. Elders Stanley Abbott and Alden Johnson disappeared in a remote area. Eleven days later, President Toronto learned they had been arrested for entering a restricted border zone. They were trying to visit a member's home on the basis of written directions, substantial enough evidence for the authorities to accuse them of "spying." With the Abbott and Johnson case pending, the authorities promulgated a new law requiring all clergy to be native Czechs,[26] and informed the U.S. State Department that the two prisoners would be released only if the other Mormon missionaries were evacuated.[27] President Toronto, seeing no alternative, asked the remaining missionaries to start packing.

Abbott and Johnson languished in prison for twenty-seven days without a change of clothing or a bath. They were interrogated, not brutally but severely, during the first three days. Thereafter, they suffered long hours of loneliness and uncertainty, isolated from the outside world, each other, and the mission. They subsisted on a diet of Postum and black bread in the morning, and soup with a floating meatball in the evening.[28]

Eleven missionaries had already departed when word came that the imprisoned missionaries would be released if Toronto could get them passage within two hours. The president raced to the airport and purchased tickets. Plainclothes guards escorted the prisoners by train from Olomouc to the Prague airport, where Toronto gave them their tickets and they boarded a flight to Switzerland. Sister Toronto arrived in time to watch the meeting from a distance and wave good-bye.[29]

The mission staff now consisted of a president, his family, and two missionaries. Unrelentingly, the secret police focused on expelling even these. The police arrived at the mission home the last day of February. Martha, bedridden by illness and frayed nerves, watched as they escorted her husband outside past a cherry tree barely beginning to bud, a harbinger of hope where there was none. After seven hours, he finally returned. The next day he took his wife and children to the train station. A crowd of Czechoslovak members gathered to bid them farewell, not unlike the mission leader's farewell that preceded the Nazi holocaust. The members proffered little packages of food—sandwiches, baked goods, apples—which they could ill afford to spare. Latecomers pushed their packages through the train window. As the train departed, some ran alongside, expressing their farewell in thrown kisses and tears. Once the train was underway, customs agents broke open the sandwiches, rolls, cakes, and cookies, even cutting into the apples to look for contraband. The family numbly watched this desecration of loving gifts.[30]

When the Toronto family arrived in New York, they discovered that the events in Czechoslovakia had not escaped the American public's attention. Reporters barraged Sister Toronto with questions and clicking camera shutters. She feared to comment, not knowing what impact her answers might have on her husband. For that matter, she knew nothing of his fate after her departure. It was not until she reached Salt Lake City that she received the welcome news of her husband's safe arrival in Switzerland. Overstrained from the sleepless delirium of the journey home, her health deteriorated further, although she eventually recovered.

After the last two missionaries departed from Czechoslovakia, the police unexpectedly granted Toronto seven days to conclude mission affairs. He set apart Rudolf Kubiska[31] as mission president and branch president in Prague, Miroslav Děkanovský[32] and Jiří Veselý[33] as his counselors, and Ceněk Vrba[34] as the branch president in Brno. Then he drove to Basel, Switzerland, where he lingered for a month, hoping to run the mission from afar. But a Czech governmental decree terminated the legal entity of the Church in Czechoslovakia on April 6, 1950. This decree eliminated the public Church, but not the one that persisted privately in the hearts and minds of its members, sundered from the main body of the Church. The circumstances did little to erase the hopes of those who gathered at the Czech mission reunion held April 7, 1950, in Salt Lake City. The group included Elders John A. Widtsoe and Ezra Taft Benson and President Arthur Gaeth, among others.[35] These leaders knew the decree was only a delay, though it turned out to last much longer than they might have hoped.

Czech Members Endure Silently

For nearly fourteen years, the Czechoslovak membership languished silently, unable to worship publicly or to enjoy any regular contact with the Church beyond its borders. During the years of isolation, a few former missionaries traveling through the country on personal or professional business occasionally visited individual members. For example, post–World War II missionary Stanley Kimball visited seven times between 1957 and 1972, staying from a week to several weeks at a time.[36] Some members were permitted to correspond with Utah members to perform genealogical research. But official contact was not possible. Though Church authorities felt great concern for these isolated members, Church theology and policy dictated compliance with civil authority. They resigned themselves to wait for the time when they would be permitted to act. President Toronto, never released from his calling as mission president, continued to provide what assistance he could from distant Utah. When possible, he corresponded and sent financial aid, clothing, medicine, and Church publications. Over the next fifteen years, he applied nine times—and received nine refusals—for a Czech visa. Every two weeks he met with fifteen to twenty former missionaries and their wives to study the gospel and preserve their mission memories.[37]

Members held formal Church meetings in Prague and Plzeň for at least two years.[38] When meetings were no longer held, the Church survived in relationships and discrete exchanges of the members who remained faithful. They visited each other in their homes and felt the strength of shared belief. Occasionally, they traveled to Dresden, Germany, and attended Church conferences, which were still sanctioned in that country.[39] Elder Kimball drove across the border with boxes of scriptures and auxiliary manuals when he visited Czechoslovakia.[40] Miloslava Krejčí in Prague translated and circulated them among the faithful.[41]

Neighbors routinely observed Church members' daily activities and reported any signs of disloyalty to the authorities. These unsolicited guardians visited the families frequently, espousing Communist doctrine and guidance. The Kučera family made a joke of the fact their "guardian" was named Angel, saying that they had their own "angel" just next door. The secret police interrogated members after President Toronto's departure in 1950. They questioned Sister Zdenka Kučerová concerning her genealogical activity, saying such information could be used to establish covers for Western spies coming into the country. Undaunted, she responded there was nothing in Czechoslovakia worth the attention of spies.[42] Ljuba Durďáková was interrogated with a light glaring in her eyes and was denied access to restroom facilities.[43] While there was an inevitable attrition, the faithful bonded together with a sense of spiritual unity that toughened under testing.

Church Leaders Reestablish Contact

In 1964, Church officials reentered the country. The General Board of the Mutual Improvement Association appointed Wallace Toronto to visit Switzerland in summer 1964. Toronto sent his passport to Swiss Mission president John Russon in advance, hoping that Russon might be able to get a visa for him to cross the border into Czechoslovakia. Permission was denied, but the European Mission president, Ezra Taft Benson, suggested Russon find an interpreter and visit Czechoslovakia. Coincidentally, Lynne Pettit, a former acquaintance and an early Czechoslovak missionary, had just informed Russon that he would be passing through Switzerland on his way home from Libya, where he and his family had just completed a U.N. assignment.[44]

On July 30, 1964, Russon and Pettit arrived in Prague with phone numbers and addresses stuffed inside their socks, later learning by experience that stuffing them outside of the socks would have resulted in notes less obliterated by sweat. Despite this measure, the information was still discernible. Over a pay phone, Pettit began using a language he had not spoken for thirty years. The acting Czech mission president, Rudolf Kubiska, was out of town and his wife was naturally suspicious and frightened. For all she knew this was a ruse of the secret police. Brother Pettit called the number for Miroslav Děkanovský, the branch president in Prague. His daughter explained that he also was out of town, but arranged for them to see a sister who had known Pettit's brother, also a former Czech missionary. Marie Veselá, who had served as the mission secretary to Wallace Toronto before the 1950 Communist expulsion, and another sister met the visitors at a hotel. The foursome strolled up a hill to Hradčany Castle, a prominent edifice overlooking Prague, and Sister Veselá began to unfold the details of those who had sustained their belief through years of isolation and oppression. Their main meeting place was the home of the Relief Society president, Sister Emilie Žďárská, located near the railroad station. Anyone desiring news would go there. Meetings were infrequent and held irregularly so as not to raise suspicion that could lead to detection and arrest or imprisonment. Brother Děkanovský returned to town on Saturday and greeted the unexpected visitors. He had been the mainstay of the Church in Prague.[45] He explained that most Church activity consisted of personal visits. He described the system of welfare they had developed out of necessity. Members kept personal tithing and fast offering accounts. When he identified a need, he would go to each member in turn and request assistance.

Knowledge of the visitors spread, and on Sunday morning a small group gathered at Sister Žd'árská's home. They arrived over the period of an hour, filtering in unnoticed until twenty were present. They held a testimony meeting, celebrating their first official Church visitors in fourteen years. To Pettit's surprise, he spoke with unexpected fluency during the meeting. One sister asked for a blessing for a heart condition and later reported that she was completely healed.

The group reconvened at 2:00 P.M., and Brother Kubiska was present. Being a Communist, he received the visitors with less warmth and considerable anxiety. His party membership, he explained, was valuable in keeping the Church membership advised of party activities that might adversely affect them.[46] On the other hand, it also required that he keep the party informed about the Church. The members kept their distance from this leader, who uneasily straddled the chasm between two loyalties.

The visitors then traveled to Brno. Ceněk Vrba, the branch president, welcomed them to another testimony meeting, which was attended by a dozen members. Afterward, the branch president showed the visitors a baptismal font in his yard. Since he worked as a veterinarian, he had passed it off as the place where he "dipped his sheep."[47]

The visit was mutually exhilarating. Russon and Pettit had entered the unknown and found the familiar: a body of fellow believers sharing with them a belief that could be shaken, but not shattered, by autocratic dictate. A comparison with East Germany is instructive. In 1945 the Communists in East Germany banned the Church, then relegalized it in 1949. Members numbering in the thousands remained faithful even though this required a commitment that could destroy opportunities for education, a good living, and a comfortable residence. The members had to rely heavily upon each other, becoming in effect a large extended clan. Their faith was sustained by occasional visits of Church officials, former mission presidents Joel Tate and Percy Fetzer.[48] Membership and legality were the two major differences between the East German and Czechoslovak groups. Because the German membership was much larger, there were sufficient youth to intermarry and raise a new generation of faithful members. In Czechoslovakia the numbers were few, and they proved insufficient to sustain internal growth. Legality meant the German members could worship openly. Conversely, the only alternative in Czechoslovakia was private meetings and fellowship in small groups.

Serving as the European Mission president in 1964, Elder Ezra Taft Benson remained attentive to the needs of the members in Czechoslovakia, some of whom he had met during his 1946 visit. Heartened by Russon's success, he sent J. Peter Loscher, president of the Austrian Mission, and his wife, Frieda, to visit families in Brno, Prague, and Plzeň, in early December 1964. The visitors and members shared embraces, kisses, and testimonies.[49] But the most momentous visit was still in the offing.

The Torontos Briefly Part the Veil

In 1964, Marie Veselá, sister to Marta Roubíčková, was granted permission to leave Czechoslovakia and visit the Roubíčeks in Salt Lake City. President Toronto arranged for her to visit Church president, David O. McKay, who asked why, if Marie could leave Czechoslovakia, Toronto could not get in. Toronto explained that he was still considered a threat. The prophet advised him to apply again, saying "[The members] have been carrying on underground long enough. They need the authority of their mission president." Within a week, the Torontos had received their visas.[50]

In late December 1964, the Torontos drove through deep winter snows from Austria to the Czechoslovak border. They passed through a barbed wire barrier, attended by dogs and armed guards, without incident. Once in the country, the Torontos headed to the Vrba home in Brno where the members, notified by Sister Veselá, smothered them with greetings, hugs, and kisses. The members shared the memories of the fourteen years that had intervened since their last acquaintance. An older sister, unaware of the guests, arrived during the meal and was astonished to find the Torontos sitting at the table.[51]

The next fifteen days were filled with similar experiences as the Torontos visited from home to home in Brno and then in Prague (illus. 3-3). Throughout the trip, the president blessed many who were sick. After consuming herbal tea and cookies at each visit, they returned to their hotel at night unable to sleep from overfilled stomachs. They visited Martha's Beehive girls, now married, and the young men, some ready for ordinations to new priesthood offices. They learned that on Sundays the priesthood brethren visited members in their homes, delivering the sacrament and gospel teachings to one family at a time. Being cautious, they had altered visiting assignments frequently, staying only twenty to thirty minutes so as not to arouse suspicion.

Despite their joy in visiting their friends, the Torontos sorrowed for a country mired in drabness and disrepair. Sidewalk tiles were broken and crumbling, loose cobblestones rattled under passing traffic, and stark buildings exhibited unadorned window displays. The sparkle they once knew was gone. Inefficient centralized control had left the once-industrious nation economically lethargic and indifferent. With the time allotted for their visit expired, the Torontos returned home.

Similar visits from outside the country continued during the next year. President and Sister Loscher returned in May 1965 and met about ten members gathered at a Prague cafe. From there the party traveled to Karlštejn on a pilgrimage to the site of Elder Widtsoe's 1929 prayer. But Brother Kubiska, the Communist Party liaison, had reported their plans, and the Loschers noticed they were being followed. In Brno the Loschers spent a good part of Sunday trying to get rid of their "tails." They zigzagged through the city, attended a Greek-Orthodox service lasting more than two hours, and visited a castle. Finally, Sister Loscher suggested they check the bushes where their "tails" were sequestered. Caught off-guard, the two agents decamped down the hill, pretending to smell flowers along the way.[52]

In July, President Toronto was permitted to enter Czechoslovakia again, this time intent on gaining legal recognition for the Church. He arrived in Prague amid the celebration of the Sokol Slet, the exhibition of mass calisthenics reminiscent of Czechoslovakia in the early days of the mission. When a Czech cameraman singled him out from a crowd of thousands and asked his impressions as an American, he replied in

Courtesy Jiří Šnederfler

Illus. 3-3. Mission president Wallace Toronto and his wife, Martha, enjoyed a brief reunion with members in Prague, Czechoslovakia, in 1965. President Toronto stands at the far right, while Sister Toronto is seated third from left.

perfect Czech that he loved the people and their land and was glad to be back after a fifteen-year absence.[53]

The government officials he visited the next day recognized him from the broadcast, but his prominence had also attracted the attention of the secret police. They arrested him, accusing him of stirring people against the regime and trying to establish the Church illegally. In a quirk of fate, Toronto was interrogated by the man he had hoped to see. He gave a history of the mission stating that the government had expelled the best friends the country ever had. Unmoved, the secret police escorted Toronto to the German border at midnight. At 1:00 A.M., guards at the West German guard station saw a lone man walking back however reluctantly to the free world.

The Longest Wait

The 1964 and 1965 visits offered a temporary respite for Church members who had persevered in silence for fifteen years and would yet persevere another twenty-five years before a new epoch of freedom dawned. Unfortunately, Toronto's visit rekindled active persecution. All Church leaders were called in for questioning, which for some lasted several days. Members' activities were severely restricted. Genealogical research for people in the West was banned.[54]

It was a difficult passage, but one they traversed. Bronja Janousková was unbaptized at age fourteen in 1965. Her mother, Ljuba (Durďáková) Janousková, was a member of the Church, but told little to her daughter so she would be honestly innocent if ever interrogated. She was able to send Bronja to a youth camp in Germany where she learned more about her mother's Church and was baptized when she returned for another youth camp the next year. Bronja was the only teenage member in Prague.[55]

The members suffered along with the rest of the nation. During the "Prague Spring" of 1968, the Czechoslovakia of old surfaced when Alexander Dubček became leader of the Czechoslovak Communist Party and instituted a series of liberal reforms, including more freedom of the press and increased contact with non-Communist countries. Encouraged by these actions, Ceněk Vrba, Jiří Šnederfler, and Miroslav Děkanovský— three stalwarts of the Church—petitioned for religious recognition.[56] However, hopes were dashed when Warsaw pact troops and tanks, under Soviet orders, crushed the progressive regime and quelled any hope of reviving the Church. Despairing at the lack of religious liberty, the Vrba family from Brno and the Kučera and Janoušek families from Prague escaped with what few belongings they could carry, not knowing what to expect in the non-Communist world, but hopeful that their situation could be no worse.[57] That same year (1968) in far-off Salt Lake City, Wallace Toronto died of cancer.[58]

The Austrian mission retained contact with the members in Czechoslovakia. In 1970 mission leaders visited on weekends and were permitted to conduct sacrament services in members' homes.[59] Later, the Germany Dresden Mission—established in 1969 as the only mission operating behind the Iron Curtain—assumed responsibility for the Czech members. President Henry Burkhardt appointed forty-year-old Jiří Šnederfler as presiding elder of the Church in Czechoslovakia in 1972 (illus. 3-4). He reestablished contact with all members throughout the country and started holding meetings.[60] Elder Šnederfler, a water resource engineer, had remained faithful since his baptism in 1949. He located members in Plzeň, Brno, Prague, and elsewhere, assuring them the Church had not forgotten them. In 1974 he organized a conference for all members in the country: only eleven came because the rest were afraid to attend. President Šnederfler described it as "a very dark time for us."[61] As he would soon discover, it is always darkest before dawn.

Church Leaders Act Amid Harbingers of Freedom

In the 1970s, contacts between the western and eastern blocs increased as international tensions decreased. It was characterized by a détente in which the superpower doctrine of confrontation was replaced by consultation. In 1972 the Church created the International Mission to care for the needs of isolated members throughout the world. In its early years, its area of concern included the scattered members of central and eastern Europe.

In April 1974, Church President Spencer W. Kimball called a special representative, David M. Kennedy, to assist the First Presidency with the explicit purpose of getting the Church into countries where it had no official presence. Because Brother Kennedy had previously held prominent positions in the U.S. government under President Richard Nixon, he had an extensive network of friends, acquaintances, and colleagues throughout the world. He was known for his honesty, forthrightness, intelligence, and decency.

At a regional representatives' meeting that spring, President Kimball set the tone for his administration with the admonition to "lengthen our stride." He then detailed a plan for taking the gospel to the whole world, including Communist countries.[62] Kennedy began visiting various

Illus. 3-4. *Left to right:* Jiří, Daniela, Petr, and Olga Šnederfler, 1965. Jiří was the presiding elder in Czechoslovakia when Church leaders could not enter the country.

nations, including those in Communist Europe. He met regularly with the First Presidency and coordinated his work with Bernard P. Brockbank, president of the International Mission, and other general authorities who succeeded Brockbank.[63]

In April 1975, Elder Thomas S. Monson[64] rededicated East Germany for the preaching of the gospel and promised its members all Church blessings, including a temple.[65] The fulfillment of the promise made in 1968 had profound implications for the rest of central and eastern Europe. His prayer included this plea: "Heavenly Father, wilt thou intervene in the governmental affairs? Cause that thy Holy Spirit may dwell with those who preside that their hearts may be touched and that they may make those decisions which would help in the advancement of thy word."[66] In August 1975, the first of the Helsinki Accords was signed, heralding a new era of cooperation between the nations of eastern and western Europe. The signers promised to respect human rights, including freedom of thought and religion. Though the terms were not fully honored at the time, it was another step toward an environment favoring the Church in central and eastern Europe.

In September 1975, Russell M. Nelson, then the general president of the Sunday School, came to Prague on a private visit and blessed Jiří

Šnederfler in his effort to maintain contact with Czechoslovak members, of which about ninety were still faithful. President Burkhardt visited Brother Šnederfler in October 1975 and set him apart as the district president in Czechoslovakia. In Prague and Brno, President Burkhardt reassured members that the Church would return to their country. He discovered that "the members in Czechoslovakia have overcome their fear. They have self-confidence, and this feeling has rubbed off on others. . . . There is love and unity among the brothers and sisters."[67] Between visits of Church officials from outside Czechoslovakia, President Šnederfler corresponded with them using coded information that went undetected by the secret police who censored the mail.[68]

Sensing the new spirit of freedom, the Church reinstated regular meetings in Prague. Although the government knew of the activity, it took no action. The renewed and increasingly regular contacts with the Church outside Czechoslovakia helped the members realize they had not been forgotten. The members shared whatever Church material they could acquire. In some cases, they even retyped the text with nine carbon copies at a time. Each of the nine recipients would, in turn, make an additional nine carbon copies and hand-deliver them to others.[69] Church members began to teach the gospel to their friends, baptizing one or two each year. Real religious freedom was still fifteen years away, but the hope of freedom had begun to flicker.

In 1975, William South, a missionary from the pre–World War II era, and his wife, Jane Brodilová South, replaced Toronto in sustaining Czechoslovak members and began making annual visits to Czechoslovakia. In 1977 when South's health started to fail, this responsibility passed to the second Brodil sister, Frances, and her husband, Calvin McOmber. By McOmber's death in 1980 a significant policy change occurred. For years the Czech government had denied President Šnederfler and his wife visas to visit the temple in nearby Switzerland, and they had little hope of ever receiving permission to visit Utah. But in 1979 the Czech government permitted President Šnederfler to attend the Church's general conference in Salt Lake City.[70] The *visited* could finally become the *visitor*.

Isolated Saints in Eastern Hungary

Czechoslovakia was not the only country in which scattered members preserved their gospel testimonies in isolation. In 1955 two lone members, János Denndörfer (illus. 3-5) and Margit Toth, lived in

Debrecen, located in eastern Hungary near the Romanian border. Although sequestered by political and social circumstances for a decade, they had not been forgotten by Church leaders. Richard Ranglack, from the East German Mission, crossed the border and ordained János an elder.[71] Brother Denndörfer used his new office to benefit Sister Toth.

As a young girl, Sister Toth had worked in Switzerland as maid to the family of a rich industrialist. The son fell in love with her, but his ardor had been cooled when she was hit by a car, causing permanent injury to her leg. She had lived with a member during her recovery and was baptized in 1937 before returning to Hungary. She married and imparted gospel principles to her children, but dared not share the entire gospel message with them for fear of government reprisal. Sister Toth's husband, Sandor, was an alcoholic.[72] When Brother Denndörfer came to visit her, she lay deathly ill with fever, beyond medical help or hope. But since he had received the priesthood, he exercised his new authority on her behalf, praying and fasting before blessing her. Afterward, she fell asleep and was able to rise from her bed the following day.[73]

Courtesy Otto Neu

Illus. 3-5. In the early 1950s, János Denndörfer (c. 1970) was one of only two Church members in Hungary. At one point, the secret police confiscated his religious texts, interrogated him, and accused him of spying. Undaunted, János remained faithful and overcame great odds. Before his death, he succeeding in doing the temple work for almost eight hundred of his ancestors.

Ranglack's visit likely would have led to further contact if political circumstances had been different. A popular uprising in Hungary during 1956 was crushed by Soviet tanks, and Hungary fell into deeper isolation. It was not until a decade later that Ezra Taft Benson, then serving as the European Mission president, learned of the faithful Debrecen members and sent J. Peter Loscher, Austrian Mission president, to reestablish contact. Accompanied by Elder Siegfried Szoke, a Hungarian speaker, President Loscher visited Brother Denndörfer, now seventy, and Sister Toth in June 1965. They gathered at the Denndörfer home in the evening, sharing tears and testimonies. Brother Denndörfer brought out a bank book and said, "Do you know what this is, President Loscher?" The president guessed it was his savings account, to which Denndörfer responded, "Yes, but note the 10 on the right corner of this book; this is my tithing that I have deposited for the last 50 years. The Church can have it anytime they want it."[74] Denndörfer then confided his desire to attend the temple in Switzerland.

Occasional Contacts and Baptisms

President Loscher visited Hungary and Yugoslavia the next year, responding to correspondence with interested individuals. In May 1966, he went with his wife and Ernst Griell, a Hungarian speaker, to Budapest and taught Louis Györkös, who had been investigating religions for three years and had even formed a religious discussion group of seventeen to eighteen people. Somehow he had obtained an English Book of Mormon. The group traveled about twenty-five miles north along the Danube, where Brother Griell baptized Györkös. In July 1966, President Loscher went to Zagreb, Croatia (a state of Yugoslavia at the time), with his assistant, Elder Ralph V. Benson, to visit Tomislav Zidar. About forty years old and very poor, Zidar lived in the bombed-out remains of an air-raid shelter with his wife and two children. He had previously had good employment in the post office, but had been fired for attempting to help a family escape the country. He had found a Church pamphlet in an old newspaper and had written to the address in it. In response, President Loscher had sent a Book of Mormon in German, a language Zidar knew well. After a single day of instruction, Elder Benson baptized Zidar in the Sava River. President Loscher acted somewhat precipitously in both cases because he had no means to continue teaching and fellowshipping these new converts. Neither remained faithful, isolated as they were and having little opportunity to associate with others or learn in the community of members what it meant to be a Latter-day Saint.[75]

Independent of President Loscher, another visitor, Brother Otto Neu, came to Hungary in 1966. Neu had been baptized in East Germany in 1928 but was living in New York City at the time of his visit. In 1964 two Hungarians had written to Church headquarters requesting information. There was no Hungarian expertise at Church headquarters, but a staff member knew of the Hungarian-speaking Brother Neu and forwarded the letters to him. Brother Neu began to correspond with the two who had written. His writing list expanded to as many as thirteen others, and it continued for the next fourteen years. Because of his language skills, Brother Neu also translated Church texts for his pen pals. August 1966 marked his first visit to Hungary since moving to the United States. He later learned from János Denndörfer that, subsequent to his visit, the police searched the homes of those he had visited and confiscated all the letters and Church literature he had previously sent them.[76] This was devastating for János, who lost not only Neu's translated material but many other prized Church texts that had nourished him spiritually for decades. The secret police interrogated János and accused him of spying. He applied for a passport and was denied, not only in 1967 but for the next seven years. In 1973 he became ill and depressed and was hospitalized for a month. Walter and Edith Krause, Church leaders in East Germany, visited him. János turned over his tithing money saying, "Now I feel worthy to shake the hand of a servant of the Lord."[77] Having recently been ordained as a patriarch, Brother Krause blessed him and promised he would be able to go to the temple. In January 1974, János received his passport, went to the temple in Zollikofern, Switzerland, received his own endowment, was sealed to his wife, and did work for almost eight hundred of his ancestors.[78]

Although the tenor of the times was auspicious the moment was not yet right for the Church to be established in Hungary. In September 1976, Gustav Salik, Austria Vienna Mission president, brought a portable font to Budapest, Hungary, and performed baptisms in an attempt to reestablish the Church there. Twenty-five people attended the service, which lasted until the early morning hours. The six converts were largely friends and relatives of John Frazer, a dual citizen of Hungary and Australia. The Hungarian secret police listened to the service, tipped off by one of the converts who was a youth leader in the Communist Party. After this event, no further effort was made.[79] Religious freedom was still more than a decade away.

Book of Mormon Translations

While the day of proselytizing was still distant, a handful of eastern Europeans joined the Church outside their native lands. At the direction of Church authorities, some began translating the Book of Mormon into their native tongues. Others did so at their own prompting. Although some of their efforts occurred before the era covered in this chapter, most of the translations were in progress while the heavy hand of Soviet authority offered little hope that they would ever be used. Nevertheless, translations were completed for the Russian, Bulgarian, Romanian, Hungarian, and Polish languages.

Andre Anastasion, a World War I Russian refugee in England, had joined the Church in 1917. In 1925 he was asked by Elder James E. Talmage to begin working on the Russian translation of the Book of Mormon. He completed the initial assignment after five years. But the job was not finished. He participated in six extensive edits, from 1945 to 1980, before the book ever made it to press. He died in 1980, having devoted a lifetime of effort to the translation so the record of ancient America could one day be read in Russian by the millions who speak it.[80]

John Coy (Kolchagov by birth) and his wife, Evangeline Kokotanova, Bulgarian émigrés to the U.S., were living in New Haven, Connecticut, in the 1930s when they joined the Church. They moved to Salt Lake City in 1932. Evangeline Coy desired to have the Latter-day Saint scriptures in her native tongue and so committed herself to the task, completing it after four years. She donated the manuscript to the Church, where it remained in the archives until missionary work expanded into their native country.[81]

Elena Perry was the daughter of Nicholas B. and Ema Filipescu Perry (Poruţiu) from Romania. Nicholas had emigrated to the United States in 1906 as a young man and succeeded in business before returning to Romania in 1921 to tend to a dying mother. He met and married Ema Filipescu, a medical doctor. Because of his connections in the U.S., he was able to introduce major U.S. manufacturers to the Romanian economy. In 1938 when Hungary, under the aegis of Germany, reclaimed Transylvania (territory that had belonged to Hungary before World War I), the Hungarians gave Elena's father, still a U.S. citizen, twenty-four hours to consign his Ford and Allis Chalmers factory to the German war effort or lose it. He lost it, returned to the U.S. in 1941, and settled with his family in New York City.[82]

Elena was converted to the Church while attending law school at George Washington University in Washington, D.C. Her parents objected to her joining the Church but agreed to attend services at the Manhattan Ward. Despite her objections, Ema decided to read the Book of Mormon. She called her daughter ten days after receiving it and said, "Elena, you and I will have to hurry up and translate the Book of Mormon into Romanian, so that we can share it with our friends." They joined the Church, and for three years, 1951–54, Ema translated while Elena typed. Elena and Ema donated the completed manuscript to the Church.

Éva Lipták, an émigré from Hungary, arrived in Toronto, Canada, in 1965. There she heard of the Latter-day Saints and learned that a Hungarian family named Teglassy had moved from Toronto to Provo. Sister Lipták became acquainted with the family and joined the Church. At the invitation of the Teglassy family, she moved to Provo. Soon afterward, she entered the library science program at Brigham Young University. This led to permanent residence in the United States and a job at the Church's Genealogical Library, cataloging the microfilms of Hungarian ancestral records acquired during the early 1960s. In 1973 the Church's Translation Department asked her to begin preparing material in Hungarian. She engaged in a work that extended over decades, translating the Book of Mormon as well as numerous manuals, brochures, hymns, and other materials.[83]

Born and raised in Poland, Maria Krolikowska converted to the Church in 1966 while living in Oxford, England. She served a mission to the Alaska-British Columbia region and eventually attended Brigham Young University to study nursing. In 1975, Sister Krolikowska was asked by the Translation Department to work on the Book of Mormon in Polish. She felt unqualified and inadequate, but she devoted five years to completing the task.[84]

Selected portions of the Book of Mormon in Hungarian, Bulgarian, and Romanian languages were published between 1979 and 1981. A complete Hungarian Book of Mormon was not published until 1991. Full editions in Russian and Polish appeared in 1981. When the time arrived for the missionaries to enter the eastern European countries, the key tool for convincing prospective members of gospel truths was available in several native tongues, the product of efforts expended over decades.

Poland Is First to Grant Recognition to the Church

Church gains in Czechoslovakia and Hungary were surpassed by a startling development in Poland. As a dramatic result of David M. Kennedy's work as special representative of the First Presidency, the Polish government recognized the Church in 1977. It was probably no coincidence that Poland was the Soviet satellite most openly antagonistic to its Communist overlords. The country's Catholic heritage had withstood the Communist onslaught against religion. In 1978, Karol Wojtyla, a Polish cardinal, became John Paul II, pope of the Roman Catholic Church. Then the Solidarity Movement that germinated from labor unrest in summer 1980 was granted legal status, becoming the first free trade union in Communist Europe.

Pieces of post–World War II Poland had previously belonged to Germany and had sizable Mormon populations. But most members had fled westward or had been expelled to Germany when the borders were realigned. A branch in Selbongen (Zelwagi in Polish), composed mostly of members of German ethnic origin, survived for several decades.[85] Though it had ceased to function as a branch in 1971, in 1975 there were thirty-five members of record in the area and thirty spoke German and five Polish.[86]

For a brief period, meetings were held in Szczecin, just east of the German border in northwest Poland. On March 30, 1975, six Church members gathered at the home of Fryderyk Czerwiński, a member who had relatives in the Church on the East German border. Church leaders visiting from the Germany Dresden Mission conducted a sacrament service in June. In July, Brother Czerwiński was appointed as the leader of the Polish group by East German Church leaders. The Polish group continued to meet monthly, having an average attendance of seven to eight. When one of the members defected to the West, the Polish government curtailed further visits by East Germans and the meetings ended.[87]

Concurrent with the activity in Szczecin, Brother Kennedy visited government officials. He went to Poland in September 1975 to become acquainted with Kazimierz Kakol, minister of religion. Brother Kennedy expressed hope that they would meet in the future. He returned in May 1976 and began negotiations in earnest. He took as interpreter Matthew Ciembronówicz, a Church member from Rockport, Illinois, and an old acquaintance from the period when Kennedy was the Chicago Stake president. At the meeting with Kakol, Brother Kennedy described the origin, beliefs, and structure of the Church. Moving to the crux of the visit, he asked what steps must be taken to obtain recognition. He returned in November and delivered a written statement with extensive information on the Church, including the twelfth Article of Faith, which defines the Church's deference to governments. He anticipated making the official request for recognition on the next visit. Kennedy's sessions with Minister Kakol were cordial, and he established a warm rapport with the minister, but after November the only response was silence.[88]

In May 1977, Kennedy made a last-minute decision to visit Poland to see if he could prompt a response. He arrived in Warsaw at 8:00 P.M., faced with an 8:00 A.M. meeting the next morning, May 26, 1977. In spite of jet lag, he worked through most of the night to finalize the petition for recognition. Minister Kakol welcomed him and, with a smile, handed Kennedy a neatly bound folder containing a document. Although Kennedy could not read Polish, he knew what it was. He commented to the minister that it was the first recognition ever granted in Communist Europe, and that its signing would be an eventful day for the Church in Europe. In response, the minister picked up a pen and signed the document.

There are various reasons that the Polish government accepted the Church. In the political realm, they saw it as a gesture of friendship to the West. In the personal realm, they were impressed with the Church's emphasis on family, sobriety, and industry. They may have also seen the Church as an instrument to diminish Catholic influence in the still-Communist state.[89]

Legal recognition gave the Church the right to own property, conduct worship services, distribute literature, and answer questions—but not to proselytize. It was not all that could be hoped for, but it was a good start. President Kimball was delighted with the news and immediately made plans to go to Poland and dedicate the land for the preaching of the gospel. He and his party arrived August 22, 1977 (illus. 3-6). (President Kimball was the first, and last, prophet to ever enter the Communist realm, primarily because the days of that realm were numbered.) Exhausted by an intensive itinerary of visits to Switzerland, Austria, Italy, and England prior to his arrival, the prophet lay sick in bed. Barely two hours before a

Courtesy Walter Whipple

Illus. 3-6. *(Left to right)* Matthew H. Ciembronówicz, President Spencer W. Kimball, Camilla Kimball, Marian Ciembronówicz, and Fryderyk Czerwiński in front of the Tomb of the Unknown Soldier in Saxon Garden, Warsaw, August 24, 1977.

formal welcome dinner he requested a blessing from Kennedy. After the blessing, Kennedy returned to his room to get ready and escort his wife to the dinner. When they arrived, President and Sister Kimball were already there. At the dinner, Minister Kakol said, "We of the government think high moral standards are very important in life as does your Church. We like those people who do right and are good human beings. With that in mind, we are happy to have your Church in Poland to help the people."[90]

Government policy required the leader of the Church in Poland be a Pole, so President Kimball called Fryderyk Czerwiński to be the presiding elder in Poland.[91] Early on the morning of August 24, a small group met in a secluded spot in the Ogrod Saski Park of Warsaw. After a short service, the prophet pronounced his dedicatory prayer. It was a small act: words of compassion for the sufferings of the Polish people, of blessing for the Polish nation, and of hope for the gospel message to be heard with gratitude. In this quiet setting, the Church took a great leap forward in central and eastern Europe.

Missionary Couples before 1980

Matthew Ciembronówicz, Kennedy's interpreter in Poland, was asked to offer his testimony at the dedicatory service. Born of Polish parents in Illinois, he had learned Polish in the home. When serving as the interpreter, his language returned as if he had always spoken it. After the dedication, he and his wife, Marian, were called to be missionaries in Poland. They served from 1977 to 1979, one of the first missionary couples to pioneer Church work in Communist Europe. They lived in Poland, except when they had to leave for renewing visas, and traveled extensively to visit members and answer questions from members of other faiths.[92] Occasionally, they were able to defray expenses by staying with relatives.[93]

For the next decade, couples shouldered the missionary work in Poland and Hungary. The concept of older couples serving in regions with no formal mission structure was new to the Church's proselytizing paradigm. Their purpose was to quietly sustain the members and continue to answer questions from interested persons preparatory to the Church gaining political recognition and establishing formal missions. Their public profile was less conspicuous than that of younger missionaries. In this early period, couple missionaries serving in central and eastern Europe reported to the International Mission.[94]

Poland. Beginning with his first baptisms on November 20, 1977, Elder Ciembronówicz eventually baptized fourteen people before his term of service ended in 1979. The Church rented an apartment in Szczecin for meetings. Fifteen people, mostly investigators, attended the first meeting there on December 1, 1977. In 1978, German members were again permitted to cross the border to help build the Church in Poland. In August 1978, the International Mission president, James E. Faust, presided over the first Polish conference (August 19–20) with twenty-eight in attendance, seventeen of them members. He established three small branches.[95] A second missionary couple, Teofilo and Dalila Rebicki from Curitiba, Brazil, served there in 1978, and a third couple, Wilford and Helen Jelinek from Salt Lake City, served for a short time in 1980 before civil unrest threatened Poland and they had to leave.[96]

In 1978 the Church purchased a small apartment in Warsaw to be used as an information center and visitor's center where Poles could visit, ask questions, and receive literature. It fit within the limitations of the recognition that did not permit proselytizing, but did allow response to inquiries. Located on a major boulevard in the downtown area, a simple plaque was the only notice of its existence.[97] Leonarda (Lona) Czerwińska, who had been baptized in 1976, a year after the death of her diplomat husband, helped establish the center.[98]

In 1979, Glen and Mildred Warner, an International Mission couple in Vienna, brought Church texts for the information center (illus. 3-7). There was little in Polish, so they brought material written in other European languages.[99] Sister Czerwińska had the center ready to be dedicated in November 1981. In December the Polish government declared martial law and outlawed Solidarity. The opening of the center had to wait, but only briefly.

Hungary. The Church used couples in 1978 to establish an unofficial presence in Hungary. Under the auspices of the International Mission, Joseph T. Bentley, a retired BYU professor and administrator, and his wife, Kathleen, resided in Budapest for eighteen months; their task was to make friends and prepare the way for regular missionary work. They arrived in Hungary in April with a list of people to contact. Some on the list were Latter-day Saints who had been baptized in the 1976 attempt to establish the Church, some were relatives and friends of Church members living elsewhere, and some were people who might be influential in helping the Church become reestablished in Hungary.[100]

The members in Hungary were not well versed in the gospel. János Denndörfer had visited them previously and reported being perturbed with their attitudes. He said they never talked about the gospel, nor were they willing to hold services in their homes. Rather, they demanded a

Courtesy Radmila Ranović

Illus. 3-7. Glen and Millie Warner (c. 1982) outside their home in Utah after completing a mission in Vienna (1979–80).

chapel and a baptismal font. He felt none of the "cordial spirit that should prevail among brethren." When János explained tithing, one member responded that it was out of the question, that the Church ought to help them for they could hardly get along.[101] When the Bentleys gave no indication that they would be of material assistance, some of the members refused to retain any allegiance to the Church. In contrast, Elder Bentley was impressed with Brother Denndörfer who, in his estimation, was a "grand ole man so full of the gospel and excited about it. He reminds me of Paul of the New Testament." At the same time, several investigators expressed the desire to be baptized as soon as the Church received legal recognition.[102]

Bentley's BYU credentials helped him establish cordial relations with the academic community in Budapest and with government officials. He assisted the Church by seeking recognition through legal channels. The Bentley apartment became a way station for other Church members and representatives coming to the country: Otto Neu visited and expressed his excitement about bringing the gospel to his native land; Kenneth Myers, Austria Vienna Mission president, and various missionaries assisted in visiting members; Dennis Neuenschwander, negotiator for the Genealogical (later Family History) Department microfilming program, visited the National Archivist, Ivan Borsa; David Farnsworth, the legal counsel to the Church in Europe, visited on several occasions to consult with lawyers about legal recognition; David Kennedy passed through to talk with Imre Miklos, head of the Ministry of Religious Affairs.

Just before the Bentley's tenure ended, the BYU folk dancers arrived and performed for a full house in August 1979. The hall was double-sold for the second night so they held two performances. The director of the tourist bureau sponsoring the folk dancers asked for a Book of Mormon, which the Bentleys happily supplied. As the troupe left, they sang good-bye to their hostess as she shed tears of appreciation.

The International Mission sent Glen and Mildred Warner to Vienna in November 1979 with a multi-country assignment to visit members in Poland, Hungary, and Yugoslavia. Glen spoke German, a commonly understood language in all three areas. They had an automobile and regularly traveled into these countries, visiting and sustaining the faith of scattered members. The Warners visited János Denndörfer in Hungary. He brought out a brown bag with his tithing accumulated since Walter Krause's 1973 visit. Because the currency was not convertible outside the country, Elder Warner spent it in Hungary and then reimbursed the Church's funds in Vienna in János's name. On one occasion, their travels even took them to visit members in Bucharest to see a couple and an elderly sister who had been baptized outside the country.[103]

In January 1980, the Church sent another couple, Theodore Verhaaren, a retired professor of German, and his wife, Nita, to Budapest. They called on János in March, but found his house dark and abandoned. None of the neighbors would talk to them. They returned the following day, and one neighbor finally revealed that János had gone to a hospital because of a heart attack, but she did not know which one. The Verhaarens tracked down his son, a Communist Party official. Probably wishing to quickly rid himself of these foreigners who might cause him trouble, he coldly told them the location of the hospital. It was Saturday and no visitors were allowed. They figured the only penalty would be to lose their visa, so they entered.[104]

The Verhaarens found a ward with seven beds. János sensed their presence, raised his arm and said, "You have come at last." Sensing the approach of death, he had been praying for someone to give him a priesthood blessing. They asked if they should seek some privacy. But he boldly replied, "Go ahead and if they ask questions I will preach the gospel to them." János passed away the following month.

David M. Kennedy paid Hungary a second visit, which coincided with the Verhaarens' service. The three of them went to the U.S. embassy unannounced, and the embassy staff scurried to accommodate the unexpected but renowned statesman. The Verhaarens were equally surprised at the status of the person they only knew as a fellow Church member. In Budapest they visited Imre Miklos, from the Ministry of Religious Affairs, but had little success. Miklos explained that the Church could have legal status only if the Hungarian state could have some control of Church leadership. After conferring with the Verhaarens and assessing the overall situation, Elder Kennedy recommended that couples temporarily be removed from Budapest. The Verhaarens left in September 1980 to finish their mission elsewhere.

The couples who served in Poland and Hungary before 1981 were overshadowed by those who followed and had greater success. An isolated handful working in obscurity during a time when progress was not discernible, they administered to scattered souls in a religious wasteland, hoping for the day when the Church could operate fully.

Europe Central Districts

The continual easing of political boundaries permitted increasing contact between the Church and its members in central and eastern Europe. In 1980, Boyd K. Packer became the first Apostle to visit Czechoslovakia since Joseph Fielding Smith in 1938.[105] In January 1981, the Church created an East European Mission headquartered in Vienna, Austria, and appointed Edwin B. Morrell, a former Czech missionary, as its president. It took over the International Mission's role in central and eastern Europe, since President Morrell supervised all Church activity in Poland, Czechoslovakia, Hungary, Yugoslavia, and Greece. In July 1982, President Morrell replaced the departing president of the Austria Vienna Mission while still retaining his other role. The East European Mission now became the Europe Central Districts of the Austria Vienna Mission, each country in the east being a separate district.[106]

Contact with Hungary after the Verhaarens' departure resumed in 1982 and continued under couple missionaries who lived in Vienna. In succession, Eldon and Virginia Hunt, Don and Marcia Merkley, and Albert and Marjorie Swensen visited and strengthened members through 1986 when a new age of opportunity arose.[107]

President Morrell was especially active in Czechoslovakia, his old mission field. He had the Czech Book of Mormon reprinted in 1984 and personally brought the first volumes into the country.[108] They were the size of a pocket hymn book, which permitted them to be carried discretely.[109] Under Morrell's guidance, President Šnederfler organized branches in Prague and Brno, appointed leaders, and kept the Church functioning *de facto* if not *de jure*. In 1983 he organized a branch in Plzeň.[110] The renewed energy of a long-restrained Church had begun to manifest itself.

Yoga Classes Help Spread the Gospel

In Brno, seventy-one-year-old Otakar Vojkůvka, a long-standing member, had become proficient in yoga and used it as a vehicle to teach gospel principles without being detected by the authorities. For example, when young Olga Kovářová (illus. 3-8) met Otakar in 1982, she wanted to understand why he seemed to have such a clear understanding of life's purpose. Later, he revealed that some of his ideas were based on the Church's teachings. He offered Olga some Church literature, which she read all night. She returned the next day to ask where she could find a member of the Church and a copy of the Book of Mormon. Otakar introduced her to his son Gad Vojkůvka, the branch president in Brno.[111]

The spirit in the Vojkůvka family was different from any other she had ever witnessed. When Olga read the Book of Mormon scripture, "Adam fell that man might be, and men are that they might have joy," (2 Ne. 2:25) she had a total change of heart. That night she awoke and felt herself filled with light. Since it was winter and there was no access to a baptismal font, she had to wait half a year to be baptized.[112]

In July 1982, Olga was baptized in a reservoir after dark. When she and the Church members arrived, they found fishermen gathered at the reservoir, even though it was late at night. The baptismal group decided to pray, and within a few minutes the fishermen left. At her baptism, Sister Kovářová learned that she was the first young Czech girl to be baptized in Czechoslovakia in the last forty years. When she began attending church meetings, she found herself surrounded by old people. Thereafter she sought to bring the vibrancy of the youth into the Church.

Brother Vojkůvka taught Sister Kovářová how to use yoga to convey the gospel. Sister Kovářová began teaching gospel principles through yoga classes in her community and at summer camps for youth and middle-aged Czechs. After class, she gave lectures on universal principles such as health or love. In lieu of prayers, they held hands and felt joy. Later, Sister Kovářová taught yoga at the University in Brno. An average of seven hundred attended the yoga classes throughout the year, and about three hundred came to the summer camps. The yoga classes offered the first step toward gospel instruction.

Students interested in learning more gathered for a "School of Wisdom" conducted on Sundays at the Vojkůvka home. When asked why so many people visited his home, Brother Vojkůvka said, "We are learning to be happy." Sister Kovářová's teaching did not go unnoticed. Police infiltrators attended the meetings occasionally. Realizing this, she read

Courtesy Olga Kovářová

Illus. 3-8. Olga Kovářová (c. 1998) helped spread gospel principles through her yoga classes in Czechoslovakia. She often faced interrogation by the secret police for suspected ideological offenses.

passages from the Bible and then supported them with the writings of a Russian author. Despite these efforts, secret police often interrogated Sister Kovářová. She always prayed for strength as she confronted her inquisitors alone, wondering if her next answer might lead to six years in prison—the standard term for an ideological offense. Nevertheless, Sister Kovářová continued teaching gospel principles and helping others discover the joy she felt in her new faith.

Between 1974 and 1984 the Church's membership in Czechoslovakia had nearly doubled to 160.[113] It was modest in comparison with membership growth in most of the free world, but in the controlled environment of Communism, each additional member was a small miracle.

A Violin-Maker's Apprentice

In the land of Chopin, music facilitated the reentry of the gospel message. Walter Whipple, a music professor from Rockport, Illinois, had listened intently one Sunday as a fellow quorum member, Matthew Ciembronówicz, described his visits to Poland. Ciembronówicz brought back a violin that impressed Whipple with its workmanship. Whipple ordered a cello from the craftsman, and when he learned the cello could not be shipped, he personally went to pick it up in May 1980. He stayed two weeks and became acquainted with Franciszek Mardula, a master violin artisan in Zakopane, a small town in southern Poland. Thoroughly engrossed by the violin-making process, Whipple made arrangements to return in 1983 and study the art. He stayed for a year, not only making violins but learning the Polish language and meeting Church members in

Warsaw who had been converted through Elder Ciembronówicz's efforts.[114] While learning to make musical instruments, Whipple was also being apprenticed to serve as Poland's first mission president.[115]

As Whipple was leaving for home in 1984, he met in Vienna a missionary couple, the Mazurs, who were in transit to Poland. The Polish political scene had quieted sufficiently that Church leaders in Salt Lake City decided to call another couple to Warsaw. While they were considering this issue, Stanisław Mazur in Fredonia, Arizona, dreamed of his native land and of seeing himself baptize his brother in the lake where they had played as children. Gwendolyn, his wife, dreamed of a telephone ringing, as if someone were trying to reach them.[116] Brother Mazur told his bishop and stake president to send him on a mission to Poland. They agreed to send him on a mission but said they could not assure him it would be to Poland. He insisted, and the stake president called Church headquarters. He learned from Elder Robert D. Hales that the general authorities had been fasting and praying to know whom they might send.

The Mazurs' first converts were two young men Brother Whipple had contacted while studying violin construction. Once baptized, they contacted their friends, bringing more people into the Church. Between June 1984 and September 1985, the Mazurs taught and baptized thirty-six Poles living primarily in four cities: Grudziądz, Warsaw, Łódź, and Zielona Góra.[117] One of the converts was the brother he had dreamed about before his mission. This type of growth in such a short time span was unprecedented behind the Iron Curtain.

A Finger in the Door

In July 1984, Spencer J. Condie arrived in Vienna to assume the presidency of the Austria Vienna Mission and Europe Central Districts. Missionary couples were then serving in Poland, Yugoslavia, and Greece. At the same time, Church leaders established the Europe Area Presidency as part of a worldwide decentralization of the decision-making traditionally performed in Salt Lake City. President Condie suggested to the newly installed Europe Area president, Joseph Wirthlin, that they hold a conference for the scattered couples. In September the missionaries traveled to Vienna for the conference. In addition to Presidents Condie and Wirthlin, the missionary couples also enjoyed the company of Elder Thomas S. Monson, who had overseen the Church in East Germany for nearly two decades, and Elder Hans B. Ringger, the regional representative over central and eastern Europe. Bringing the missionary couples together engendered a sense of unity and spiritual renewal that they carried back to their assignments.[118] Emphasizing the tenacity they must employ, Elder Monson declared, "In each of the countries where you labor, wherever we can, we will get a foot in the door, or a hand in the door, or a finger in the door."[119]

More significant than the conference for couple missionaries was the existence of an Area President and counselors with local decision-making authority. Decentralization of Church administration had matured over the decade since 1976 when regional representatives were given limited line authority, and the First Quorum of Seventy was expanded to assist the Twelve Apostles in administering Church affairs worldwide. Various forms of area supervision were tried until Area Presidencies were created in 1984. Concurrent with the development of the Area Presidencies was the emergence of area offices acting as the Church's headquarters for a region. Central and eastern Europe came under the purview of the area office in Frankfurt, Germany. The area office provided legal advice, physical facilities, and other support.[120]

Communism's Failure

The Soviet Union dominated central and eastern Europe much as the empires that preceded it. Scattered Church members continued to nurture their faith, even when that meant the constant danger of retribution. The largest community of members in Czechoslovakia enjoyed the occasional visit of Church authorities. Then, unexpectedly, Poland granted the Church legal recognition. It was one evidence among many that religion had survived decades of public abuse and desecration. The Communists could not, in the end, maintain the external suppression of inner belief.

By 1985 the Soviet empire's western edge had begun to slough the doctrine of Communism, permitting Latter-day Saint missionaries to reach out to long-lost members and interest a new generation in its teachings. Senior missionary couples, a novel proselytizing force fitted to conditions in central and eastern Europe, played a key role in this process. If officials could not implement the Church's regular program, they could insert those who knew the program and who could sustain isolated members without attracting the undue attention of political authorities. The missionary couples could also do what was legally permitted, such as respond to questions. It was not the most efficient approach to spreading the gospel, but it was the only feasible one under the circumstances.

When the opportunity arose for the Church's complete program to enter this realm, it was laid on a foundation established by the dedicated and unseen efforts of these senior emissaries.

Further south a similar scenario was transpiring in the maverick Communist state of Yugoslavia. Senior missionaries functioned there as elsewhere in Communist Europe, but this country was the first to see young missionaries since the early days of the Czechoslovak Mission (1929–50). They faced a seemingly impossible task, serving behind the Iron Curtain of Communism without legal recognition.

Notes

1. Arthur Gaeth, "Ex-Mission Head Reports on Czechoslovakia," *Church News*, published by *Deseret News*, December 15, 1945, 4. Also a source for the next paragraph.

2. Gaeth, "Ex-Mission Head Reports," 4.

3. Czechoslovak Mission, directory, 1945, Church Archives, The Church of Jesus Christ of Latter-day Saints, Salt Lake City.

4. "First Report Comes from Czechoslovakia," *Church News*, July 21, 1945, 9. Source for the next paragraph as well.

5. Hoyt Palmer, "Young Czech Convert Guides Mission during War Period," *Church News*, February 14, 1951, 13.

6. Ezra Taft Benson, *Labor of Love: The 1946 European Mission of Ezra Taft Benson* (Salt Lake City: Deseret Book, 1989), 68–70; Gaeth, "Ex-Mission Head Reports," 4.

7. Palmer, "Young Czech Convert," 7; Czechoslovak Mission Manuscript History, June 28, 1946, Church Archives.

8. Sterling Beesley, interviewed by author, February 5, 1990, Bountiful, Utah.

9. Martha Toronto Anderson, *A Cherry Tree behind the Iron Curtain: The Autobiography of Martha Toronto Anderson* (Salt Lake City: M. T. Anderson, 1977), 38–39.

10. Anderson, *Autobiography,* 40–41.

11. Anderson, *Autobiography,* 40–46.

12. Anderson, *Autobiography,* 48.

13. Czechoslovak Mission, annual genealogical report (Form E), Family History Library, The Church of Jesus Christ of Latter-day Saints, Salt Lake City.

14. Anderson, *Autobiography,* 43.

15. Stanley Kimball, "The Church in Czechoslovakia, 1946–1950," typescript, 1957, 3–4, Church Archives; Czechoslovak Mission Manuscript History, August 7, 1947.

16. "Pres. Toronto Reports Condition of Saints Left in Czechoslovakia," *Church News*, May 28, 1950, 4.

17. Anderson, *Autobiography*, 49–50.

18. Otakar Vojkůvka, born in 1911, was an active nonmember in the Mutual Improvement Association of the Brno Branch when he married Terezie Kudelová in 1939. He was baptized in July of that year and served as the Brno branch president during World War II. He owned a large factory that was confiscated and nationalized by the Communists when he was imprisoned. Czechoslovak Mission Manuscript History, June 1950.

19. Czechoslovak Mission Manuscript History, June 1950.

20. "Mission Basketball Team Contacts Thousands of Investigators Enroute," *Church News*, March 27, 1949, 14–15; Czechoslovak Mission Manuscript History, January–June 1950.

21. Czechoslovak Mission Manuscript History, June 1949.

22. Kimball, "Church in Czechoslovakia," 5–7; Anderson, *Autobiography*, 56–57.

23. Czechoslovak Mission Manuscript History, June 1949; Czechoslovak Mission, annual genealogical report (Form E).

24. Czechoslovak Mission, annual genealogical report (Form E).

25. "Pres. Toronto Reports Condition of Saints," 4.

26. Dana Adams Schmidt, "Loyalty to Prague Sworn by Bishop," *New York Times*, February 18, 1950, 4.

27. "Czechs Release Two Missionaries after 27-Day Imprisonment," *Church News*, March 5, 1950, 3.

28. "Czechs Release Two Missionaries," 4; Stanley Abbott and Alden Johnson, interviewed by author, March 31, 1990, Salt Lake City.

29. Anderson, *Autobiography*, 59.

30. Anderson, *Autobiography*, 60–63. Source for the next paragraph as well.

31. Rudolf Kubiska was born in 1903 and baptized in 1948. Joseph Roubíček, the previous president in Prague, had emigrated to Canada in September 1949. The brief sketches in notes 31–34 are derived from Czechoslovak Mission, annual genealogical reports (Form E) and Zdenka Kučerova, telephone interviewed by author, January 12, 1992.

32. Miroslav Děkanovský was born in 1898 and baptized in Prague in 1946. In the words of one of the members there, he was a kind and dedicated man who would do anything to be helpful. He died in 1974.

33. Jiří Veselý was born in 1935. He was fifteen when he became a counselor. Inquisitive and scholarly, he later became a psychoanalyst.

34. Cenĕk Vrba was born in 1919 and baptized in 1947. In the words of one of the members, he always knew what to do and gave the members a sense of security and a feeling of peace.

35. Czechoslovak Mission Manuscript History, June 1950.

36. Stanley Kimball, telephone interviewed by author, January 19, 1999.

37. Czechoslovak Mission Manuscript History, June 1950; Anderson, *Autobiography*, 77.

38. Jiří Šnederfler, interviewed by author, July 25, 1990, Salt Lake City.

39. Zdenka Kučerová, conversation with author, January 12, 1992.

40. Kimball, telephone interview.

41. Spencer Taggart, telephone interviewed by author, July 12, 1992.

42. Zdenka Kučerová, interviewed by author, February 14, 1990; January 12, 1992, Salt Lake City.

43. Bronja Janousek Nibley, telephone interviewed by author, March 25, 1991.

44. John Marshall Russon, interviewed by Richard L. Jensen, 1975, California and Utah, typescript, 26–32, James Moyles Oral History Program, Church Archives. Unless otherwise cited, source for the next four paragraphs.

45. Zdenka Kučerová, interviewed by author, March 15, 1991.

46. Russon, interview, 31.

47. Russon, interview, 26–32.

48. Douglas F. Tobler, "Before the Wall Fell: Mormons in the German Democratic Republic, 1945–89," *Dialogue: A Journal of Mormon Thought* 25 (winter 1992): 21.

49. J. Peter Loscher, *J. Peter Loscher* (n.p.: privately published, 1976), 121–22.

50. Anderson, *Autobiography*, 76–77. During his absence from the mission, President Toronto had served as the executive secretary for the Utah Chapter of the American Cancer Society.

51. Anderson, *Autobiography*, 83–95. Source for next paragraph as well.

52. Loscher, *J. Peter Loscher*, 126–27.

53. Anderson, *Autobiography*, 100–105. Source for next paragraph as well.

54. Austrian Mission Manuscript History, August 27, September 22, 1965, Church Archives.

55. Nibley, telephone interview.

56. Šnederfler, interview.

57. Nibley, telephone interview; Edwin Morrell, interviewed by author, July 7, 1990, Provo, Utah; Kučerova, interview, March 15, 1991. For example, the Kučera family received permission to attend a funeral in Vienna. Once outside the country they did not return.

58. "Cancer Crusader W. F. Toronto Dies," *Deseret News*, January 10, 1968, B1, B5.

59. Ruediger Tillmann, interviewed by author, March 9, 1991, Draper, Utah.

60. Šnederfler, interview.

61. Gerry Avant, "He Was Paul before Agrippa," *Church News*, August 31, 1991, 10.

62. Martin Berkeley Hickman, *David Matthew Kennedy: Banker, Statesman, Churchman* (Salt Lake City: Deseret Book, 1987), 334–37.

63. Hickman, *David Matthew Kennedy*, 343.

64. Elder Monson served as the apostolic advisor to Church leaders over affairs in central and eastern Europe, a position he held until 1985.

65. Tobler, "Before the Wall Fell," 24. He had made a similar promise in 1968 when he first visited East Germany.

66. Bruce A. Van Orden, *Building Zion: The Latter-day Saints in Europe* (Salt Lake City: Deseret Book, 1996), 202.

67. Henry J. Burkhardt, "Travel Report by President Henry J. Burkhardt and President Gottfried Richter, Saturday, October 18, 1975, and Sunday, October 19, 1975," typescript, Church Archives; Šnederfler, interview; Marvin K. Gardner, "Jiři and Olga Šnederfler: A Closer Look at Two Czech Pioneers," *Liahona*, September 1997, 20.

68. Gardner, "Closer Look at Two Czech Pioneers," 20.

69. Gardner, "Closer Look at Two Czech Pioneers," 20.

70. Gardner, "Closer Look at Two Czech Pioneers," 21.

71. Douglas F. Tobler, "Alone with God," *Ensign* 23 (April 1993): 52.

72. Loscher, *J. Peter Loscher*, 127–28; Spencer J. Condie, interviewed by James B. Allen, March 15–22, 1989, Provo, Utah, audio tape 3, in the possession of the interviewer, Orem, Utah.

73. Tobler, "Alone with God," 52.

74. Loscher, *J. Peter Loscher*, 127–28.

75. Austrian Mission Manuscript History, 1964–67, Church Archives.

76. Otto Neu to author, September 12, 1991.

77. Dell Van Orden, "Season in Church for Building Temples," *Church News,* May 8, 1993, 12.

78. Tobler, "Alone with God," 52.

79. Margaretha Tetzl, meeting minutes, 1976, in Hungary Budapest Mission, Historical Records and Minutes, 1991 report, Church Archives.

80. Gary Browning, *The Restored Church in Russia* (Salt Lake City: Deseret Book, 1997), 13–14.

81. Victor Coy, conversation with author, February 13, 1997, Salt Lake City.

82. Elena V. Johnson, telephone interviewed by author, January 7, 1997. Source for the next paragraph as well.

83. Éva Lipták, interview, February 14, 1997, Salt Lake City; Éva Lipták, information sheet, May 5, 1997, in possession of the author.

84. Maria Krolikowska Eppich, telephone interviewed by author, February 20, 1997; Kerrill Sue Rollins, "'The Book of Mormon in Polish," *Ensign* 12 (June 1982): 74–75.

85. Gilbert Scharffs, "The Branch that Wouldn't Die," *Ensign* 1 (April 1971): 30–33.

86. Gerry Avant, "Reunion Revives 'Spirit of Selbongen,'" *Church News,* October 14, 1989, 7; Gary L. Schwendiman to Joseph B. Wirthlin, January 9, 1976.

87. "Record of the Sacrament and Sunday School Meetings of The Church of Jesus Christ of Latter-day Saints Held in Szczecin in 1975," Church Archives.

88. Hickman, *David Matthew Kennedy,* 350–55. Unless otherwise noted, source for next four paragraphs as well.

89. Edward L. Kimball to author, February 28, 1999.

90. Edwin B. Morrell, "Last Laugh Belongs to Poles," *Daily Universe,* September 23, 1980.

91. Matthew Henry Ciembronówicz, telephone interview by author, December 4, 1996.

92. Ciembronowicz, telephone interview, December 4, 1996.

93. Matthew Henry Ciembronówicz, telephone interview, December 18, 1996.

94. W. Grant Bangerter, interviewed by author, February 18, 1998, Alpine, Ut.

95. Ciembronówicz, telephone interview, December 18, 1996; "Record of the Sacrament and Sunday School Meetings . . . in Szczecin." A source for the next paragraph as well.

96. Walter Whipple, telephone interviews by author, January 31, February 6, 1997; Matthew Henry Ciembronówicz, Letters, March 1978–April 1979, Church Archives. After the 1978 conference, Brother Czerwiński was released and replaced by Przemystaw Zarzycki of Warsaw. Walter Whipple, interviewed by Matthew K. Heiss, October 4, 1991, Warsaw, Poland, typescript, 17, copy in possession of the interviewee, Provo, Utah; Walter Whipple, telephone interview by author, February 5, 1997.

97. Condie, interviewed by James B. Allen, audio tape 1.

98. Grace Whitaker, "Pioneer in Poland," *Latter-Day Sentinel* 3 (February 26, 1982): 14–15.

99. Mildred Warner, telephone interview by author, December 3, 1996.

100. Joseph T. Bentley, *Life and Family of Joseph T. Bentley: An Autobiography* (Provo, Utah: J. Bentley, 1982), 141–80. Unless otherwise noted, also the source for next three paragraphs.

101. János Denndörfer to Otto Neu, February 25, 1977, translated by Neu.

102. Whipple, interview, October 4, 1991.

103. Mildred Warner, telephone interview.

104. Nita Verhaaren, telephone interview by author, November 21, 1995; Nita Verhaaren, "New Article Sparks Memory of Hungarian," *Church News*, December 5, 1992, 4. Same sources for the next two paragraphs.

105. Šnederfler, interview.

106. Morrell, interview.

107. Don Merkeley, telephone interview by author, January 5, 1991.

108. Morrell, interview.

109. Condie, interview, audio tape 2.

110. Šnederfler, interview.

111. Carri Jenkins, "After the Revolution," *BYU Today* 45 (March 1991): 30, 32–33.

112. Olga Kovářová, talk, BYU Women's Conference, April 11, 1991; Olga Kovářová, talk, Czech Mission Reunion, April 6, 1991; Olga Kovářová, talk, Church Educational System Experienced Personnel Convention, May 10, 1991, audio tape; Olga Kovářová, "Spreading the Gospel under Communism," Sunstone Symposium 13, audiotape. For further information see Olga Kovářová, *Saint behind Enemy Lines* (Salt Lake City: Deseret Book, 1997). Sources for the rest of the section as well.

113. Condie, interview, audio tape 2.

114. Ewa Boguslawska, Slavomir and Jolanta Bylicki, and Urszula Demczuk; Whipple, interview, October 4, 1991, 1.

115. Whipple, interview, October 4, 1991, 1–4; Walter Whipple, telephone interview by author, November 25, 1996.

116. Susan Turley, "I Saw Myself in a Vision in Poland," *Latter-day Sentinel,* September 6, 1986, 20.

117. Stanisław and Gwendolyn Mazur, talk, November 13, 1985, Salt Lake City; Condie, interview, audio tape 1.

118. Condie, interview, audio tape 1.

119. Spencer J. Condie, note on draft manuscript, 1997.

120. Kahlile Mehr, "Area Supervision: Administration of the World Wide Church, 1960–1999," *Journal of Mormon History* 27 (spring 2001): 192–214.

4

Mission Impossible

1972–1991

In 1918, Yugoslavia ("Land of the South Slavs") arose from the ashes of Austro-Hungary. The land of the southern Slavs was a political veneer concealing ethnic diversity and ill will. The flames of strife leading to the first World War continued to smolder below the superficial unity of its disparate states: Slovenia, Croatia, Bosnia-Herzegovina, Montenegro, Serbia, and Macedonia. Yugoslavia fell under Communist rule after World War II. Though the government soon disavowed any subordination to Moscow, it retained the Communist disposition toward religion, fostering the element of godlessness in a land of uncertain peace.

The Church's early history in Yugoslavia was brief and sporadic. Mischa Markow preached there in 1899. Arthur Gaeth visited several times in the 1930s and baptized a man living in Zemun. However, in 1972 Church leaders ventured into what at the time seemed like an impossible mission: teaching about God and the gospel of peace in a land where both were denied. For twenty years the Church tested a government's will to exclude its emissaries and struggled with the pride of a people harboring deep antagonisms. The effort likewise tried Church leaders' will to maintain hope when their labors resulted in little visible progress. In 1991 the underlying political and cultural tensions in this unhappy land exploded in a bitter four-year civil war followed by a crisis in Kosovo at century's end. Did the results of the Church's efforts expended over twenty years before the civil war justify the expenditure in time and personnel?

Basketball Emissary

Communist control over Yugoslavia remained impenetrable and forbidding in the 1960s. In 1967, President Rendell Mabey of the Swiss Mission (1965–68) received a letter from Tomislav Zidar, a man baptized in Yugoslavia in 1966, requesting a Bible. President Mabey met him at his home and delivered the Bible. Visiting a second time, President Mabey found Zidar working in a large factory surrounded by a fence. Zidar came to the perimeter, and they exchanged only a few words before a passerby intervened and suggested that Mabey leave. Zidar wrote again, this time saying his wife wanted to be baptized and that he needed glasses. On the third visit, President Mabey was not able to contact the family, left the glasses, departed, and was unable to maintain any further contact.[1]

But change was imminent. In 1972, forty years after the first visit of President Gaeth, another tall and lanky church representative came to Yugoslavia. Imbued with the same enthusiasm and hope of his early pre-decessor, this representative was different in a significant way. He was not an intervening stranger, but a welcome native son. Krešimir Ćosić was a basketball hero in a country that was passionate about the sport. He played the game better than anyone else there. Nevertheless, he accepted an invitation to play college basketball at Brigham Young University (BYU) in Provo, Utah (illus. 4-1). After his junior year, he returned home for the summer as a newly baptized member of the Church.

The events leading up to this circumstance began at the 1968 Olympics in Mexico City, where Ćosić played on the Yugoslav basketball team that garnered a silver medal.

Courtesy Mark Philbrick

Illus. 4-1. Krešimir Ćosić goes for a hook shot during a basketball game against the University of Utah.

Unbeknown to Ćosić, a BYU player from Finland was there to scout him out. Vako Vajno befriended Ćosić and was excited to learn that the Croatian wanted to play for a school in the United States. Vajno raved about this potential recruit to BYU coach Stan Watts, who then undertook a successful recruiting effort.[2]

In late 1969, young Ćosić arrived at BYU, unruly, fun-loving, and undisciplined. He stood 6 feet 11 inches tall and wore a size four-teen sneaker. Ćosić was unpre-pared for a campus environment where religion mattered, and he was even more appalled to learn that although he was an Olympic star he could not play during his freshman year.[3] Despondent, he quietly and abruptly packed up and headed for the airport. Fortunately, a vigilant BYU sports staff caught him before his departure and convinced him to stay.[4]

At this troubled juncture, Ćosić confided in a friend that, despite his disappointment, he knew he was not going home. He explained that even before coming to Provo, he had seen himself in a dream playing in a place between the mountains and a lake. His confidante was Christina Nibley, girlfriend of Ćosić's Yugoslav roommate, Zdravko Minček, a BYU tennis player. Christina explained that her father had also dreamed dreams such as his. Ćosić began to question her about her beliefs and eventually sought guidance from Christina's father, BYU professor Hugh Nibley.[5] After his sophomore year (1970–71), Ćosić played with the Yugoslav national team over the summer. When he returned to school in the fall, he immediately visited Professor Nibley and requested baptism. When asked why, Ćosić said that he could think of a hundred reasons why not but only one reason why: "Because it is true." He shared more details with the Truman Madsen family, who had befriended him: "I read the Book of Mormon. It was true. I was baptized."[6]

The conversion took many on the BYU sports staff by surprise. The flamboyant, unruly Ćosić had never seemed to be disposed toward religion. When Floyd Johnson, a member of the sports staff, heard the rumor that Ćosić had been baptized, he replied, "That guy will *never* be baptized, and if he is, the water will never stop boiling." In a conversation with Johnson's colleague, Rod Kimball, Ćosić asked, "What you do if I tell you that I be Mormon?" Rod replied, "Kresh, if you ever get to be a Mormon, I'll apostatize." Ćosić responded, "Rod, one thing we Mormons don't like is man who say he do something and then not do it." When the event was confirmed and Johnson learned the ordinance had been performed by Hugh Nibley, he wondered how "the smartest man at BYU had been so dumb" as to baptize Ćosić.[7]

Krešimir Ćosić achieved U.S. attention as a player, and he became very popular on campus. He was simply one of a kind:

> He galloped like a camel, he jumped like a gazelle, shot eighteen-foot hook shots, made length-of-the-court passes, lead the fast break, passed like a man with a third eye, shot double-pump lay-ups, all the time smiling that familiar and contagious Ćosić smile. Kresh played basketball like it was really a game. None before or since ever played the game with more outward enthusiasm for the sheer joy of it like Krešimir Ćosić.[8]

He was the first foreign player to ever earn All-American honors.

Brother Ćosić devoted equal zest and intensity in serving his Church. He had no intention of hiding his new faith. Rather, he began making plans to introduce it to everyone in his native land. Even then he was well on his way to becoming not *a* national hero but *the* national hero, a combination of Babe Ruth, Larry Bird, and Muhammad Ali all wrapped into one.[9] This prominence gave him the "podium" he desired to deliver an ever-greater message than basketball prowess to his countrymen.

Ćosić arranged to have two films of BYU basketball games produced with special half-time features inserted: one was the 1964 World's Fair film produced by the Church, *Man's Search for Happiness,* and the second was *Meet the Mormons.* Brother Ćosić personally narrated the audio for the half-time shows in Serbo-Croatian.[10]

The intentions of the young enthusiast received support from the highest echelons of Church leadership. In two private conferences during spring 1972, Elder Gordon B. Hinckley spoke with Brothers Ćosić and Neil D. Schaerrer, the incoming president of the Austria Vienna Mission about plans to establish the Church in Yugoslavia.[11] Elder Hinckley also set Ćosić apart as a missionary.[12]

During summer 1972, Elder Ćosić returned to his hometown of Zadar, a town of about seventy thousand inhabitants, halfway down the Adriatic Coast of Yugoslavia. Concurrently, Elder Hinckley implemented another plan conceived earlier that year. Many people in Zadar spoke Italian. Hugh Nibley's son Paul was serving in the Italy North Mission. Acting on a request from Brother Ćosić for the assistance of his mentor's son, Elder Hinckley called President Dan Jorgenson of the Italy North Mission and directed him to send Paul Nibley to Yugoslavia.[13]

Elder Nibley and his companion, Gale McOmber, spent almost two months (May–June 1972) in Zadar and the surrounding vicinity, engaging in a variety of proselytizing activities.[14] They taught discussions in Italian to Ćosić's friends and neighbors. They showed the basketball films several times after hours at a nightclub where Ćosić's friends played in the band. They also took a film to the island where Ćosić's grandparents lived, playing it on a bed sheet hung between the walls. So many people came that some had to watch it backwards from the other side of the sheet. As a result, one of Ćosić's friends, Vladimir Perić, was converted, and Ćosić baptized him in the Adriatic Sea.

The missionaries returned to Italy, and Ćosić headed for the Yugoslav Olympic basketball training camp in the resort center of Kranjska Gora, located in the northwest corner of the country, just south of the Austrian border. Ćosić led his team to a bronze medal at the Munich Olympic

Games and then returned to Zadar. In early September 1972, the Schaerrers and missionary assistants traveled down the coast to Zadar. Ćosić's name was their passport. Elder Ruediger Tillmann, who was driving, failed to communicate in German with the heavily armed border guards. He finally said, "Krešimir Ćosić! Basketball!" and they waved the car through. When they reached Zadar, Elder Tillmann stopped a passerby and said, "Krešimir Ćosić!" Within fifteen minutes, Ćosić was there to greet them.[15]

On September 17, they held a sacrament and testimony meeting with six locals, three of them members and three not. The group expressed great hopes for the future, hopes that were not fulfilled immediately. The next day, the visitors and Ćosić consulted with Milan Vladovic, an attorney in Zadar. He informed them that door-to-door proselytizing—the main proselytizing technique—was prohibited. Though pessimistic about the outcome, he outlined the procedure for obtaining recognition and agreed to file a petition with the Department of Religious Affairs.[16]

Shortly afterward, Ćosić returned to BYU for his senior year. His success on the court led to professional contract offers in America that would have earned him millions, but he opted to return home, manage the Zadar basketball program, and play on the Yugoslav national team. When asked why he returned, he responded, "It was the right thing to do. I would have enjoyed playing in the NBA, and maybe I did lose something by not doing so. But I don't regret it. I regret when I do something wrong. But I never regret when I do something right."[17] His decision reflected not only love for his native land but also a desire to help establish his new faith there.

Krešimir Ćosić made Yugoslavia a basketball powerhouse in world and European championships, first as a player and later as a coach. At the same time, he served as the country's district leader. His religion may have grated on Communist leaders, but his prowess on the court curtailed reprisals.[18]

From 1973 to 1975 Ćosić remained in Zadar. Doug Richards, a fellow basketball player from BYU, joined him during the 1974–75 basketball season and helped with the sport while also teaching the gospel. Richards noted that Ćosić took advantage of every opportunity "to help the light of the gospel seep through the iron curtain." Richards's fiancée, Kerry, spent six weeks there as well. The couple answered questions about the Church since many Yugoslavs had some knowledge of English. The Zadar team became the national champions and played in the All-Europe tournament, taking third place.[19]

Ćosić's proselytizing methods were often unique, not unlike his style of basketball. He asked Floyd Johnson at BYU for all the old T-shirts that had "Brigham Young" printed on them. When kids followed him around and asked for a shirt like his, he pulled out an Articles of Faith card and said, "If you will memorize what's on the card, I will give you a T-shirt just like mine."[20]

Ćosić's friends from all over the country visited him in Zadar. Yet his missionary efforts were punctuated only occasionally by conversions. The task proved more insurmountable than any challenge on the court. Some of Krešimir's long-time friends joined—Mladen Dunatov, and Mišo and Ankica Ostarčević. The Ostarčevićs' baptism occurred in the Adriatic at 2 A.M. to avoid attracting any unwanted attention. They were the first couple to join the Church in Yugoslavia and the only one for a decade. The fledgling branch met in homes and rented a house for a short time in 1974. Most Yugoslavs, however, showed little interest in Ćosić's religion and regarded his conversion as an insignificant blemish on his ever-growing status as a national hero.[21]

The Attempt to Create a Yugoslav Mission

Attempts to obtain legal recognition proved futile. In October 1974, First Presidency representative David M. Kennedy visited Beograd, the capital city of Serbia and the federation of Yugoslavia, to seek recognition for the Church as a precursor to permitting standard missionary work in the country. On the tail of Kennedy's visit, the Schaerrers made a series of official visits to Ljubljana, Zagreb, Zadar, and other small cities in between. President Schaerrer contacted attorneys, language specialists, printing companies, and the Seventh-Day Adventist and Jehovah's Witnesses churches to get a feeling for how to proceed.[22]

Hoping for the best in Yugoslavia, mission leaders mounted an effort in Austria to begin teaching the half million Yugoslav émigrés. In November 1974, President Schaerrer appointed Elders Rulon Orton and Andre Zivkovic to proselytize exclusively among the émigrés. A Sunday school was soon established in Vienna. Two Austrian members, Charlotte Dospil and Katarina Jokl, translated for the meetings.[23] At the same time, the Church's Language Training Center in Provo, Utah, began training missionaries in Serbo-Croatian. A group of missionaries assigned to Austria arrived there in January 1975, but their assignment was changed to Yugoslavia. They studied two languages—first German then Serbo-Croatian.[24] However, Yugoslav visas were never granted. Members of this missionary group either continued working among the émigrés or were reassigned to proselytize among Austrians. A second group of Yugoslav missionaries arrived during 1975.[25] Brother Ćosić crossed the border to visit and help the missionaries, but neither of these two missionary groups was ever permitted to work in Yugoslavia.

In 1975 the Church sent missionaries and a leader to preside over the anticipated Yugoslav Mission. In May, Brother Kennedy visited Beograd in the company of Gustav Salik, who had served for a year as the president of the Brazil Rio De Janeiro Mission but was in the process of being reassigned to Yugoslavia. The visit was an attempt to get him a visa. Anticipating that eventually he would receive one, President Salik returned in July 1975 with his family to live along the Yugoslav border until his visa was granted. Although the Saliks were from Brazil, Gustav had relatives in Yugoslavia and neighboring countries.[26]

By 1975 six Church members lived in Zadar. Because they needed seven to petition for recognition in that city, they invited a Church member from Trieste to stay in Zadar for a few months, giving them the required number to receive recognition.[27] The impact of this recognition was only local and never extended to the entire country. President Salik spent a year trying, in vain, to organize a mission in Yugoslavia, and when it was clear that this would not be feasible, he was assigned to preside over the Austria Vienna Mission for the last year of his presidency. This did not mean the Church had given up entirely, for in 1977 more contingents of Yugoslav missionaries arrived in Austria as replacements to be ready when the border opened.[28]

While President Salik was working from the outside, Brother Ćosić was drawn away from Zadar by other responsibilities. During 1975 and 1976 he spent his obligatory time in the military and then focused on preparing for the 1976 Olympics in Montreal. There his team garnered the silver medal, further adding to his national stature. Brother Ćosić could not continue to foster the Church in Zadar while he was away. And to exacerbate the situation, Mišo Ostarčević and his family lived temporarily in Provo while he played basketball for BYU (1975–77); the Nibley family helped solidify his testimony as they had done previously with Ćosić.[29] With two key individuals gone and the missionaries still prevented from crossing the border, the Church in Yugoslavia temporarily idled.

Student Missionaries Challenge the Limits

In 1977, Brother Ćosić took up residence in Ljubljana, capital of Slovenia, near the Austrian border. He suggested to President Kimball that missionaries enter Yugoslavia without white shirt and tie,[30] and

President Kimball agreed. Although his policy was to always enter by "the front door," he hoped to find the door only shut and not locked.[31] Missionaries, instructed to dress casually, were sent into Yugoslavia as students studying the language and culture. They did not openly proselytize, but were allowed to answer questions if anyone approached them. It was an unusual tactic for the missionaries to pose as students, but the impelling desire of a prophet to take the gospel to all nations and the urging of a devoted follower led to an atypical missionary experience.

President Salik sent missionaries into the country for only short periods during 1977. At his recommendation, in early 1978, the duration of their stay was extended to the full term of their missions. President Salik noted in a report to Church President Spencer W. Kimball, "It looks safe. The government knows they are not doing anything wrong, and they should recognize that" (illus. 4-2).[32] These missionaries had to leave every three months to renew their visas, but this was done without too much trouble at the border instead of going to the Yugoslav embassy in Vienna. Elders Kirk Barrus and Michael Meyer left Austria for Zadar on February 1, 1978, the first set of missionaries to work in Yugoslavia full-time. Todd Zagorec, Dennis Wilson, Kurt Bestor, and David Parr soon followed.[33] They served not only in Zadar, but also in Zagreb, Croatia, and Beograd, Serbia.

Sending young missionaries into a Communist society was risky. Missionaries could either succeed in building a membership that would make the Church a fait accompli, or antagonize civil authorities who would become even more stubborn in their opposition. The effort received no publicity within the Church, much less without. It was a mission with little prospect of success and with real dangers to those involved. Yet it was not without precedent. Missionaries had struggled at the edges of legality in Europe for decades, especially around the turn of the twentieth century. After being banished from parts of the German Empire in 1903, the missionaries continued to operate out of Switzerland, crossing the border into proscribed territory. From the Church's perspective, religious imperatives sometimes outweighed civil impediments.

By 1978, Brother Ćosić and the Ostarčevićs had returned to the country and once again helped promote the Church, which in turn helped the missionary effort. As Croatians, they were most involved in the western area of Yugoslavia. Little work had occurred among the Serbs or other nationalities within the country. When the missionaries entered Beograd, Serbia, they received the unanticipated but welcome assistance of a newly baptized stalwart, Radmila Ranović. Born in

Courtesy Edward Kimball

Illus. 4-2. Church President Spencer W. Kimball and Gustav Salik, who spearheaded the early missionary efforts in Yugoslavia in the late 1970s, meet at the Vienna airport.

Sarajevo, Bosnia, but raised in Switzerland from a young age, she was baptized in Zürich in 1975. She received a patriarchal blessing in 1977 which stated, "It wasn't by an accident that you became acquainted with the Church of Jesus Christ, because Father in Heaven chose you for a great mission. You will continue to act as a witness for Christ in your home country."[34]

For a year, Sister Ranović had strong feelings that she should return to Yugoslavia. She finally decided to visit Beograd to determine if the time had come to fulfill the dictum of her blessing. Upon arrival in March 1978, she noted in the newspaper that Krešimir Ćosić was playing a game in Beograd that evening. She went and met with Ćosić but did not reveal her membership. Rather she expressed interest in the Church, and he arranged to meet her the following day. When Sister Ranović revealed her true allegiance, Ćosić was overjoyed. Her visit had been favorable, and she decided to move and continue her education in Beograd. When she returned in May, two missionaries, Elders Zagorec and Bestor, were there to greet her.[35]

Testing the boundary of religious toleration, the missionaries had to be innovative and circumspect in their approaches. Elder Bestor, a musician, played the piano in a lounge and gave piano lessons. Missionaries joined games of soccer and basketball and ate at student restaurants, seeking to develop friendships with youth. They got to know shopkeepers, merchants at the marketplace, bank tellers, postal workers, or anyone else they came in contact with during the normal course of a day. They enrolled in language classes to meet fellow students as well as to study the language. They even served as Scout den leaders and physical education teachers. The most pervasive technique was street contacting, or engaging passers-by in casual conversation, hoping to turn the conversation to religion. For instance, when they asked for directions, people noticed their accent and talked with them a little longer. Ćosić's name also served as an icebreaker, since his identity as a member of the Church was well-known. The discussion of religion was legal as long as the missionaries only answered questions. Occasionally, the missionaries received referrals from members in other countries or from those who visited Church sites while abroad.[36]

As permitted under these unusual circumstances, the missionaries wore casual clothes and let their hair grow to shoulder length (illus. 4-3). It befitted their ostensible role as "students." But in 1979, they experimented with white shirts and ties for a short while, which produced mixed results. Elders Everett Smith and David Zivkovic donned them to visit a group of psychologists that had been to the Polynesian Cultural Center, a Church visitors' center in Hawaii. Unfortunately, white shirts and ties attracted the wrong type of attention because the average citizen wrongly identified this type of dress with the attire of the secret police.

The mission president in Vienna rotated the Yugoslav missionaries into Austria for short periods to give them the standard missionary experience of wearing suits and tracting. They also traveled every few months to missionary conferences held in Austria. Otherwise, the Yugoslav missionaries functioned separately from their Austrian counterparts. Though they reported to the same president, the Yugoslav missionaries were isolated by language and the great distance at which they operated from Vienna. Glen Warner, one of the couple missionaries working out of the mission home, referred to them jokingly as the dirty dozen.[37]

From April to September 1979, missionaries worked in Skopje (the capital of Macedonia), the southern-most city of Yugoslavia. They taught American-style football to the youth, at the same time involving American exchange professors and U.S. embassy staff in the games. The major problem they encountered was obtaining funds from Austria, since the money was often held up at the border. The elders hitchhiked to Beograd, borrowed money from the elders there to get to Vienna, received the needed funds from the mission president and returned to Skopje, a 1,000 mile round-trip. In the end, the post was too remote for the missionary effort to be sustained, and no more elders were sent to Macedonia.[38]

Meanwhile a project initiated by Brother Ćosić in 1974 finally came to fruition—translating the Book of Mormon into Serbo-Croatian. He employed a Catholic priest who had been in a car accident and, as a result, could devote nearly all his time to the project. Ćosić saw this as an unexpected but effective way of getting the job done. Although the translation was not ready in 1978 when the missionaries entered Yugoslavia, they helped edit the Book of Mormon as it neared completion. Before its publication in late 1979, they taught principally from the New Testament.[39]

Something Different, Maybe Even Dangerous

The missionaries' efforts resulted in only a few baptisms. In 1978, for instance, there were just two.[40] Once the initial barrier of finding someone to listen was overcome, the missionaries had to convince people to join a Church with a few scattered members. Those who joined faced an uncertain future in the hands of the authorities. Near the end of his mission, Elder Bestor taught a mother and three children in Karlovac. This family had read an article about the Osmonds, a well-known Latter-day Saint performing family, and had sent for information, which was how the missionaries discovered them. However, the family chose not to join because they feared losing their jobs. They explained, "It may be true but we can't do anything about it."[41]

While the missionaries' American ties may have drawn attention, this did not translate into trust or an interest in their message. Some citizens welcomed them into their homes and treated them hospitably. And the fact that missionaries took the time to learn the language intrigued many Yugoslavs. The missionaries dispelled the limited understanding of America that was usually based on imported U.S. television programs.[42] Once the discussion got to religion, the barriers rose. When Sister Ranović, the young convert living in Beograd, presented copies of the Book of Mormon to her friends or introduced them to the missionaries, they began to distance themselves from her. As she explained, their eyes seemed to say: "She's something different, something maybe even dangerous. She's around those Americans, who knows what they are doing." She told people she was a Mormon, the same as Krešimir Ćosić, and that was it. They never asked questions about it.[43]

Courtesy Radmila Ranović

Illus. 4-3. Elders Kurt Bestor *(left)* and Todd Zagorec *(right)*, in Yugoslav missionary attire, with Radmila Ranović in Beograd, c. 1978.

The common attitude toward religion in Yugoslavia was apathy. Few practiced any religion, and often those who did were older. The Communist regime had achieved widespread results over the thirty years it had disparaged religion in the schools. The missionaries found little common ground to serve as a basis for religious discussion. Only the more sophisticated and well-educated people were able to consider the new doctrine of the gospel so the missionaries often went to universities to find such people.[44]

Ethnic and cultural tensions within Yugoslavia militated against charitable thoughts and actions. The people harbored resentments based on deep cultural distinctions. Croatian society evolved under the Austo-Hungarian Empire. Croatians were traditionally Catholic and culturally oriented to the West. Serbian society, on the other hand, developed under the influence of the Ottoman Empire. Serbians were Orthodox and, as slavophiles, faced eastward. Both Croatians and Serbians snubbed the Muslims, who symbolized centuries of Ottoman aggression to the Croats and Ottoman servitude to the Serbs. All sides had little tolerance for ethnic mixing. Added to these long-held prejudices was the memory of the genocidal slaughter in concentration camps of Serbs by German-backed Croats during World War II.

Economic conditions began to deteriorate after 1980, with the death of Marshall Tito, the country's leader and foundation block of national unity since World War II. By 1982 people had to stand in line for milk, meat, butter, oil, and laundry detergent. Electricity stopped every second day for several hours so it could be exported to Austria in exchange for hard currency.[45]

Because Yugoslav society was male dominated, missionaries encountered difficulty when it came to teaching wives who had expressed interest. It was not socially acceptable for women to be taught if their husbands were not present. Sister Ranović had a cousin with two children in Beograd who showed some interest by asking questions. When alone she was interested, but when her husband was around she did not ask questions. After a while, she even stopped associating with Ranović.[46]

Besides facing a seemingly apathetic people, the missionaries feared exceeding the bounds of the law and attracting the attention of local authorities. Neighborhood officials asked landlords what the missionaries were doing. Responding to their landlords, the missionaries said they were working with members and learning the language and the culture.[47] In one instance, the police called in and interrogated one of the missionaries' language instructors. The teacher was surprised to learn that the authorities knew many details about the missionaries' past activities, not only in Yugoslavia but in America.[48]

Elders Zagorec and Bestor learned the hard way about registering their presence with local police when working in a new area. They traveled an hour by train, forty-five minutes by bus, and walked thirty minutes up a mountainside to visit a contact who was not home. The parents of the contact invited them in for a sumptuous meal and to stay for the night. To everyone's surprise, the police burst in during the night, then searched, arrested, and jailed them at the police station. The missionaries learned they had been mistaken as spies because of their facility with the native language. The police finally released them at 4:00 A.M.[49]

In at least one instance, boldness and honesty paid off in missionary dealings with the authorities. Because the missionaries entered on tourist visas, they had to leave the country every three months to get them renewed. After a visa transaction in April 1979, Elders Smith and Zivkovic were reentering Zagreb when the guard suspiciously asked why they kept saying they were tourists. Smith candidly said they represented the Church, so the guard called the secret police. The missionaries entered the secret police's office and the agent pulled out a gray folder labeled "Mormons" containing the names of and information on the missionaries. Smith noted the information was woefully out-of-date and helped update the file. His helpfulness impressed the officer.[50]

During their meeting, the agent asked for a fuller explanation of the missionaries' activities. Elder Smith explained that they simply talked to people. The officer said they had received complaints that the missionaries looked for people who had died. Smith explained that a few referrals were several years old and that some people had passed away before they had been contacted. The officer also asked about the literature they carried. Elder Smith gave him the Book of Mormon, the *Joseph Smith Story*, and some other pamphlets. The officer concluded that the two men were more than tourists and ordered them to go to court. Smith, equally honest at court, pleaded guilty and was fined $50. Elder Zivkovic did the same. The court ordered the missionaries to go back to the secret police and file for missionary status. Because they had befriended the officer, he granted them entry for ninety days as missionaries.

Occasionally, the somber reality of Church circumstances in Yugoslavia was punctuated by visits from Church authorities. In August 1978, James E. Faust, International Mission president, visited Yugoslavia as part of a tour through central Europe.[51] He boosted the morale of missionaries and members alike.[52] H. Burke Peterson of the Presiding

Bishopric visited not long thereafter. He said the missionaries and members had the full support of President Kimball, though some general authorities had begun to question the Yugoslav venture; the Church had just closed a low-key mission in Iran, similar to the one in Yugoslavia. Elder Peterson advised renewed caution to avoid any confrontation that would endanger the Church's presence or themselves.[53]

Anxiety about the political authorities and lack of conversions were compounded by a sense of isolation. A missionary companionship often had little contact with missionaries in other towns and met only once every two or three months with President Smith in Vienna. Phone calls often proved very troublesome because of problems with scheduling or making connections. Packages sent to the missionaries were ripped apart, and mail was weeks or months late. Psychologically it was difficult. The missionaries referred to the situation as "Mission Impossible," after a television series of the same title.[54]

Faced with these circumstances, some missionaries questioned the reason for their presence in Yugoslavia. Success could not be measured by numbers of discussions, baptisms, or tracting hours—the standard activities of missionaries elsewhere. Elder Bestor found success in the feeling that he worked as hard as possible even though the circumstances were trying.[55] Elder Smith viewed his mission as plowing furrows that would be ready when seeds could be planted at some future date.[56] The Church's presence in the Communist world was indeed frail and its prospect anything but promising.

Despite the small number of members, the missionary force increased to a total of fourteen by September 1980. Then, on September 22, Elders David Angerhofer and Krayton Davis were unexpectedly expelled from the country for being teachers of religion and were given forty-eight hours to leave.[57] Other expulsions followed. President Edwin B. Morrell arrived in January 1981 to manage missionary efforts and members in central and eastern Europe and found himself in the middle of the crisis. Because of the expulsions, Church leaders stopped the flow of missionaries from the States. Six missionaries completed their missions in February 1981, leaving eight still serving in the country. Elder Gordon B. Hinckley, newly appointed counselor in the First Presidency, visited Zagreb with the Young Ambassadors, a Brigham Young University performing group. After examining the missionaries' dismal circumstances, he decided to remove the elders and send in couple missionaries like those serving elsewhere in central and eastern Europe. The last four elders were transferred in October 1981, completing their missions elsewhere.[58]

A Novel Addition: Couple Missionaries

For five years senior missionary couples sustained the Church in Yugoslavia. A senior couple from the International Mission, Glen and Millie Warner, had operated from Vienna in behalf of Yugoslavia and other eastern European countries during 1979 and 1980.[59] Others worked in Poland and Hungary as previously noted. In June 1981, the first missionary couple to live in Yugoslavia arrived in Zagreb. Vaughn and Esther Stosich entered as students and dutifully paid their money to attend classes at the university. Meanwhile, they sustained the members and built on the contacts of the exiled missionaries.[60]

The experiences of the next couple to serve in Zagreb, Ralph and Elaine Gibbons (1983–85), are indicative of the conditions all couples encountered there. There was little privacy. Telephone calls were tapped. The secret police employed many informers to report those who might exhibit non-Communist sentiments. Inflation as well as shortfalls in consumer goods and services plagued the daily life of the populace. The missionaries heated their apartment with a portable radiator and froze one day out of four when the electricity was shut off. Their bed consisted of a mattress on the floor. The couple's apartment also doubled as the meeting place on Sundays. Although the Gibbons eventually moved to a better apartment, they had to pay a hefty rent.[61]

The law prohibited meetings of over five people without permission from the secret police, thus limiting the ability of anti-government forces to organize. When members visited the Gibbons, they came and left in ones or twos to avoid attention. Whenever they had more than five people— a common circumstance—they shuddered when the doorbell rang, fearing it might be the police ready to expel the missionaries from the country and do even worse things to the members. They knew that those who were incarcerated could expect only bread and water unless relatives or friends brought additional food.[62]

The Gibbons faced one particular danger without fully realizing it at the time. They knew that there were import duties and other restrictions on goods brought into Yugoslavia. Giving it little thought, Elder Gibbons arranged for the Vienna Austria Mission president to purchase a portable electronic organ in Graz. He and Sister Gibbons accompanied a consulate group of American, British, and European wives who traveled by bus to Graz each month to buy food they could not get in Yugoslavia. He picked up the organ and placed it in the back of the bus. At the border where they reentered, the guards began to search the compartments under the bus and the packages each person carried inside the passenger compartment. Everyone was tired and anxious because one of the ladies had been strip-searched on an earlier trip. Elder Gibbons argued with the guards to let them pass, and the search was called off just before an inspector reached the back of the bus. Once they crossed the border, Elder Gibbons realized the organ would have been regarded as electronic equipment, a strictly prohibited import item, and was extremely relieved that the search had ended before it was found.[63]

The senior couples were a novel addition to the traditional missionary force since they operated outside the standard mission structure. They were isolated, exposed to the whims of a government that could, at the least, expel them for infractions of a governmental system adverse to religion. In spite of the danger, they quietly sustained Church members and remained ready to answer questions from people interested in learning about the gospel. While their success was not measurable in numbers, their value was sufficient that Church leaders continued to send couples into other countries with regimes similar to those of the old Soviet bloc, such as Mongolia and Vietnam. In a broader frame of reference, senior missionaries became more common in the 1980s as the Church began to recruit them more heavily. Their service was an important innovation in missionary work during the last half of the twentieth century, and their antecedents were this stalwart handful that operated in obscurity behind the Iron Curtain.

A Meager Membership

Despite the best efforts of elders and senior missionary couples, the Church barely survived in Yugoslavia. A few small pockets of members sustained their faith, virtually isolated in an environment hostile toward those who professed religion, particularly a religion outside the traditional faiths of Catholicism and Orthodoxy. Krešimir Ćosić served as the Yugoslav District president, responsible for the overall direction of the members in the country. As he traveled to basketball games, he often visited missionaries and members. The missionaries in Beograd saw him every several weeks. For example, on Sunday he might show up at 7 A.M. and say, "We have Church now; you give talk; you give prayer," and the service would proceed. Because it was illegal for a foreigner to baptize or perform any religious ordinances, Brother Ćosić did all the baptisms and confirmations in the 1970s.[64]

In Ćosić's hometown of Zadar, a small branch met under the leadership of Mišo Ostarčević. Having returned in 1977 from playing basketball at Brigham Young University, Brother Ostarčević served as branch president until Ćosić left temporarily for Italy in 1979, and he succeeded him as Yugoslav District president. Brother Ostarčević continued in that position until 1984, except when his work was temporarily interrupted by mandatory military service from 1979 to 1980.[65]

Despite the meager membership, Kenneth Myers and Briant Smith, successive presidents over the Austria Vienna Mission, continued to seek official recognition. In March 1979, President Myers held a Church conference in Zadar and announced it was time to fully organize the Church in Yugoslavia. David Farnsworth, legal counsel to the Church in Europe, explained to the four members present that according to the Church's interpretation of Yugoslav law all that needed to happen was for a meeting place to be obtained and recognition sought by petition. However, the prospects were not inviting. Although names of about thirty members appeared on Church rosters, only the handful present were active.[66] Despite President Myers's initiative, there was no immediate result.

Around the same time, the lone member in Zagreb, Tomislav Zidar, had lost interest in the Church. The missionaries' greatest support was Ivan Valek (illus. 4-4), an architect and a long-time acquaintance of Brother Ćosić. He had two apartments and let the missionaries stay in one, rent-free, while he stayed in the other with his mother. He read voraciously and even studied books on the Church.[67] He finally joined the Church in 1981, crossing the border into Austria long enough to be baptized by Elder Stosich.[68] Brother Valek was soon called as the branch president in Zagreb, and he eventually became a leader over all members in Yugoslavia.

Brother Ćosić also lived in Zagreb after returning from Italy. He continued to sustain members and represent the Church to the nation. Still considered the best basketball player in the country, he was often the center of national attention. In a nation where being openly religious could have serious repercussions, Ćosić was unflinching. He was known to have responded on national television, "Well, yes, I guess I am the number one star of the game, but that's because I don't drink or smoke, I take care of my body, and I'm a member of the Church of Jesus Christ of Latter-day Saints!"[69] Ćosić retired from playing to begin coaching the Yugoslav national team in 1985.[70] In 1986 the team won the bronze medal in the World Basketball Championships, keeping alive Yugoslavia's twenty-three-year streak of finishing in the top three. (They missed the final by a single point, dropping a 91–90 overtime decision to the Soviet Union.)[71] In 1987 he accepted a coaching position in Italy.[72] For nearly fifteen years, Brother Ćosić was a figure who could not be dismissed or

Courtesy Radmila Ranović

Illus. 4-4. Church gathering in Zagreb, October 1982. Ivan Valek is next to last at the far right beside Radmila Ranović. Krešimir Ćosić is next to last on the far left.

silenced by authorities. Though he had his flaws, his Croatian nationalism and authoritarian disposition sometimes grating on others,[73] Brother Ćosić was the undisputed bedrock of the Church in Yugoslavia until his departure for Italy.

In 1984 a valiant convert joined the Zagreb branch and became instrumental in establishing a facility for Sabbath services. Juraj Vuković read the Book of Mormon, which he obtained from a friend who had received it from his brother in Germany. Vuković came looking for the Church. He arrived at the Gibbons apartment and "soaked up the Gospel like a sponge." He was baptized in Graz, Austria, a day's trip from Zagreb. Brother Vuković soon became involved in acquiring a Church facility in Zagreb.[74] The site selected was two second floor side-by-side apartments located on Svačićev Trg in downtown Zagreb. The facility was renovated during 1984. Elder Gibbons acted as the liaison, working with contractors and city officials.[75]

Contractors completed the remodeling in October 1984. Brother Vuković then took it upon himself to gather approximately thirty permits that had to be signed by all the organizations required to approve the location of a meeting place. He faced embarrassment, delay, and lost two jobs in the process, but he succeeded. The facility included a chapel area, a Relief Society room, a baptismal font room, and a small missionary apartment.[76]

There was Church activity further east in the capital city of Beograd. Sister Radmila Ranović was one of two members there from 1978 to 1980. The other, Dušan Tabori, a man in his seventies, met the missionaries at the train station in Basel, Switzerland, where he had gone to exchange money, and joined the Church in October 1977 (illus. 4-5).[77] Brother Tabori was faithful but enfeebled, and his wife had some mental difficulties, making her incapable of comprehending the gospel message.[78]

Sister Ranović and Brother Tabori began holding church services with the missionaries in his apartment. They sat around Brother Tabori's kitchen table, had a Sunday School lesson, a talk, and then the sacrament. Others, mostly curious younger people, attended occasionally. The few who were baptized did not remain active. At least once a year, Sister Ranović traveled to Zadar and visited the Ostarčevićs.[79]

The circumstances discouraged members, all of whom were young in the Church and isolated from the fellowship of others. Sister Ranović's feelings were perhaps indicative of members' feelings.

> I didn't have a bishop, I didn't have a stake president, I didn't really have a mission president. Well, the mission president was there and he would come occasionally. But I felt he was mostly concerned for the missionaries. And I did feel the missionaries were there to help me, and they did. I mean, actually it was more helping each other. They didn't know what to do, I didn't know what to do, and so we

Courtesy Radmila Ranović

Illus. 4-5. Missionary couple John and Arlene Irwin (*left*) with Beograd members Brother Tabori and Sister Ranović, 1982.

were together a lot. I don't know if it was good or bad, but it did keep us active in the Church.[80]

After the 1979 meeting with President Myers, Sister Ranović began seeking recognition for the Church in Beograd in March 1980. She and Brother Tabori convinced a Presbyterian priest to agree to let them meet in his church. She sent a petition to the authorities and was summarily called into the police station. The officer explained other parts of the process: the meeting place had to be inspected to determine if it were safe and if the neighbors had any complaints, and the Church must also have a formal, rather than a verbal, agreement with the Presbyterians. When Radmila asked the priest for a written rental arrangement, he referred her to his lawyer. The lawyer quizzically asked why just two or three members wanted a church. David Farnsworth, the Church's legal counsel in Europe, visited to help take the request to the Presbyterian Synod. But the outcome was to no avail. The fruitless effort absorbed ten months.[81]

In December 1980, David Farnsworth and Elder Robert D. Hales, Executive Administrator of Central Europe, visited Sister Ranović in Beograd. Having no advance notice of their exact arrival date, she opened the door unsuspectingly. They came in, and Elder Hales said, "I hear you want to go on a mission." She had previously discussed the possibility with Glen Warner, a senior missionary serving in Vienna. Sister Ranović soon left to serve in the Canada Montreal Mission and became the first Yugoslav as well as the first eastern European to perform a full-time mission.[82]

Isolated from contact with the other members who might have provided multiple examples of gospel living, members had difficulty relinquishing attitudes and dispositions that were contrary to the gospel's ideal of unity. When Sister Ranović returned from Canada in October 1982, she found little had changed in her absence. It was still just Brother Tabori and herself. Only now he was frequently sick, and when this was the case, no church service was held. But the loneliness was about to end. The Stosichs visited Beograd with some referral names. One was the Stipica family—Ivo, Vuka, Maja, and Bata. Because the Stosichs did not speak the language adequately, they delivered a first discussion mostly by having the Stipica family read it. Sister Ranović contributed by relating the Joseph Smith story and testifying it was true. She was startled to see a response in the family and to feel they had been touched by the Spirit. Sister Ranović continued to teach them alone once a week. Despite a heart attack a few years earlier, Ivo Stipica was smoking two packs of cigarettes a day. At Sister Ranović's urging, he quit on October 20, the anniversary of Beograd's liberation at the end of World War II. In the meantime,

Courtesy Radmila Ranović

Illus. 4-6. Beograd branch members, April 1983. Branch President Ivo Stipica is standing on the far left.

Ivo's sister, Alemka, joined the Church while on an extended visit in Switzerland. The rest of Ivo's family became serious investigators.[83]

In January 1983, Lee and Marilyn Manwill arrived in Beograd as the first missionary couple to serve in that city. With Sister Ranović's help they taught Zorica Jovic, a friend of Maja Stipica. She and the Stipicas were baptized in May. The group held family home evenings with the mission-ary couple and with nonmember friends. The future of the Church in Beograd finally appeared hopeful.[84] By November 1983, the Beograd membership had grown large enough to be organized as a branch (illus. 4-6), and it was a time of great excitement among the members. However, it was also the beginning of adversity in the Church. Because the members were isolated from contact with the rest of the Church, some had diffi-culty relinquishing attitudes and dispositions that were contrary to the gospel's ideal of unity.

The Manwills left in 1984 and were replaced by Joseph and Melba Padovich.[85] A year later, in May 1985, Brother Tabori died of old age. In August, President Morrell, no longer serving over Yugoslavia, came to Beograd while conducting a tour group from Utah. A member of the tour group met Sister Ranović and offered to sponsor her as a student at BYU. Radmila eventually accepted the chance to obtain a four-year degree, something for which she had longed.[86]

Momentous Proceedings

The meeting place in Zagreb had been nearly finished for a year when the members unexpectedly learned on September 17, 1985, that Elder Thomas S. Monson would arrive in Zagreb to dedicate the building, and, more important, to dedicate the land of Yugoslavia for missionary work.[87] Church leaders felt confident that with the approval for the building in hand they could proceed with no adverse repercussions. In a flurry of activity, workers hung drapes in all the windows, mounted chalkboards, and installed display shelves and a sound system.[88]

Just prior to dedicating the chapel on October 30, 1985, Elder Monson delivered words of greeting from President Spencer W. Kimball.[89] It is perhaps fitting that the President whose vision sent the missionaries into Yugoslavia in 1978 should live to learn of the momentous proceedings in that land. The chapel dedication was one of the final acts of Kimball's presidency, as he died six days later. Brother Ćosić arranged to have government officials present and a camera crew on hand to record the dedication (illus. 4-7).[90]

Courtesy Jeffrey Moore

Illus. 4-7. Zagreb meeting place located on the second floor of a building.

On Thursday, October 31, at a smaller gathering during the work day, Elder Monson dedicated the country for missionary work. Explaining that dedications were normally performed outdoors, he said that instead he would proceed with the windows open, symbolic of blessing the entire country. He uttered many promises, some of which soon began to be fulfilled. Among these was that the missionaries would go forward with their work unhindered and successfully.[91]

Though the impact was uneven and there were still valleys as well as peaks, the various ethnicities of Yugoslavia began to take the gospel message seriously in ever greater numbers. While the number of baptisms did not skyrocket, they occurred with much greater frequency than previously. Only a week after the dedication, Elder William Wilson, part of a senior couple that replaced the Padovichs in Beograd, set Sister Ranović apart as a district missionary. Missionary work started to develop much faster than before, and she and the couple missionaries had their hands full teaching new investigators. Investigators came independently to the missionaries' apartments asking questions. During winter 1985–86, the Wilsons and Sister Ranović taught discussions every single night.[92]

The relationship with officials remained tentative as different offices made conflicting decisions. In 1985, Beograd officials ordered the Wilsons to leave. In spite of this, the Yugoslav embassy in Vienna gave them a yearlong visa to reenter.[93] The couple missionaries made numerous contacts in 1986 until Sister Wilson suddenly died of complications from one of her prescribed medications.[94]

Young Missionaries Return

Sensing the dissipation of antireligious sentiment, Church leaders again sent young missionaries into Yugoslavia. Elder Spencer J. Condie, Austria Vienna Mission president, supervised their activities. In July 1986, Elders Kirk Teske and Brian Peterson entered on tourist visas. Later, Elder Greg Tayler replaced Elder Peterson. Fifteen baptisms occurred in a six-month period, an unprecedented success.[95]

One of the first people the young missionaries baptized was Nena Okeke, a Nigerian student. Nigerians came to Yugoslavia for four or five years of schooling. As a group they listened more attentively to the gospel message, and at the time they constituted about a third of the active membership in Zagreb. The missionaries then baptized a family from Split that had been converted by earlier missionaries. Elder Teske felt he and his companion had harvested the work of his predecessors.

This activity was noticed by the civil authorities, who abruptly expelled the missionaries after a few months for exceeding their privilege as tourists. Shortly afterward these same missionaries reentered the country as students and enrolled in language classes at the University of Zagreb. In 1987, Elders Teske and Tayler were expelled a second time, this time with the proviso that they could not return to the country for at least nine months.[96] Prior to the missionaries' second expulsion, they baptized the Fulepp family.

To smooth out the situation with missionary expulsions, Elder Russell M. Nelson, Hans B. Ringger (Europe Area president), Spencer J. Condie (Austria Vienna Mission president), and Krešimir Ćosić visited top officials in Croatia and Serbia in April 1987. They received assurances that there would be no future problems. From the Church's perspective, permission had now been granted to proselytize, if not in all of Yugoslavia at least in Croatia. When missionaries entered Croatia in summer 1987 they did so as missionaries instead of students or tourists. In August 1987, Elder Kevin Field obtained the first residency permit granted to a missionary.[97] Regardless of recognition at higher levels, local officials still kept a close eye on missionary activity, and expulsions occurred randomly.[98] The situation in Serbia was more daunting than in Croatia. Though attempts were made, a meeting place could not be secured in Beograd. Despite this situation, missionaries began registering as missionaries there as well as in Croatia.[99]

Missionary methods in Yugoslavia were altered, though not entirely, following political reconciliation in 1987. The missionaries still engaged mainly in sports, attempting to make friends first and proselytize later. But changes did come. In 1987, Yugoslavia and the rest of central and eastern Europe came under the auspices of the newly created Austria Vienna East Mission, with Dennis Neuenschwander as president. The new president wanted to increase missionary discipline and have the missionaries stretch the limits of their proselytizing opportunities. He believed some missionaries had become lax by spending too much time in non-proselytizing activity.[100]

Whereas the missionaries had previously attempted to blend in, the new approach was to attract attention. One new innovation was street displays,[101] which attracted the attention of the police, who kept watch on the events to ensure compliance with proselytizing restrictions. They occasionally shut down the meetings with no explanation.[102] The missionaries were now clean shaven. They wore suits and short hair, and they smiled a lot. At times they even wore name tags. It seemed to one missionary that at bus stops every single face on the bus was planted against the window just staring at them.[103]

In 1988 the civil authorities began to delay granting extended visas and provided no explanation.[104] In addition, public indoctrination continued to hold sway. From their youth, Yugoslavs had been instilled with the concept of "self-management," or the idea that individuals could take care of themselves alone without need of any divine assistance.[105] Those who listened and considered spiritual matters were usually put off by the Word of Wisdom.[106] To some missionaries, there was a palpable atmosphere of spiritual darkness that parted only when they left the country every three months to attend missionary conferences and renew their visas.[107]

Deteriorating economic conditions distracted the populace from exploring religion. Political, social, and economic unrest surfaced in strikes and political demonstrations. In 1989 missionaries exchanged money once a week because of inflation. Sometimes they even received letters that had been slashed open, searched for valuables, and then clumsily resealed with tape.[108]

Public behavior was sometimes inexplicable by Western standards. Beginning in 1991, the Church directed all missionaries to render four hours of humanitarian service each week. In Yugoslavia missionaries who tried to follow this rule faced the official government policy that there was no need for volunteer service. When some missionaries cleaned up a park, they did so against the advice of the people in the apartment where they lived. The second time they did it, a policeman came and said, "If you do it again, we'll throw you into jail."[109]

Still unsure of official censure, the missionaries proceeded cautiously in their activities. Casual contacting continued to be the norm. As Elder Kim Simpson described it: "Ten-hour extroversion, canned conversation, and street contacting." He concluded, "If serving in Yugoslavia seemed a formidable task upon arrival, it seemed impossible later."[110] Each missionary had to face and personally resolve the question of whether their effort was of value. Elder Simpson described his resolution of the issue:

> I stood looking out the window at the same old park, the same old people from the same old block, and felt myself asking that old missionary cliché question so seriously it scared me—"Is it really worth it?" Then immediately I rediscovered the Comforter, was purged, and sat down to write about it. Of course it's worth it.[111]

A Providential Beginning in Slovenia

In 1990, President Neuenschwander decided to send the missionaries into Slovenia, the northernmost state of Yugoslavia and the most western oriented of the confederation. Its population, comprising less than ten percent of pre–civil war Yugoslavia's twenty-three million people, had long been neglected by the Church since leaders sought first to establish a base in the country's major urban centers. The shift of attention was providential. In contrast to the years of waiting for legal recognition further south, it was only a matter of months before Slovenia granted legal recognition. When Yugoslavia dissolved into civil war in 1991 (as will be discussed in chapter 6), Slovenia was touched only briefly by the holocaust. While missionaries did not continue working in other places in the country during the civil war, they did keep working there.

The assignment to open Slovenia was given to veteran missionary Jeffrey Moore and his companion Corey Bodily, fresh from the Missionary Training Center. They entered Ljubljana late in November 1990 and immediately visited the university to investigate language classes since neither missionary knew the language. They met a lady who befriended them, and she gave names of contacts who could help. That Sunday the missionaries held a sacrament meeting. After praying to find people to attend church, someone knocked on their apartment door. The stranger identified himself as the lady's husband and explained that his wife had been very impressed by them. He had biked twenty miles to meet them himself. His home became the first in Slovenia to be visited by the missionaries.[112]

In February 1991, President Neuenschwander entered Slovenia to conduct a fireside. Nine people came. The president strongly encouraged the missionaries to get the names and addresses of those who attended. However, no one in the audience would volunteer this information. When there were only two people remaining, Elder Moore bore his testimony and asked again if they would give their names and addresses. One girl said yes. When they visited her, she confided that she had opened her mouth to say no, but the wrong word had come out. On March 30, 1991, Suzana Klenovšek became the first convert in Slovenia. Her friend Dušanka Punčec became the second on April 13.[113]

There were two members already living in the vicinity who would provide future leadership: Albin and Boža Lotrič. Albin had been baptized in Norway and had later taken Boža to Austria to be baptized before they were married. They lived about an hour and a half from the town of Ljubljana. There was also a student from Novi Sad named Andre Stupavsky. The first services with members were held in this student's apartment.[114]

The missionaries wanted better quarters for meetings, and after about two months they started going door-to-door to buildings where they thought people might let them meet. An employee at the Chamber of Commerce was favorably impressed by the young men and gave them a reference. The missionaries soon discovered their reference was the vice-president of Slovenia. They found themselves in a huge office abounding with secretaries and even an interpreter. The vice-president asked, "What can I do for you?" Elder Moore responded, "We're missionaries for The Church of Jesus Christ of Latter-day Saints and we want to establish our Church here, and we need to find a place where we can have church meetings." The man called the president of Slovenia, who responded favorably. The missionaries were then referred to the Ljubljana mayor's office, which was less grandiose and had no interpreter. Even though the mayor tried to speak English, Elder Moore instead spoke in Slovenian, this time with a facility far beyond anything that could have been expected after just two months of study. The mayor pulled out a city map and pointed to the very center of the city. The Church was promised the use of the Communist Party offices on Sunday.[115] The missionaries agreed to it because President Neuenschwander had previously told them to accept any quarters offered.

The appointment to register the Church in Slovenia was March 1, 1991. Ivan Valek, who had replaced Brother Ćosić as Yugoslav District president in 1987, arrived from Zagreb for the important meeting. Some government and police officials were not particularly happy about the Mormon missionaries' success and the troubled President Valek said, "They could exile me, they could fine me, they could take away my job." The meeting with the Secretary of Religious Affairs went poorly, and the petitioners were dismissed. Hesitating as they made their departure, President Valek said, "I will go back. I need to go back." The minister was in the process of boxing up his papers, but he listened a second time, and while they were there he had a document prepared. He signed it and the Church was officially recognized.[116] Considering the Church's history in Yugoslavia, something extraordinary had happened.

Mission Unfinished, 1986–1991

Since the beginning, the Church in Yugoslavia struggled against seemingly overwhelming problems. The membership consisted primarily of individuals, not families. For a decade, the Ostarčević family in Zadar was the only couple belonging to the Church. They were joined in 1983 by the Stipicas in Beograd and in 1987 by the Fulepps in Zagreb. A Church focused on families simply did not function fully and effectively without them. To exacerbate the situation, many of the faithful, active members did not remain in Yugoslavia.[117] Another problem was that several members lived in remote areas and missed the fellowship of weekly services. If they did not read the Book of Mormon and pray regularly, their chances of remaining active in the Church were slim. Missionary couples traveled to outlying areas to visit these scattered members and administer the sacrament, but their visits, of necessity, were brief.[118] Until 1991 the membership never matured to fulfill the Church's vision of a unified group rendering service to each other.

In 1987, the year Krešimir Ćosić left Yugoslavia for Italy, the Zagreb branch struggled with an average attendance of fifteen to twenty. The Ostarčević family came from Zadar, and Andre Stupavsky traveled from Slovenia for conferences. Baptisms occurred infrequently. One was Rudolph Ruter, baptized October 23, 1987, in Zagreb, the city in which he had been raised. He met the missionaries at baseball practices, where they invited him to attend Church. After reading the Book of Mormon and responding to its spiritual power, Brother Ruter accepted baptism against the will of his mother and friends. On his baptismal day, he felt like he was "on the moon" because he was so light. He tried to explain his feelings to his friends and relatives, but to no avail. However, they respected his decision, and he later served as a missionary in Salt Lake City, reciprocating the blessings so many missionaries had brought to his country.[119]

By early 1988, the branch had grown sufficiently to require the calling of a Relief Society president. Sister Ljiljana Fulepp served as president in the Zagreb Relief Society, which was first organized March 27, 1988. The Relief Society fall social, held on September 10, 1988, was well attended. Forty-two people, including thirty-six investigators, enjoyed eating dinner, listening to a program, and dancing and singing. Elder Johann Wondra, the Church's regional representative over Yugoslavia (assisting President Neuenschwander in supervising members), conducted the first training for the branch in June and November, explaining that the purpose of Church leaders was to bring people to Christ through covenants and ordinances and then help them endure to the end.[120]

The situation in Beograd remained unremittingly dismal. The Stipica family were the only active members in late 1986. Two people were baptized in 1987, but both lived outside Beograd.[121] In the next few years, Ivo Stipica's health declined and the family eventually fell into inactivity. In January 1988, the Church rented a suitable facility in Beograd to serve as a meeting place and a residence for the missionaries.[122] A stable membership continued to be an elusive goal, as seen in the case of Željko Križanac. He arrived in the city to complete his training as a priest, and as he had heard many rumors about the Church, he decided to eavesdrop clandestinely outside the window on Sundays to report any lawbreaking to the authorities. Favorably influenced by the services, he eventually decided to enter and while there felt a sense of peace. The missionaries taught Željko the gospel and baptized him, but the opposition of his friends made him reconsider. He entered the chapel to announce his rejection, but once again felt enveloped with a peace that washed away his indecision. Željko was called on a mission to England a year after being baptized. He later married and remained in England.[123] Although he served faithfully elsewhere, the branch in Beograd did not benefit from his conversion.

Even though Church success in Yugoslavia after 1985 exceeded that of the earlier proselytizing effort, a mature membership was still something to be hoped for in the future. Those joining often had significant personal struggles to overcome before leading others. On the night of her baptism, a prospective member in Zagreb paced nervously through the waist-high water, ringing her hands and repeating "I don't know . . . I don't know" as the missionaries waited patiently to perform the ordinance. Another family smoked their last cigarettes between baptism and confirmation.[124] Among the more promising converts was Ivica Babin, baptized just before the country's civil war. Unfortunately, he stepped on a land mine during the war and was killed.[125]

On March 22, 1991, responsibility for Yugoslavia returned to the Austria Vienna Mission, presided over at the time by Kenneth Reber. He went into the country on April 29, 1991, with President Neuenschwander to hold conferences with missionaries and members. Twelve missionaries and two senior couples served in Beograd, Zagreb, and Ljubljana (illus. 4-8). Nearly a hundred members appeared on the rolls, but only twenty or so were active. Some members could not be found, usually those who had been baptized elsewhere and who lived in remote areas. In Zagreb about thirty-five people attended the members' district conference,[126] not much to show after twenty years' work. Yugoslavia was still a mission unfinished, a handful of active members and missionaries dependent on the Austria Vienna Mission.

There are several parallels between the Yugoslav experience until 1991 and the one in Hungary before World War I. The technique of casual contacting used by Elders Biesinger and Jennings in Budapest during 1885 was essentially the same (except for casual clothing and long hair) as that used by the missionaries during the early years in Yugoslavia, 1978–81. The imperial authorities monitored the missionaries in Hungary from

1901 to 1914 much as the Communist authorities did in Yugoslavia until 1991. In both cases, the people were basically unreceptive, and a majority of those who joined usually left or drifted into inactivity. The Church desisted in Hungary when faced with no response. The same nearly happened in 1980 when the Church extracted the young missionaries from Yugoslavia. There the parallel ends.

In 1980 the Church varied its approach from the past by implementing the new tactic of sending in senior couples, a concept already tested in Poland and Hungary. This resource became available in the later half of the twentieth century when Church members retired in greater numbers, many having sufficient funds and adequate health to serve missions. The Church took advantage of this opportunity to call them on missions. Their service in Communist Yugoslavia provided a vital element in sustaining an embryonic Church until Communism self-destructed and young missionaries were able to return.

A Worthwhile Endeavor?

Was the effort from 1978 to 1991 worthwhile? The country never developed a stable and self-sustaining community of faithful members as did Czechoslovakia before World War II. The Church fielded the manpower, developed language skill in its representatives, and sustained its commitment over time. Yet few Yugoslav citizens converted. Political and social strife along ethnic lines, distrust engendered by a repressive regime, and deeply ingrained traditions seemed to foment a pall over the country's religious climate. Despite his prominence and popularity, Brother Ćosić was not able to generate a similar response from his countrymen for the religion he espoused. Those who did join faced the difficulty of learning to live gospel principles with little guidance and few examples to follow. Although the conversion of one soul is of inestimable worth, in the aggregate, the effort in Yugoslavia did not succeed well.

Political turmoil canceled the 1991 basketball season. On the eve of civil war, the Ostarčević family came to Utah. The visit was intended to last a few months, but it extended into years.[127] Of the early leaders, only President Valek lived in the country. A civil war that had threatened since the death of Communist president Josip Tito a decade earlier finally erupted. Paradoxically, the threat of civil war began to revive religious aspirations, offering hope to a mission that had previously seemed impossible. Before this transition occurred in Yugoslavia, the rest of central and eastern Europe entered a new age of inquiry and hope.

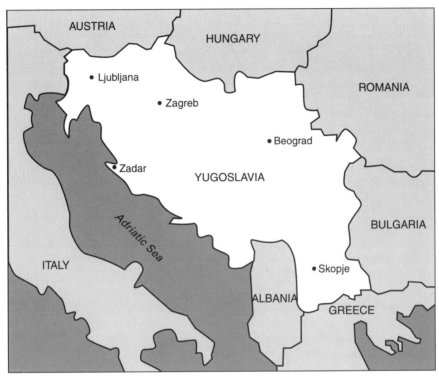

Illus. 4-8. Areas of Latter-day Saint missionary work in Yugoslavia, 1972–90.

Notes

1. Rendell Mabey, telephone interviews by author, October 30, 1995; January 15, 1996.

2. Glen Tuckett, speech, Memorial Service for Krešimir Ćosić, May 31, 1995, audio tape (Marriott International Audio Visual Operations Department); Carri P. Jenkins, "Kresimir Cosic Moves from Basketball to Diplomatic Courts," *BYU Today* 46 (November 1992): 10.

3. Floyd Johnson, *Touchdowns, Tipoffs, and Testimonies: A Look at the Spiritual Side of BYU Athletics* (Orem, Utah: Alba Publishing, 1989), 15–16; Tucket, speech.

4. Phyllis Nibley, telephone interview by author, November 24, 1995.

5. Phyllis Nibley, telephone interview.

6. Truman Madsen, speech, Memorial Service for Ćosić, May 31, 1995.

7. Johnson, *Touchdowns, Tipoffs, and Testimonies,* 15–16.

8. Tuckett, speech.

9. Tuckett, speech.

10. Paul Nibley, telephone interview by author, November 22, 1995; "Yugoslavian History," in Austria Vienna Mission Manuscript History, 1968–77, Church Archives, The Church of Jesus Christ of Latter-day Saints, Salt Lake City.

11. "Yugoslavian History," 1.

12. Phyllis Nibley, telephone interview.

13. Paul Nibley, telephone interview. Unless otherwise noted, source for the next paragraph as well.

14. Jay G. Burrup, "Church History in Italy," 1996 Directory (Ogden, Utah: John R. Halliday Italy Milan Mission Organization), unpaginated.

15. Ruediger Tillmann, interviewed by author, March 9, 1991, Draper, Utah.

16. Austria Vienna Mission Manuscript History, August 30, 1973 report, entry for September 16–19, 1972, Church Archives; "Yugoslavian History," 1–2. Sources for the next paragraph as well.

17. Jenkins, "Kresimir Cosic," 10.

18. Lee Davidson, "Cosic as a True Man of Principle," *Deseret News,* June 3, 1995, A-9.

19. Mildred Austin, "The Zadar Mormons," *Monday Magazine,* September 22, 1975, 7–8.

20. Johnson, *Touchdowns, Tipoffs, and Testimonies,* 18.

21. William T. Black, *Mormon Athletes* (Salt Lake City: Deseret Book, 1980), 29–30; Dick Davis and Duane Hiatt, "Kresimir Cosic—Basketball and Baptism," *New Era* 4 (February 1974): 10; Ankica Ostarčević, telephone interview by author, February 23, 1996; Mišo Ostarčević, interviewed by author, February 28, 1995, Salt Lake City; Austria Vienna Mission Manuscript History, 1974–75 report, entry for October 1974.

22. Austria Vienna Mission Manuscript History, 1974–75 report, entry for October 1974.

23. "Yugoslavian History," 3.

24. Jeff Anderson, telephone interview by author, February 21, 1996.

25. Kevin Pinegar, telephone interview by author, October 27, 1995; "Yugoslavian History," 1.

26. Austria Vienna Mission Manuscript History, 1974–75 report, entry for July 2, 1975; "Yugoslavian History," 4; Anderson, telephone interview.

27. Ankica Ostarčević, telephone interview.

28. Kevin Pinegar, telephone interview.

29. Mišo Ostarčević, interview.

30. Spencer J. Condie, interviewed by James B. Allen, March 15–22, 1989, Provo, Utah, audio tape 3, in possession of the interviewer, Orem, Utah.

31. Martin Berkeley Hickman, *David Matthew Kennedy: Banker, Statesman, Churchman* (Salt Lake City: Deseret Book, 1987), 342.

32. Kurt Bestor, telephone interview by author, November 20, 1995; Gustav Salik, "Mission President's Report on Brazil, Yugoslavia, Hungary, Romania, Austria" typescript, 20–21, in possession of author.

33. Austria Vienna Mission, Historical Records and Minutes, 1978 report, entries for February 1, 11, 1978, and April 26, 1978, Church Archives.

34. Radmila Ranović, interviewed by Matthew K. Heiss, 1988, Provo, Utah, typescript, 24, James Moyle Oral History Program, Church Archives.

35. Ranović, interview, 26–30.

36. Kurt Bestor, interviewed by author, October 18, 1995, Provo, Utah; Everett Smith, interviewed by author, June 22, 1995, Kingston, Canada; Charles Lamb, "Early Missionaries in Yugoslavia," undated and unpaginated ms., repository; Ranović, interview, 35–36. Unless otherwise stated, these are the sources for the next three paragraphs as well.

37. An allusion to a movie of the same name.

38. Eric L. Anderson, "The Church in the SFR of Macedonia," typescript, June 28, 1997, repository.

39. Ranović, interviewed by author, 43; Smith, interview.

40. Austria Vienna Mission, 1978 report, entry for November 31, 1978.

41. Bestor, interview; Bestor, telephone interview.

42. Bestor, telephone interview; Smith, interview.

43. Ranović, interview, 31, 37.

44. Bestor, interview; Bestor, telephone interview. Sources for the next paragraph as well.

45. Ranović, interview, 61.

46. Ranović, interview, 37; Smith, interview.

47. Bestor, interview; Bestor, telephone interview; Smith, interview.

48. Ranović, interview, 41–42.

49. Bestor, interview.

50. Smith, interview. Source for the next paragraph as well.

51. Austria Vienna Mission, 1978 report, entry for August 13–18, 1978.

52. Ranović, interview, 40; Bestor, interview.

53. Smith, interview.

54. Bestor, interview; Bestor, telephone interview.

55. Bestor, interview.

56. Smith, interview.

57. Austria Vienna Mission, 1980 report, entry for September 22, 1980.

58. Edwin B. Morrell, telephone interview by author, November 20, 1995; Austria Vienna Mission, 1980 and 1981 reports, entries for September 22, 1980, January 20, 1981.

59. Austria Vienna Mission, 1980 report, entry for November 6, 1980.

60. Esther Stosich, telephone interview by author, February 21, 1996. The Stosichs served in Zagreb until November 1982. John and Arlene Irwin joined them in August 1981 and served until April 1983. Ralph and Elaine Gibbons served there from September 1983 until January 1985. They were followed by William and Barbara Williams, and later by Fred and Margarit Glowa. The missionary couple of Lee and Marilyn Manwill were sent to Beograd and served there from January 1983 until April 1984. Joseph and Melba Padovich replaced the Manwills in Beograd for the period March 1984 to July 1985. They were followed by William and Joann Wilson and later by Blaine and Thelma McKinley. The Glowas and McKinleys were there when the young missionaries returned. Morrell, telephone interview.

61. Ralph Gibbons, "Our Mission to Jugoslavija, 1983–1985," typescript, 2–6.

62. Gibbons, "Our Mission to Jugoslavija," 9.

63. Gibbons, "Our Mission to Jugoslavija," 9–10.

64. Bestor, interview; Bestor, telephone interview; Smith, interview; "Y.'s Ćosić Again in Limelight; Coaches Yugoslavian Team," *Church News*, published by Deseret News, July 27, 1986, 11.

65. Wrst name Ostarčević, interview.

66. Ranović, interview, 38–39.

67. Bestor, interview.

68. Stosich, telephone interview.

69. Gibbons, "Our Mission to Jugoslavija," 11–12.

70. Condie, interview, audio tape 2.

71. "Y.'s Ćosić Again in Limelight," 11.

72. Condie, interview, audio tape 2.

73. Kenneth Dudley Reber, interviewed by Matthew K. Heiss, 1994, Salt Lake City, typescript, 50, copy in possession of the interviewee, Sandy, Utah; Bestor, telephone interview; Radmila Ranović, "Missionary Reunion," talk given at Yugoslav Missionary Reunion, October 28, 1995, typescript, 9, in possession of the author.

74. Gibbons, "Our Mission to Jugoslavija," 6–7.

75. Gibbons, "Our Mission to Jugoslavija," 7; Morrell, telephone interview; Ranović interview, 83–85.

76. Gibbons, "Our Mission to Jugoslavija," 7; William G. and Barbara T. Williams, dedicatory conference program and notes, October 30–31, 1985, typescript, 9.

77. Ranović, interview, 28–29.

78. Bestor, telephone interview.

79. Ranović, interview, 37–38.

80. Ranović, interview, 44.

81. Ranović, interview, 45–46.

82. Ranović, interview, 46–47.

83. Ranović, interview, 60–63.

84. Ranović, interview, 63–65; Ranović, "Missionary Reunion," 5–6.

85. Ranović, interview, 70–74.

86. Ranović, interview, 81–83.

87. Williams, dedicatory conference program and notes, 10.

88. Williams, dedicatory conference program and notes, 10.

89. Williams, dedicatory conference program and notes, 12–13.

90. Ranović, "Missionary Reunion," 7.

91. Williams, dedicatory conference program and notes, 5, 16–17.

92. Ranović, "Missionary Reunion," 8.

93. Condie, interview, audio tapes 2 and 3.

94. Ranović, interview, 88–90; Condie, audio tape 3.

95. Spencer J. Condie, interviewed by author, August 5, 1991, Frankfurt, Germany; Condie, interview, audio tape 2.

96. Kirk Teske, telephone interview by author, February 20, 1996. Source of next two paragraphs as well.

97. Arlene B. Darger, comp., "Europe Area Historical Report: A History of the Work and Growth of the Europe Area," August 15, 1986–August 15, 1989, bound typescript, 410; Condie, interview, audio tape 2.

98. Kevin Field, telephone interview by author, February 21, 1996.

99. Darger, "Europe Area Historical Report," 410, 412.

100. Field, telephone interview.

101. "Jugoslavija District—Zagreb Branch Annual Report," in Darger, "Europe Area Historical Report," 416.

102. Jeffrey Moore, interviewed by Jeff Anderson, 1991–92, Salt Lake City, typescript, pt. 1, p. 13; pt. 2, p. 9, copy in possession of the interviewee, Orem, Utah.

103. Moore, interview, pt. 1, p. 15.

104. Kim Simpson, "Crows," *Dialogue: A Journal of Mormon Thought* 25 (winter 1992): 151.

105. Moore, interview, pt. 2, p. 6.

106. David Garner, interviewed by author, May 12, 1995, Provo, Utah.

107. Field, telephone interview; Simpson, "Crows," 151.

108. Moore, interview, pt. 1, p. 19–20; pt. 2, p. 1.

109. Reber, interview, 31.

110. Simpson, "Crows," 152, 154.

111. Simpson, "Crows," 154.

112. Moore, interview, pt. 2, p. 19–20.

113. Moore, interview, pt. 2, p. 22–23.

114. Moore, interview, pt. 2, p. 18.

115. Moore, interview, pt. 2, p. 18–21.

116. Moore, interview, pt. 2, p. 21–22.

117. Rudolph Ruter, interviewed by author, April 7, 1995, Salt Lake City; Mišo Ostarčević, interview.

118. Reber, interview, 36.

119. Ruter, interview; Field, telephone interview.

120. "Jugoslavija District—Zagreb Branch Annual Report," 415–16.

121. Blaine McKinley, telephone interview by author, February 22, 1996.

122. "Jugoslavija District—Zagreb Branch Annual Report," 415.

123. Gerry Avant, "Plans Changed, but Dream Is Fulfilled," *Church News,* November 14, 1992, 5.

124. Simpson, "Crows," 153.

125. Simpson, "Crows," 155; Reber, interview, 52.

126. Reber, interview, 46, 57–58.

127. Ankica Ostarčević, telephone interview.

5

The Curtain Rises

1985–1991

The year 1985 was a defining moment for the Church in Soviet-dominated Europe for three reasons. First, Mikhail Gorbachev came to power in the Soviet Union, auguring an era of unprecedented reform in the Communist system. Second, the Freiberg Germany Temple was dedicated in East Germany, becoming the only Church building ever constructed behind the Iron Curtain. It hinted at a new era of religious freedom in eastern Europe. Third, Ezra Taft Benson, obdurate opponent of Communist ideology, became President of the Church, living to witness the crumbling of the system he had long opposed.

Gorbachev was a gamble for the Soviet Politburo. As the junior member of this body at the pinnacle of Soviet power, he took control with the promise to reverse the country's economic disintegration. He instituted a program of economic reform termed *perestroika* (restructuring), which decentralized economic decision-making and rewarded improved productivity. Gorbachev soon realized that restructuring the workplace had little benefit unless people's minds and hearts were changed from following orders, as they had done for decades, to controlling their own destiny. He instituted a political policy of openness (or *glasnost*) in which the government tolerated public expression of dissenting opinions. Gorbachev viewed himself as a Communist and hoped that as the party permitted such freedoms, it would reap popular support. Instead, he unleashed forces far beyond his ability to direct. Economic reform did not bring prosperity, and political reform did not empower the masses.[1]

Gorbachev began altering the religious environment in 1988 when he received Russian Orthodox Church leaders in a formal meeting. It was the first such meeting in fifty-five years. The government supported the 1988 millennial celebration of Orthodox Christianity in Russia, Belarus, and Ukraine. The next year, the long-suppressed Greek Catholic Church emerged on the Ukrainian scene. When Gorbachev visited Rome to meet with Pope John Paul II, tens of thousands of Ukrainian Catholics converged in the streets of L'viv, the former seat of their religion, demonstrating for recognition. New congregations of Protestant faiths, existent in the former Russian realm, began to achieve recognition as legal entities in 1988 and 1989. In September 1990, a new law on religious freedom was enacted, separating church and state and guaranteeing full legal status to churches as well as equality for all faiths. Religious bodies received the right to own their meeting places, to proselytize, and to publish or import religious literature from abroad.[2]

Freedom of expression and participation unleashed latent feelings of nationalism among the Soviet citizens. The Communist parties in Eastern Bloc nations crumbled in the face of popular demonstrations. Even the independent Communist parties in Yugoslavia and Albania that had broken away from Soviet Communism in 1948 and 1961, respectively, disintegrated. Lithuania declared independence in March 1990, and by the end of the year the Iron Curtain had risen on a new drama on the European stage. Having waited for decades on the western edge of the Slavic world, the Church was prepared to take advantage of the opportunity.

New Leaders and New Missions

The Church's role in the events of the east was, in the beginning, shouldered by four leaders. In 1985, Elder Russell M. Nelson was appointed to assume the role held previously by Elder Thomas S. Monson, that of the apostolic point of contact for the Church in central and eastern Europe. A surgeon of international fame, Elder Nelson tirelessly importuned

Courtesy Church Archives

Illus. 5-1. Hans B. Ringger, a Swiss architect, served as a counselor in the Europe Area Presidency before becoming the Europe Area President in 1989.

government officials to grant the Church recognition in their respective lands. In April 1985, Hans B. Ringger (illus. 5-1), a Swiss architect, was called to be a general authority, and in August he was appointed to serve as a counselor in the Europe Area Presidency with a specific assignment to supervise the eastern countries. In 1989, Elder Ringger was appointed as the Area President. He acted as the constant companion of Elder Nelson and frequently visited the region. The uniqueness of a surgeon and an architect representing a church was most unusual and disarming to government leaders accustomed to dealing with those who had been clergymen for their whole careers.[3] The third leader was

Courtesy The Church of Jesus Christ of Latter-day Saints

Illus. 5-2. Dennis Neuenschwander presided over the newly created Austria Vienna East Mission from 1987 to 1991. As circumstances permitted, he began sending young missionaries into countries such as Poland, Hungary, Romania, Ukraine, and Bulgaria.

Dennis Neuenschwander (illus. 5-2), who held a doctorate in Russian and who had been a frequent visitor to central and eastern Europe since 1975 as a negotiator for the Genealogical (now Family and Church History) Department of the Church. Beginning in 1981, Neuenschwander helped supervise the Europe Central Districts as a counselor to Presidents Edwin B. Morrell and Spencer J. Condie. In 1987 he was installed as the president of the newly created Austria Vienna East Mission and given the assignment of introducing young missionaries into the various countries of central and eastern Europe as circumstances permitted. The fourth leader, Johann Wondra, a prominent leader in Austrian theater and previously the first Austrian stake president, was called in 1985 to be a regional representative with responsibility over members in Austria, southern Germany, Yugoslavia, Czechoslovakia, and Poland. He trained many new members in the principles of gospel leadership. These four leaders comprised the Church's early emissaries to the nations that soon emerged from the moribund autocracies of Communism.

Under Elder Nelson's leadership, during the next five years, five new missions—Finland Helsinki East, Poland Warsaw, Czechoslovak Prague, Hungary Budapest, and the German Democratic Republic Dresden—were organized in the former Communist world with more in the offing. This first wave of mission presidents began creating congregations in the East. The eastern frontier of the Church expanded as representatives forged past the Communist satellite nations at an ever-increasing pace to the heartland of the waning Soviet empire: Russia and its confederated republics.

In the political realm, another leader operated behind the scenes to develop and maintain Church contacts with foreign governments. In 1984, Beverly Campbell was appointed the director of the Church's public affairs office in Washington, D.C. Her assignment was to develop contacts and foster a positive and accurate Church presence in the national and international media, alleviating problems and misunderstandings as the Church expanded into other countries. The following year, the office received a mandate to work in the nation's capital as an intermediary between the General Authorities and ambassadors of foreign governments. While David Kennedy worked with officials abroad, Beverly Campbell worked with officials at home. When David Kennedy's assignment ended in 1987, the office was renamed the International and Public Affairs Office, and Sister Campbell became the key figure in obtaining for Church leaders an audience of government officials.[4]

Two other people made significant contributions in the legal realm. David Farnsworth was the Europe Area legal counsel from 1977 to 1982 and again from 1986 to 1991. (His efforts in Yugoslavia are discussed in chapter 4.) The meager gains of his earlier stint were greatly exceeded in the 1980s. He often accompanied ecclesiastical officials and was responsible for concluding the necessary legal arrangements to ensure that the Church's foundations in the East had consent from the governments granting entry. At the international level, BYU Professor W. Cole Durham Jr., an international authority on religious liberty, taught the principles of religious freedom throughout central and eastern Europe. During a trip there in early 1990, Durham made contacts that led to an invitation to teach in Hungary. This in turn led to contacts among decision makers who shaped legal reforms in former Communist nations. His influence was pervasive and outside the limelight.[5]

In June 1991, the Tabernacle Choir toured the East. Its choruses reverberated in the hearts of listeners, not only at the concerts but through televisions at home. Its songs of devotion and hope advanced the missionary effort. The choir sang while the East was still Communist, but by the end of the year that ideology, long dead in the people's hearts, was swept off the nations' political stages.

A Miniseries on Utah

With the coming of the 1980s, the religious apathy the Church had encountered among Hungarians in the early part of the twentieth century appeared to have been replaced by a new spirit of inquiry. This development reflected the Hungarian yearning to rejoin the Western world. Hungarian National Television sent an advance team to the United States in 1984 to identify a broadcasting project that would interest the Hungarian nation. After visiting many American sites, the vice-president of Hungarian National Television told Church officials that in Utah he had found a place and a people that met all his expectations, a model society in a scenic environment. The special was filmed in fall 1984 and broadcast as a miniseries in November and December 1985.[6]

The broadcast resulted in a deluge of requests for more information from Church headquarters in Utah. Although the program had not given the Church's address, this did not deter correspondents who sent their mail in general terms to such locations as "Mormons, America," and "Missionary Center, Utah." The Church headquarters forwarded the mail to the Austria Vienna Mission president, Spencer J. Condie, who now presided over the East Central Districts.[7] President Condie began traveling into Hungary with Karl Trinkl, a native Hungarian living in Vienna, to teach the gospel in private homes. Anyone wishing to be baptized came to Vienna for the ordinance.[8]

Among those interested were some future Church leaders in Hungary. Dr. Gedeon Kereszti, an ear, nose, and throat surgeon who had watched the broadcast pored through back issues of professional journals to locate an article that he remembered had been written by someone living in Utah. Assuming that the author, Dr. R. Kim Davis of the University of Utah Medical School, was a Latter-day Saint, Dr. Kereszti sent him a request for more information about the Church. Dr. Davis sent a picture of his family and a letter with his testimony via President Condie and Brother Trinkl in February 1986. Missionaries soon traveled to Ajka, Hungary, to visit Dr. Kereszti and his family, who were not only anxious to learn more but who also spoke fluent English. Their son Zsolt, who was away at medical school, traveled halfway across the country to hear the missionaries during their visits. Six months later, the Keresztis traveled to Vienna to be baptized. Gedeon became the first native to be called as the district president in Hungary.[9]

An orthopedic surgeon in Budapest, Dr. Peter Varga, read an article in a medical journal by Dr. Ralph Cloward, a Church member living in Hawaii. In an uncommon instance, a footnote mentioned that Dr. Cloward was a Latter-day Saint. Dr. Varga wrote his fellow surgeon,

> I have some very good friends, all of us Calvinists, but separated from Hungarian Calvinist Church some years ago. We make our introspections among ourselves from this time. Six months ago, after a meeting with a Mormon believer in Vienna, we are keenly interested in the Mormon-religion. . . . I would like to ask you to send us some pieces of the Mormon literature which are the best for us, in your opinion, to get us acquainted with the religion.[10]

Dr. Cloward responded via President Condie, and Dr. Varga joined the Church in Vienna on April 9, 1987. He would later be called as the first branch president in Budapest.

New Representatives in Budapest

In April 1987, the Church sent new representatives into Hungary after a seven-year hiatus. Wayne and Linnea Johnson from Midvale, Utah, filled the new assignment. At the Missionary Training Center they received some Hungarian language instruction from Éva Lipták, the Hungarian who had translated the Book of Mormon into her native tongue. After arriving in Europe, the Johnsons witnessed the baptism of Dr. Varga in Vienna and then accompanied him and two young missionaries—Elder Zoltan Nagy-Kovacs, raised by Hungarian parents and serving in the Germany Frankfurt Mission, and Elder Jean-Marc Frey of the Austria Vienna Mission—to Budapest.[11]

The Hungarian border was only the second Communist border in central Europe to be crossed by young missionaries, the first having been Yugoslavia (see chapter 4). As had been the case in Yugoslavia for nearly a decade, missionaries entered on temporary visas that had to be renewed each month. They had some referrals for Hungarians who had come in contact with the Church abroad or who had requested information through the mail, some following the 1985 television broadcast. However, most of the referrals came from younger people curious about the West from which they had long been isolated. Many of them spoke some English and could assist the Johnsons, whose Hungarian was limited.[12]

The missionaries were soon followed by the visit of Elder Nelson, who visited Hungary in April 1987. The visit came at the invitation of the Hungarians. In late 1986, the ambassador had contacted Francis A. Madsen, a bishop in the Washington, D.C., area and a high-ranking official in the U.S. Senate, with the hope of making a deal that would bring money into

Hungary as the Freiberg Temple had brought into East Germany. The ambassador knew of Bishop Madsen through a Hungarian member of his congregation, Miklos Karoly Radvanyi, previously a state prosecutor in his homeland who had fled to Germany and joined the Church in Munich. Madsen served on the Church's Public Affairs Advisory Committee in the Washington, D.C., area and had worked with the General Authorities, keeping them informed on congressional matters of interest to the Church for a decade. After a number of visits to the Hungarian embassy, Madsen negotiated a deal that would permit the Church to have missionaries in Hungary though they would not be able to proselytize openly. Elder Nelson and President Benson both approved the arrangement, thus laying the groundwork for the April meeting.[13]

On Easter Sunday, April 19, 1987, Elder Nelson dedicated Hungary for missionary work on Mt. Gellért, located on the shore of the Danube across from downtown Budapest. He recounted later, "There had been a lot of people, a lot of traffic in the park. But all of a sudden, the people had gone home, and I had a sweet, peaceful feeling that this [was] the spot." It was the fifth dedication in the East, preceded by Russia (1903), Czechoslovakia (1929), Poland (1977), and Yugoslavia (1985). The newly baptized Dr. Varga was able to attend the dedication ceremonies.[14]

Two days later, Elder Nelson met with Miklos Imre, director over the Ministry of Religious Affairs. The Apostle was accompanied by Elder Ringger and Miklos Radvanyi, who acted as an interpreter. The minister had previously listened to overtures made by David Kennedy. Elder Nelson said to the minister, "I have come 10,000 miles to know if I am welcome in your country."[15] He also felt impressed to let the minister know that he "had offered a special apostolic prayer for his country and for its people." A meeting originally scheduled for half an hour stretched out to an hour and a half. "And he [Miklos Imre, the Minister of Religious Affairs] was visibly moved. Even as I relayed that message to him through an interpreter, he was able to perceive that we were not there to exploit, but to bless the people of that country."[16]

Long-Awaited Recognition

In July 1987, the Austria Vienna East Mission assumed jurisdiction over Hungary. Elder Christopher Jones, a new missionary trained in Hungarian at the Missionary Training Center in Provo, Utah, joined Elder Nagy-Kovacs. In September another senior couple arrived, Alan and Ruth Macfarlane of Salt Lake City. President Neuenschwander visited the missionaries in Hungary monthly. He gave them the same commission the Bentleys had been given a decade earlier: to establish a circle of friends and contacts and be available to answer questions about the Church. A retired physician, Elder Macfarlane was a natural for associating with the medical colleagues of Peter Varga and Gedeon Kereszti. The Macfarlanes also shared the gospel with their landlord, their Hungarian language tutor, people living in their neighborhood, those they met on public transportation, and others they came into contact with in their daily activities.[17] In early 1988, Elder Trevor Andreason replaced Elder Nagy-Kovacs, who had completed his term of service.[18]

Hungarian law required a membership of at least twenty before legal recognition could be granted.[19] The missionaries worked to obtain the desired number. Among the early contacts was Ferenc Csapo, a cabinetmaker who lived in Dunaújváros, sixty kilometers south of Budapest. He and his family came looking for the Church and knocked on the missionaries' door. The missionaries began visiting his home, teaching him and his family the gospel. Ferenc read the Book of Mormon and the promise of Moroni to pray about its message. Even as he thought to pray, and before uttering a word, the witness came.[20] Ferenc later became the second branch president in Budapest, and he continued to build a strong congregation in Dunaújváros.

While the missionaries worked among the people, negotiations for official recognition continued at a higher level, with Elder Ringger of the Europe Area Presidency playing a key role. In late spring 1987, representatives of the Hungarian State Office visited the Frankfurt Germany Temple open house in West Germany and discussed granting recognition. Church officials made a follow-up visit in October. The official request was submitted in December. In continuing negotiations, Elder Nelson visited Hungary a second time in January 1988.[21] On June 1, the document granting the long-awaited recognition of the Church as a legal entity in Hungary was signed. Coincidentally, it was granted on the centennial of Elder Ferdinand Hintze's 1888 visit. Elder Nelson received the document in a formal ceremony at the end of June. The Minister of Religion had invited the media to the recognition ceremony. Twenty reporters attended a press conference later in the day and generated seventeen articles—all positive.[22] On the evening of June 25, 1988, Peter Varga baptized his wife Erika, the first baptism of a new Church era in Hungary.[23]

A Metamorphosis of Interest

The recognition unleashed an unexpected onslaught of interest and baptismal success not previously witnessed in central and eastern Europe. The two elders were inundated with teaching appointments, going steadily from eight in the morning until ten at night. People came to the missionaries' apartment, asking if it were the Latter-day Saint Church. The impact of the 1985 television broadcast seemed to still be fresh in many people's minds, but until now they had not known where to find the Church. When inquiries reached the desk of the Minister of Religious Affairs, he gave out the missionaries' address and phone number.[24] Some Hungarians even tried to contact the Church by calling the Communist Party headquarters. To accommodate the Hungarians' interest in the gospel, two more missionaries were sent in by year's end. In early 1989, the four missionaries had to make teaching appointments three weeks in advance.[25] When Elder Jones left in spring 1989, he had participated in the conversion of approximately eighty people.[26] By the end of 1989, eight missionaries worked in the country, and by the end of 1990 there were twenty-five. When the Hungary Budapest Mission came into being in July 1990, Church membership had risen to 250 members in the cities of Budapest, Györ, Szombathely, Debrecen, and Szekesfehervar.[27] The first great flowering of missionary success had begun to realize the hope expressed by Elder Hintze a century earlier when he wrote that Saints would yet be found "in those places."[28]

In at least one instance, the success in Hungary extended far beyond its borders. A Hungarian member attending a hydrology course in St. Petersburg (then known as Leningrad) became acquainted with Liudmila Terebenin. The Hungarian invited Liudmila, her husband, Yuri, and daughter, Anna, to Budapest. She persuaded the visiting Russians to be taught by the missionaries while the friend translated. The family was baptized on July 1, 1989, and returned to Russia.[29]

In April 1989, the Church purchased a former Rothschild mansion in Budapest to be renovated into a meeting place (illus. 5-3). The building had been found with the assistance of Brother Varga, who had many connections in Hungarian society. It was owned by a carpenter-renovator and was located near many foreign embassies. He was performing a first-class renovation when Church representatives visited in 1989. New floors were already in, and he was almost ready to paint and install carpet. The Church architect from the Frankfurt Area Office proclaimed it to be the best built structure he had ever seen in all of Europe. Though contacted by several nations that wanted it as an embassy, the carpenter decided he wanted the Church to have it.[30] In April when the Church purchased the building, the government abolished the State Office for Religious Affairs, which had regulated religions during the Communist period.[31] By October 1989, the renovations were completed, and

Courtesy Mary Kay Stout

Illus. 5-3. This building was used as the first meeting place in Hungary, 1991.

Elder Monson dedicated the mansion as a chapel. Over a hundred people, including many investigators, routinely gathered there every weekend during 1990 for Sabbath services.[32]

In time it became evident that circumstances had changed over the decades, and Hungarians were now receptive to the gospel message. Illustrative of this is the experience of Attila Böröcz. Having just graduated from high school in July 1990, he walked past a street display in which he saw a print of Jesus Christ. He asked the young man in front of the display what he must do to get one. The young man kindly offered him something else, a Book of Mormon and an invitation to a baptismal service. Attila attended the service, and as he watched the two people dressed in white descend into the font, he felt overcome by a gentle burning sensation. The false feeling of satisfaction about his life vanished, and he began to realize that something was missing. One missionary sensed the young visitor's feelings and boldly asked if Attila would like to be baptized also. Without hesitation, Attila said, "I do want to be baptized!" For the closing hymn they sang "I Am a Child of God." The message of the hymn was a truth that Attila had never considered before. Eight months after his own baptism, Attila filled out papers to serve a mission.[33]

When Wayne and Linnea Johnson received the notification of their call to Hungary in 1988, President Condie sent them a letter stating they "would be on the cutting edge of a miracle." They witnessed several. During the year of Church recognition (1988), the Hungarian Communist Party became the first in the Soviet dominion to recognize additional political parties, edging the country closer to a democratic society. The

Johnsons saw the impact most clearly at the Hungarian-Austrian border where they crossed once a month to renew their visas. When they first entered Hungary, the border guards had conducted rigorous searches. But prior to their departure in August 1988, the check consisted of glancing at their passports.[34] More significantly for the Church, they witnessed a metamorphosis of interest in religion. The decades-long suppression of religious liberty had whetted, rather than extinguished, Hungarians' desire for religious fulfillment. Conditions for missionary success were reversed from those experienced in the early twentieth century. Civil authorities no longer hindered missionary activity, and the Church's messengers were now preceded by a positive image, unlike the public caricatures that had preceded them in the past.

New Senior Missionary Couples in Poland

Juliusz and Dorothy Fussek, from Salt Lake City, replaced the Mazurs in September 1985. As with the Mazurs, the husband was a native Polish speaker. The Fusseks' mission call, originally intended for two years, lasted for five. Their extended term of service provided important continuity during a formative period. The Fusseks became good friends with public officials and directed the growth of an infant membership. As they served, they witnessed the transfer of power from autocracy to democracy and the dawn of true religious freedom.

The Fusseks' example not only sustained the early Church in Poland but also opened the path for others to follow. In May 1986, Elder Nelson, Elder Monson, Elder Ringger, and Elder Wondra arrived in Poland and met with Adam Łopotka, the head of the Religious Affairs Ministry. He said, "You may build your buildings, you may send your missionaries. You are welcome in Poland. This man," and he pointed to Juliusz Fussek, "has served your church well. You can be grateful for his example and his work."[35]

Three other missionary couples soon followed: Neil and Leotha Slagowski, Don and Joanne Schultz, and Hyrum and Ruth Cieslak. The Slagowskis served in Kraków and Sopot; the Schultzs in Zielona Góra and Sopot; and the Cieslaks in Wrocław (illus. 5-4). As with many of the early couples in the East, they were often isolated. The first night in Kraków, Leotha Slagowski stared out the apartment window into darkness and wondered how they would fare with a poor knowledge of the language, separated by hundreds of miles from other missionaries and members. She returned to bed and wept until a voice spoke to her spirit

Illus. 5-4. Cities where Mormon missionaries served in Poland, 1985–91.

saying, "The Priesthood is in Kraków." Realizing that they were not really alone, she relaxed and slept.[36]

The Slagowskis spent seven and a half months in Kraków, making friends and handing out copies of the Book of Mormon. They addressed letters to each person on their referral list, requesting an invitation to visit, and enclosed a stamped, self-addressed postcard for a response. If they received no response, they wrote a second time and then dropped by, uninvited, taking a small gift of flowers or candy.[37] To improve their Polish, the Slagowskis attended a course at the Jagellonian University. Although the director cautioned them that the course was designed for young students who could study hard, he did not dissuade them. Neil and Leotha graduated at the top of the class, and when they received their diplomas, the young students stood up, clapped, yelled, whistled, and stomped their feet in appreciation for their achievement.[38]

The problems the Slagowskis faced were encountered by many missionary couples in the East. While some couples had good language skills, many had to depend on the English knowledge of their contacts. They found it was difficult to proselytize without a support system of other members or a designated building. Crowded living conditions offered limited privacy for teaching investigators. Fear of antagonizing the authorities also made them hesitant. The people's devotion to the Catholic Church over a thousand years limited their interest in other religions, particularly in Kraków, seat of the former archbishop, Karol Wojtyla, chosen as Pope John Paul II in 1978.[39]

The Slagowskis served the second part of their mission in Sopot, on the Baltic shore of northern Poland. They finally baptized two women, one of them a divorcee with two sons, a tiny one-room apartment, and a poor job. Though her temporal situation in life did not change because of baptism, she seemed to sparkle spiritually afterward.[40]

One missionary summed up the contribution of the Polish missionary couples: "Their example and spirit have left a lasting impression upon hundreds, I'm sure, if not thousands. Because of their faithfulness and humbleness and courage, the doors to this country are opening and great strides are in the making."[41]

The First Young Missionaries Enter Poland

Elders Matthew Binns of Seattle and Sean Peterson of Salt Lake City, the first two young missionaries called to serve in Poland, spent the first year of their missions in the Chicago area waiting for the Polish government to grant entry. They received notice in late 1987 that the hour had arrived for them to go. President Neuenschwander gave them an orientation in Vienna on January 18, 1988. After he had detailed the scope of their responsibility and their role in deciding the future of the Church in Poland, they both felt terrified. Elder Peterson's disquiet peaked as they descended by plane into Warsaw: "As we were approaching the runway my heart sped up 100% and I just couldn't believe we were within seconds of landing behind the Iron Curtain. When the wheels touched ground it was as if my whole life just disappeared from my memory and I was trapped."[42] Young missionaries had now crossed the borders of a third country under Communist domination.

President Neuenschwander of the Austria Vienna East Mission accompanied them on the trip and took them to the *biuro* (bureau) of information, or visitors' center, in downtown Warsaw. It also served as the Fusseks' residence. The president drilled the missionaries for a couple of hours on what they were to say at their appointment with the Minister of Religious Affairs. At the meeting, Minister Rilewski reviewed the terms of their agreement to represent the Church, which in brief was that they could answer questions but not proselytize. In response, the missionaries took turns telling him in Polish something about themselves. Speaking second, Elder Peterson went beyond his script saying, "I'm very happy to be here in this country and I love the Polish people." The minister bowed his head and said, "Well, I hope you can say that in one year."[43]

That evening Elder Peterson confronted the reality of their adventure: "I am back in the apartment having broken a lamp, boiled some water to drink, unclogged the bath tub, plugged in the alarm clock which goes twice as fast, . . . and wondering what . . . I'm doing here in Poland." The next day they registered with the police and ate in a cafeteria—"cold noodles with [sour] cream, a scoop of sugar, a side of apple marmalade and a cup of soggy strawberries to drink." Elder Binns gagged and Elder Peterson got an upset stomach. During the first week they learned that finding necessities occupied many hours. They trekked from store to store, standing in long lines, and "bellowing out" what they wanted to purchase. On preparation day, Elder Peterson spent three and a half hours laundering his clothes by hand.[44]

The lot of the first two missionaries in Poland was less than a high adventure. They spent five to six hours a day waiting for visitors to show up at the biuro on the Nowy Świat (New World) thoroughfare in downtown Warsaw. With only a handful of visitors each day, they had plenty of spare time on their hands. The temptation was to spend too much of it in wasted conversation. They disciplined themselves by memorizing the missionary discussions in Polish, a version they had brought with them from Chicago. The Fusseks played the role of a language-wise senior companion by listening and critiquing their ability to deliver the first discussion. While they were not alone, they missed the comradeship of fellow missionaries their own age.[45]

The monotony was punctuated by a wide range of inquirers at the biuro, including a young girl interested to know why Latter-day Saints practiced polygamy and a "born-again prophet" who wanted to preach rather than listen. In March 1988, a preponderance of theology students began to visit the biuro, and they continued to be regular customers as word spread. Occasionally, the missionaries left the biuro to visit people who had asked for more information at Latter-day Saint visitors' centers abroad, or who had been referred to the missionaries by relatives or friends. They soon became accustomed to their new life. In March, Elder Peterson recorded, "I'm turning more and more Polish by the minute. I poured strawberry sauce all over my noodles!"[46]

Like the young missionaries, the new converts of the 1980s brimmed with enthusiasm. They came a half hour before services and, after the three-hour block of meetings, stayed for two more hours to socialize. They ate, enjoyed each other's company, and sang or listened to hymns.[47] When he first attended services, Elder Peterson was surprised to see "everybody hugging and kissing like one big huge family."[48]

It was a period of unity and spiritual growth in the membership. Elder Wondra held a leadership training meeting that impressed both young missionaries. The last Sunday of February, twenty-eight people attended church, the largest congregation since the young missionaries' arrival. Religion permeated the members' lives as they lived gospel principles. The missionaries were touched when the Warsaw Branch president, Brother Wojcieszek, dropped by to give them dinner one evening. Since food was scarce and expensive, it was a real sacrifice. In early March, at a baptismal service for people taught by the Fusseks, Elder Binns felt a sense of unity that enlivened his love for the members specifically and the people of Poland generally.[49]

President Neuenschwander visited frequently to encourage and challenge the missionaries. At the March baptism, he started a conversation with two investigators and told Elder Binns to translate. Elder Binns later wrote, "Well, we talked a little, things were okay but a little sporadic. It

was weird translating, the first time I've ever done it." President Neuenschwander also set the example by delivering a conference talk in Polish,
a language he had learned on his own initiative.[50]

The missionaries finally experienced a conversion in April 1988.
Zaneta Świercz, a niece of a recent convert, came to the biuro to be
taught. After the first meeting, there was no doubt in either missionary's
mind about her eventual baptism. She sought her parents' permission to
join the Church and returned to say that they had left the decision to her.
Elder Peterson later recorded, "She was glowing like crazy. I've never
seen anyone so happy before."[51]

Growth and Challenges in Poland

The gospel filled the converts with new hope for the future. Urszula
Adamska was converted the year before Sister Świercz. At the time of her
baptism, Urszula was twenty-three years old and unhappy with life. Her
mother was dead and her father expected her to keep house. She had no
marriage prospects and no future until she encountered a newly baptized
member of the Church who sparked her marriage interest. Her acquaintance with him caused her to begin reading the Bible, but with little com-
prehension. She read the Joseph Smith story her friend had given her
and, encouraged by his experience in seeking God, prayed to understand the Bible. For the first time in her memory, she felt something wonderful. Her initial visit to a Church meeting was inconclusive because she
could only think of how she was betraying her Catholic tradition. But
during the testimony meeting, she felt the same wonderful feeling she had
experienced earlier. She accepted the Fusseks' instruction and was baptized two weeks later, in September 1987. This had displeased her father,
and out of deference to him she stopped going to church. Two months
later, she was miserable and returned to seek the Fusseks' counsel. It was
the same day the young elders arrived in Warsaw.[52]

The missionaries gave Sister Adamska a vision of how young and
active Church members could find happiness in life. During vacation
time in late summer 1988, she volunteered to help the missionaries teach
discussions and found it very enjoyable. Elder Peterson mentioned this to
President Neuenschwander, who asked Sister Adamska if she would
like to serve a mission. She said yes, but did not tell the president she
wanted to serve in the United States. She later expressed her feelings,
"The missionaries were here and they were giving these things to me
here, in this country, and I wanted to go do that in their country." In 1989,

Sister Adamska received a call to serve in the Washington Seattle Mission, the very mission from which Elder Binns had left for Poland. It was an answer to her deepest desire. Set apart by President Neuenschwander on July 3, 1989, Sister Adamska became the second missionary, after Radmila Ranović from Yugoslavia, to leave central and eastern Europe in order to serve an overseas mission.[53]

The story of each individual conversion includes feelings similar to those experienced by Sister Adamska. But after conversion there was no guarantee that this spiritual renewal led to continuing commitment. In Sister Adamska's absence the membership grew, but not without problems and setbacks. One member stopped coming to church after a month because he decided wine and unleavened bread should be used for the sacrament. The branch president had to leave Poland to earn money abroad. Attendance slipped to a low of thirteen in September. One convert, an ex-Catholic priest who had lived in a monastery for seventeen years, joined the Church in June 1988. He confided in Elder Binns that since his baptism he had felt something that he had never before felt. Yet within a month, he was hospitalized and began smoking again. He started making progress and blessed the sacrament by September, only to begin smoking again in November.[54] In October, Zdzisława Chudyba, a member who had been living in England for nearly a year, returned to Warsaw. She was a strong member who immediately had a positive impact on the branch. She revived the young adult program and helped Sister Świercz face the opposition of her uncle, who had apostatized and was trying to pull her away as well.[55]

In July 1988, two more young missionaries arrived in Poland. Elder Peterson and his new companion, John Mitchell, were assigned to work with the Cieslaks in Wrocław. Elder Binns and Stephen Thomas, the other new missionary, continued to serve in Warsaw. It was pleasant for the two veteran missionaries to finally have others there. Elder Peterson also enjoyed being in Wrocław: "I really like being a normal missionary again and not a biuro of information missionary."[56]

Additional strength came from a gathering of east European zone leaders and their companions at Vienna in September 1988. Among others the group included Christopher Jones (Hungary), Kevin Field (Yugoslavia), Matthew Binns, and Sean Peterson (Poland). President Neuenschwander informed the group that each had been hand-picked for their assignments. Their pioneering efforts were of interest to those who directed the Church's missionary effort and to the Quorum of the Twelve Apostles. Elder Jones remarked on the feeling of unity and love among them, saying, "This is what Zion must be like." President Neuen-schwander counseled and encouraged each of the missionaries privately. When the interview with Elder Peterson ended, the president gave him a big hug and said he was the best they could ask for. He and the others left refreshed to face the challenges of their different assignments.[57]

Church permanence in this still Communist world was manifest by the construction of the first chapel. After negotiations from 1986 to April 1989, the Church received some of the finest land in Warsaw, Poland, for a building, with the only requirement being that the structure be beautiful.[58] The groundbreaking occurred on June 15. Elders Nelson and Ringger presided over a gathering of about two hundred people including mem-bers, government dignitaries, and religious leaders from various faiths.[59]

The year of the groundbreaking, Lech Walesa, leader of a newly revived Solidarity, pressured and obtained government concession to hold new elections. Victory for Solidarity at the polls in March 1989 continued the decline of Communist control in central and eastern Europe. Later that year, the reconstituted government passed a revised law on religious liberty, allowing foreigners to direct Polish congrega-tions.[60] The way was open for a mission to be established.

Baptismal success was slow in comparison to Hungary. Twenty-four baptisms occurred in Poland during 1988 and thirty-eight baptisms in 1989.[61] But to the missionaries, witnessing a single conversion was equal to the effort. Włodzimierz Zeniewski, who joined in January 1989, was excited to live the Word of Wisdom after he heard it. It startled Elder Binns so much that he thought, "This man is either about the biggest blessing the Lord has given me on my mission or a KGB agent who is trying to get into the Church."[62] In 1989 the missionary ranks in Poland began to swell. Many of them came into the country having been taught Polish at the Missionary Training Center in Provo, Utah, by Walter Whipple (illus. 5-5), the 1983 violin apprentice.

In a series of coincidences, Brother Whipple was in the right place at the right time when the need arose to create the Poland Warsaw Mission. In 1988 he had entered BYU on sabbatical leave from Rockford Col-lege. In January 1989, he was called to teach missionaries headed for Poland. At the inauguration of BYU President Rex Lee in October 1989, Brother Whipple met Elder Nelson. Brother Whipple introduced himself and, in response to Elder Nelson's questions, explained his violin-making experience and his service teaching Polish to the missionaries. What Brother Whipple did not know was that the Quorum of Twelve

Courtesy Walter Whipple

Illus. 5-5. Walter Whipple and his family in Warsaw, June 27, 1993. Walter Whipple *(back)*, his wife Mary *(right)*, with their children Timothy *(left)* and Elisabeth *(center)*.

Apostles had voted on the previous day to establish a mission in Poland. In the words of Elder Nelson, "Within twenty-five hours of voting to establish a mission, the Lord delivered a mission president into our hands."[63]

Events in East Germany

Concurrent with the unpublicized entry of missionaries into Yugoslavia, Hungary, and Poland, missionaries publicly entered East Germany. In October 1988, Elders Monson and Nelson and President Ringger, along with several local priesthood leaders, met with Chairman Erich Honecker to ask permission for missionaries to serve there. President Honecker addressed them with this salutation: "We know you are good citizens in whatever country you claim as home; we have observed that. The floor is yours. Make your desires known."[64] The president granted permission, and the first missionaries entered on March 30, 1989. Elder Monson announced the event at the April 1989 general conference. Two months later, the first missionaries from East Germany left for service elsewhere, and, on July 1, Church officials established the Germany Dresden Mission.

By January 1990, Czechoslovakia was the lone country on the western edge of Communism that had not yet permitted the missionaries to enter, though this soon changed. However, Church leaders were interested in more than just this slice of the Communist realm. An opportunity to enter the Russian Empire at the beginning of the twentieth century had not been pursued, and Church officials would not let that happen again.

Train Contacting in Helsinki

In 1988 the Church's closest mission headquarters to the Soviet Union was in Helsinki, Finland (illus. 5-6). President Steven Mecham sanctioned a train-contacting program directed at Russians. Sister Leena Riihimäki, a Finnish missionary who spoke Russian, and Sister Carina Mahoney talked with Russian passengers arriving on the daily trains from Moscow and St. Petersburg (known as Leningrad until 1991). President Mecham chose two elders who knew some Russian, Clarence Dillon and Bruce Bunderson, to continue the program after the conclusion of Sister Rihiimäki's mission in November 1988. These missionaries developed their Russian language skills by going to the Russian Cultural Center in Helsinki. Most of their contacting occurred at the train station, where they approached nearly everyone. The Russian embassy called the mission office and requested that the missionaries stop interfering with passengers in business suits. Thereafter, the program became more selective. In March 1989, Elder Bunderson was reassigned to work at Joensuu with a new missionary, David Reagan.[65]

David Reagan also had some background in the Russian language. He had taken a year of Russian in high school and a semester of Russian at BYU before his mission. When he got his mission call to the Helsinki Mission, everyone in his Russian class said he would go to Russia, but he discounted their comments.

Elder Kevin Dexter, who had studied Russian in high school, was appointed to work with Elder Dillon on the train-contacting program. Elder Dillon unexpectedly developed a lump on his leg and was sent home to receive medical attention. In October 1989, Elder Reagan joined Elder Dexter, and the two soon entered the Soviet Union.

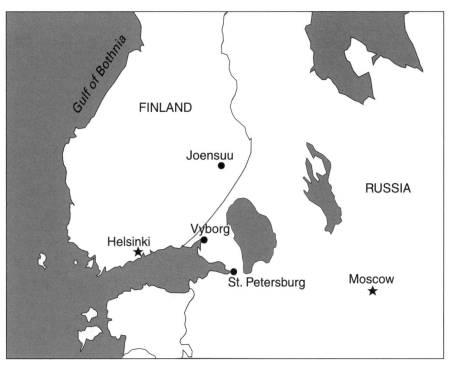

Illus. 5-6. In the late 1980s, missionaries serving in Helsinki, Finland, often shared the gospel with Russian travelers from St. Petersburg at the Helsinki train station.

Soviets Abroad and Latter-day Saints at Home

At the governmental level, Beverly Campbell made the necessary contacts prior to the Moscow visit of Elders Nelson and Ringger in June 1987. In August 1989, arrangements were made to discuss the possibility of a Church presence with the Chairman of the Soviet Council on Religious Affairs. They were told that recognition was possible when a minimum of twenty Soviet citizens, all residing in a political district, petitioned for it. Official recognition would permit the Church to own buildings, worship freely, and proselytize openly.

Church leaders wanted their entrance into the Soviet Union to be welcomed rather than opposed. Because of the legal requirement of having members obtain recognition, leaders faced the dilemma of obtaining members without sending in missionaries. The resolution of this dilemma began with the Gorbachev policy of *glasnost,* which increasingly permitted Soviet citizens to leave the country and experience the world outside their borders. While vacationing abroad, several of these citizens encountered more than new sights and faces—they also discovered a new faith.

Valttari Rödsä departed Tallinn in his native Estonia to visit relatives in Finland. During his trip, he noticed two young men on bicycles. He felt prompted to stop and meet the cyclists, and discovered that they were Mormon missionaries. This chance encounter led to Valttari's conversion, and when he returned to Estonia in July 1989 he did so as a Church member. President Mecham assured Valttari that in due course he would visit him in Estonia. Anticipating that day, Valttari wasted no time in telling his friends and relatives of his new faith.[66] Concurrently, the Terebenin family returned from Budapest, where they had joined the Church, to St. Petersburg. They, like Brother Rödsä, did not keep their new religion a secret. Soon their acquaintances were learning the basics of the restored gospel. Another was Olga Smolianova, an eighteen-year-old from Moscow, who visited friends in Italy for two weeks in September 1989. Among the friends was a Church member who introduced her to the missionaries. At the end of her visit she was baptized. As she crossed the border to go home, Olga began to weep, knowing that she returned to a city of eight million, alone, facing an uncertain future in a land where her church had no official presence.[67]

Not only did Soviets stream abroad, but an increasing number of foreigners crossed the border to experience the Soviet world. In summer 1989, Church members Aimo and Nellie Jäkkö went canoeing with a

Soviet group in Karelia, across the Finnish border in northwestern Russia. Around the campfire one evening, they introduced their religion to a twenty-four-year-old doctor, Andrei Semionov from Vyborg. Andrei often encountered the suffering and death of young children, and he questioned the reasons for this. His new Finnish friends offered a satisfying answer to this question, preceding his eventual conversion.[68]

President Mecham sent Finnish members across the border on various missionary errands. He asked Matti Ojala, a construction engineer who often visited St. Petersburg, to teach the Terebenin family. In September, Brother Ojala took twenty-five copies of the Book of Mormon across the border. Sister Riihimäki went to Moscow as a student after her mission and train-contacting experience. At President Mecham's request, she spent time in St. Petersburg, visiting the Terebenins and teaching some of their friends before returning home.[69] She returned for more visits, and through this personal network she contacted Anton Skripko. She met him at the Kazan Cathedral in downtown St. Petersburg and gave him a Book of Mormon.[70] In September 1989, while Anton studied the book, Misha Penkin and Yuri Kuverov crossed the border and became the first of several Russians to be baptized in Finland.

Other contacts came through unanticipated circumstances. Raija Kemppainen, the wife of Jussi Kemppainen, a counselor to President Mecham, met Svetlana Artiomova, from St. Petersburg, in a Helsinki park in April 1989. She maintained the acquaintance and learned later that after failing to purchase a Bible in either St. Petersburg or Helsinki, Svetlana had miraculously found one in the forest while searching for mushrooms. Svetlana accepted a Book of Mormon from Sister Kemppainen, received both the traditional and the new scriptures into her life, and later joined the Church.[71]

Decision at the Budapest Conference

In October 1989, the mission presidents of Europe met in Budapest—the first time they had been able to congregate in a central European capital since the Prague conference fifty-seven years earlier. Elder Nelson and Elder Ringger, now the Europe Area President, told Presidents Steven Mecham of the Finland Helsinki Mission and Dennis Neuenschwander of the Austria Vienna East Mission that the time had come to move ahead in the Soviet Union. They were also told that this decision would be attested to by unmistakable physical manifestations.[72] The next month, the Berlin Wall was breached.

In Vienna, President Neuenschwander had watched during summer 1989 as Hungarians clogged the roads in and out of Vienna. "It was a common sight to see washing machines, refrigerators or other appliances tied to the tops of their little cars making their way to Hungary." After the Berlin Wall opened, thousands of people from Czechoslovakia swarmed into Vienna. Special parking lots had to be set up outside of the city with bus service into town. "There was a festive atmosphere throughout the city."[73] Borders so long impermeable became porous.

In the month prior to the Budapest conference, President Neuenschwander, by assignment, had visited President Steven Mecham in Helsinki and then traveled into the Soviet Union with David Farnsworth to assess the possibilities for sending in missionaries.[74] President Neuenschwander found the Terebenin family of St. Petersburg still firm in their commitment to the gospel. They also had a growing circle of friends who were interested in learning about the Church.

At the Budapest conference, responsibility for northern Russia and the Baltics was transferred from the Austria Vienna East Mission to the Finland Helsinki Mission. The Austria Vienna East Mission retained responsibility for southern Russia and Ukraine.[75] President Mecham in Helsinki had been told when he was set apart in 1987 that new doors would eventually be opened to the missionaries and that he would be instrumental in accomplishing this task.[76]

Following the mission president's conference, Neuenschwander visited Moscow in November 1989 and contacted Sister Smolianova as well as American Church members working at the U.S. embassy in Moscow. One of these members, Dohn Thornton, had just obtained an apartment in the city, outside the embassy compound. The president counseled the group to begin holding meetings in Thornton's apartment where Russians could worship with them, something that was not possible inside the embassy grounds.[77] Sister Smolianova now had contact with fellow members.

In late 1989, President Mecham called several Finnish couples who spoke Russian to fellowship new Russian converts and answer questions from prospective members in Russia. In January 1990, he appointed Jussi Kemppainen, his counselor in the Finland Helsinki Mission, to preside over these couples and direct the affairs of what was termed the Baltic District.[78] These Finnish couples served in their missionary calling for six months.[79] One such couple, Antti and Leena Riihimäki Laitinen, entered St. Petersburg in early 1990. They tried to visit Svetlana Artiomova, Sister Kemppainen's Helsinki Park contact. No one was home, but a couple down the hall opened their door and asked if they were Latter-day Saints.

In the neighbor's apartment, the missionaries learned that this couple had become acquainted with the Church while on a visit to Warsaw and had been hoping for missionaries to arrive because they wanted to be baptized.[80]

The first weekend of December 1989, President Mecham and his wife, Donna, visited St. Petersburg. He convened a sacrament meeting on December 3 in his hotel room. Eleven people attended, including the Terebenins and Anton Skripko.[81] Anton had told his friends of his religious studies, and when one of his friends claimed the Church was wrong, he replied, "I need this Church. I feel that my soul is not empty; I have gained something."[82] By February 1990, the twenty members needed for registration had been baptized, primarily by crossing into Finland to receive the ordinance.[83] The stage had been set for the final act of sending in missionaries.

Missionaries Enter the Soviet Union through Estonia

On Friday, December 8, 1989, a passenger liner crossed the churning Baltic from Finland to Estonia. The turbulence could hardly dispel the buoyant spirits of several passengers: President and Sister Mecham, President Kemppainen, and Elders Kevin Dexter and David Reagan, the first young full-time missionaries to pass the Soviet border. It was the fourth Communist country, after Yugoslavia, Hungary, and Poland, to have young elders. President Mecham was finally able to fulfill the promise he had made six months earlier to Valttari Rödsä. Brother Rödsä introduced the group to friends and relatives who were interested in the gospel. One young man, Alari Allik, proclaimed, "I have always known, ever since I was a young boy that the true Church of Jesus Christ would come to Estonia. And that in that organized church would be apostles and prophets and priesthood." Another young man, Jaanus Silla, explained, "I want to be a missionary for the Church." Though still only a dream at the time, President Mecham said, "You will be."[84]

On the Sunday of their visit, President Mecham piqued the interest of his Tallinn cab driver, Peep Kiviit, by telling him they were headed to the most important meeting to ever be held in Estonia. The driver attended the meeting, and when he asked to learn more, President Mecham said they would not only teach him but that when he was converted he would serve as a branch president.[85] Peep Kiviit was later called as the first native branch president in Estonia.

Elder Reagan and Harri Aho, a native Finnish missionary, returned to Tallinn on December 16–17 and taught four young Estonians: Alari

Allik, Jana Lass, Kristi Lass, and Eve Reisalu. Having taught three discussions in succession, the missionaries felt prompted to issue a baptismal challenge. When the investigators accepted, the missionaries sought a place to perform the ordinances. After protracted negotiations with the hotel sauna attendants, they were granted some exclusive time. These four youth became the first Estonians baptized in their native land and the first converts to receive baptism in the Soviet Union, which at that time still included Estonia. Reflecting on his experience, Elder Reagan felt as if angels were present: "It was the single most spiritual experience of my mission."[86]

President Mecham returned a week later and, as in his previous visit, engaged another cab driver in a gospel conversation. The man professed atheism but said his mother had always believed in God. The mother came to the meeting the next day and asked how she could help. President Mecham explained that the Church had a woman's organization and that after she joined she would be set apart as its president. Marina Saarik replied, "I do not know what that is, but I'll be a good one."[87]

On January 5, 1990, Elders Dexter and Aho traveled to Estonia and baptized Jaanus Silla and Urmas Raavik, the two young contacts from the first visit. The young men immediately began to contact others, providing new people for the missionaries to teach.[88] Thirteen months later, Jaanus Silla was called to the Utah Salt Lake City South Mission and was permitted to leave his country as the Church's first missionary to serve from the Soviet Union.[89]

Missionary work continued even though the government had not yet recognized the Church. However, the important step toward recognition was not being ignored. Presidents Mecham and Kemppainen went to Tallinn and visited Ants Liimets, Estonian Minister of Religion. Later, the minister attended a conference in Helsinki and was stranded there when Soviet President Gorbachev closed Estonian ports during the independence crisis in early 1990. Liimets called President Mecham, his only personal acquaintance in Helsinki, and was impressed with the hospitality and warmth of the visit. He returned to Estonia, promising to personally deliver the papers needed to grant recognition through the government bureaucracy.[90]

A Second Chance in Russia

Circumstances at the beginning of the twentieth century that preceded missionary work in Russia were not as daunting as the century concluded. The Church had the missionary force, the ability to teach language skills, and the resources to mount a sustained effort. Gorbachev's *glasnost* had untapped a wellspring of Russian interest in the West generated over years of isolation behind the Iron Curtain.

On January 13, 1990, young missionaries began to enter Russia, though only for short visits. Elder Reagan and President Jussi Kemppainen visited the Terebenins in St. Petersburg for three days and held several large group discussions. The next weekend, Elders Reagan and Dexter entered for two weeks. On February 3, at the end of their visit, they baptized Anton Skripko, the first baptism in Russia since before the 1917 Revolution. Anton had entered a new course in life, seeking spirituality and giving up smoking and drinking. Frustrated at first because of his limited understanding and inability to explain the gospel to his friends, he persisted and eventually was called as the first native Russian to serve a mission for the Church.[91]

Even though in early 1990 the Church had not received political recognition, President Mecham started sending in more missionaries. He had laid the groundwork with the appropriate officials, and they knew the missionaries would hold meetings and proselytize on a referral basis only. By year's end, the officials began issuing visas for longer periods, initially ranging from days to weeks and later to months.[92]

Elder Dexter began to serve exclusively in Estonia and Elder Reagan in St. Petersburg. Elders Bert Dover, Kurt Wood, and William McKane joined them. President Mecham also sent in two young women, Sisters Heidi Moffett and Stefanie Condie, in March 1990. Coincidentally, they had known each other at BYU, graduating at the same commencement. At graduation, Heidi, who had received her mission call to Finland, said, "See you in Finland," although Stefanie had not yet received her call. When she was also called to Finland she wrote in jest to Heidi, "Perhaps we shall open up Russia together."[93] When they did, the two were particularly helpful in teaching single women and establishing the Relief Society program.

At the end of February 1990, Elder John Webster, Elder Don Leavitt, the Kemppainens, and the Jäkkös traveled to Vyborg and held a meeting for approximately thirty people, including Andrei Semionov, at the local library. The following day, Andrei decided to attend a church service with them in St. Petersburg and was baptized that evening.[94] Brother Semionov was a strong and charismatic leader.[95] He later became the first Russian to receive the Melchizedek Priesthood.[96] Elder Ivan Stratov soon joined Elder Webster in Vyborg and, with Brother Semionov's help, the missionaries baptized forty people there within a six-month period.[97]

Many of these early missionaries had begun preparation for preaching in Russia, perhaps unknowingly, long before their missions. David Reagan, Kevin Dexter, Clarence Dillon, and William McKane had all studied Russian in high school. As a fourteen-year-old, William McKane, on his own initiative, began studying the Book of Mormon in Russian.[98] David Reagan, Bert Dover, Heidi Moffett, and Stefanie Condie had taken Russian classes at BYU. Ivan Stratov, son of a Russian father, had learned Russian in his Australian home. Kurt Wood had a degree in Russian from Stanford University. When the time came, there was an abundance of missionaries in Finland with the background to either speak Russian or learn it quickly (illus. 5-7).

With little Church literature available in Russian, the missionaries relied heavily on the Russian Book of Mormon. There were no Russian discussions, except for a few translated by Elder Dillon. The missionaries encountered widespread interest and taught constantly. Russian curiosity about the West attracted many to the young Americans. Others were equally fascinated by religion, having long been treated only to a steady diet of Communism's atheistic tenets. In Finland the missionaries had struggled to find someone to teach. In Russia they struggled to find time to teach, and baptisms came easily—perhaps too easily, as Russians who joined the Church without understanding the full extent of the commitment soon faded back into the masses. When this trend was noted, missionaries began lengthening the teaching process.[99]

Sunday services were always an adventure with new members and numerous people of other faiths. In testimony meetings, investigators as well as members would testify or comment on random subjects such as astrology or reincarnation. The first Relief Society meeting of six sisters was conducted under a huge portrait of Lenin that had to remain up because they were in a rented facility.[100]

The first missionaries in Russia had to be registered at a motel because they entered on tourist visas, so during the first four months they stayed at a motel in Ol'gino, on the outskirts of St. Petersburg. The main problem was that to reach the city center, they had to walk half a kilometer, ride a bus twenty kilometers to reach a subway station, and then spend an additional half hour on the subway. By summer the members, who fulfilled a legal requirement by issuing invitations that gave the missionaries visas for longer periods, had helped to arrange apartments for them.[101]

Because the missionaries had little time to wait in food lines and no kitchen facilities, they ate at hotels, restaurants, and members' homes.

Illus. 5-7. Missionaries attending a conference of the Finland Helsinki East Mission in Leningrad (St. Petersburg), October 1990.

Though they were strained themselves because of limited food supplies, the members generously fed the missionaries. Over time the sisters began to dress more Russian, and instead of being approached by Russians trying to exchange money on the black market, they were approached by people asking for directions.[102]

The Moscow Branch

Missionaries were not sent to Moscow for most of 1990 as the Church proceeded slowly and cautiously in Russia. Expatriate Church members undertook the missionary work there. Dohn Thornton was particularly active in this effort. As with the missionaries, he had prepared himself early in life. He had studied Russian in junior high school, and after serving a mission to Finland (1985–87) he took two semesters of Russian at BYU. He had a great desire to work in Russia and arrived in March 1989 on a two-year contract to work in the U.S. embassy. While there, he hired Russian language tutors to further his studies.[103]

Brother Thornton held Sabbath services in his apartment. The presence of Russian members and investigators had a significant impact on the meetings: "No one seemed to want to leave once church was over.

A new spirit had entered our group; a spirit of missionary work. Ever since Russian investigators began coming to church, the Spirit seemed to increase in intensity." President Neuenschwander visited the branch on the first Sunday in February 1990. Galina Goncharova, an investigator, bore her testimony at the fast service. "She poured out her soul in gratitude to Heavenly Father for blessing her so much. . . . She said that her life had changed completely since she learned about the church six months ago." It was the first service in Moscow where Russians outnumbered Americans. Beginning in March 1990, Dohn initiated a Wednesday evening study group for Russians to read the Book of Mormon. Sister Smolianova helped him teach this group. Attendance grew from between fifteen and twenty in April 1990 to thirty and forty by September. Having received permission from President Neuenschwander, Brother Thornton baptized Sister Goncharova on June 10, 1990. She was the first Muscovite to be baptized in Russia.[104]

Dedications in the Soviet Union

Elder Nelson and Elder Ringger visited Estonia and Russia in April 1990 to help obtain legal recognition. Elder Nelson took advantage of the opportunity to dedicate both countries for the missionary work that had already commenced. The dedication in Estonia occurred on April 25 at Laululava, an amphitheater (illus. 5-8) where a national folk song festival is held every five years. The festival consists of a thirty-six-thousand-member choir and an audience exceeding three hundred thousand.[105] "Some Estonians say the soul of their country resides there."[106]

The following day, the group of Church leaders arrived in St. Petersburg. Elder Nelson announced that the dedication of Russia would be at the Summer Garden, the site of Elder Lyman's 1903 prayer. They arrived at the garden to find it closed. President Mecham requested a guard's permission to enter. He stonily refused at first but eventually softened and directed them to a gate that could be opened with a little force.[107] Surrounded by somnolent trees and statuary of Greek gods and goddesses, the small group stood in a closed park as Elder Nelson offered the prayer. That same day, they met with government officials and made further progress toward recognition for the Church in St. Petersburg.[108]

In both Tallinn and St. Petersburg, Elder Nelson gave firesides attended by approximately two hundred people including missionaries and members. Emilia Alexandrovna told a story at the St. Petersburg fireside. Her daughter Katia, baptized that month, had gone on a Komsomol (a Communist youth organization) boat trip outside of St. Petersburg. A storm arose that threatened to sink the boat. The Komsomol advisor asked if anyone believed in God. Katia said, "I do." The advisor pleaded for her to do something. Katia prayed, the storm abated, and the group returned safely to shore. The advisor thanked Katia's mother adding that she was no longer an atheist.[109]

The atheism of many Russians, instilled by the system from youth, was being shed by some. Lilia Chuprovoi wrote to Sister Condie, who had taught her the gospel:

> Soon you will go home, get on with your life, maybe get married, and gradually forget about us. But we will not forget you. The impression is this: as if we have lived in an old, run-down shed, half-falling apart, and so cramped that with every step we bumped into something. You came along, took me by the hand, and set me on the road leading to a beautiful garden, and there—light, fruit, and joy.[110]

Little was known of these events in the United States. In April, Iurii Dubinin, the Soviet ambassador to the United States, visited Salt Lake City. He was hosted by Utah industrialist Jon M. Huntsman. After a brief news conference outside the Huntsman home, a reporter approached the ambassador and broached the subject of a Church mission in the Soviet Union. He was startled when the answer came back that the Church was

Courtesy Kahlile B. Mehr

Illus. 5-8. Choral amphitheater at Laululava (1998), where Elder Russell M. Nelson dedicated Estonia for missionary work in April 1990.

welcome.[111] As the reporter wrote his scoop, he kept thinking that a premature announcement could damage the reputation of the ambassador and cause repercussions for the Church.[112] What he did not know was that even then a group of about a dozen missionaries were working in St. Petersburg, Vyborg, and Tallinn as a virtual, if not a formal, mission under President Mecham in Helsinki. A month later, Church leaders decided to move ahead and make the mission a reality. Gary Browning, a Russian-language professor at Brigham Young University, had been called in January 1990 to serve as the Finland Helsinki Mission president. At the end of May 1990, he was notified that he would now preside over the Finland Helsinki East Mission, the word *East* meaning beyond the borders of Finland.[113]

The cause prayed for by Elder Lyman at the beginning of the twentieth century found fruition ninety years later. The Church had the resources and the commitment to pursue the opportunity presented by political reform. Even more important, they found the people, who had been denied religious freedom for decades, disposed to renew their faith. Some were receptive to a new message, a condition not present at the beginning of the century. The slavish devotion witnessed by Elder Lyman was no longer the norm. It was as if Communism had accomplished the opposite of its intent. Instead of eliminating religion, it had only abetted it.

The Long Wait Ends in Czechoslovakia

An ultraconservative regime delayed the arrival of missionaries into Czechoslovakia. However, members who had remained faithful for decades succeeded in doing their own missionary work. They were helped, it seemed, by unseen forces. After the Freiberg Temple dedication, the baptismal rate in Czechoslovakia jumped from a handful each year to twenty. District president Jiří Šnederfler opened new branches in Uherské Hradiště in 1986 and Jičín in 1987 (illus. 5-9).[114] The hopes of a small band of missionaries proclaiming the gospel in a Slavic country in the early twentieth century had begun to take form.

Elder Nelson and Elder Ringger visited Czechoslovakia annually to request recognition. Each visit ended with the disappointing assertion that the request was still being studied.[115] The members continued to meet in homes, but always with a sense of foreboding. The forty members who attended a conference at the Šnederfler home in Prague in November 1986 sang in hushed tones so as not to attract unwanted attention.[116]

Illus. 5-9. Church branches in Czechoslovakia, 1987–91.

In 1987, Czechoslovak officials told Elder Nelson and President Ringger that the petition for recognition could only be made by a native member of the Church. The two informed President Šnederfler of the requirement (illus. 5-10). Pausing only briefly he responded, "I will go. I will do it. . . . This is for the Lord, and His work is more important than our freedom or life." After forty years of remaining in the shadows, he knew that he risked everything by stepping forward to announce his allegiance to the Church. The membership fasted and prayed every third Sunday for six months before he carried the petition to the authorities in December 1988. The response was not encouraging. President Šnederfler was interrogated every month until the "velvet" revolution in November 1989 dethroned Communism in Czechoslovakia.[117] Nevertheless, he remained free and able to perform his duties. In November the petition was resubmitted to a new government. The desired recognition became a possibility when the new regime established religious freedom for all faiths in January 1990. Official recognition of the Church came in February.[118] On February 6, Elder Russell M. Nelson ascended the wooded knoll by Karlštejn and, in the presence of a small group of Czech Saints, offered a new prayer of dedication, reconfirming the blessing of Elder Widtsoe delivered six decades earlier.[119] Elder Widtsoe's vision of thousands gathering under the auspices of the restored gospel had finally begun to materialize.

In April 1990, former Czechoslovak missionaries, Czechoslovak émigrés, their families, and others gathered in Salt Lake City to attend the annual Czechoslovak Mission Reunion. Twelve missionaries were present

Illus. 5-10. Elder Russell M. Nelson between Olga Šnederfler and Jiří Šnederfler in 1988.

from the pre–World War I period and thirteen from the period between the wars. Frances (Brodilová) McOmber was there, dressed in the costume of her native land and surrounded by many of her descendants who were similarly dressed. On the stand sat a newly called mission president, Richard Winder (a former Czechoslovak missionary) and his wife, Barbara (previously the Church's Relief Society General President), along with four missionaries appointed to serve in Czechoslovakia. They had all gathered to celebrate a new epoch in mission history, the opportunity to present their message to a country now free to hear it once again.

After a forty-year absence, missionaries again entered Czechoslovakia May 2, 1990, crossing the fifth Communist border after Yugoslavia, Hungary, Poland, and the Soviet Union. Transferred to the Austria Vienna East Mission from missions in Austria and Portugal, the four missionaries studied the Czech language in Vienna before entering the country. When the elders arrived in Brno, the members finally believed they were free to worship openly. The branch members hugged and kissed the missionaries, but it was the members themselves who had prepared the way. Within a week, the missionaries in Brno performed ten baptisms.[120] A majority of the converts were young, well-educated, and vibrant in their new faith. And there were the older ones, those who faithfully withstood the test, resolutely living the gospel through decades of isolation, believers who had endured to see a brighter day.

New Missions in the East

Not much was accomplished during the sixty years after Elder Widt-soe established the first mission on the edge of the Slavic world. In July 1990, the Church took advantage of the new religious opportunities in the East to mold four new missions from the Austria Vienna East Mission. New mission presidents helped shoulder the responsibility President Neuenschwander had borne alone for the previous three years. The Czechoslovak Prague Mission, the Hungary Budapest Mission, and the Poland Warsaw Mission covered the nations for which they were named. The Finland Helsinki East Mission covered the northern Soviet Union (Russia and Estonia). The Austria Vienna East Mission, which President Neuenschwander continued to direct during a fourth year of service, cov-ered the other areas of eastern Europe.

Czechoslovak Prague Mission. President Richard Winder presided over the Czechoslovak Prague Mission (illus. 5-11). When he had attempted to enter Czechoslovakia through Switzerland and Austria as a young missionary in 1948, he was refused permission to cross through the Russian Zone of Austria. He reached Prague by a circuitous route, through the American Zone of Germany. Expelled before completing his service, President Winder returned in 1990 to finish the task. In Brno, the center of membership in the country, he was able once again to converse with Otakar Vojkůvka, who was still faith-ful after four decades.

Courtesy Jiří Šnederfler

Illus. 5-11. Detail of a picture of Czechoslo-vakia Prague Mission President Richard Winder and his wife, Barbara, in 1986.

President Winder was not the only missionary from an earlier period to return. Other former missionaries also came to serve with their wives as couple mission-aries.[121] By the end of the year, there were 353 members clustered in five cities: Praha, Plzeň, Jičín, Brno, and Uher-ské Hradiště. Three new cities were opened to mission-ary work during 1991, and 247 baptisms swelled the membership to 600.[122] In

March 1991, Martin Pilka, one of the converts from the yoga class taught by Brother Vojkůvka and Sister Kovářová, arrived at the Missionary Training Center in Provo, Utah, prior to serving as the first missionary from his country.[123]

Hungary Budapest Mission. Prior to his call as the president of the Hungary Budapest Mission, James L. Wilde (illus. 5-12) had established a connection with Hungary, having volunteered a decade of labor to trace that country's nobility for the Family History Department of the Church.[124] When he arrived in Budapest in July 1990, there were almost 250 members in the newly established mission. With influxes of new missionaries, six new cities were opened and six new branches established between July 1990 and December 1991. In September 1991, thirty-six members visited the Freiberg Temple in Germany as part of the first Hungarian temple trip. In November, Brother Attila Böröcz left for Idaho, becoming the first member from Hungary to serve a mission for the Church. The Hungarian membership doubled in 1991 to approximately six hundred.[125] Just before Christmas, Johannes Gutjahr, a translator from the Church's area office, brought in sixteen hundred copies of the newly translated Hungarian Book of Mormon. In a herculean effort, the books saw distribution in ten cities throughout Hungary in time for Christmas services on the Sabbath.[126]

Poland Warsaw Mission. Walter Whipple presided over the new mission in Poland. In early 1991, the government eased restrictions on religious proselytizing. Previously confined to answering questions, the missionaries could now contact people at will on trams, on the street, or elsewhere.[127] The missionary force grew to almost fifty during 1991, and the membership increased to a total of approximately three hundred. The hundred baptized from 1985 to 1989 had

Courtesy James Wilde

Illus. 5-12. President of the Hungary Budapest Mission, James Wilde and his wife, Patricia, 1990.

Courtesy Walter Whipple

Illus. 5-13. Warsaw chapel, March 1991.

been augmented by a second hundred in 1990 and a third hundred in 1991.[128] Members lived primarily in six cities: Warsaw, Sopot, Wrocław, Łódź, Katowice, and Bydgoszcz.[129] Eleven members received temple ordinances in Freiberg, Germany, in May 1991. Prior to their departure, the visa requirement was dropped, making it much easier to cross the border. Sister Urszula Adamska, who had on her mission helped translate the narrative used in the temple ceremony, now accompanied this first group of fellow Poles on their temple trip.[130]

In June 1991, the Warsaw chapel, the first constructed by the Church in the former Soviet world, was dedicated (illus. 5-13). Situated in an excellent location next to a beautiful park and a cemetery, it put the Church on the Polish map. During that year, inquiries from all over Poland poured in daily.[131] When the site was obtained, the average attendance at the Warsaw Branch was only fifteen.[132] However, 140 people attended the first meeting held there in November 1990.[133] The chapel's completion confirmed the reality of the Church in Poland, becoming to Polish members like "food and water to a human being."[134]

Finland Helsinki East Mission. Gary Browning (illus. 5-14) presided over the Finland Helsinki East Mission, which covered northern Russia and Estonia. As a former Finnish missionary in 1963, he had had the opportunity to accompany a tour of Finnish teachers to Moscow before being released. The train stopped in Vyborg for an hour, and the young man set foot on Russian soil for the first time. Little did he imagine that twenty-seven years later, in July 1990, he would again set foot in that city as the president of the first Russian mission. The mission had over a hundred members in branches in Tallinn, Vyborg, St. Petersburg, Moscow, and other scattered locations.[135]

Estonia granted the Church recognition on July 2, 1990. After a six-month wait, and largely through the efforts of Yuri and Liudmila Terebenin, the St. Petersburg Branch received official recognition on September 13, 1990. Similarly, Vyborg was recognized on November 1.

Courtesy Gary Browning

Illus. 5-14. Gary Browning, president of the Finland Helsinki East Mission (1990–93), renamed the Russia Moscow Mission in February 1992, and his wife, Joan, c. 1990.

These recognitions were preceded by a quiet drama in the lives of newly baptized members, who were required to sign a petition for the government to consider granting recognition to the Church. Remaining anonymous among the masses had been a protection under Soviet rule when attracting attention for religious activity might lead to severe repercussions such as losing a job, being forced from an apartment, or even suffering physical harm. It took courage for these new members to affix their names to a list that dispelled that protective anonymity.[136]

In October a new Soviet law took effect that ended the state's persecution of organized religion and guaranteed freedom of worship throughout the nation. On October 16, 1990, Sister Zdzisława Chudyba from Poland arrived in Russia as the first young missionary specifically called to serve there, rather than being transferred in from another mission. That same month, five missionaries opened up Moscow (illus 5-15). In 1991, Jaanus Silla departed Estonia and Anton Skripko departed Russia to serve their missions in Utah. Mission membership stood at three hundred by the end of 1990 and over seven hundred by the end of 1991.[137]

The Tabernacle Choir Tours Central and Eastern Europe

In June 1991, the Tabernacle Choir visited the capitals of central and eastern Europe: Budapest, Prague, Warsaw, Moscow, and St. Petersburg.

Illus. 5-15. First Latter-day Saint meeting place in Moscow, 1990. *Left to right:* Stefanie Condie, Zdzisława Chudyba, Rick Robinson, Albert Walling, William McKane, Adam West, Heath Thompson, and Aleksandr Goncharov.

The 313-member ensemble enthralled audiences, both in concert halls and through nationwide broadcasts. The audience enthusiastically solicited encores with standing ovations, rhythmic clapping, or stamping feet. They touched audiences in each country by singing at least one number in the people's native tongue. The choir's performances fostered a new appreciation for a church that many perceived to be an obscure foreign faith, and the concerts garnered a multitude of new contacts for missionaries.[138]

Equally significant were dinners held in conjunction with the performances. Beverly Campbell obtained private funding and, with the assistance of the Church's area office in Frankfurt, orchestrated these events attended by government leaders; embassy and consular officials; prominent figures in education, science, the arts and business; as well as various local officials. Mingling with them were members of the choir and local Church leaders. Demonstrative of the mutual appreciation encouraged by these dinners, the deputy minister of culture at the Moscow dinner said, "You are sending us your love and beauty, and we are looking for the same things." The tour also included four firesides and sacrament meetings to share testimonies and promulgate the gospel. Hundreds came to these meetings.[139]

At the Budapest concert on June 15, the choir sang the national anthem, and the audience was on its feet even before a note was sung, many shedding tears. After a standing ovation, it took eight curtain calls and seven encores before it ended. Coincidentally, the last Soviet soldier left Hungary the day of the concert.[140] In Prague at Smetana Hall on June 18, the Tabernacle Choir sang "Teče, Voda, Teče" (Flow, Water, Flow), a song banned previously because it spoke of liberty and freedom. A great hush filled the hall, and over a third of the audience stood, some with arms upraised and others weeping openly.[141] Again the choir received a standing ovation. The president of Prague Television commented to President Winder that never before had he witnessed a standing ovation there.[142] At a packed opera house in Warsaw, the choir sang many encores, including "Boze cos Polske" (May God Bless Poland), which fascinated and moved the audience.[143] Sister Urszula Adamska made the announcements at the concert. As she presented the Tabernacle Choir to her nation, her hands shook but her heart felt peaceful.[144]

The Moscow concert ended only after five encores, including its signature number, "The Battle Hymn of the Republic." An older man outside the theater called out, "Lenin—first revolution! Tabernacle Choir—second revolution!"[145] At the dinner hosted by Church leaders after the concert, Alexander Rutskoi, Russian vice president, read the announcement issued on May 28, 1991, that the Church was now legally recognized by the Russian state.[146] The Church had indeed been made welcome in Russia. At the concert in St. Petersburg, six encores were performed to an enthused audience. As the crowd left, one man exclaimed, "Wonderful! Wonderful! Spiritual! Spiritual! Leningrad is happy again! This is a holiday."[147] The next day at a fireside, Elder Nelson announced that he and Elder Dallin H. Oaks had broken ground only a few days earlier in Vyborg to begin construction of the first chapel in Russia.[148]

Upon their return to Salt Lake City, Elder Nelson and Elder Oaks reported to President Ezra Taft Benson on July 3, 1991, and showed him the certified copies of the documents granting the Church recognition in Russia. Joy filled the elderly president's countenance. They recalled President Benson's own experience, speaking from a church pulpit in Moscow twenty-five years earlier, saying, "Our Heavenly Father is not far away. . . . Be unafraid, keep His commandments, love one another, pray for peace, and all will be well."[149]

The Attempted Coup in the Soviet Union

The catalyst permitting the Church to reenter central and eastern Europe came from inside, rather than outside, the Communist sphere.

Soviet leader Gorbachev's policies were the key that opened the door. Eventually, however, the forces he unleashed by his policies of openness and restructuring superseded his ability to control them. In August 1991, he was vacationing at his resort in Crimea. Soviet officials, representing major power factions in the Soviet government, instigated a coup. Army troops surrounded the capital cities of the Soviet republics and threatened to quell any civilian authority or popular demonstrations. For three days, the fate of the Soviet Union balanced on whether or not the military leaders would obey their orders and impose martial law. They disobeyed. Gorbachev survived the coup, but his political power did not. Between August 20 and October 27, all former republics of the Soviet Union, except for Russia and Kazakhstan, declared their independence. The Soviet empire had collapsed and Communist power dissipated. Gorbachev resigned on Christmas Day 1991, and on December 31 the Soviet Union ceased to exist on paper as it had already ceased to exist in reality.[150] The unanticipated political maelstrom ultimately created new religious opportunities in the Soviet realm. The long-awaited moment arrived between 1985 and 1991, and the Church became a player on a stage which it had formerly been permitted only to observe.

The Drama Unfolds

The dissolution of political power that had long opposed the entry of Western-based religions into the Soviet Bloc was but a prelude to a groundswell of interest in spiritual renewal. This was evidenced in the missionaries' busy teaching schedules and the quick growth of the Church in the early years of missionary effort in central and eastern Europe. By 1991 the Church's worldwide missionary force had grown to forty-three thousand, much greater than the hundreds it fielded at the turn of the twentieth century. With this enlarged missionary force, the Church now had the capacity and the desire to commit language-qualified missionaries to central and eastern Europe. The new, open political environment facilitated this move. However, the final ingredient was the willingness that many people had to listen to the gospel. Curiosity about the West opened many doors, but curiosity did not lead to conversion and commitment—these were experienced only by those who pondered the missionaries' message more deeply.

Notes

1. Howard L. Biddulph, *The Morning Breaks: Stories of Conversion and Faith in the Former Soviet Union* (Salt Lake City: Deseret Book, 1996), 27–29.

2. Biddulph, *Morning Breaks,* 29–34.

3. Russell M. Nelson, "Drama on the European Stage," *Ensign* 21 (December 1991): 8.

4. Beverly Campbell, telephone interviews by author, January 30, 1997, January 15, 1998; Lee Davidson, "Ambassador Opens Doors for LDS Church," *Deseret News,* October 4, 1997, A-1, A-3.

5. "W. Cole Durham Jr.," *Brigham Young Magazine* 52 (winter 1998): 22–23.

6. Wayne K. Johnson, telephone interview by author, December 23, 1996.

7. Spencer J. Condie, "God Has Not Ceased to Be a God of Miracles," typescript, 1, in possession of the author.

8. Spencer J. Condie, interviewed by James B. Allen, March 15–22, 1989, Provo, Utah, audio tape 3, in possession of the interviewer, Orem, Utah.

9. Condie, "God Has Not Ceased," 2–3; Condie, interview, audio tape 3. Source for next paragraph as well.

10. Peter Varga to Ralph Cloward, November 10, 1985, copy in author's possession.

11. Johnson, telephone interview; Christopher Jones, telephone interview by author, October 12, 1989; Alan Macfarlane, telephone interview by author, April 18, 1990.

12. Johnson, telephone interview.

13. Francis A. Madsen Jr., interviewed by author, July 1, 2000, Aalborg, Denmark.

14. Dell Van Orden, "Church Granted Legal Recognition in Hungary," *Church News,* published by *Deseret News,* July 2, 1988, 13. Also a source for the next paragraph.

15. Condie, interview, audio tape 3.

16. Nelson, "Drama on the European Stage," 11; Van Orden, "Church Granted Legal Recognition," 13.

17. Alan Palmer Macfarlane, journals July 1987–January 1989, 41ff, Church Archives, The Church of Jesus Christ of Latter-day Saints, Salt Lake City.

18. Jones, telephone interview; Macfarlane, telephone interview.

19. Condie, interview, audio tape 3.

20. Christopher Jones, interviewed by author, February 3, 1996, Salt Lake City; Jones, telephone interview.

21. Arlene B. Darger, comp., "Europe Area Historical Report: A History of the Work and Growth of the Europe Area," August 15, 1986–August 15, 1989, bound typescript, 409, in possession of author.

22. Condie, interview, audio tape 3.

23. Alan Palmer Macfarlane, Journals, July 1987–January 1989, Church Archives.

24. Johnson, telephone interview.

25. Condie, interview, audio tape 3.

26. Jones, telephone interview.

27. Hungary Budapest Mission, Historical Records and Minutes, 1990 report, Church Archives.

28. Ferdinand Hintze, Journal commencing November 1, 1886, entry dated March 10, 1888, 176, Ferdinand Friis Hintze, papers, 1882–1916, Church Archives.

29. Liudmila Terebenin, interviewed by author, May 19, 1993, St. Petersburg, Russia.

30. Johnson, telephone interview.

31. Darger, "Europe Area Historical Report," 409.

32. Macfarlane, telephone interview; "Meetinghouse Dedicated in Hungary," *Church News*, November 11, 1989, 3–4.

33. Attila Böröcz, "I Am a Child of God," typescript, 8–9, in possession of the author.

34. Johnson, telephone interview.

35. Thomas S. Monson, "To Learn, To Do, To Be," *Ensign* 22 (May 1992): 48.

36. Leotha Wade Slagowski to family, April 1, 1987, Missionary correspondence April 1987–May 1988, Church Archives.

37. Neil Slagowski, missionary report for 1987 in Leotha Wade Slagowski, Missionary correspondence April 1987–May 1988, Church Archives.

38. Leotha Slagowski to family, May 20, 1988, 8, Church Archives.

39. Neil Slagowski, missionary report.

40. Leotha Slagowski to family, May 20, 1988, 5, 8.

41. Matthew Robert Binns, Journal 1987–88, May 22, 1998, Church Archives.

42. Binns, Journal, December 21, 1987; Sean Kenneth Peterson, Journal 1987–89; December 21, 1987; January 20, 1988, Church Archives.

43. Peterson, Journal, January 20, March 25, 1988; Martin Berkeley Hickman, *David M. Kennedy: Banker, Statesman, Churchman* (Salt Lake City: Deseret Book, 1987): 355–56.

44. Binns, Journal, January 21, 1988; Peterson, Journal, January 20, 21, 26, 28, 1988.

45. Binns, Journal, February 23, 26, May 29, 1988; Peterson, Journal, February 4, 8, 11, 27, 1988.

46. Binns, Journal, March 16, 28, 1988, January 23, 1989; Peterson, Journal, February 19, 24, March 2, 21, April 28, 1988.

47. Condie, interview, audio tape 4.

48. Peterson, Journal, January 24, 1988.

49. Binns, Journal, February 14, 27, 29, March 9, 1988; Peterson, Journal, February 14, 1988.

50. Binns, Journal, March 24, May 22, 1988.

51. Binns, Journal, March 30, April 5, April 13, 1988; Peterson, Journal, April 5, 1988.

52. Urszula Maria Adamska, interviewed by Matthew K. Heiss, October 5, 1991, Warsaw, Poland, typescript, 12–17, James Moyle Oral History Program, Church Archives.

53. Adamska, interview, 18–22.

54. Binns, Journal, May 8, June 14, 18, 27, July 18, September 12, 23, November 28, 1988; Peterson, Journal, May 16, June 14, 1988.

55. Binns, Journal, October 14, 31, November 7, 1988, February 27, 1989; Adamska, interview, 18.

56. Binns, Journal, July 14, 1988; Peterson, Journal, July 7, 13, 15, 17, 1988.

57. Binns, Journal, September 2, 4, 1988; Peterson, Journal, September 3, 6, 7, 1988.

58. Condie, interview, audio tape 2.

59. "Happy Day for Poland," *Church News*, July 1, 1989, 4.

60. Darger, "Europe Area Historical Report," 409.

61. Poland Warsaw Mission, Historical Records and Minutes, baptism statistics dated January 3, 1995, Church Archives.

62. Binns, Journal, January 9, 12, 18, 1989.

63. Walter Whipple, interviewed by Matthew K. Heiss, October 4, 1991, Warsaw, Poland, typescript, 6, copy in possession of the interviewee, Provo, Utah; Stephen Jerome Bardsley, Journal excerpts, June 22, 1991, Church Archives.

64. Dennis Neuenschwander, "Reflections on Establishing the Gospel in Eastern Europe," *Liahona* 22 (October 1998): 44–45.

65. Mecham, interview; David S. Reagan, interviewed by author, February 17, 1991, West Jordan, Utah; Finland Helsinki Mission, Historical Records and Minutes, 1989 and 1990 reports, Church Archives. Sources for the next three paragraphs as well.

66. Steven R. Mecham, devotional address, Church Educational System Experienced Personnel Convention, May 10, 1991, Salt Lake City, copy of transcript, 2.

67. Dohn Thornton, "The Beginnings of the Moscow Branch," copy of typescript, 3, in possession of author.

68. Ralph Gibbons, "Our Mission to Jugoslavija, 1983–1985," typescript, 11–12, in possession of author.

69. Browning, *Russia and the Restored Gospel*, 22–23.

70. Anton Skripko, interviewed by author, December 19, 1992, Farmington, Utah.

71. Browning, *Russia and the Restored Gospel*, 24, 41–42.

72. Steven R. Mecham, interviewed by author, May 24, 1991, Salt Lake City.

73. Shaun D. Stahle, "Foothold of Faith in Europe," *Church News*, November 22, 1997, 7.

74. Gary Browning, *Russia and the Restored Gospel* (Salt Lake City: Deseret Book, 1997), 23–24.

75. Neuenschwander, "Reflections," 46.

76. Mecham, interview.

77. Thornton, "Beginnings of the Moscow Branch," 3.

78. Browning, *Russia and the Restored Gospel*, 24.

79. Mecham, devotional address, 7–8; Browning, *Russia and the Restored Gospel*, 24.

80. Browning, *Russia and the Restored Gospel*, 41–42; Don Woodward, ed., *Muistamme, 1947–1997* (Salt Lake City: Artistic Printing, 1997), 135.

81. Finland Helsinki Mission Historical Records and Minutes, 1989–90 report, Church Archives.

82. John L. Hart, "I Feel That My Soul Is Not Empty," *Church News,* November 16, 1991, 6.

83. Browning, *Russia and the Restored Gospel,* 39.

84. Mecham, devotional address, 3.

85. Mecham, devotional address, 4.

86. Reagan, interview.

87. Mecham, devotional address, 5.

88. Kevin Dexter, interviewed by author, March 29, 1991, Orem, Utah; Jaanus Silla, interviewed by author, June 18, 1992, Salt Lake City.

89. Finland Helsinki East Mission, Historical Records and Minutes, 1990 report, Church Archives.

90. Mecham, devotional address, 6.

91. Skripko, interview.

92. Mecham, interview.

93. Heidi Moffett, interview, February 27, 1991, Centerville, Utah.

94. Browning, *Russia and the Restored Gospel,* 43.

95. Stefanie Condie, interviewed by author, April 8, 1991, Salt Lake City.

96. Browning, *Russia and the Restored Gospel,* 92.

97. Scott Suggs, interviewed by author, November 1, 1992, Kiev, Ukraine; Browning, *Russia and the Restored Gospel,* 56.

98. William McKane, interviewed by author, February 17, 1991, West Jordan, Utah.

99. Stefanie Condie, interview; Moffett, interview.

100. Moffett, interview.

101. Stefanie Condie, interview; Moffett, interview.

102. Moffett, interview.

103. Dohn Thornton, telephone interview by author, March 12, 1992.

104. Thornton, "Beginnings of the Moscow Branch," 3–7.

105. Russell M. Nelson, "Dedicatory Prayer for Estonia," typescript (copy), in possession of the author.

106. Nelson, "Drama on the European Stage," 15.

107. Mecham, devotional address, 8.

108. Mecham, devotional address, 8–9; Nelson, "Drama on the European Stage," 15.

109. McKane, interview.

110. Stefanie Condie, devotional speech, Family History Library Technical Services staff, April 10, 1991, Salt Lake City.

111. The ambassador had been favorably influenced by Church assistance after a 1988 earthquake in Armenia, the homeland of his wife (a story told in chapter 7). But the statement also reflected the Gorbachev policy of *glasnost* and the attendant freedom to grant religious expression in the Soviet Union.

112. Robert H. Woody, "Reliving 'LDS Question,'" *Salt Lake Tribune,* October 15, 1995, A-1, A-4.

113. Browning, *Russia and the Restored Gospel,* 51, 53.

114. Jiří Šnederfler, interviewed by author, July 25, 1990, Salt Lake City.

115. Nelson, "Drama on the European Stage," 10.

116. Spencer J. Condie, interviewed by author, August 5, 1991, Frankfurt, Germany.

117. Gerry Avant, "He Was as Paul before Agrippa," *Church News,* August 31, 1991, 6, 10.

118. Nelson, "Drama on the European Stage," 10.

119. Šnederfler, interview.

120. Olga Kovářová, speech, Czech Missionary Reunion, April 6, 1991, Salt Lake City.

121. Van Orden, *Building Zion,* 275.

122. Czechoslovakia Prague Mission, Historical Records and Minutes, 1990 and 1991 reports, Church Archives.

123. "Religious Freedom Opened Way for First Czech Missionary," *Church News,* March 16, 1991, 5.

124. James L. Wilde, telephone interview by author, February 7, 1997.

125. Hungary Budapest Mission, Historical Records and Minutes, 1990 and 1991 reports, Church Archives; Europe area baptismal statistics, December 1992, typescript, Europe Area Frankfurt Office.

126. Jeffrey S. McClellan, "Christmas Gift for Hungary," *Ensign* 26 (December 1996): 7–9.

127. Stephen Todd Bunnell, interviewed by Matthew K. Heiss, October 4, 1991, Warsaw, Poland, 5, James Moyle Oral History Program, Church Archives; David L. Chandler, interviewed by Matthew K. Heiss, October 6, 1991, Warsaw, Poland, 3–4, James Moyle Oral History Program, Church Archives.

128. Poland Warsaw Mission, Historical Records and Minutes, 1991 report, Church Archives; Poland Warsaw Mission, Historical Records and Minutes, baptism statistics, dated January 3, 1995.

129. Whipple, interview, 7, 11.

130. Whipple, interview, 17; Adamska, interview, 29, 37.

131. Whipple, interview, 18.

132. Binns, Journal, December 8, 1988.

133. Walter Whipple, telephone conversation with author, January 31, 1997.

134. Chandler, interview, 10.

135. Browning, *Russia and the Restored Gospel,* 53, 57, 340.

136. Dennis B. Neuenschwander, conversation with author, December 2, 1999, Salt Lake City.

137. Finland Helsinki East Mission, Historical Records and Minutes, 1990 report, Church Archives; Browning, *Russia and the Restored Gospel,* 340.

138. Jay M. Todd, "An Encore of the Spirit," *Ensign* 21 (October 1991): 35, 38.

139. Todd, "Encore of the Spirit," 36.

140. Bardsley, Journal, June 17, 1991.

141. Todd, "Encore of the Spirit," 46.

142. Bardsley, Journal, June 19, 1991.

143. Whipple, interview, 19–20.

144. Adamska, interview, 38.

145. Todd, "Encore of the Spirit," 32, 35.

146. Gerry Avant and Matthew Brown, "Church Is Recognized by Russian Republic," *Church News*, June 29, 1991, 3; Browning, *Russia and the Restored Gospel*, 151.

147. Todd, "Encore of the Spirit," 48.

148. Bardsley, Journal, June 28, 1991.

149. Sheri L. Dew, *Ezra Taft Benson: A Biography* (Salt Lake City: Deseret Book, 1987), 343.

150. Biddulph, *Morning Breaks*, 46–47, 52–55; Browning, *Russia and the Restored Gospel*, 170–72, 198.

6

Mission Accomplished

1990–1992

In late 1990, missionaries crossed new borders into Bulgaria, Ukraine, and Romania, extending the eastern edge of missionary work deep into the interior of the former Communist realm. At that time, these countries were still components of the Austria Vienna East Mission directed by Dennis Neuenschwander, who watched the Soviet Empire crumble from the former imperial city of Vienna. Concurrently, he witnessed the same fate befall the Communist confederation of Yugoslavia. By early 1993, missionaries had also crossed the borders of Latvia, Lithuania, and Belarus (a pocket of nations in northeastern Europe along the Baltic Sea) as well as Albania (which sits in southern Europe across the Adriatic Sea from Italy). The seemingly impermeable barriers had finally given way to patiently waiting Church representatives. The task that had seemed so impossible for forty years was accomplished in less than four.

The Austria Vienna East Mission, which had been partitioned into four additional missions in Poland, Czechoslovakia, Hungary, and Russia (Finland Helsinki East Mission) in July 1990, was further dismantled. Additional mission presidents assumed responsibility for the remaining pieces of the mammoth mission field President Neuenschwander had nurtured since 1987. Still his task was not finished. In 1991, President Neuenschwander was called as a General Authority and appointed to serve in the Europe Area Presidency with Elder Ringger, continuing his efforts to shepherd missionary work in the East but at a broader level of responsibility. In the normal course of rotating responsibility among the Twelve, Elder Russell M. Nelson's responsibility as first contact for central and eastern Europe passed to Elder Dallin H. Oaks, who continued to probe the eastern edges of the Church's frontier in Europe.

A Revival of Faith in Bulgaria

Of the countries still without missions, Bulgaria was the first to be opened (illus. 6-1). The 8.7 million inhabitants of Bulgaria were primarily Orthodox. Orthodox monasteries staved off Turkish assimilation by preserving the Bulgarian language, literature, and religion through five centuries of Ottoman rule. In 1878 the Bulgarians ousted the Ottomans with military assistance from the Russian army. The country was independent until the end of World War II, but in 1944 their liberators became their captors. The Soviet army rumbled into Bulgaria and installed a Communist regime that, like the Ottomans, attempted to efface Bulgaria's Christian past.

Bulgaria was one of the most loyal satellite states under Soviet Communist hegemony. Nevertheless, on November 11, 1989, two days after the dramatic fall of the Berlin Wall, Todor Zhivkov, the Communist Party leader in Bulgaria for thirty-five years, was arrested and forced to resign. The nation installed a more democratic regime, opening the door not only for political reform but also for religious and social reawakening. The Communists had eliminated Bibles, but, as elsewhere in eastern Europe, a Christian tradition had survived to nurture a revival of faith. The Bulgarian Orthodox Church of the pre-Communist past reawakened, and many other religions from outside the country began to establish themselves in Bulgaria.

Deviating a little from the normal process seen elsewhere in the East, the first Church representatives into Bulgaria were not missionaries assigned to preach, but volunteers assigned to teach English. Because the ability to speak English is highly valued in much of the world, missionaries from the United States have often shared their language, as well as their faith, by teaching English classes. Indeed, English classes are currently taught in many missions. In Bulgaria, however, the primary purpose of the first Church representatives sent in 1990 was to teach English in Bulgarian schools. While teaching their language, these volunteers shared their beliefs and tapped a wellspring of curiosity in a nation long denied unfettered religious worship.

Bulgarian Officials and Church Leaders Get Acquainted

Elder Nelson and Elder Ringger visited Sofia in October 1988. Tsviatko Tsvetkov, of the Religious Affairs Ministry, was unimpressed. Through his interpreter he said, "Nelson? Ringger? Mormons? I've never heard of you." Elder Nelson replied, "That makes us even. We have never heard of you, either. It's time we got acquainted." They did,

Illus. 6-1. Church volunteers assigned to teach English worked in these Bulgarian cities in 1990.

but much was left undone. When the two returned to Sofia in February 1990, the government was no longer Communist and the reception was more cordial. Prior to meeting with government officials, Elder Nelson consulted with John Menzies, the Public Affairs Officer at the U.S. Consulate, and asked for advice on how to deal with the Bulgarians. Menzies suggested that Elder Nelson offer English instruction. The government was amenable to the idea, and Menzies set up an appointment for Elder Nelson to meet with the St. Cyril and Methodius Foundation, a cultural exchange organization that knew how to get instructors into the country. Fortuitously, Elder Nelson was also able to assist in arranging for cancer treatments for a Bulgarian government official, an effort that had a lasting impact.[1]

Elders Nelson and Ringger concluded their visit to Bulgaria in Sofia's Park of Liberty on February 13, 1990. They were accompanied by Baird King, a Church member then working at the U.S. embassy, his wife, Susan, and their children. There in the early morning, shrouded by fog and falling snow, Elder Nelson dedicated Bulgaria for the preaching of the gospel and left a blessing of hope that the nation would develop in peace—politically, economically, and socially.[2]

Missionaries Teach English in Bulgaria

Bulgaria's request for English teachers came back to Church headquarters in Salt Lake City and landed on Ross Ekins's desk, since he processed assignments for missionary couples. Around the same time, Morris and Annetta Mower, a retired couple who wanted to serve a mission, contacted Roy King, a former acquaintance and a director in the Missionary Department, to inquire about missionary opportunities. King referred the Mowers to Ekins. Since Morris held a doctorate in education and was a retired principal and Annetta was a nurse who had also worked as a schoolteacher, they expressed their willingness to accept a call to teach in Bulgaria if it were extended to them.[3] Coincidentally, the Mowers met Elder Nelson outside the Church Administration Building several weeks later. Learning of their call to Bulgaria, he asked them to visit his office, where he predicted that people would come to the Mowers seeking religious guidance. Then he told them they not only would teach English, but would also teach the gospel and baptize.[4]

Another couple, Delbert and Marilyn Fowler, was also called to serve in Bulgaria. Delbert had been a high school principal in Salt Lake City. Marilyn had taught one year of high school. Although they were not seeking a mission call when they had an interview with their stake president, they learned that their names had been suggested by George Brooks, a newly appointed mission president who had been the personnel manager of the Salt Lake City School District. The Fowlers accepted the call.[5]

A fifth English teacher, Judith Gubler, also accepted a call to Bulgaria. A schoolteacher from Provo, Utah, Sister Gubler had felt the desire to serve a mission even though she was older than the typical single missionary. After submitting her mission papers, she sought confirmation of her feelings while attending a temple session. The response was clear and unequivocal. She heard the words, "You are needed now." In her mind's eye she saw people who did not look American. Sister Gubler was confused when her mission call came and it was to North Carolina. However, she served there for only a week and half when the Missionary Department called, explaining her assignment was being changed to Bulgaria.[6]

President and Sister Neuenschwander met Sister Gubler in Vienna with a bouquet of flowers. The president told her the Church had been trying to establish the English instruction program all year but had encountered delays because of turmoil in the new government. Sister Gubler later met her missionary companion, Rose Marie Daigle, from Maine, who had been working as a companion to an older Church member in Finland.

When the Mowers and Fowlers arrived in Vienna, they met Sisters Gubler and Daigle. The group then flew to Sofia, arriving on September 12, 1990.[7] Representatives of the hosting organization, the St. Cyril and Methodius International Foundation, greeted them at the airport and transported them to their assignments. The single sisters went to Smolyan, site of the Bulgarian National School of Language, the Fowlers taught in a high school north of Sofia at Pravets, and the Mowers worked in Sofia.[8]

Sofia English Classes

The realization that they were in totally foreign circumstances sank in as the Mowers encountered their first challenges. The former residents of the apartment that had been secured in their behalf had not entirely moved out when the Mowers arrived. When they finally starting moving in, the lights went off. At the time, it was a common occurrence to have insufficient electrical power to service all customers twenty-four hours a day. Since it was already dark, the Mowers decided to dine out. They sat at a table for six, where, in the usual Bulgarian manner, four seats were already occupied. Since they knew no Bulgarian, they ordered by pointing and succeeded in securing a sour cheese dish, not something to which their palates were accustomed. They returned to the apartment before the lights came on, found stubby candles but no matches, and resigned themselves to an evening in the dark.[9]

Two interpreters from the Foundation took the Mowers on a city tour the next day. As they passed the U.S. embassy, Baird King emerged. He had been alerted to the Mowers' arrival by his parents, acquaintances of the Mowers. They were relieved to find someone to talk to in the foreign environment. King inquired, "Who told you what to bring?" Elder Mower answered, "No one." King responded, "This is going to be a hard winter." And it was. The food stores were empty. Food lines for cheese, bread, and eggs were long, the wait tedious, and the Mowers had no time to waste. Yet these circumstances soon became insignificant as they started teaching.

The Mowers could hardly have anticipated the conditions they encountered at the first class. The podium was a rickety platform. Students sat at grade school desks. The chalk was hard, and writing on the chalkboard was more difficult, in Elder Mower's words, than "writing on cement." Erasers did not exist, so they had to clear the board with a wet sponge or rag and then wait for it to dry. The classroom windows were broken, and the rooms had no heat. Moreover, the Mowers had to provide their own texts. The students were mostly young adults at the graduate level preparing for the Graduate Record Examination that, if passed, would permit them to study abroad. The class met under these conditions three hours a day for two weeks. When the weather turned colder, Elder Mower decided to move the class to his apartment where accommodations were slightly better.[10]

Sister Mower started teaching separately during the second week, doubling their teaching capacity. They taught several different classes a day, sometimes in rotation with Bulgarian teachers of English. The classes lasted for two, four, or six weeks and were held evenings as well as days. The Mowers learned where they would teach only a week before each class began. Depending on the location and the weather, they either walked to class or used public transportation. Sister Mower even taught one class in an army installation. The couple rendered their service gratis. It was particularly inspirational to them that, in spite of not knowing the language, they were always able to make appointments, deal with the customs, and run into people they needed to contact. Each felt divine assistance constantly, even in small matters.[11]

Elder Mower stumbled upon another way to help their students. When he unpacked, he discovered five boxes of personal checks and no neckties. He remembered having intended to pack the ties and not the checks, not expecting to need them in Bulgaria. Then he learned the English testing service at the U.S. embassy did not accept payment in Bulgarian currency. U.S. dollars could not be bought in Bulgaria at the time, but the testing service would accept U.S. checks. As a service to his students, Elder Mower paid for their tests, and they returned the payment to him in Bulgarian money at the official rate of exchange. Before U.S. dollars became available to Bulgarians, he went through four boxes of checks.[12]

Whatever their success in teaching English, the teachers' efforts to establish the Church flourished. Four members lived in Bulgaria when the English teachers arrived: Dr. Kafeero G. Williams, from Uganda, baptized in London and attending medical school in Sofia; Ivan Miranov, baptized in Hungary and married to a Bulgarian; Gabor Todorov, baptized while attending school in Switzerland; and Snegina Filipova, baptized in France.[13] When the Mowers' assignment concluded in March 1992, they left a Church membership of several hundred and a mission with the third-highest baptismal rate in Europe.[14]

The Mowers exerted a religious influence through their English instruction. Because no restriction was placed on the subject of their classes, they incorporated Church literature into their lessons. Due to the long absence of religion from Bulgarian culture, discussion of religion piqued the students' interest.

President Neuenschwander visited Sofia the weekend after the first English class. He proposed holding a fireside, and the Mowers invited their students. Twenty came. President Neuenschwander, who had earned a doctorate, described graduate school and then taught from the scriptures. The students' reactions were mixed. In the following week, one said the Joseph Smith story sounded like a fantasy, while another, Mirella Lazarova, asked to learn more.[15]

On October 7, 1990, the Mowers held a church service in their apartment and invited their students. Twenty-three came to this meeting. Mirella interpreted for Sister Mower and Kafeero Williams for Elder Mower. In later church meetings, students from the English classes taught lessons even though they were not yet members. Within a month, fifty-four attended a Latter-day Saint Church service, leaving standing room only.

The Mowers also made contacts wherever they were, such as when they waited in food lines. When a woman, excited to speak English, helped them understand the price of bread, the Mowers invited her to

Illus. 6-2. Elders Garner, Elggren, and Kuta, President Neuenschwander, and Elder Warner on their first day in Bulgaria, November 14, 1990.

attend church. She later served as a pianist and a chorister. In another food line, the Mowers met a woman who accepted their invitation to go to church, and she even brought her granddaughter. At the time, the child's mother was in Italy, where she ended up joining the Church. Likewise, the grandmother was baptized, and she become one of the first Relief Society teachers and a translator of lesson material.

On November 14, 1990, four proselytizing missionaries arrived in Bulgaria (illus. 6-2).[16] Ten days later, six converts were baptized in the first Bulgarian baptismal service (illus. 6-3). Among these were Mirella Lazarova and her husband, Ventsislav. Ventsislav was later called as one of the first native branch presidents, and Mirella as the first native Relief Society president.

The Mowers coordinated their efforts with the proselytizing missionaries. They arranged for the missionaries to attend the English classes, adding a new dimension to the lessons. One missionary, for instance, told the students about his experiences rock climbing, rappelling, and camping in America.[17]

Food was scarce during the first winter. Living in Sofia, the Mowers did not know what they would be able to buy or when they could buy it. Yet in Elder Mower's words, "We were fed by the ravens." Victor Coy, an American of Bulgarian descent, who was a Church member, came

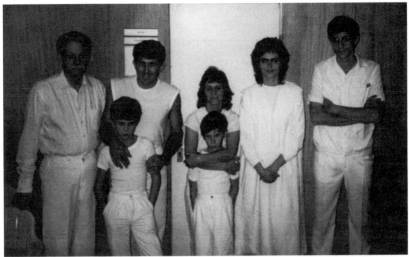

Courtesy Morris and Annetta Mower

Illus. 6-3. Morris Mower, on the far left, with the Khristov family (*middle*), and Mirella and Ventsislav Lazarov, the first Bulgarian converts, November 24, 1990.

to visit his cousins during Christmas. He brought food and shared it with the missionaries. He even went to Greece and returned with food. Baird King also delivered food from Greece, and President Neuenschwander brought food from Vienna. Still, the Mowers were down to a few onions, potatoes, and some dried milk in late February 1991 when John Dinkelman, an embassy employee in Beograd, and four missionaries from Yugoslavia drove through a snowstorm to bring in a vanload of food. In spite of the "ravens," Elder Mower lost thirty pounds during the first winter.[18]

Pravets and Smolyan English Classes

The food situation was not as dire in Pravets, where the Fowlers taught at an elite boarding school. There they could eat at least one meal a day with the students. But they faced challenges, too. Whisked away upon arrival, the Fowlers found themselves isolated in a small village, totally unlike the area where they had lived in Utah. However, they had little time to ponder their fate, for they immediately immersed themselves in teaching English. They found some comfort in the fact they could converse with four Bulgarian English teachers at the school.[19]

The school taught computer use to approximately eleven hundred students who had qualified to attend by achieving high entry-test scores.

A computer company stood adjacent to the school, and some students were employed part-time in computer manufacturing.

Elder Fowler taught third- and fourth-year English language students, while his wife taught second-year students. In contrast to most U.S. schools, the teachers, rather than the students, went from class to class. This caused considerable hardship for the older couple, who had to lug their materials up and down stairs. Unlike the Mowers, the Fowlers did not teach gratis because their salary would have been dropped from the school's budget if they had not accepted the money. However, they used the money to buy hard-to-obtain supplies, such as tape, and gave them to the school. The Fowlers had the same chalk problem as the Mowers, but they solved the problem by shipping in good chalk from Utah.

The main disadvantage for the Fowlers was their isolation. They traveled to Sofia at least monthly to, in Elder Fowler's words, "recover their sanity" and to assist with Church services. In Pravets they had only each other. They were told not to teach the gospel to the students unless the parents were present. Since the parents lived elsewhere, the Fowlers were not able to proselytize. They had served in Pravets for seven months when, in March 1991, they were temporarily transferred to Vienna. There they learned how to manage a mission office and then returned to Sofia in June 1991 to establish and run the mission office of the newly created Bulgaria Sofia Mission.

In Smolyan, Sisters Gubler and Daigle also fared well in a boarding school where food was available. Smolyan was located on the southern border of Bulgaria, about six hours by bus from Sofia. The sisters taught in the Ivan Vasov Language School, which included students in grades two through high school who were taught primarily German and English. The language school where the sisters taught was also an elite school, accepting annually only about fifty out of two thousand applicants. They, like the Fowlers, accepted salaries to preserve the school's budget and returned the money to the school by donating supplies. They expanded their students' cultural experiences by importing bats, mitts, and balls from Utah and teaching them how to play baseball.[20]

Sister Gubler did not leave religion out of the classroom. She may have been the first person to teach the Bible as literature in a public school in Bulgaria since the advent of Communism, but she did it at the insistence of the students. When the students invited her to meet their families, who lived out of town, Sister Gubler explained that on Sunday she needed to study the Bible as well as hold church services with Sister Daigle. The students were shocked to learn she had a Bible. One boy said, "When they come to take you away, you call me and I will protect you." They asked to come to her services, and, on the first Sunday, fourteen students showed up at the teachers' apartment.

When school officials learned of her weekend activities, they summoned her to explain. She offered the defense that the students had asked to come and that it did little good to tell teenagers what they could not do. The officials decided that if the students were that curious, they would allow her to teach the Bible in school where they could observe. They had only one qualification: that she teach the Bible without a religious emphasis. She said that was impossible. The school officials then suggested the subject not be brought to their attention again, so the discussion stopped, and the classes continued.

Along with English classes, the sisters taught other subjects in the evenings: culture one night a week, music another, and the Bible yet another. They continued to hold meetings on Sunday, and the number that attended grew. When twenty students came regularly, they started looking for another place to hold meetings. Assistance came from a dentist, who arranged for the group to meet in the dental clinic's library. Eventually, school officials let them meet on school premises in the music room so they could have a piano. When German-speaking missionaries arrived later, the group held services in three languages, and students interpreted between Bulgarian, German, and English. When the group reached forty-five people, Church officials authorized them to rent a facility in a youth center.

Young Missionaries Proselytize in Bulgaria

Similar to missionaries in Russia and Czechoslovakia, the first four missionaries sent to Bulgaria were serving elsewhere when the assignment came. Elders David Garner and Trent Warner were already part of the Austria Vienna East Mission but had served in the neighboring country of Yugoslavia. Elders Christian Elggren and Timothy Kuta came from Germany, where they had been more immersed in teaching discussions, unlike the missionaries from Yugoslavia. They had a mix of skills to prepare the way for a much larger contingent of missionaries to follow.[21]

The foursome entered Bulgaria on student visas because the Church did not yet have legal status in the country.[22] They were hosted by the St. Cyril and Methodius Foundation as an extension of the agreement that had brought in the English teachers. The foundation arranged for quarters and assigned them to two Bulgarian instructors—women who spoke neither English nor German. Their textbooks were entirely in Bulgarian, and bilingual dictionaries were scarce and had to be shared. Because Serbo-Croatian is related to Bulgarian, the two Yugoslav missionaries had a rudimentary ability to communicate.[23] For two months, the missionaries attended language classes six hours a day, four days a week.[24] In the evenings, they taught gospel discussions to students from the Mowers' English classes or to Bulgarians who had encountered the Church while traveling abroad. Until they obtained some mastery of the new language, the missionaries taught in a mixture of English, German, and Serbo-Croatian.[25]

The missionaries worked in a grim world of stark, drably decorated architecture and polluted air. People wore dark clothes and hunkered in seemingly endless food lines. The entire stock of Sofia's central department store consisted of some tools and blue work clothes.[26] Eating establishments offered a single entree to the few who could pay. One had to get up early and stand in long lines to buy meat. For one hour of three, the electricity went out.[27] But for Elder Elggren the shock, the gloom, and the sadness dissipated as he became involved with the people.[28] The missionaries quickly discovered Bulgarian hospitality. On her own volition, the coordinator of the Bulgarian classes stood in line for two hours to buy the missionaries some bologna.[29] Although food was in short supply, the people they visited always fed them, even when the missionaries requested they not do so.[30]

Originally, the missionaries were to provide humanitarian service after they had become proficient in the language, but at the end of their training the service was not requested. Since they were there, they continued to teach. They did not proselytize in public; there was no tracting door-to-door, no street contacting with displays, and no attempts to reach contacts through the media. Nor did they wear name tags.[31] Still, they taught a constant flow of people as interest rippled through the English language students to their relatives and friends. The Bulgarians were curious about the missionaries from America, and for some the spiritual message the missionaries presented brought hope for a better future.

The missionaries found many opportunities to converse with people in public. On the bus, a missionary might ask a person, "Do you mind if I talk with you? I am learning the language." Inevitably the conversation led to religion. One couple, desiring to learn more, invited the missionaries straight off the bus into their home.[32]

Interest in religion ran high, and the missionaries had full teaching schedules. On December 8, 1990, Elder Elggren reported in his journal that there were thirty-five investigators at church. He lamented that "with our [language] class, we don't have enough time to teach them all." On January 12, 1991, President Neuenschwander spoke to more than two hundred people at a fireside. Elder Mower introduced each missionary and invited people to ask them questions. By January 27, there were eighty-five people at church, although membership rolls listed only fifteen (illus. 6-4). On February 9, six more Bulgarians were baptized. Elder Elggren commented in his journal, "I have no doubt in my mind that these people were prepared to begin the work here and to be the future leaders. The level of spiritual sensitivity is awesome. What a great blessing it is to be a messenger of the true gospel in this choice land with these people." The following month, Elder Elggren wrote, "We have over 200 referrals to look up and this weekend Pres. Ringger of the Quorum of Seventy is coming down to speak at the [National] Palace of Culture to (get this) get us more contacts! . . . It's called adding injury to pain. We can't do all."[33]

Additional referrals came in with the visit of the Lamanite Generation, a Brigham Young University performing group, in June 1991. Since ticket sales were sluggish, the Mowers bought a thousand tickets and

Courtesy Chris Elggren

Illus. 6-4. Elder Dennis B. Neuenschwander amid missionaries in Bulgaria outside the meeting place at P. Parchevich, no. 49, in Sofia, c. 1991.

gave them to former students, missionaries, neighbors, and people they had met in the customs department, the post office, the airport or anywhere else. They finally generated an audience of two thousand. The sisters in Smolyan supported the group's production in Plovdiv.[34] The performances provided another dimension of the Church as more than a Sunday affair and generated many investigators.[35] Among the baptisms resulting from the group's visit was Liubomir Traikov, who later became the first Bulgarian to serve as a missionary for the Church.[36]

The Kiriakov Family Escapes Bulgaria and Joins the Church

The first group of missionaries called specifically to Bulgaria arrived for language training at the Missionary Training Center in Provo, Utah, on February 13, 1991, the first anniversary of the dedicatory prayer pronounced by President Nelson in the Park of Liberty.[37] Julia Kiriakov Caswell, a native Bulgarian, greeted the new missionaries at the Missionary Training Center. The ability to speak Bulgarian was a rare skill in the Church, and Sister Caswell had accepted an invitation to move from Virginia to Provo for the purpose of teaching her native tongue.[38]

In 1963 the Kiriakov family—parents Kiril and Nevenka and children Julia and Peter—lived in Sofia. Kiril worked as a dental technician. One day he learned that a post in Algeria was available, so he applied. The other people in his section applied because with it went the promise of seeing the world outside the Communist realm. To avoid conflict in determining who should go, the seven colleagues decided to draw slips of paper, six marked "no" and one marked "yes," out of a hat. Because Kiril was a junior colleague, the others protested when he drew the winning paper. They drew a second time, and again Kiril drew the "yes." Believing the repeat was a coincidence, the group demanded a third draw. A fourth draw had the same result. Kiril was blindfolded for the fifth draw. On the sixth, someone else drew for him. And on the seventh, Kiril drew last. Each time he ended up with the "yes" slip. The group sadly abided by their agreement.[39]

After completing two years in Algeria, Kiril applied for a visa to vacation in France. His unspoken intent was to flee. The Bulgarian embassy granted him a visa but did not grant visas to his family. Julia offered a solution. She had been taught to forge signatures in school as part of the training offered Bulgarian children in anticipation of them defrauding their foes in the West. She forged the words "and family" after the father's name. Fortuitously, the scheduled departure was during a time of political turmoil, and, in a state of public confusion, the authorities granted the whole family visas. They escaped to France. Eventually, the Bulgarian intelligence network located them and threatened Kiril with death and his family with life imprisonment if they did not return. After the family had moved around France for a year, Mormon missionaries knocked on their door. The family was baptized in July 1966. In time, Julia received a scholarship to Brigham Young University, and in 1969 the Kiriakovs immigrated to the United States. While living in Virginia, Julia obtained a broadcasting job for the Voice of America in Washington, D.C. When Todor Zhivkov was deposed in November 1989, it was Julia who broadcast the information to the world.

Kiril knew that one day he would preach the gospel to his relatives because of a blessing he received from a Church patriarch.[40] The prospect of returning to face a death sentence was not enticing, but when the call came, he accepted. Two days before receiving a call to serve as the Bulgarian mission president, he lay in a hospital bed with a gangrenous leg. The surgeon intended to amputate it, but Kiril refused the operation, requesting a priesthood blessing instead. The next morning he walked out of the hospital on a sound leg. While Julia taught Bulgarian to the missionaries in Provo, her father prepared to serve as the mission president in Bulgaria.

Transition to the Bulgaria Sofia Mission

Because of legal considerations, the Church entered Bulgaria not as a religion but as an association. In January 1991, Elder Mower began the process, filing and refiling the necessary papers to resolve the government's questions and objections to its request for recognition. Church members in Bulgaria had submitted a petition for recognition in April 1991. The St. Cyril and Methodius Foundation leaders also used their influence in the Church's behalf and had a critical impact on the final recognition, which was granted July 10, 1991, just after President Kiriakov's arrival.[41]

President Kiriakov served only six months before being released because of poor health. On his way to Bulgaria, he had slipped in a Zurich hotel bathtub and broken two ribs, though the extent of injury remained unknown till he arrived in Bulgaria. This and other medical problems led to his release in January 1992. Still, his blessing had been fulfilled.[42]

Elder Mower, one of the senior missionaries in Bulgaria, served as acting mission president during February 1992.[43] In March, Dale Warner, the permanent replacement, arrived with his wife, Renée. President Warner had been a Russian teacher and educational administrator.

Sister Warner had taught geography and history. Incidentally, Dale had been Dennis Neuenschwander's first Russian teacher.[44]

In 1990 the Warners had been initially considered to serve as English teachers in Bulgaria, but Elder Nelson changed the assignment when he learned of Brother Warner's Russian language skill. The Warners were the first missionaries called to the Finland Helsinki East Mission, serving as the office couple who supported the first young missionaries entering Russia. The Warners had been home only two days from their mission when they received a call from Elder Oaks, asking them to visit him in Salt Lake City. The Warners assumed he wanted a report on their service. Instead, Elder Oaks called them to serve in the land to which they had nearly been called two years previously. President Warner entered Bulgaria in March 1992, with the administrative skills needed to organize inexperienced members and young missionaries into a united, functioning whole.[45]

The English contract with the St. Cyril and Methodius Foundation expired in 1992 and was renewed for two more years. Afterward, the mission began to sponsor its own English classes. The Church also provided school supplies, giving the school in Smolyan forty thousand English books in 1994.[46] After returning home, the Fowlers stayed in touch with the school in Pravets and in 1994 were still sending it supplies.[47]

Of the original six English teachers, the Mowers were the last to leave, doing so in March 1992.[48] President Warner altered the English program by phasing out full-time English teachers and assigning proselytizing missionaries to teach faculty and staff at schools and hospitals. He always taught the first English class to determine the level at which the class could be taught and then assigned missionaries to continue the instruction.[49] The program's impact continued into the future for those who learned not only English but something of even greater worth.

Initial Missionary Activity in Ukraine

Ukraine is mostly a flat plain that stretches along the southern flank of Belarus and Russia (illus. 6-5). The country's peasant soldiers were hired by Poland and Russia in the sixteenth and seventeenth centuries to protect them from Tatar invaders. The term *Ukraine* is a Slavic word meaning borderland. The Cossacks formed self-governing communities based on democratic principles. The word *Cossack* is of Turkic origin and means free person. Polish and Lithuanian rulers held sway over the area until the mid-1700s when the Russian Empire assimilated it. With a population of fifty-two million, Ukraine is the second most populated

Illus. 6-5. Ukrainian cities where Mormon missionaries labored, 1990–92.

country in eastern Europe. Subordinate to Russia and then Soviet hegemony until the fall of Communism, its Cossack heritage still provided a separate identity.

In late November 1989, President Neuenschwander visited Kiev, the capital city, attempting to contact two people who had requested information about the Church. He was accompanied by Lynn Carson, a Church employee responsible for negotiating the microfilming of eastern European genealogical records. Missionaries had not yet crossed the Soviet border, and the possibility of them successfully entering that realm remained doubtful. Neuenschwander and Carson visited the churches in the city and found them resurgent in the new environment of political and religious freedom. At the hotel room, President Neuenschwander gazed out the window contemplatively and after a while stated simply and conclusively, "I can see missionaries here."[50] He returned a year later on October 7, 1990, with Elders Ivan Stratov of Melbourne, Australia, and Brian Bradbury of Seattle, Washington, both transferred from the Finland Helsinki East Mission. They arrived with a list of Ukrainian referrals and made enough contacts to gather seventeen people for an evening meeting at the Writers' Union Hall in early October.[51]

October 1990 was momentous for Ukraine. Political liberty was being contested on the streets, and religious liberty hung in the balance. During the month, thousands of students and then workers of Kiev fought against Communist Party attempts to squelch a Ukrainian nationalist opposition group known as *Rukh* (Hand). Even as the first Latter-day Saint Church service was held, demonstrations raged in Parliament mere blocks away.[52]

Regardless of the distracting turmoil, the future Church leaders in Ukraine were converted before the close of the first year. Among the six who were baptized in Kiev before the end of 1990 were Valery Stavichenko, the first branch president; Aleksei Roms, the first Ukrainian missionary; and Aleksandr Manzhos, future mission president and the first national representative of the Church to the Ukrainian government.[53]

The missionary corps grew by two more on December 10 with the arrival of Gregory Christensen of Washington, D.C., and Nathan Coulter of Sandy, Utah. During 1991 the total number of missionaries increased to twenty-five.[54] Among the young missionaries was Elder Scott Suggs, who had taken Russian in high school because he had wanted to be a Russian missionary some day. Sister missionaries also arrived that first year: Melanie Gamble from the U.S. and Minna Vähänikkilä from

Finland.[55] A missionary couple, Charles and Susan Creel from Nevada, came in June.[56]

Missionaries had to go to Vienna every month for visas. At the same time, President Neuenschwander interviewed them on their work progress. In summer 1991, Ukrainian officials began issuing six-month visas. Initially living in expensive hotels, the missionaries eventually migrated into apartments with monthly rents costing half of one day's hotel stay.[57] As was true throughout eastern Europe, the young missionaries encountered living conditions and customs completely different from any they had previously encountered. One missionary assessed the situation:

> The apartments here are very small and I can't believe people actually live in them. But the people are nice. They feed you every time you go to their house and they make you eat it. Borscht is pretty good but when they give you this milk that has lumps in it and has been sitting on the shelf for about 6 weeks, I advise you not to drink it.[58]

The missionaries were led by Ivan Stratov, who served as the zone leader. A few years older than the average missionary, he had completed a doctorate in medicine, minus the practicum and residency, prior to his mission. His father had been raised in Novorossiysk (just beyond the eastern border of Ukraine). Captured by the Germans in 1943 and unable to return home after the war, Ivan's father had emigrated to Australia. Ivan was tall with a pleasing personality and an excellent command of the Russian language.[59]

Ukrainians quickly responded to the young missionaries' message. By June there were forty members and a regular meeting attendance of about a hundred.[60] The first Ukrainian branch was organized in Kiev on June 9, 1991.[61]

During 1991 the Church began dismantling the Austria Vienna East Mission. On May 1, 1991, Yugoslavia was transferred to the Austria Vienna Mission; on June 1, 1991, Romania was transferred to the Hungary Budapest Mission; and on July 1, 1991, Bulgaria became a separate mission, leaving only Ukraine in the Austria Vienna East Mission. Elder Neuenschwander was sustained as a member of the Second Quorum of the Seventy in April Conference. In July he began serving as a counselor in the Europe Area Presidency, continuing to supervise the work in the East under the direction of Area President Hans Ringger. He turned over the reins of the Austria Vienna East Mission to Howard Biddulph.

"The Standard of Truth" Is Erected in Ukraine

Even though Howard Biddulph worked as a political science professor at the University of Victoria in Canada at the time of his appointment, he had a connection to Ukraine going back three decades. As a political science graduate student at Indiana University in 1961, he participated in a study group that took a river boat down the southern stretch of the Volga to the city of Rostov. As they approached a small settlement upstream from Rostov, Brother Biddulph studied the streets of a dreary village, not unlike countless others in southern Russia. Suddenly he thought he saw the future when missionaries walked those streets and congregations grew up in that village and the vicinity. Brother Biddulph learned that the village was named Aksai and recorded his experience in his journal on August 13, 1961. He later learned that the Soviets began that very day to erect a wall in Berlin, Germany, symbolizing Communist isolation from the West.[62]

The Soviet Union had intrigued President Biddulph since his youth. His patriarchal blessing also hinted at his future involvement there. This knowledge influenced his career choice as a political science professor specializing in the Soviet Union. On a visit there in 1990, he learned of the missionary work in St. Petersburg and Moscow. Howard visited the branch in St. Petersburg and was invited by the branch president, Yuri Terebenin, to speak in a sacrament meeting. Witnessing the advent of the gospel in the Soviet Union touched his emotions deeply. He returned home and confided to his wife, Colleen, his desire to serve a mission there. Anticipating this possibility, she began studying Russian. The Biddulphs received an opportunity to serve there, and on June 27, 1991, they arrived in Vienna to supervise Ukraine from afar.[63]

President Biddulph was visiting the missionaries in Kiev in August when a coup was attempted against the Soviet leader Mikhail Gorbachev. He listened to the radio announcement that all political gatherings were banned and Gorbachev's human rights enactments suspended. Cut off from the outside world, President Biddulph gathered with the missionaries to assess their situation. He discovered that Kiev was surrounded by Soviet troops who might advance at any moment. Opening his scriptures to address the missionaries, his eyes fell on Doctrine and Covenants 35:24–27, which concluded with the phrase, "Fear not, little flock, the kingdom is yours until I come." Through inspiration, President Biddulph realized that the crisis would pass, that they need not fear, and that they should stay in the country. He watched the Ukrainian flag flying outside his window, thinking they were safe as long as it continued to fly.

He knew the coup had failed on the third day when he heard an old man shouting outside his window: "Thanks be to God; we are free!"[64]

The missionaries assembled again in fasting and thanksgiving. Elder Stratov stood and, with no pretension or melodrama, cited from memory Joseph Smith's words written a century and a half earlier:

> The Standard of Truth has been erected; no unhallowed hand can stop the work from progressing; persecutions may rage, mobs may combine, armies may assemble, calumny may defame, but the truth of God will go forth boldly, nobly, and independent, till it has penetrated every continent, visited every clime, swept every country, and sounded in every ear, till the purposes of God shall be accomplished, and the Great Jehovah shall say the work is done.[65]

Elder Packer Dedicates Ukraine for Missionary Work

After Ukraine declared itself independent from Russia, it initiated the process of establishing a new political system. President Biddulph feared the new bureaucracy might not legally recognize the Church before the scheduled visit of an Apostle to dedicate the new country for missionary work in September. The application had been submitted prior to Biddulph's arrival by the members in Kiev. Viktor Cherinko, a deputy of the city council, visited the fast and testimony meeting in September. Cherinko's impression was positive and his influence sufficient to get the council to pass a bill granting recognition in Kiev on September 9, two days before the arrival of Elder Boyd K. Packer, Elder Dallin H. Oaks, and Elder Dennis Neuenschwander.[66]

In the early morning hours of September 12, 1991, a group of forty Church leaders, members, missionaries, and investigators gathered at a Kiev park overlooking the Dnieper River. Standing at the base of the statue of Prince Volodymyr, the fabled ruler who brought Christianity to the Kievan Rus, the group listened as Elder Packer dedicated Ukraine for the preaching of the gospel. He said that tens of thousands would join the Church in the future. He also spoke the words of an early Apostle, Parley P. Pratt: "The morning breaks, the shadows flee; Lo, Zion's standard is unfurled! The dawning of a brighter day; Majestic rises on the world." At the conclusion of his prayer, the clouds briefly parted, and streaming light shone over the Dnieper River and the city of Kiev. It seemed that the elements themselves had announced the gospel morning in Ukraine. After the dedication, the Apostles watched as Ukrainian workmen began to dismantle a sixty-foot statue of Lenin on the main square in Kiev.[67]

That day the visiting authorities held a zone conference for the eighteen missionaries and later a public meeting at the House of Artists on Lviv Square. A total of 475 attended, only 75 of them members.[68] After the authorities departed, the missionaries' work load increased dramatically. In November, one missionary wrote home, "We had 10 baptisms last week and expect to have the same this week."[69] That month membership reached 140 with 250 attending Sabbath meetings.[70]

Mission Leaders Explore Eastward

Church leaders knew little about eastern Ukraine and southern Russia, countries which had long been unfriendly to Western visitors. Like President Arthur Gaeth in Czechoslovakia half a century earlier, President Biddulph toured the unknown area. Commissioned by the Area Presidency, he and Elder Stratov visited scattered members who had been baptized elsewhere, contacted new referrals, held meetings for investigators, and determined the prospects for future missionary work. They sought information on food availability, languages spoken, economic conditions, politics, and religious activity. They successfully negotiated through the inadequate public transportation, receiving unexpected assistance at almost every juncture.[71]

On November 20, 1991, President Biddulph and Elder Stratov departed by rail for Dnepropetrovsk, Zaporozhe, Donetsk, Lugansk, and Rostov. In Dnepropetrovsk they met a friend of a Kiev member who dropped everything to guide them through a successful fourteen-hour day on trams and buses. Through the member's friend, President Biddulph and Elder Stratov met a university student who arranged for a meeting with ten students and faculty. Everyone in the group signed their names on a list to have the missionaries teach them later.

South of Zaporozhe, President Biddulph and Elder Stratov visited the collective farm of Vasylivka. This was the home of Dina Ivanovna Shakhovskaya, who had written to President Biddulph every month since his arrival. She had heard of the gospel through a man in Estonia. President Biddulph had previously mailed her copies of the Book of Mormon and some Gospel Principles manuals. Dina had convened weekly meetings on the Sabbath for a group of thirty-one relatives and friends to study the Bible and Church literature. The jovial peasant woman, flanked by three adult sons, their wives, a married daughter, and several grandchildren, warmly greeted the visitors.

For three hours, President Biddulph and Elder Stratov answered the well-conceived questions of seventeen inquirers. The peasants had notebooks filled with doctrinal questions for which they wanted answers: How do we know Jesus is Jehovah? How is baptism for the dead performed? Where is it taught that Lucifer was once the brother of Christ? When one of the sons disputed a point, Dina said, "Don't argue; that will only waste time. They are messengers of God bringing us the gospel and we want to hear as much as there is time to receive."

Following the session, the group feasted on a huge meal. Afterward, the family gave the president their tithing, which by then equaled several months wages for a collective farm family. Paying their tithing was something they wished to do even though they were not yet members. President Biddulph wrote, "I'll never forget the scene as we drove away: Dina Ivanovna, her family, her friends, beaming, waving, crying; small children reaching outward as if saying goodbye to a prophet. . . . Even the dogs stood at attention."

In the nearby village of Marganets, the president and missionary visited cousins of Elder Stratov's father, who during the war had fled from Novorossiysk in Russia (at the east end of the Black Sea). It was a poignant experience for Stratov to become acquainted with relatives he had never met.

In Donetsk, President Biddulph and Elder Stratov were hosted by members of the Donbas Ukrainian Dancers Ensemble, which had performed at Ricks College in Rexburg, Idaho, several years earlier. Having been befriended by Church members during their tour, they sought to return the favor of their hosts. They also expressed an interest in the gospel. Before President Biddulph and Elder Stratov left the city, the missionaries had a list of twenty people from the group who wanted to learn more and a total of twenty-eight in Donetsk. Later, the missionaries contacted a Baptist pastor, Ivan Medvedev, a referral from a Church member in Rexburg. Medvedev invited them to attend a council of elders that was in progress. They also attended a Sunday evening prayer service at the Baptist church and were even given seats of honor. President Biddulph met with Medvedev the following day and found they shared much common ground in rejoicing for the religious freedom in Ukraine. They prayed, and at the end of the prayer Medvedev put his arms around Biddulph and kissed him on each cheek, a truly Russian gesture. That night, President Biddulph dreamed of a future Church stake in Donetsk. Within two years, the city experienced significant membership growth and became the headquarters for a second Ukrainian mission.[72]

Arriving in Rostov, the president and elder visited Aksai, the village Biddulph had seen from the river boat three decades earlier while visiting Russia as a student. He now stood on the wharf looking toward the river, partially fulfilling the vision of that long-remembered day. Rostov later became the headquarters for a Russian mission.[73] The two travelers returned to Kiev to greet four new missionaries brought by Sister Biddulph from Vienna. Then, on December 1, President Biddulph and Elder Stratov left again, flying to Sochi on the eastern shore of the Black Sea.

A small congregation of seven Church members had come into being through the efforts of Vladimir Fyodorov, baptized in St. Petersburg in 1990. The congregation awaited the day when missionaries would come to stay and help them establish the Church more fully.[74] President Biddulph and Elder Stratov continued on their journey to Krasnodar and Gelendzhik. They visited Krasnodar twice during their excursion. On the first visit, they met a Peruvian Church member, Jesus Condori, who was studying agronomy at the Kuban State Agricultural University. Brother Condori agreed to arrange a group meeting for students to hear the missionaries upon their return. That evening, Biddulph and Stratov visited Galina Ostroikh, a high school principal, who had been to Salt Lake City and Temple Square. Not notified of their pending arrival, she confided:

> Last night I had a dream that indicated that two important strangers would be knocking on my door with something vital for me. I realize the value of your Church and would be your greatest proselyter in this city, but I am personally an atheist. Yet, maybe I should review that position after my dream. Certainly something supernatural prompted me of your coming.

The following day, they needed to find a taxi for a three-hour trip to Gelendzhik, south of Krasnodar. No taxi would take them because of the distance. While they were examining their alternatives, an old Ford van stopped in front of them. The driver was a Russian named Valery, but he was dressed in the garb of Crocodile Dundee, including a close replica of the character's hat. He asked where they were from and where they needed to go. When Stratov said Australia, he exclaimed, "Get in!" Valery had worked as a miner in Australia for several years and was excited to tell Elder Stratov of his many exploits. While Elder Stratov was given the front seat, the president sat on a three-legged stool in the back of the van. This proved to be a difficult circumstance as "Crocodile" Valery sped along the tortuous mountain route to Gelendzhik. The stool bounced on the van's floor, causing the president to hang on as best he could to Stratov's seat. When the van stopped abruptly, the president's momentum carried him into the back of Stratov's seat, sliding it and the missionary into the dashboard. The van stalled at the top of a pass during the middle of a blizzard. When Valery determined that he had only run out of gas, he filled the tank from a spare can and exclaimed, "I wouldn't have known how to fix anything anyway."

In Gelendzhik, President Biddulph and Elder Stratov met with Aleksei Kolomysev, who had been baptized in Moscow. They taught five of Kolomysev's friends, and one was ready for baptism. Early on December 4, Elder Stratov entered the Black Sea, breaking though a thin sheet of ice, and baptized Olga Shaganova. The missionaries then departed for Novorossiysk, ancestral residence of the Stratov family, where Ivan could meet his relatives and represent the Church. The two travelers returned to Krasnodar by dark and arrived in time to teach Brother Condori's student gathering. Eighteen of those in attendance requested missionary lessons when possible.

On December 5, President Biddulph and Elder Stratov addressed several groups of students and faculty at Galina Ostroikh's high school. She introduced them saying, "This Church is the answer to the moral crisis left by Communism's collapse." Fourteen students and seven faculty signed their names to receive future instruction.

After two weeks, the travelers returned to Kiev and held a baptismal service for twelve, eight of them having been taught previously by Elder Stratov. President Biddulph asked the missionary in passing how many he had baptized during his mission. Elder Stratov demurred, but the president persisted. He learned that the missionary had privately committed with the Lord to baptize a soul for each week of his mission and that night, his last day of service, he had achieved this goal.

In late December 1991 and early January 1992, President Biddulph and Elder Brian Bradbury (the other missionary to open Ukraine with Ivan Stratov) visited the cities of southern Ukraine and Crimea, gathering information needed for future Church activity in those areas.[75] The baptismal rate began to soar during the new year, and even severe winter weather did not stop people from receiving the ordinance. At 8:00 A.M. on January 1, 1992, Elder Suggs baptized three people in the Dnieper River, despite the four inches of ice that had to be broken before the baptism could proceed. The candidates had prepared for the baptism by taking cold showers for days in advance. The baptismal service was brief and people returned to their apartments quickly for warmth.[76] Personal discomfort did not dissuade those who were ready to make the baptismal covenant.

The Austria Vienna East Mission was discontinued in February 1992. The name was changed to the Ukraine Kiev Mission, since Ukraine was the only country remaining after the other eastern European missions had been created in 1991.[77] The Biddulphs moved from Vienna to Kiev in March 1992 to establish both a residence and a mission office in a four-room apartment, spacious by Ukrainian standards.[78] The mission that had operated beyond the borders of the Communist world now resided in its heart.

Humanitarian Service Missionaries in Belarus

Belarus has always been a rural area, dependent on Russia for its political and economic needs. Situated between Poland and Russia, the country has been culturally and religiously tied to this eastern neighbor. Though it became independent along with the other republics of the former Soviet Union, Belarus remained closely aligned with its long-term benefactor. Its 10.4 million inhabitants make it equal in size to Hungary.

Anatoly Neverov lived in Minsk, the capital of Belarus. He was interested in religion and was an active member of a Protestant evangelical group. As a graduate of the Institute of Foreign Languages in Minsk, he spoke English well. Anatoly corresponded with President Biddulph to learn about the Church. His interest was sincere, his questions deep and probing. When President Biddulph learned the Church would send a humanitarian service couple (the nature of this calling will be discussed in chapter 7) into Belarus, he remembered his faithful correspondent in Minsk. Acquainted with the Church only by correspondence, Anatoly met Karl and Hanna Borcherding from Germany at the Minsk airport in January 1993 and became their welcome assistant. He found them an apartment, took them shopping regularly, acquainted them with the city transportation system, and introduced them to many of his friends. He also helped arrange for visas since he worked in the travel industry. Anatoly and the Borcherdings spoke English to one another, and Anatoly translated for the couple daily as they dealt with everyone from the ordinary person on the street to prominent government officials. In March 1993, the Borcherdings were joined by four young missionaries: Matt Ericson, Cody Hill, Daniel Reneau, and Liubomir Traikov (from Bulgaria). Because they performed a humanitarian service mission, the missionaries taught the gospel only to those who requested it.[79]

Illus. 6-6. Centers of Latter-day Saint missionary
activity in the Baltics during the early 1990s.

Ethnic Issues in the Baltic States

In 1990, Estonia was part of the Finland Helsinki East Mission, along with the country of Russia. The Church had not yet tried to enter the other two Baltic states (illus. 6-6), Latvia and Lithuania. Unlike most of the area covered by this mission, these three countries presented daunting language and ethnic problems to missionaries and members. The Baltic States were assimilated into the Russian Empire during the eighteenth century and remained so until 1918. During this period they retained their native languages, Western cultural heritage, and faith as either Lutherans or Catholics. When Russia collapsed after World War I, each of the Baltic states achieved independence and remained free for three decades. First the German war machine and then Soviet arms reversed the fate of these nations, and during the next four decades they functioned as Soviet satellites, having the Russian language and culture imposed on them. Achieving new political freedom with the collapse of Communism, the majority of the populace preferred to speak the native tongue rather than Russian and spurned those unable to do so. Yet sizable portions of the population in all three countries were of Russian extraction and spoke only that language.

Some of the early missionaries had to learn a third language in addition to their prior attempts at learning Russian or Finnish. Finding it necessary to teach both Russians and non-Russians, many became equally fluent in two mission languages. Church literature in the native languages was virtually nonexistent, forcing early converts to consider the gospel message in Russian or Finnish regardless of their preference. Language and its concomitant ethnicity caused tensions among a few of the members, resulting in the creation of separate branches for speakers of Russian and speakers of the ethnic languages.

In February 1992, the Finland Helsinki East Mission was divided and the name dropped. The eastern portion of the mission became the Russia Moscow Mission. The western portion, including Estonia, came under the supervision of the newly created Russia St. Petersburg Mission. Charles and Susan Creel, who had served for eight months as the mission office couple for the Austria Vienna East Mission, were called to direct the new mission. President Gary Browning continued to preside over the Church in the rest of Russia. Charles Creel knew Russian from a stint in the U.S. military in 1954. After serving in the military he became a successful businessman, working as director of real estate for the Hughes Corporation.[80] President Creel continued to mold the

Church effort in St. Petersburg and Vyborg while he sustained the members in Estonia and sent missionaries into the other Baltic states of Latvia and Lithuania.

Missionaries Continue the Work in Estonia

Estonia, the northernmost country of the Baltics, was subjected to Danish, German, Swedish, and then Russian rule for seven hundred years. Native Estonians are traditionally Lutheran and comprise 61 percent of the 1.6 million people in the country. Russians comprise 30 percent of the population and are primarily Russian Orthodox. The Russian minority that once ruled the country is now disparaged as a second-class minority.

Missionaries had visited Estonia on the weekends until Elder Nelson dedicated the country (see chapter 5). During summer 1990, missionaries began staying in the country, leaving just once a month for visa renewals. The early missionaries were Christopher Gooch from Washington; Kevin Dexter, Alan Johansen, and Ryan Rogers from Utah; and Harri Aho from Finland. The elders initially taught in Finnish because of the many Finnish speakers in Tallinn and because it was intelligible to Estonian speakers. However, the missionaries realized the difficulty many Estonian speakers had in understanding gospel principles in Finnish or Russian. They began studying the new language under the tutelage of Brad Woodworth and his wife, American members living in Tallinn at the time.[81] Along with the missionaries who had learned Finnish and now struggled with Estonian were those who had transferred from Russia and had taught in Russian.[82]

In late 1991, missionaries began working in Tartu, the second largest city in Estonia. During that same month, a Russian-speaking branch was organized in Tallinn.[83] In October 1991, Jussi and Raija Kemppainen moved from Finland to Tallinn for Jussi's job at IBM. The Kemppainens brought a broad background of Church experience that helped the Church mature in Estonia, and there were 116 members by late 1992.[84]

Latvia Is Opened

Latvia is wedged between Estonia (to the north) and Lithuania (to the south). Historically rural like the other Baltic States, the country was conquered by the German Teutonic Knights, who ruled for nearly three centuries. The Swedes, Poles, and Russians followed as conquerors. Latvian nationalism, based on its distinctive language, Lutheran faith, and Western heritage, developed during the nineteenth century. When

Soviet rule was established, Russians came in and developed Latvian industry. Of the 2.5 million inhabitants, 56 percent are Latvians and 30 percent
are Russians; small groups of Belarussians, Ukrainians, and Poles round
out the population.

Similar to Yugoslavia and Poland, the Church's foundation in Latvia
was laid by a native son. In 1924, Boris Schiel was born in Riga of mixed
Latvian and Russian parentage. At the beginning of World War II, when
Boris was fifteen, the family fled to Germany where he learned German
and studied English, adding to his native skill in Latvian and Russian.
Boris and his wife, Ilse Rosenwald, joined the Church in 1954. They
moved to America, where his wife passed away and he remarried. He
retired in 1989. With his second wife, Liselotte Haertl, he served a temple
mission at Friedrichsdorf, Germany.[85]

In 1992 the couple was called to serve in the Russia St. Petersburg
Mission, which was then responsible for Latvia. They vacationed in
Europe prior to their reporting date and visited Elder Hans B. Ringger
in Frankfurt. The Schiels learned that Elder Ringger was going to meet
President Creel in Riga on May 16, the same date they would be there on
vacation. Providentially, the four gathered in Riga and began planning for
the Church's entry into Elder Schiel's native country. Later in the vacation, the Schiels met the Schafers, Church members from Iowa who had
just completed a teaching assignment at the University of Latvia. They suggested that the Schiels take over the apartment they would soon vacate.[86]

Prior to the Schiels' visit, a Latvian couple, Gvido and Velga Senkāns,
were converted while living and studying in Moscow. Baptized in early
1992, they were preparing to return to Riga when they sought the advice
of the missionaries about what they should do as the only known Church
members in their land. The missionaries, also unaware of plans for Latvia,
encouraged them to depend on prayer, but not to expect missionaries for
five to ten years. The converts heeded the advice to pray, and within only
a few months, missionaries were sent.[87]

On June 17, 1992, the Creels and four missionaries—Dale Franklin,
Dennon Ison, Matthew H. Lyman, and Michael G. Van Patten—flew
to Riga. Unaware of the Schiel's apartment site, the newly arrived missionaries secured a meeting place on the other side of the street. It was
a fortuitous circumstance that permitted the Schiels' apartment to be a
convenient site for missionary meetings and teaching investigators. The
Schiels returned on June 30. Because of his skill in multiple languages,
Elder Schiel talked to government officials, attorneys, realtors, home own-
ers, translators, and others in their own language. He taught investigators

Courtesy Kahlile B. Mehr

Illus. 6-7. The first Latter-day Saint meeting place in Riga, Latvia, was located in the middle building, 1997.

in Latvian or Russian, coordinated the work of various Church agencies, and interpreted for visiting Church authorities. His influence was pervasive and essential in establishing the Church in Latvia.

Shepherded by Elder Schiel, the Church took shape rapidly in Latvia during 1992. They held a church service on July 5 at the Artists' Building on Vaļņu iela 9 (illus. 6-7). Twenty-eight attended: two members, twenty investigators, and six missionaries. Before the month ended, Gunārs Kavals was baptized on July 25 in the forest-encircled Silver Lake, ten miles east of Riga (illus. 6-8). On September 6, seventy-five people attended church services, an all-time high. Primary, Sunday School, Priesthood, and Relief Society organizations were all established before year's end. Church services were conducted in Russian. Because little gospel literature was available in Latvian, Elder Schiel was asked to supervise the translation work done by local translators to help make up for the deficit.[88] By the end of 1992, a fledgling membership of twenty-seven existed.[89]

Lithuania Is Opened

Lithuania, the most southern of the Baltic states, has a population of 3.8 million. The country differs from the others in two distinct ways: it is traditionally Roman Catholic and it has a heritage of independence, never succumbing to the German Teutonic Knights. In the fifteenth century, it was one of the largest and most powerful European states, with a domain

Courtesy Boris Schiel

Illus. 6-8. Gunārs Kavals (in the white shirt) was the first native Latvian to be baptized into the Church in that country on July 25, 1992.

stretching from the Baltics to the Black Sea. A Polish-Lithuanian commonwealth forged in 1569 lasted just over two hundred years, and in 1795 Lithuania was absorbed into the Russia Empire. Large-scale insurrections failed several times during the nineteenth century. Lithuania was the first of the Baltic states to declare independence from the Soviet Union. Gorbachev attempted military intervention to subdue the nation, but failed. Its independence was confirmed with the failed coup against Gorbachev in August 1991 and the demise of the Soviet Union.

Even though Lithuania was the first to achieve independence, it was the last of the Baltic States to receive missionaries. Similar to the other Baltic States, it was slow to welcome the gospel message. Before missionaries entered Lithuania, the swell of interest in the West had begun to diminish, and the hard realities of living in strained economic conditions preoccupied the nation. The ingrained presence of a Catholic tradition presented another deterrent to Church growth. As in Poland, Catholicism had been a mainstay of the national identity during the Communist period, and it was a satisfactory faith to most of the population.

Robert and Ruth Rees arrived in Kaunas, Lithuania, on November 17, 1992. He was a professor from UCLA, she an accomplished musician. As humanitarian service missionaries, they taught at the University, consulted with the Ministry of Education, and worked with the media. They also used folk music to teach English at a local public school, visited orphanages, and held worship services in their apartment for friends and acquaintances.[90]

Young missionaries came to the capital city of Vilnius in December 1992, flying in with the Creels to Vilnius from St. Petersburg. The four elders were Neil Checketts, Greg Lorenzon, Spencer Glende, and Jason Swenson. A blanket of snow covered the city, and "everything was a pristine and sparkling white."[91] To Elder Swenson, it symbolized the opportunity to serve where no missionary had ever been previously. Given the initial rapid growth of the Church elsewhere in central and eastern Europe, it was discouraging to work hard with no apparent success. An average of only eight people attended meetings during the first few months.

By the end of 1992, virtually all the borders of the former Communist world in eastern Europe had permitted the missionaries to pass through.[92] Within the space of only three years, the long-awaited opportunity to bring the gospel message to many millions of people had arrived. The arduous process of not only converting, but teaching, training, sustaining, and building a faithful membership had begun.

Yugoslavia Collapses

Even as the Soviet Union collapsed in 1991, Yugoslavia separated into disparate segments. The disruption of Yugoslav society caused great suffering among the innocent. The Church, along with many others, attempted to assuage the people's suffering. These circumstances temporarily interrupted proselytizing activity, but in the end the civil war caused greater interest in the gospel of peace. The first blow fell unexpectedly in Slovenia.

Elder Jeffrey Moore, one of the first missionaries in Slovenia (see chapter 4), witnessed the transition to a new order with the change in flags. When he arrived in Maribor, Slovenia, two flags flew at official buildings—the red Yugoslav flag with a star symbolic of Communism next to a Slovenian republic flag with a similar star. One day the star was gone from the Yugoslav flag. Then the Yugoslav flag was missing altogether, and the republic flag with a star flew alone. Finally, the star disappeared.[93] All symbols of a Communist or a Yugoslav past were being erased.

On June 28, 1991, Slovenia declared its independence. The day after the declaration of independence, military jets flew over the city. Heavily armed guards were posted at city hall. Emptied of the civilian population, the streets bristled with armed soldiers. Missionaries in Maribor, a city opened in the previous month, watched television footage of tanks running over cars. Telephones did not function, and missionaries had no contact with the outside. Finally, a call got through to them with the message to leave. They bought train tickets and waited. The train never left. They later learned that fighting had occurred on the border as the Yugoslav army tried to secure the crossings into Austria. Their train would have traveled through the middle of the fighting. On the streets, the two missionaries found an Austrian who invited them to take a taxi with him through the mountains. They pulled up to the border, and the guard cocked his machine gun as they exited the car. Still, they were permitted to cross into Austria.[94]

The civil unrest in Slovenia was relatively brief and bloodless, lasting for approximately three days. When it appeared that civil war would erupt in Croatia, President Kenneth Reber brought the Croatian missionaries to Vienna on July 1, 1991. The Halgrens, a senior missionary couple, stayed in Zagreb. Elder Halgren had been a World War II pilot and had combat experience. On one occasion, October 4, 1991, when the bombing occurred around Zagreb, President Reber telephoned the Halgrens to leave. As they prepared to depart, an air raid alert forced them to wait in a cellar. Afterward, they decided to stay. In the midst of war, they continued their work, baptizing several new members each month.[95]

President Reber sent the young missionaries back into Slovenia in August 1991. In the wake of war came a new appreciation for religion. The missionaries began having more success. The president sent additional Yugoslav missionaries to Slovenia until there were twenty, more than had ever served at one time in all of the former Yugoslavia. Interest in the Church increased: seventy-six people (though there were only four members in Slovenia at the time) attended a Church conference held in Ljubljana in December 1991. President Ringger of the Europe Area Presidency commented to President Reber, "In all my days I never expected to see this many people gathered together in a church meeting in Yugoslavia." A branch in Ljubljana was organized during the conference, and President Reber later sent missionaries to open the cities of Celje and Kranj.[96] Twenty people had joined the Church by late 1992.[97] Success such as that in Slovenia was not isolated, since similar growth occurred further south.

In October 1991, President Reber sent missionaries back into Beograd where there was no fighting. Two months later, the Church purchased a building in Beograd after a five-year effort. Thirty-five people attended the first fireside held in the new facility. On January 28, 1992, the building passed sanitation inspection, which meant that Serbia officially recognized the Church. Missionaries could now receive permanent visas. In February 1992, the missionaries entered Novi Sad, the second city opened for missionary work in Serbia.[98]

Receiving recognition in Serbia did not translate immediately into a regular program of proselytizing. The local police needed to be informed before the long-established restrictions were eliminated. The missionaries had to be retrained to work openly rather than indirectly, as they had done for over twenty years. Elder Moore, now serving as assistant to the president, went to Beograd and trained them in the techniques he had found successful in Slovenia. He startled the missionaries by talking about the Church to a perfect stranger on the bus. They had had no one in their contacting pool for years, and in one day Elder Moore helped them get seventeen names. Eventually the missionaries began tracting, contacting people on the streets, and proselytizing openly anywhere they wished.[99]

President Reber sent missionaries back into Croatia in February 1992. They had been absent from the country for eight months. In addition to elders, he sent in a companionship of sisters. The fighting had not stopped, but it was confined to the border areas, so the missionaries were not in harm's way. In summer 1992, missionaries resumed the work in Karlovac and began laboring in Varaždin.[100]

Proselytizing had become just the opposite of what it had been for the previous twenty years. The civil war provided an immediate topic of conversation. With some listeners, the missionaries were able to turn the conversation to religion. Despite the civil war, Slovenia, Croatia, and Serbia boasted 22 baptisms during 1991.[101] In 1992 these same countries had 106 baptisms.[102] While not overwhelming by standards elsewhere, it was remarkable in comparison with previous experience. Teaching opportunities abounded to the degree that Austrian missionaries envied their Yugoslav counterparts.[103] Unfortunately for the Church, this pattern did not presage a trend.

By 1992 the civil war had spread into Bosnia. On the edge of the conflict, the Church did not remain idle. In March the Vienna Stake sent relief supplies to a children's hospital in Sarajevo. President Reber took it across the Croatian border in the middle of the night, hoping to avoid confiscation of the precious cargo. He concealed the supplies in the car's trunk. During the guard's inspection, President Reber gave the young man a Book of Mormon with Krešimir Ćosić's signature. The guard looked no further. Later, district president Ivan Valek successfully transported the medications from Croatia into Bosnia. During the same period, European stakes sent relief supplies to help refugees in Croatia and Serbia.[104]

The civil war found Church members on either side of a battlefront. One sister from Macedonia served in the Yugoslav army that occupied eastern Croatia. President Valek crossed the lines once a month to visit her in the barracks. A teenaged brother in Croatia sent a letter to Church leaders in Serbia saying, "We're praying for you every day, your protection, and that the war will end so that we can be together again." In Serbia they read it during a church meeting and posted it on the bulletin board. Then they wrote back, "We're praying for you and we pray for the same thing and we want to be together again."[105] Although ethnic tensions precluded missionary work in Bosnia and Macedonia, the Church survived much during its first twenty-five years among the southern Slavs, indicating its determination to remain.

Mission Finally Accomplished

The Austria Vienna East Mission existed briefly to cross the threshold of the Communist world. It operated for only five years (1987–92), expanding the efforts of the East Central Districts that had been in place since 1981. Missionaries worked in a previously forbidden realm, striving to deal with a spiritual vacuum created by decades of state-imposed atheism. From thirty-four missionaries working on half a continent in 1987 to hundreds of missionaries in five missions (with many more in the offing) in 1992, the Austria Vienna East Mission had accomplished its purpose of establishing the Church in eastern Europe.

The chronicle of this effort followed a basic pattern. Church officials sent in a few missionaries to test the limits of religious freedom in a chaotic environment of political and social upheaval. Concurrently, it sought legal recognition to function openly. More missionaries went in, and a mission was established. The people were curious about the West, and they listened to this new religious message. Converts trickled in at first, and then baptismal rates increased, particularly during the first several years. The members experienced challenges to their new faith and not all could sustain their commitment to the religion. The rate of conversion slowed as people grew more accustomed to general foreign influences and the novelty of the missionaries' presence diminished. This pattern varied somewhat in Bulgaria and, as the next chapter shows, in Romania, Albania, and Armenia. There, Church leaders attempted to meet urgent temporal needs as well as spiritual ones.

Notes

1. Russell M. Nelson, "Drama on the European Stage," *Ensign* 21 (December 1991): 13; John Menzies, telephone interview by author, May 23, 1998.

2. Russell M. Nelson, "Dedicatory Prayer of the Land of Bulgaria," typescript, copy in possession of author. See Kahlile Mehr, "Keeping Promises: The LDS Church Enters Bulgaria, 1990–1994," *BYU Studies* 36, no. 4 (1996–97): 67–105.

3. Morris Mower and Annetta Mower, interviewed by author, November 3, 1993, Salt Lake City; Morris Mower, telephone interview by author, January 20, 1995. Unless otherwise indicated, these are the sources for material through the section on Pravets.

4. Morris Mower, telephone interview.

5. Delbert and Marilyn Fowler, telephone interview by author, December 31, 1994; Marilyn Fowler, telephone interview by author, January 15, 1995.

6. Judith Gubler, telephone interview by author, December 31, 1994. Unless otherwise noted, this is also the source for the next two paragraphs.

7. Marilyn Fowler, telephone interview.

8. Mower and Mower, interview, November 3, 1993; Morris Mower, telephone interview.

9. Mower and Mower, interview, November 3, 1993. Also source for the next two paragraphs.

10. The apartment was located on Tsar Asen I, no. 22A. The Church later obtained a meeting place on Parchevich, no. 49. Morris Mower, telephone interview by author, March 21, 1997.

11. Morris Mower and Annetta Mower, interviewed by author, April 27, 1994, Salt Lake City; Mower and Mower interview, November 3, 1993.

12. Mower and Mower, interview, November 3, 1993; Morris Mower, telephone interview by author, June 30, 1995.

13. Morris Mower, telephone interview by author, January 30, 1997.

14. Mower and Mower, interview, April 27, 1994; Keith Hansen, interviewed by author, October 22, 1992, Sofia, Bulgaria.

15. Mower and Mower, interview, November 3, 1993; Morris Mower, speech given at Bulgarian fireside, Salt Lake City 20th Ward, April 21, 1994. Sources for next three paragraphs as well.

16. Christian Elggren, interviewed by author, August 4, 1994, Salt Lake City.

17. Mower and Mower, interview, November 3, 1993.

18. Mower and Mower, interviews, November 3, 1993, April 27, 1994; Mower, telephone interview by author, December 9, 1994; Trent Warner, telephone interview by author, November 30, 1994.

19. Fowler and Fowler, telephone interview, January 15, 1995; Marilyn Fowler, telephone interview, January 15, 1994. Also the sources for the next three paragraphs.

20. Gubler, telephone interview by author, December 31, 1994. Also the source for the next three paragraphs.

21. Trent Warner, telephone interview; Christian Elggren, interview.

22. Mower and Mower, interview, November 3, 1993.

23. Timothy J. Kuta, "Apostles to the Slavs: Gospel Messengers in Bulgaria," *Latter-Day Digest 3* (August 1994): 27–28.

24. Christian Elggren, interview.

25. Kuta, "Apostles to the Slavs," 28.

26. Trent Warner, telephone interview; Elggren, interview.

27. David Garner, interviewed by author, May 12, 1995, Provo, Utah.

28. Elggren, interview.

29. Kuta, "Apostles to the Slavs," 29.

30. Christian Elggren, Journal, March 11, 1991.

31. Trent Warner, telephone interview.

32. Garner, interview.

33. Elggren, Journal, December 8, 1990; January 17, 28, February 18, March 11, 1991.

34. Mower and Mower, interview, April 27, 1994.

35. Olia Botcheva, interviewed by author, August 4, 1994, Provo, Utah.

36. Hansen, interview.

37. Julia Caswell, interviewed by author, January 21, 1995, Salt Lake City.

38. Caswell, interview.

39. Caswell, interview. The story is also available in Edwin O. Haroldsen, "To Be Free," *Ensign* 1 (October 1971): 10; Kuta, "Apostles to the Slavs," 24–27. These are also the sources for the next two paragraphs.

40. Each member of the Church may receive a patriarchal blessing typically once in a lifetime. The blessing identifies the possibilities the person can achieve if faithful. See William James Mortimer, "Patriarchal Blessings," in *Encyclopedia of Mormonism*, ed. Daniel H. Ludlow, 4 vols. (New York: Macmillan, 1992), 3:1066–67.

41. Garner, interview; Morris Mower interview, March 21, 1997, Salt Lake City.

42. Mower and Mower, interview, April 27, 1994; Kuta, "Apostles to the Slavs," 27.

43. Hansen, interview.

44. Dale Warner, interviewed by author, December 26, 1994, Ogden, Utah. This is also the source for the next paragraph.

45. Renée Warner, conversation with author, January 11, 1995.

46. Dale Warner, interview.

47. Marilyn Fowler, telephone interview, January 15, 1995.

48. Morris Mower, speech given at Bulgarian fireside.

49. Dale Warner, interview.

50. Lynn Carson, telephone interview, January 6, 1997.

51. Howard L. Biddulph, *The Morning Breaks: Stories of Conversion and Faith in the Former Soviet Union* (Salt Lake City: Deseret Book, 1996), 38–42; Dennis B. Neuenschwander, telephone interview, January 17, 1997.

52. Biddulph, *Morning Breaks*, 38–42. Source for the next paragraph as well.

53. Biddulph, *Morning Breaks*, 42–43.

54. Austria Vienna East Mission, Historical Records and Minutes, 1991 report, Church Archives, The Church of Jesus Christ of Latter-day Saints, Salt Lake City;

Howard L. Biddulph, "A Journey to Explore New Proselyting Areas in the Eastern Ukraine and North Caucasus: Journal Entries, November 20 to December 7, 1991," typescript in Austria Vienna East Mission, 1991 report.

55. Scott Suggs, interviewed by author, November 1, 1992, Kiev, Ukraine.

56. The Creels would later be transferred to Russia, where Charles would serve as the Russia St. Petersburg Mission President.

57. Suggs, interview.

58. Karl Mueller to parents, June 2, 1991.

59. Howard L. Biddulph, "Journey to Explore New Proselyting Areas."

60. Karl Mueller to parents, June 15, 1991, in possession of author.

61. Austria Vienna East Mission, 1991 report. Also a source for the next paragraph.

62. Biddulph, *Morning Breaks*, 6–8.

63. Biddulph, *Morning Breaks*, 8–12; Biddulph, comments on manuscript draft, March 1997.

64. Biddulph, *Morning Breaks*, 46–53.

65. Biddulph, *Morning Breaks*, 54.

66. Biddulph, *Morning Breaks*, 58–59.

67. Karl Mueller to parents, October 1, 1991, in possession of author; "Two Republics in USSR Are Dedicated," *Church News*, published by *Deseret News*, September 28, 1991, 3.

68. Austria Vienna East Mission, 1991 report; Mueller to parents, October 1, 1991.

69. Karl Mueller to parents, November 4, 1991.

70. Biddulph, "Journey to Explore New Proselyting Areas."

71. Biddulph, "Journey to Explore New Proselyting Areas"; Biddulph, comments on manuscript draft, March 1997. Sources for the rest of this section unless otherwise noted.

72. *1997–1998 Church Almanac* (Salt Lake City: Deseret News, 1997), 397.

73. *1997–1998 Church Almanac*, 382.

74. Austria Vienna East Mission, 1991 report; Karl Mueller to Doug Mueller (his brother), June 17, 1991, in possession of author.

75. Biddulph, *Morning Breaks*, 62–63.

76. Suggs, interview.

77. "3 New Missions Established in Russia, Ukraine," *Church News*, February 15, 1992, 3.

78. Howard L. Biddulph, telephone conversation, December 20, 1999.

79. Biddulph, *Morning Breaks*, 66–68.

80. "New Mission Presidents," *Church News*, February 29, 1992, 4.

81. Kevin Dexter, interviewed by author, March 29, 1991, Orem, Utah.

82. Brigham Redd, interviewed by author, July 1993, Draper, Utah.

83. Gary Browning, *Russia and the Restored Gospel* (Salt Lake City: Deseret Book, 1997), 179.

84. Steven R. Mecham, "Missionary Work Starts in the Former Soviet Union," in *Muistamme, 1947–1997* (Salt Lake City: Artistic Printing, 1997), 136. Baptismal

statistic from "State of the Mission January 1994," in "Latvia-Riga Mission Year-book, 1993–1994," unpaginated manuscript, in possession of author.

85. Boris A. Schiel, "Short Life Story of Elder Boris A. Schiel," in "Latvia-Riga Mission Yearbook."

86. Boris A. Schiel, "The History of the Latvia Riga Mission of The Church of Jesus Christ of Latter-day Saints, June 17, 1992–December 14, 1993," typescript, 1, in possession of author. Also the source for the next paragraph.

87. Gvido Senkāns, interviewed by the author, Salt Lake City, Utah, October 27, 2000.

88. Schiel, "History," ii–iii, 1–5.

89. Schiel, "History," 3–9. Totals derived from accounts of baptismal services, plus the three members baptized elsewhere before there was a mission.

90. Robert and Ruth Rees, "Elder and Sister Rees," in "Latvia-Riga Mission Yearbook."

91. Jason Swenson to Sister Moretti, December 7, 1993, in "Latvia-Riga Mission Yearbook." Except as otherwise noted, also the source for the rest of this paragraph and the next paragraph.

92. Moldova, a landlocked country between Ukraine and Romania, was the only exception. Missionaries did not enter there until 1997.

93. Jeffrey Moore, interviewed by Jeff Anderson, 1991–92, Salt Lake City, typescript, pt. 1, p. 20, copy in possession of the interviewee, Orem, Utah.

94. Moore, interview, pt. 2, p. 25–28; Kenneth Dudley Reber, interviewed by Matthew K. Heiss, 1994, Salt Lake City, typescript, 61–63, copy in possession of the interviewee, Sandy, Utah.

95. Reber, interview, 1994, 63–65.

96. Reber, interview, 1994, 57, 63, 73; Kenneth Dudley Reber, interviewed by author, October 28, 1995, Sandy, Utah.

97. "Member list," computer database output, Europe Area Frankfurt Office, November 5, 1995.

98. Reber, interview, October 28, 1995; Reber, interview, 1994, 65–66; Moore, interview, pt. 2, p. 35. For more details on the complications of obtaining the building see Reber, interview, 1994, 48.

99. Reber, interview, 1994, 52; Moore, interview, pt. 2, p. 34–35.

100. Reber, interview, 1994, 70.

101. Austria Vienna Mission, Historical Records and Minutes, 1991 report, Church Archives.

102. "Europe Area Convert Baptisms, December 1992," typescript, Europe Area Frankfurt Office.

103. Reber, interview, 1994, 46, 51.

104. Reber, interview, 1994, 67, 71–72.

105. Reber, interview, 1994, 51–52.

7

Exemplary Lives

1989–1993

During the 1980s the Church began directing its humanitarian work, long focused primarily on helping members, toward the under-privileged of any religion. There were precedents such as the ship-ment of food and supplies to San Francisco after the 1906 earthquake, grain to quake-devastated China in 1907, and flood relief assistance to the Netherlands in 1952. However, these were isolated incidents, not part of a general plan. A watershed event in the process of worldwide humani-tarian service consisted of two Church-wide fasts during 1985 in behalf of African famine victims. The total donation toward the purchase of food-stuffs amounted to $10 million.[1] In December 1986, the Welfare Depart-ment officially commenced an international welfare program with Isaac Ferguson as director.[2] While direct assistance continued to grow, indirect aid emerged in the form of the Church's humanitarian service workers.

This international welfare program consists of older Church mem-bers being called to donate knowledge and skills, developed during a life-time of work, to nations needing medical, educational, or other assistance. The primary objective of the volunteers is less to satisfy immediate need than to develop long-term benefits through educating local workers and professionals. The humanitarian service workers are an incarnation of a basic tenet in the Church's welfare program: self-reliance.

Where immediate need was identified, these service workers drew upon the expanded services of Deseret Industries, a Church-run thrift operation. In 1991, Deseret Industries established a Humanitarian Service Center, commonly known as the "sort center," to select and package sur-plus clothing, medical equipment, and other supplies as requested by service workers or Church representatives. In time, it began to ship books in English to eastern Europe, a world where such books had been available only to Communist elite. The shipments included publishers' donations of unsold textbooks superseded by more current editions. A newer aspect of the program consists of Church groups volunteering to prepare or make inexpensive items such as first aid kits, quilts, toys, and student packets with paper and pens for shipment worldwide.[3] From 1985 to 1997, the value of Church humanitarian aid amounted to $162.5 million.[4]

Elder Russell M. Nelson, a surgeon of international renown prior to being called as a member of the Quorum of the Twelve Apostles, was particularly attuned to the value of welfare in demonstrating, beyond words, the principles of the gospel. He incorporated the changing nature of the welfare program into the Church's overall program in the Eastern Bloc. Though welfare assistance was provided throughout the area, it was particularly evident in the southern tier of the old Communist realm. Humanitarian service workers crossed the Romanian border in September 1990. Similar workers entered Armenia in 1991 and Bulgaria and Albania in 1992. Through these pioneering efforts, humanitarian service demonstrated the Church's commitment to bettering the situation of all humankind. The humanitarian service program, administered independent of missionary work, helped the Church establish a presence in some central and eastern European countries.

Earthquake Disaster in Armenia

The Church entered Armenia during one of the country's bleakest hours. In 1988, Armenia was devastated by an undeclared war and a major earthquake. The war over the right to self-rule in Nagorno-Karabakh (an ethnically Armenian enclave entirely within Azerbaijan) pitted the traditionally Christian Armenians against the Moslem Azeries. Neighboring countries aligned against the frail Soviet republic, creating a blockade with dire results. The earthquake, which hit on December 7, left fifty thousand dead and a seventh of Armenia's three million people homeless. The events signaled the beginning of another bitter chapter in the history of a hapless nation beset with misfortune for centuries. Yet the tragedy offered opportunities for the rest of the world to provide needed and welcome assistance.

The Church contributed to the relief effort. Just a week after the quake, Elder Nelson presented a $100,000 check (from the Church's disaster relief fund) to the Soviet ambassador in Washington, D.C., to be used for assistance in Armenia. The money had been generated by voluntary contributions from numerous Church members for emergencies such as this. In the letter of donation, the Church also offered further assistance upon request.[5]

Prominent among others contributing to the relief effort were Jon Huntsman from Utah and Armand Hammer from California, both successful in business and well known for their philanthropic works. Together they established the American-Armenian Bridge of Friendship, offering assistance to build short-term housing or to pursue other projects according to the beleaguered nation's wishes. The Church became a third party to the agreement, offering workers skilled in building trades to help the nation recover.[6]

David Horne, a Salt Lake City contractor and member of the Church, became the point man for the short-term housing initiative. Unacquainted with David prior to this date, Huntsman employed him upon the recommendation of Elder M. Russell Ballard of the Quorum of the Twelve.[7] Actual contact with David was made by Elder Nelson, a personal acquaintance of Horne when they served in the presidencies of adjacent stakes.[8]

Elder Nelson originally asked Brother Horne to spend three months building temporary housing for earthquake victims, but the project evolved into the construction of a concrete plant, which in turn evolved into the establishment of the Church in Armenia. This effort became the focus of Brother Horne's life for the next six years and probably would have lasted longer had it not been for his untimely death.[9] His contributions to Armenia were emulated by others who followed. The exemplary lives of Church service missionaries taught a gospel of works as well as of words.

The telephone call came on July 21, 1989, and in a few days David Horne left for Armenia. Armenians in Turkey and Syria had joined the Church around the turn of the century, but no Church representative had ever visited Armenia proper. Brother Horne met Peter Huntsman, Jon's second son, in Germany, and they flew to Yerevan. Anticipating being picked up by members of the German Red Cross, they were surprised to be met by a chauffeur with a black limousine. Brother Horne inquired with humorous naiveté if the limousine were from the Red Cross. The man bluntly corrected him, explaining it was from the prime minister's office.[10]

Over the next few days, the two Americans witnessed heart-rending scenes. At Spitak, epicenter of the quake, they saw nothing but rubble. The mayor, who had lost his wife and two children, continued to direct relief efforts even though he suffered from a broken back and broken legs. He was living in a tent and stated that he would do so until everyone in the city had homes. Four other families shared his tent. Horne and Huntsman went to Gumri and visited a sixty-five-year-old woman living in a fourth-floor apartment, one of the few buildings still standing. Her two sons and their wives had been killed, leaving her responsible for eight grandchildren. Water came only once a week, and the children hauled it up the staircase to the apartment.

By consulting with the central government, Horne and Huntsman learned that permanent rather than temporary housing was the greater need. On August 7, they reported this need to Elder Nelson, Elder Hans B. Ringger (the Europe Area president), and Jon Huntsman, who were all in Moscow with the Armenian leaders for the signing of the American-Armenian Bridge of Friendship agreement; the document was signed the next day. David returned to Armenia and learned that government leaders wanted to alter their request again, this time to upgrade concrete plants. David toured existing plants and returned in October 1989 and February 1990 with groups of engineers, who ultimately decided to bring in American technology and build anew rather than upgrade outdated Soviet technology. The final concept was to build a completely new facility that would create concrete slabs to be used in construction. A concrete factory on the site for the proposed factory was torn down and carried away, along with mountains of trash.[11] Work on the plant progressed sufficiently that it was ready for dedication in June. In August 1991, another Huntsman representative, Roger Doxey, accompanied by his wife, Jewell, arrived to work as the plant's superintendent.[12]

Susanna Sarkissian, who worked part time as an interpreter for the Ministry of Foreign Affairs, was intrigued by these people who had come to help rebuild her country. When she first met them in May, she was particularly struck by their demeanor and pleasant dispositions.[13] The next month, she interpreted at the plant dedication.[14] Later, she happened to meet Brother Horne in a store, and she invited him and his colleagues to dinner. The Horne and Doxey families accepted the invitation. Susanna and her family were amazed that people would voluntarily leave the comforts of their American homes to live a Spartan life in Armenia. Sergei, the father, opened his bar and offered his guests something to drink. They declined. The family was surprised and impressed with people who strictly adhered to their principles and lifestyle.[15]

Meanwhile, the Church was busy identifying couples who would volunteer to assist in the construction and running of the concrete plant. Most of them arrived the day after Thanksgiving, November 28, 1991: Scott and Erma Lee Hurst, Marvin and Mona Lee O'Donnal, Joseph and Catherine Rickman, and Hanley and Nola Vinson. Scott Hurst, from Utah, was a concrete specialist with more than forty years of experience as a contractor. Marvin O'Donnal, from Washington, had manufactured concrete pipe for thirty-five years. Hanley Vinson, from Colorado, was an electrician. Joseph Rickman, from Georgia, was skilled in repairing electronic equipment. The last couple, Roy and Carol Stephens from California, arrived in January 1992. Roy was an engineer who specialized in earthquake-resistant construction.[16]

Most of the materials and means to build the plant were not readily available. Sand came from twenty miles out of town. A small locomotive moved the sand by rail to the plant site. The main concrete-making machinery came from Wisconsin. Approximately 450 people helped construct the plant, which was finally completed in March 1992.[17]

When brought into service, the slab-laying machine simultaneously dumped three layers of concrete. The first was relatively dry and the two on top successively wetter so that all three layers would dry evenly. Machines poured the concrete over taut metal cables that gave the slabs rigidity. Additional panels were then poured on top of the drying panels. Poured in lengths of several hundred feet, the slabs, when dry, could be cut to size for construction.[18]

Although the old factory had been replaced, the sixty employees from the former plant were retained. They had to develop work habits that differed from their previous experience. Some were caught stealing, a practice endemic to operations throughout the former Soviet states. When a few were fired, also uncommon under the Soviet system, the problem ended. Compromising with the old system, Horne and Huntsman retained the excess personnel even though the plant was overstaffed.

Brother Horne made an impression on the workers. He worked alongside them, not shirking even the lowliest job. He made sure the plant was clean and tidy, unlike most Soviet workplaces. Horne always smiled broadly when shaking hands with the workers. In the springtime, he often brought fruit to the plant because he knew it was too expensive for the workers to buy. Approaching seventy years of age, Horne was the image of good health. He joked that his only sickness was work. In the words of an Armenian journalist, "Those people who were around David Horne somehow began to look at the world through his eyes, to appreciate life in all its many facets: nature, the smile of a child, a kind word, a delicious dinner, visiting a friend, heartfelt conversation and prayer." He looked for opportunities to serve. When driving through the streets of Yerevan, Horne commonly offered to give others rides.[19] He frequently carried a Polaroid camera, giving children pictures of themselves, a rare possession for an Armenian child.[20]

Brother Horne was not there when the humanitarian service workers arrived in November 1991, though he had already arranged for their apartments. He returned to Armenia in July 1992 with his wife Jeanne to take up residence.[21] Even while living there, Horne was often gone for two or three weeks at a time, traveling to neighboring countries as well as to Church headquarters in Frankfurt, Germany, and Salt Lake City, Utah, to find and courier needed equipment and supplies. One of his many tasks included ensuring the arrival of convoyed goods.

In late 1992, a forty-foot container of parts for the plant started out for Yerevan from St. Petersburg, Russia. The container took nine days to travel by rail to Krasnodar in southern Russia, where Brother Horne joined it. He and the truck driver made it into Chechnya, where the truck's motor blew up, forcing them to find another truck. In a stretch of sixty kilometers, they were stopped by armed bandits thirteen separate times. They had to bribe each group to continue. Horne and the driver also had to bribe the police for passage. At Bezlem they joined a convoy of 175 trucks to the Armenian border. They arrived two weeks after leaving Krasnodar, a distance of only 450 miles.[22]

As the representative for Huntsman and unofficial representative for the Church, Brother Horne managed continuing relief efforts and other projects in Armenia.[23] In December 1989, ten thousand pounds of powdered milk from the Church welfare system dairy farms were shipped to Armenia.[24] During the winter of 1991, Horne brought thirty thousand boxes of relief supplies from Turkey and distributed them throughout the country.[25] Later, the Church sent in shipments of clothing.[26] Huntsman continued to expend monies in Armenia, his total contribution reaching $18 million by 1998.[27]

The original couples and successive missionaries continued to work at the concrete plant until July 1994, when daily operations were handed over to the Armenians.[28] In the short term, the service workers had fulfilled their responsibility at the concrete plant. In the long term, their contribution to the Church and to Armenia was much greater. While operating the plant, they necessarily lived in a destitute country that took notice of their sacrifice, and many closely watched their every act, asking themselves, "Why?" Some received an answer that would alter their lives.

Couple Missionaries Enter Armenia

Elder Russell M. Nelson offered a prayer in Moscow prior to the ceremony for the signing of the American-Armenian Bridge of Friendship Contract, mentioned previously. The prayer focused not on disaster relief but on religious renewal and the entry of the gospel message into Armenia. David later reflected that had temporary housing been built, this event probably would have never occurred. But the concrete factory and the need for skilled volunteers were long-term requirements that made the spreading of the gospel a possibility and provided the opportunity to fulfill Elder Nelson's blessing.[29]

Early in the morning on June 24, 1991, Elder Dallin H. Oaks, Elder Nelson, and Elder Ringger gathered with Jon, Peter, and Brynn Huntsman, David and Jeanne Horne, and David Farnsworth, the Church's legal counsel in Europe, at the Mother of Armenia statue overlooking the capital city of Yerevan. With Mt. Ararat in the background, Elder Oaks offered a dedicatory prayer for the introduction of the gospel into that country. He asked that the country would "hear the song of liberty."[30] Within months, the Soviet Union crumbled, and Armenia gained its independence. Shortly thereafter, the humanitarian service workers arrived to shepherd operations at the concrete plant.

Prior to their arrival, Brother Horne presented the Armenian government with a plan to build housing for Church service workers. They agreed, but, after numerous delays he began renting apartments located in various parts of the city. Narina Sarkissian, Susanna's sister and a good friend of the Hornes, located the apartments. Inadvertently, this created a situation where the service workers were spread throughout the city, widening the opportunities to reach people. Eventually, their apartments served as meeting places for those curious to know more about their beliefs.[31]

The missionary couples arrived and were dropped off at the different apartments. They began a bewildering new existence, where the conveniences they had taken for granted were either sparse or nonexistent. It was winter, but there was no heat. Water and electricity were available only sporadically. One of the men shaved under an umbrella because the ceiling leaked.[32]

The routine of missionary life for these early couples was simple and basic. A driver picked up the husbands each day to go to work at the plant. Once a week, the driver took the wives shopping. During the rest of the week, the wives fixed up the apartments. Saturdays were their only day of leisure since they held Sabbath services and an official report meeting on Sundays. Monday evenings they all gathered for a light supper and social.[33]

The service workers held a fast and testimony meeting December 2, 1991, in which they resolved to invite Armenians to their services. Several Armenians attended the following Sunday: Mikhail Belousov, a graduate student who lived across the hall from the O'Donnals; Narina Sarkissian; and Anna Sargsian and her husband, Andernik, neighbors of the Hursts.

Andernik was asked to give a lesson in Russian from the *Gospel Principles* manual lent to him by the American visitors. Anna was asked to sing in church. She had not slept well Saturday night, feeling anxious about what to expect and thinking about her family heritage as early Bolsheviks in Armenia. She remembered her grandfather saying religion was for weak people. But she overcame her hesitations, sang and felt accepted when everyone gave her a hug.[34]

Still, Anna worried about her new foreign neighbors when she looked up the term *Mormon* in the Soviet encyclopedia and learned about polygamy. Again she slept poorly, wondering how many wives Elder Hurst had. The next day, she asked him, and he explained that it was a doctrine practiced only in the previous century. Her apprehension was allayed, and soon she found further evidence to trust these foreigners.

One day Anna's neighbor confided in her that she needed bread. Fortuitously, the Hursts brought bread the next day and, without knowing of the neighbor's need, gave her some. Anna was now worried that they knew much more than they disclosed. She and the neighbors covertly observed the behavior of the Hursts, noting their kindness to children, spending hours with them, and teaching them a little English. The Hursts bought kerosene heaters and gave them to families in need. When Anna visited one day, she found the Hursts wrapped in blankets, having given their own heater to a neighbor. She felt the service workers attracted the people because, "They sacrificed everything to be in Armenia to bring the gospel."

The situation in Armenia was dire in the winter of 1991–92. Armenia endured a blockade because of the war with the Azeries. Its atomic power plant, damaged by the quake, was closed. With energy in short supply, heating was shut off, and people froze indoors since electricity came on sporadically. Sufficient food was available only to the small minority who had the money. These conditions, coupled with soaring inflation and bewilderment in the attempt to hold elections and establish a democracy, discouraged the citizens.[35]

Invitations to church services in December and January were extended to specific people because the service workers did not want to overstep the boundaries of their primary commission to run the plant. They awaited the arrival of Elder Ringger and Elder Neuenschwander, members of the Europe Area Presidency, in January to visit the Minister of Religion and seek legal recognition for the Church. The minister did not prohibit proselytizing, but he counseled the Church leaders to have the humanitarian service workers keep a low profile and only respond to unsolicited questions about their faith.[36]

Acting on the permission to answer questions, the service workers extended invitations to a larger group of Armenians to attend a fast and testimony meeting in February 1992. The missionaries were surprised when more than forty came. Attracting such a large group after such a short period may be explained in part by the couples' presence: their willingness to give up the comforts of America aroused the curiosity and inspired the trust of those they met.

The person conducting the meeting explained to the Armenian guests, through an interpreter, the nature of a fast meeting. One or two of the service workers bore their testimonies. Then the Armenians started to speak. They expressed their feelings about the service workers and how they had felt religious yearnings under Communism. Armen Babakonian, who had played at the Gina Bachauer piano competition in Salt Lake City, stood and described his experiences at Temple Square. He explained how he had felt alone and nervous during the event, but when he went to the temple grounds he found peace and renewed strength while sitting before the statue of Christ. Armen said he felt the same way at the fast meeting.

Recognizing that a government agent also attended this meeting, the service workers decided that general meetings had too high a profile. Instead, future meetings were held for smaller groups in each of the missionary's apartments. But they could hardly slow the interest of the Armenians. Within three or four months, approximately a hundred Armenians attended church services at the various apartments. A year later, the Hursts, who had the smallest apartment, were hosting over thirty and the Stephens, with the largest apartment, upwards of seventy-five.[37]

As Americans, the service workers aroused the curiosity of many Armenians. While standing in line for food, some Armenians practiced speaking English to them. Armenians living near the service workers frequently visited them in their apartments. At times it was difficult to find any privacy. Indeed, the Armenians treated them as celebrities. After the press wrote about them, the service workers were recognized on the streets wherever they went. Beyond the curiosity to learn about Americans, many Armenians soon became interested in the service workers' faith.

The Spiritual Yearnings of Armenians

For decades prior to the arrival of the service workers, the Communist regime had forbidden people to own Bibles. It was one more episode in a tragic history through which Armenians had survived because of their Christianity, a faith dating back at least sixteen hundred years in their country. Narina Sarkissian obtained a Bible after they became available as a result of Gorbachev's reforms. But she had difficulty comprehending the scriptures. While this did not diminish her faith in Christ, she could not recognize the wisdom in his teachings.[38] Her story, as follows, is illustrative of the spiritual yearnings felt by many Armenians and the courage that had sustained them over the ages.

Prior to meeting the service workers, Narina had worked at a school of fifteen hundred students, aged seven to seventeen. She was responsible for the students' moral and ethical education, ideological work, parent-teacher relationships, and social activities. Even though she was twenty-eight years old and a relatively young staff member, the principal asked her to be the vice-principal. The prospect was exciting, but she could fill the position only if she joined the Communist Party. Even though her parents were top Communist officials, she refused. Skirting the requirement, the principal made her acting vice-principal. Narina did the work but did not receive the salary. Recognized as a leader by her peers, she instigated a protest against the misappropriation of Armenian earthquake relief funds by Soviet overlords. Although many people sympathized, most chose not to go public with their feelings. When it came to signing a protest addressed to Gorbachev, only three—including Narina—out of a hundred teachers did so. KGB agents visited her, insisting she join the party. She again refused. In May 1989, the KGB told the principal to disqualify her for the promotion. Later that weekend, as the principal pondered Narina's fate, seventy thousand people demonstrated in Freedom Square. On Sunday, three hundred thousand people were on the square, and by Monday the Communist Party had been dissolved. Enjoying their new freedoms, the staff elected Narina to be the vice-principal.[39]

Soon after their arrival, the service workers requested that Narina teach them Armenian. She had the time since the schools were closed due to lack of electricity, transportation, and fuel. Narina not only taught but also learned. She had studied many religions but had never received answers that seemed to "echo in her heart and brain like the absolute truth." After a week of teaching the service workers, Narina had a dream. She viewed a tall building with spires and circular windows along the top of the walls. It was engraved with sun stones, a typical symbol of eternity in ancient Armenian architecture. Light filled the building, and the people inside it sang magnificent music. Although she walked around the building, she could find no entrance. She awoke with the lingering expectation that something momentous would happen in her life.[40]

The service workers wanted to pay Narina for the Armenian language instruction. Her salary as vice-principal was the equivalent of four dollars per month, an amount that would buy a pound each of meat, butter, and sugar, as well as two dozen eggs. She needed the money but still refused. Instead, she surprised the service workers by asking to be baptized. Then she told them of her unusual dream. Since she did not ask them for an interpretation directly, the workers hesitated to explain the dream. Instead they told Narina to write it down, that it might be important in her life. She and her daughter began taking missionary discussions from the service workers. One day, at a missionary's apartment, she was startled to see a new picture hanging on the wall. It was of the building from her dream. The couple explained that the picture was of the Salt Lake Temple and that the package it had arrived in came from Germany.[41]

Excited with the gospel knowledge she was receiving, Narina invited the service workers to her school. She described the experience: "Can you imagine 300 teenagers sitting in the room with not a single movement, not any single noise for about two-and-half hours listening to the missionaries, to what they were teaching, then running after them up to the bus station begging, asking them to come back again."[42]

During January 1992, the Doxeys moved into a rented home on the outskirts of Yerevan. The house had a tub that could accommodate baptisms. Mikhail Belousov was baptized there in late March 1992, the first Armenian to join the Church in that country (illus 7-1).[43] As the day for Narina Sarkissian's baptism approached, the weather turned cold and bitter with over a foot of snow on the ground, freezing pipes and making

Illus. 7-1. David Horne and the first convert in Armenia, Mikhail Belousov, 1993.

Courtesy Kahlile B. Mehr

it impossible to fill the baptismal font until the weather softened. However, on April 4, the weather was resplendently sunny and warm. Although the font water was still cold, Sister Sarkissian felt so warm inside that the water did not seem cold enough to her. Fifty people—the school principal, friends, relatives, and neighbors—came to the baptism.[44]

Narina returned to her job at the school. "I was . . . flying. My life had changed. I was full of knowledge, full of spirit and emotions and I wanted to share it with everybody." The next school day she asked her students, "What are we studying now?" They said, "The Second World War." She said, "Do you know when the war started?" They said, "Yes." "Do you know when it was over, how many people died, and what a tragedy it was for history?" They said, "Yes, of course we know." She said, "Okay, that's enough of history, now we're going to study the Plan of Salvation."[45]

Armenians responded to the music of the Church. Anna Sargsian, the Hursts' neighbor, was the third Armenian to join the Church. As a music teacher, Sister Sargsian first embraced the Church hymns. She had taught for thirteen years at an exclusive music school for talented children. Once a week, she met with Nola Vinson to start translating the hymns. At a recital in May 1992, she directed a choir that sang, "I Know My Father Lives," "I Am a Child of God," and "Love One Another." Prominent Armenian composers and teachers were in attendance. Later, Sister Sargsian's friends took the music to their schools.[46] Sister Sarkissian also translated hymns and taught them at her school. Elementary students in many Armenian schools were soon singing Primary songs.[47] Sister Sargsian had them sing in English, as well as Armenian, to teach them the English language. The songs were even sung on national television. Hymns such as "A Poor Wayfaring Man of Grief" reached the choir at the university. Armen Babakonian, the pianist who had played in Salt Lake City, made his own arrangements of the hymns and used them as encores in Armenian concert halls.[48]

The fledgling group of members welcomed the visits of Church authorities. Elder Howard W. Hunter visited Armenia in September 1992. The six newly baptized members of the Church in Armenia attended a banquet with Elder Hunter at the prime minister's complex. President Neuenschwander, from the Europe Area Presidency, visited in December 1992 and spoke to more than a hundred people at the American University auditorium.[49]

Church members suffered with their fellow countrymen during the tragic winter of 1992–93 but found spiritual unity in an effort to stay the elements. The nation teetered on the edge of a catastrophe. The cold was incredibly severe. Some peoples' fingers and toes froze in their own apartments because there was no fuel for central heating. Schools closed. People sat listlessly at work for a couple of hours, then went home to continue freezing.[50] There was little or no electricity to run appliances or heaters. And it snowed constantly. People cut the limbs from trees throughout Yerevan to burn for warmth. Food was scarce or unaffordable. The public health ministry expected a cholera epidemic that would kill one hundred thousand people.[51]

The service workers held a special fast, in hopes of assuaging the elements, that concluded during church services on January 24. They asked the handful of members to invite friends to join in the fast. As many as four hundred people participated. The morning of the fast, the Azeries blew up the last gas line coming into the country. At the end of the priesthood meeting, Elder Hurst prayed for a blessing on the country, for the people to be able to tolerate the cold, and for the hearts of the enemy to be softened. The next morning, there was no snow, the sun came out, the electricity came on, and the service workers went to work at the plant. By Tuesday, two days later, the gutters were full of runoff from the melted snow. A few people even walked outside in short sleeves. There was still more winter to endure, but for three weeks the weather stayed moderate. The augured epidemic never materialized.

The nation discovered it had also been saved from a man-made tragedy. Monday afternoon, Sister Sargsian came home from the U.S. embassy, where she had been working for several months, with a startling announcement. A Russian pilot, paid by the Azeries to bomb Stepanogerk in Nagorno-Karabakh, had reconsidered, landed the plane in Yerevan, and turned it over to the Armenians. While it was broadcast in Armenia, the event was never publicized outside of Armenia to protect the Russian's family back in his homeland.[52] A nation on the edge of calamity began to right itself. Even more significantly, its spiritual roots began to revive.

The Tragic Legacy of a Romanian Dictator

Wedged between Ukraine and Bulgaria in southeast Europe, Romania's population of twenty-one million ranks it second to Poland in eastern Europe (illus. 7-2). Romanians speak a Latin-based, non-Slavic language. As in Armenia, service workers introduced the Church in Romania. Though unknown to anyone there, Temesvár (later Timişoara, Romania) had been the site of Mischa Markow's greatest baptismal success in eastern Europe in 1901.

Illus. 7-2. Sites of two early twentieth-century branches (Temesvár and Brassó) and cities opened by missionaries (Bucharest and Ploieşti), 1990–93.

Nicolae Ceaucescu, the Communist dictator from 1965 to 1989, impoverished the county to bankroll himself and his supporters. Romanians endured shortages because he exported much of his nation's crops and manufactured goods to other countries. Consumed with the idea of further prostrating the population of his nation, he taxed couples, even the barren, who failed to have at least five children. He outlawed birth control and ordered monthly checks of pregnant women to ensure against abortion. A scarce food supply and minimal wages left parents unable to provide for their children. Malnourished mothers could not nurse their babies, and many mothers gave them over to orphanages that were ill-equipped and poorly staffed to nurture them. The babies received little attention, and disabled children received even less care. One in five infants died.[53]

Romanians were enlivened with new hope as Communist barriers began to fall elsewhere in Europe. In mid-December 1989, large demonstrations occurred in Timişoara, known as Temesvár when the city had belonged to the Austro-Hungarian Empire. In an effort to quell the crowds, government security forces fired on the masses, and hundreds were slaughtered. Rather than being cowered, the rest of the nation rose in revolt. Security forces in Bucharest fired on demonstrators there, and the death toll rose into the thousands. Army units began to battle with security force in defense of civilians. In December, Ceaucescu was deposed, and on Christmas day he was executed.

Welfare Initiatives in Romania

On February 8, 1990, Elder Nelson, Elder Ringger, and Peter Berkhahn (Europe Area Director of Temporal Affairs) arrived in Bucharest. They visited Cismigiu Park and invoked a blessing upon the country, its people, and its leaders. They also prayed that the gospel message might be received there. Later, the men met with national ministers and local officials. When Elder Nelson asked how the Church could be of help, he was informed of the problems in the orphanages. Officials estimated that Bucharest alone had more than thirty thousand orphans.[54]

Elder Nelson reported his experience to the Quorum of Twelve. At the Church's next general conference, Elder Thomas S. Monson announced that action had already been taken to begin tending to the needs of these innocent victims.[55] The Europe Area Presidency set up a Romanian relief committee, and it sponsored an assessment team from

Austria, Finland, Germany, and the United States to determine specific needs and to help develop a strategy for action. The project targeted orphans and other children in various child-care institutions. The step the Church representatives took of asking what was needed in Romania made a difference. One hospital director stated, "Many are helping, but you are the first ones to ask us what we really need."[56] European Church members were asked to donate money and goods to the project. Among other efforts throughout the continent, Church members in the Netherlands initiated a nondenominational effort to gather food and shipped twelve truckloads to Romania.[57]

Church leaders began to mobilize relief workers from the United States to go to Romania. Arrangements were made to have a team of specialists examine hearing-impaired students at a vocational school. The team consisted of Glen K. Lund, an ear, nose, and throat doctor from Bountiful, Utah; Kim B. Leishman, director of speech and hearing services for Intermountain Health Care in Utah; and C. Rex Scott, owner of Audiology Associates of Salt Lake City. Headed by Dr. Lund, the group tested some 200 hearing-impaired children and dispensed 160 hearing aids. They taught local professionals to use the test equipment and left it in the country for future examinations. Dr. Lund observed that professionals there were doing their best, but that they were severely limited by lack of equipment. During the team's trip in August 1990, truckloads of supplies began arriving from the Church's European headquarters. Peter Berkhahn's office contacted companies throughout Europe, many of which donated or gave substantial discounts on equipment and tools. The vocational school where Dr. Lund and his team worked was given wood planes, rubber boots, and rubber aprons to support a carpentry program.[58]

In the meantime, Church officials looked for volunteers not only to administer humanitarian aid but also to provide extended humanitarian service. In September 1990, eight service workers entered Romania: Harold Davis, an electrical engineer from Idaho Falls, Idaho, the project coordinator, and his wife Enid, a social worker; R. Reed Fife, a retired pediatrician also from Idaho Falls, and his wife Dorothy, a nurse; Alvin Price, a BYU professor of family science and his wife Barbara, a high school teacher of home economics; Beverly Cutler, a BYU professor of special education; and Virginia Bruse, a nurse from Salt Lake City. The small group felt overwhelmed by the immense task before them of serving the children, distributing supplies, and updating the training of professionals in child care, development, and education.[59]

The government gave the service workers living quarters and secured a warehouse to store supplies for distribution as need arose. The service workers visited orphanages, schools, and hospitals. Not speaking Romanian, the Americans often found English speakers on the staff, but sometimes they just engaged in mutual guessing. Occasionally they were invited to examine the patients and offer suggestions for treatment. They gave classes to orphanage staff members and university students on child development, methodology, communication, and relationship skills. They met with psychologists, educators, and social workers to help devise long-term training for their staffs. In addition, they organized a support group for mothers of disabled children and trained personnel at orphanages and schools for the disabled. The service workers also distributed chalkboards, clipboards, overhead projectors, and video training tapes that had been dubbed into Romanian.

Romanians appreciated the missionaries' contributions. Sister Cutler taught child development and educational methodology to a group of orphanage teachers for nine months. At the end of her course, one student said, "For 45 years we in Romania felt as though we were in prison. But then came freedom. And then came you to help us teach our children."[60] Dan Cristescu, the director of the Secretariat of the Handicapped who dealt with many organizations, said: "[Yours] was a very good mission because it was discreet, without noise, without publicity."[61] This was a welcome commendation to the Church's desire for meeting needs.

The Special Olympics Comes to Romania

Probably the most successful effort of the humanitarian service workers was the institution of the Special Olympics for disabled children in June 1991. It was an example of the Church's desire to initiate projects the Romanians could continue on their own. The Prices trained Romanian leaders, then let them do most of the planning. Sponsorship and donations for the games came from throughout the world. A company in France donated racing wheelchairs while a company in the United States donated tennis shoes to every participant.[62]

Under the Communist regime, disabled children had been on the bottom rung of Romanian society. They could not go to school or participate in youth activities. In some extreme cases, disabled children spent their time squatting unclothed on the floor and staring at each other. Some who had never been outside their orphanage participated in the first Romanian Special Olympics. Approximately two thousand spectators watched with tear-glistened eyes as the five hundred contestants filed into the stadium. They were led by a young girl in a wheelchair, disabled during the 1989 revolution, carrying the torch to light the Special Olympics flame. The Prices greeted them with hugs and tears at the end of the track. A steady rain finally stopped as the games began. The children participated in foot races, team sports, and other activities. Every participant received recognition—a medal or a ribbon, a T-shirt, and a photograph of themselves. The Romanian prime minister, along with ambassadors' wives, helped present the awards. The games publicized the plight of children with disabilities and helped change attitudes about how to treat them. As evidence of its success, Romanian leaders began planning future Special Olympics that would involve the whole country, and laws were later passed favoring disabled children.[63] The Prices' contribution was not forgotten. When welfare representatives visited Romania in 1995, the national director of the program expressed his gratitude for the Prices' work and explained that the program was now completely self-sufficient.[64]

More Service Projects in Romania

Another beneficiary of a Church-sponsored effort was the Central University Library in Bucharest. Romania's craving for materials written in English was made known by Hack Miller, a *Deseret News* columnist who toured Romania in late 1989. His tour guide explained that Romanians wanted "gum wrappers if they have English written on them. Newspapers, magazines, books—anything!"

During the December upheaval, a fire destroyed many valuable collections of books and periodicals at the Central University Library. Responding to the crisis, George S. Barrus, an emeritus BYU communications professor, and Elder Russell M. Nelson encouraged BYU to sponsor a book project.[65] A campus-wide effort netted twenty thousand volumes that arrived in Romania in August 1991. The 922 cartons represented the largest single book acquisition from the United States to restock the library. The library staff formed a chain line fifty people long into the library and cheerfully unloaded the cartons.[66] In gratitude, the library director created a library exhibit with a banner that read, "A Presentation of The Church of Jesus Christ of Latter-day Saints."[67]

The first team of humanitarian service workers left by February 1992. This did not signal the cessation of humanitarian efforts, however, since other service workers followed. Romania continued to be the beneficiary of Church-sponsored projects. From 1991 to 1992, the Germany Duesseldorf Stake gathered food, sanitary supplies, clothing, and toys, and delivered them to Romania. In September 1992, funds to help renovate two orphanages and a nursing home were raised in a benefit concert sponsored by the Wuppertal Ward in the Duesseldorf Stake. Construction supplies were purchased, and stake members personally helped refurbish the facilities. The tools were left behind for future use by Romanians.[68]

Young Missionaries Arrive in Romania

Young single missionaries entered Romania soon after the service workers. Although service work preceded the missionaries, there was no direct connection between the two—they were simply concurrent. Still, they complimented each other since the service workers attended to massive social ills and the missionaries to spiritual malaise.

During Elder Nelson's visit in February 1990, Elder Christopher Jessop entered the MTC bound for Italy. He had served ten months when he was notified that he had been selected, along with fellow Italian-speaking missionaries Ryan Osborne and Ray Van Wagoner, to serve in Romania. These missionaries were chosen because of the kinship between Romanian and Italian languages. The missionaries left for Vienna on December 4, having been reassigned to the Austria Vienna East Mission. Dan Peterson, fresh from studying Croatian in the MTC but unable to obtain a Yugoslav visa, also joined them in Romania. President Neuenschwander appointed Elder Jessop as the district leader. Anticipating the culture shock and deprivation of everyday life in Romania, the president blessed the missionaries to see inside the people and not judge by exterior appearances. Initially, Elder Jessop was taken aback by the grime and dreariness of a nation benighted by a self-serving dictatorship, but he recalled the president's blessing and, with his companions, began the task at hand.[69]

The missionaries celebrated Christmas soon after their arrival. It was the first opportunity Romanians had had to commemorate the occasion in forty-five years. In January the missionaries contracted a professor of English at the University of Bucharest to teach them Romanian.

Membership was minimal. The Munteanu family, a lone family of members, lived in Sibiu, located in the northwestern Romanian region of Transylvania. The parents and their son had been baptized in Germany. Although isolated from the missionaries by distance, the family was visited by them as occasion permitted. Another member living in Bucharest soon proved to be untrustworthy, absconding with some of the food and supplies of the service workers.

Church services were held at one of the service workers' apartments. Romanians began attending the meetings, and when the apartment became overcrowded, the missionaries arranged for a room in a vocational school. There was no heat the first winter so they met for only an hour. A visitor who attended regularly, Gheorghie (Bigi) Banu, quipped that they should close the windows so the people outside would not get cold.

Elder Jessop was discouraged by the seeming lack of progress when he went to Vienna January 18–21, 1991, for a conference with other missionary leaders from eastern Europe under the Austria Vienna East Mission (illus. 7-3). There he heard the glowing reports of Elders Stratov and Bradbury from Ukraine and Elder Garner from Bulgaria. But President Neuenschwander counseled him to be patient and attend to all his duties no matter how small.

Meanwhile, Church leaders called new missionaries to Romania and sent them to the MTC in Provo to learn Romanian. Arriving in the country in spring 1991, the missionaries carefully enlarged the scope of their

Courtesy Christopher Jessop

Illus. 7-3. Missionary leadership seminar for the Austria Vienna East Mission in Vienna at the mission home, January 18–21, 1991. Back row *(left to right):* Brian Bradbury (Ukraine), Ivan Stratov (Ukraine). Middle row *(left to right):* Kerry Holt (Yugoslavia), President and Sister Neuenschwander, Ryan Cox (Yugoslavia). Front row *(left to right):* David Garner (Bulgaria), Darren Jepperson (Yugoslavia), Chris Jessop (Romania), Brother and Sister Harman (Vienna mission home).

activity. One example of this was that they began wearing name tags a couple of months after arriving. Although the missionaries knew they were watched and followed, no one interrupted their activities. In December 1991, they did the first street displays, but only after obtaining permission from local authorities.

International circumstances came to their aid unexpectedly. Concurrent with the arrival of the service workers and the missionaries, a massive international adoption effort arose almost spontaneously as couples from around the world tried to ease the Romanian orphans' suffering. Interestingly, visiting members hoping to adopt children had an influence that indirectly led to the first baptisms in Romania.

International Response to the Romanian Orphan Crisis

Albert Choules Jr., a counselor in the Area Presidency, witnessed the orphanages' needs:

> These typical tendencies for children to love became especially apparent to me on my first visit to Romania. I remember it vividly. Sister [Marilyn] Choules and I went to various institutions with our humanitarian missionaries who were serving there. At an orphanage we saw a rather long, narrow, glass-enclosed room where twenty or so children were playing. They were about three years of age. Most of their daytime hours were spent entertaining themselves and each other, apparently with very little adult care. I asked the supervisor if I could open the door and take some pictures. She agreed. Upon opening the door, many of the children rushed out. I was reminded of days in my youth, when in like manner I saw cattle and horses rush to freedom when a corral gate was opened. These children, however, were not rushing to be free. They hungered for love. Soon we had one or more grasping at each of our legs, reaching up for the love for which they were so starved.[70]

In April and October 1990, ABC's *20/20* aired programs describing the orphans' plight. The October program received a greater response than any other broadcast in its history. Some Americans disrupted their own settled lives and traveled to Romania to adopt and ease the burden of the children.[71]

Cheryl and Steve Worsley of Santa Anita, California, had a family of daughters ranging from age ten to twenty-six. They discussed the Romanian orphans with their extended family—three sisters, a brother, and their respective spouses—and concluded to arrange for adoptions in Bucharest.[72] The Worsley's Romanian violin instructor referred them to a cousin,

Octavian Vasilescu, who lived in Bucharest. Serving as a chauffeur, Octavian helped the Worsleys in their adoption activities and then took them to the Church's meeting place to attend Sabbath services on November 18, 1990. Octavian, not much interested in religion, was startled when Alvin Price told him, "You're a good man." Octavian replied, "How do you know?" Alvin's response was, "I do." After that exchange, Octavian decided to attend the services. President Neuenschwander, also in attendance that day, talked about honesty and spending time with children. The message was timely for Octavian, who was disconcerted by the events in his country and lamented the lack of integrity that seemed to prevail. Because of his Communist background, Octavian had the idea that all churches were strange, but this service impressed him deeply. He received a Book of Mormon and started reading it. A few weeks later, he began translating at Church services.[73] Another Worsley contact, their landlady, Doina Biolaru, also began attending church.[74]

In addition to the Worsleys, other Church members from America traveled to Romania and, while struggling through stressful adoption proceedings, found solace at church meetings. Although the service workers were under strict orders to remain apart from adoption matters, they provided medical assistance, and the priesthood holders gave blessings as requested. The parents, however, could continue their associations with one another after church services, supporting each other as they wended their way through the Romanian bureaucracy, a process that often took months.[75]

David Stoddard, Cheryl Worsley's brother, also traveled to adopt children in December 1990. Octavian helped him during that month and again in February 1991. He confessed to feeling guided while helping the Stoddards. For example, the adoption temporarily stalled for want of birth certificates until he realized he had obtained them—without being asked—several months earlier and that they were in his car. The Stoddards involved Octavian in many gospel conversations, and he began to feel a sense of brotherhood.[76] The Stoddards, Worsleys, and other siblings succeeded in adopting eleven children.[77] More significantly for the Church in Romania, the family had fellowshipped two of the first Romanian converts, Octavian Vasilescu and Doina Biolaru.

Romanian Branches

Anticipating conversions and baptisms, the Church remodeled a house and fitted one room with a baptismal font. It was ready for service in early 1991.[78] On March 24, three Romanians were baptized. In

Courtesy Christopher Jessop

Illus. 7-4. In February 1991, Octavian Vasilescu, a native of Romania, was the first to be baptized into the Church in that country. Left to right: Octavian Vasilescu, Sister Choules, Elder Choules, Doina Vasilescu, Sister Neuenschwander, and President Neuenschwander.

addition to Brother Vasilescu and Sister Biolaru was Camelia (Cami) Ionescu. Brother Vasilescu eventually became the first branch president, Sister Biolaru the first Relief Society president, and Sister Ionescu the first translator (illus. 7-4).[79]

Sister Ionescu's boyfriend had been baptized into the Church while on a trip to France. One day she answered a telephone call from Elder Jessop, inviting her boyfriend to attend services. After listening to the elder struggle with Romanian for a minute, they switched to conversing in English. Prior to her baptism, Sister Ionescu had already translated the hymn "Because I Have Been Given Much" for the service. She later translated the discussions and forty-five other hymns. Cami gave the translations to Elder Jessop, who entered them on the Davis's laptop computer. He added diacritics and then pasted the Romanian text on the music. Afterward, the material was ready for use in church services.[80]

In August 1991, a woman attended a church meeting with her daughter. The mother was a journalist, and she threatened to blacken the reputation of the Church if it harmed her daughter. Then one particular Sunday, the two women fasted to know if the Church was true. Elder Jessop felt as if there were electricity in the air when they arrived. He was relieved and overjoyed when they bore testimony that they had received their answer. Both women were baptized six days later.

This family added their strength to the first branch in Romania, organized July 28, 1991 in Bucharest. Elders Boyd K. Packer and Dallin H.
Oaks visited in September 1991, tending to the needs of the new congregation. By the end of 1991, fifty-five baptisms had been performed.[81]
Though the missionaries attempted to baptize only those they felt were
fully committed, disaffection and inactivity still occurred. New members
could not always withstand adversity and adhere to the Church's requirements. Some could not abstain from tobacco and coffee. Some were
offended by other members. In spite of these problems, a second branch
was created in Bucharest on September 1, 1992, and a third branch on
February 14, 1993. By then, there were nearly three hundred members,
including a small branch of eight to ten individuals in Ploeşti.[82]

The Armenian and Romanian experiences were similar in that the
Church's entry was blazed by humanitarian service workers. However,
the Romanian experience followed the traditional model, where young
missionaries presented the gospel message early, with that as their primary
purpose for being in the country. The humanitarian service workers were
not there to proselytize, but their very presence relayed the message that the
Church had a temporal as well as a spiritual mission. Conversely in
Armenia, the service workers assumed the dual role of teaching the
message as well as performing humanitarian service. In Romania this
task remained secondary.

Contacts in Albania

Service workers and missionaries in Albania worked in tandem to
establish a Church presence in the country. Situated across from Italy
on the Adriatic littoral of the Balkan Peninsula, Albania is a small country of approximately 3.5 million people. Communism had isolated the
country from the West and also from its neighbors. Albania was the
only Communist nation in Europe to adopt the Chinese variant of that
political doctrine, which rejected the policy of coexistence with non-
Communist nations.

From the international airport to Tirana, Albania's capital, there are
lines of concrete machine-gun pillboxes like ranks of gray beetles on every
defensible ridge. Intended to protect the nation from any army trying
to reach the seat of government, many have been knocked off their foundations and lay upside down, like empty tortoise shells. Albanian youth
grew up under the specter of an enemy at their doorstep when, in reality,
most foreigners forgot the country existed. Ruled after World War II by

a Communist tyrant as maniacal as any in history, Albania remained a poor, underdeveloped country as Europe entered the modern age. Student demonstrations in 1990 and political unrest in 1991 finally resulted in the first democratic election. Still, the national situation was not conducive to democratic development. Over half the population did not have jobs. Housing and food shortages forced two and three generations to live together in very small apartments. The country's infrastructure was dilapidated and barely functioning.[83] On March 22, 1992, the newly elected president, Sali Berisha, formerly a physician and cardiologist, addressed a victory rally of sixty thousand jubilant supporters: "We are saying farewell to Communism once and for all. It will never return. The long night of Communism has ended. Albania celebrates the greatest day in its history!"[84] But he faced a nearly impossible task in overturning decades of economic and social deterioration.

A year earlier, in 1991, an Albanian had walked into the office of Kenneth Reber, president of the Austria Vienna Mission. Esat Ferra introduced himself as a computer analyst who had defected from Albania. He explained that he had previously met President Wilde in Budapest, Hungary, and that he sought President Reber's assistance for his country. Initially, the president was skeptical because he had met many defectors with hidden agendas. Ferra gave the president a list of ten of his friends along with information about how they could assist the Church to help his country. Later, those references proved to be the key in making contacts that gave the Church exposure at the highest levels of Albanian society.[85]

Meeting the Needs of the People in Albania

Church emissaries entered the country in 1991. Beverly Campbell in Washington, D.C., working through the Albania delegation to the U.N. in New York, made the necessary arrangements for Elders Oaks and Ringger to visit the country's leaders in April 1991.[86] In October, Elder Ringger returned to Albania, this time with President Reber, who received the charge to supervise Church work in Albania, and Lloyd Pendleton, welfare specialist from the Church's area office in Frankfurt, Germany. They talked with officials at the Department of Agriculture, explaining their willingness to meet the nation's needs. When the minister, Nexhmedin Dumani, asked for two hundred tractors, Elder Ringger had to explain the limits of Church assistance. Dumani informed them that many people had come with promises, but nobody had done anything yet.

As they talked, President Reber realized that one of the senior missionaries in Vienna had worked as a soil research specialist and had analyzed soils in the Middle East. During a pause in the translation, he told Elder Ringger. Elder Ringger continued speaking to the minister, "And furthermore, we've got a soil scientist right now in Austria. He could be here next week." Then President Reber remembered that another senior missionary had been a horticulturist and a farmer. He leaned over to Elder Ringger with the information. "And furthermore," Elder Ringger continued to Dumani, "we can have a practical farmer . . . here next week as well."[87] Theron Sommerfeldt, the soil specialist, and George Niedens, the farmer, went to Albania the following week.

Two humanitarian service couples were called to perform longer terms of duty in Albania: Dr. Thales Smith, a retired pediatrician and former stake president from Utah, and his wife, Charone, a nurse; Melvin Brady, a professor of economics from California, and his wife, Randolyn, a teacher of English as a second language. President Reber entered Albania in January 1992 to procure apartments for them. He contacted a name on Ferra's list: Dr. Kodra, the vice-rector at Tirana University. Dr. Kodra helped President Reber contact "practically everybody who was anybody" to make the needed arrangements for the service workers who would arrive soon. He introduced the president to Dr. Anastas Suli, an English-speaking child psychiatrist, and his wife, Sophia. The Sulis were willing to let the missionaries use half their home at no cost, even though the normal apartment rent to foreigners was $400 a month.

When President Reber visited government offices he found a new cast of Albanian leaders. Dr. Kodra, who knew all the replacements, introduced them to the president. At the School of Economics, the dean could not believe that an American professor (Melvin Brady) was willing to teach at the university gratis for eighteen months. Dr. Kodra also took the president to meet Baskim Kopliku—who later became the vice-prime minister—the mayor of Durrës, the second largest city in Albania.[88]

The month after President Reber made arrangements, the couples arrived in Albania. They faced a challenging experience, much as the service workers had in Armenia. That winter the electricity worked erratically and frequently went out for hours at a time. Water ran early in the morning, afternoon, and at night for only two hours at a time. There was little or no heat. When the couples first arrived, they nearly froze. At sunset, they often burrowed under their bed covers, seeking what warmth they could find.[89]

The Smiths worked primarily at the Dystrophy Hospital, a center for treating malnourished children. The conditions at the hospital were tragic. One-third of the windows were broken, the lighting was poor, the rooms stark and gray. The infants lay motionless and unresponsive, staring at the ceiling. The couple approached the problem by developing the trust and confidence of the staff. Lack of supplies had caused much of the problem. In particular, the short supply of baby formula was in fact a home brew with insufficient nutrients. So Elder Smith improvised and produced an adequate baby milk formula. Another pressing problem was that the caretakers received low wages, and running their own households simply wore them out, resulting in mediocre work performance.

Sister Smith began cuddling and exercising the limbs of several children (illus. 7-5). Within two weeks, they began focusing their attention on her face and started making pleasurable sounds. Thereafter, others began to emulate what she was doing. The babies remained Sister Smith's central task for the next eighteen months.

To help alleviate some of the shortages and improve the children's conditions, Church leaders sent a large container of humanitarian

Courtesy Thales and Charone Smith

Illus. 7-5. Charone Smith with children in Albania, c. 1992.

supplies in October. It included soap, diapers, bottles, nipples, clothes, blankets, and medical and cleaning items. In time, the windows were repaired and the walls painted. Elder Smith also taught at the university. He was appalled to find that the most current pediatric text was twenty-five years old. Consequently, he started holding lectures to help the local doctors become current in the field. While in Albania, Elder Smith also treated acute cases of infant diseases, many of which he had seldom seen previously while practicing in the West.[90]

The other set of missionaries was just as busy as the Smiths. Elder Brady taught at the School of Economics and ultimately was appointed as the assistant dean. He helped the college plan its curriculum for the year and was instrumental in obtaining English textbooks from California universities as well as a few copy machines. Meanwhile, Sister Brady taught the professors English so they could use the textbooks.[91]

A third set of missionaries arrived in summer 1992. Farmer George Niedens and his wife, Nancy, extended their mission for several months so they could return to Albania, this time to help establish a honey co-op.[92]

As was the case with all service workers, none of these couples proselytized, but they did answer questions. They held a meeting in the Sulis's garden in May 1992, and forty people came. Elder Ringger and President Reber were also there. Even though many audience members asked to be taught the gospel, they were advised to be patient.

Elder Ringger and President Reber requested approval from Albanian authorities for the entry of four new service workers. In June 1992, Elders Matthew Wirthlin, Mark Slaybaugh, and Paul McAllister, from German missions, and Beau Jarvis, from the Austria Vienna Mission, arrived in Albania. They studied the native language from 8:00 A.M. to 2:00 P.M., then did humanitarian service until the evening when then resumed their language studies. Part of their service involved helping Sister Smith at the hospital twice a week. On other days, they worked at an orphanage. Finally, through the minister of culture, arrangements were made for the elders to be involved in youth activities such as basketball. These young service workers impressed the minister, and he even invited them to his home for dinner (illus. 7-6).[93]

An Albanian Foothold

Young Blendi Kokona heard about the Americans and decided to attend a church service with the idea of practicing his English. After the meeting, the young missionaries asked him how he felt. Blendi said, "It

Illus. 7-6. The first Mormon missionaries in Albania, c. 1992. Back row *(left to right)*: Elders Jarvis, McAlister, Wirthlin, and Slaybaugh. Front row *(left to right)*: Sister Niedens, Melvin and Randolyn Brady, Sister and President Reber, Charone and Thales Smith, and passersby.

was good." They made an appointment to meet him later that week at the statue of Skanderbeg, legendary hero of Albania in its battle against Turkish domination. The men found a park bench, and Blendi began learning about new and interesting principles. That evening he prayed as the elders had taught him, and Blendi felt as if someone in heaven were listening. On July 25, 1992, Blendi Kokona became the first convert in Albania. He later served in San Diego, California, as the first missionary from his country.[94]

Baptisms occurred regularly in the following weeks (illus. 7-7). While Albania is 70 percent Muslim, years of Communism had limited the degree of their devotion. They were starved for anything spiritual, intellectual, or from the outside. The missionaries did not have to tract to find contacts. People came to them. Even on the first day they arrived in the country and toured the city, at least fifty people asked who they were. However, the missionaries made prospective members wait until they were assured they understood the commitment that baptism entailed.[95]

During their May visit, Elder Ringger and President Reber approached officials in the Ministry of Religion about granting recognition for the Church. Government authorities were hesitant to discuss the issue, but the two Church representatives obtained an audience with President Sali Berisha. Elder Ringger and President Reber had several contacts to

Courtesy Thales and Charone Smith

Illus. 7-7. Humanitarian service workers Melvin (*far left*) and Randolyn Brady (*far right*) pose with two newly baptized Church members in the early 1990s.

the Albanian president. For example, Dr. Suli's wife, who allowed the Smiths to live in her house, was a friend of Berisha's wife. And one of Sister Brady's first English pupils was Berisha's daughter. During the meeting, President Berisha explained that the parliament did not want to address the issue, preferring to have only the three traditional religions—Islam, Eastern Orthodox, and Catholicism.[96]

The Albanian president remained very friendly toward the Church. In September, Elder Ringger brought the president of the Swiss Parliament, his personal friend, to Albania. The trip culminated with a dinner that honored the parliamentarian visitor. Fifty people came, including Baskim Kopliku, the vice-prime minister, the U.S. ambassador, and various government ministers. Just as the meal began, the door opened and in walked Sali Berisha. The ambassador turned to Sister Smith and asked, "How did you get him here? I've been trying to see him for six weeks."[97]

The Church continued to grow without any adverse reaction by the government. As President Reber explained, "In Albania, since there was no constitution, no laws or regulations, it was kind of just do what you had to do, so all of the arrangements were made."[98] On April 23, 1993, Elder Oaks returned to Albania along with Elder Neuenschwander. Elder Oaks invited all members in the country to attend the dedication service. They rented a bus and traveled to the southeast end of the city. In the park surrounding the Monument of Heroes, Elder Oaks blessed Albania and dedicated it for the gospel.[99] At the end of the Smiths' service in August 1993, there were 130 members and three branches: two in Tirana and one in Durrës.[100]

That same month, Pope John Paul II visited Albania, the first Pope ever to cross the Adriatic for this purpose. Mother Teresa, a native Albanian, was part of his entourage. One of the doctors at the Dystrophy Hospital made arrangements for several members of the staff, including Sister Smith, to visit her for about fifteen minutes. In good English, Mother Teresa explained, "We cannot love God and man and do nothing to lessen human suffering." In recognition of Sister Smith's contributions to Albania, Mother Teresa, the fabled benefactor of the poor, honored Sister Smith by giving her a silver medallion of her order (illus. 7-8).[101]

The service program worked in tandem with the missionary program in both Romania and Albania. Undoubtedly, Church leaders hoped the service program would engender favorable feelings and indirectly pave the way for proselytizing missionaries. However, there is no evidence to suggest it was ever used as a bargaining chip for that purpose. The primary purpose was temporal welfare, regardless of any secondary

Courtesy Thales and Charone Smith

Illus. 7-8. Mother Teresa visited the orphanages in Albania in 1993 and awarded Sister Charone Smith a medal of her order for her service to the children there.

purpose it might have served. Indeed, the service workers sometimes followed the young missionaries. Such was the case in Bulgaria.

Service Workers Aid Bulgarians

Humanitarian service workers arrived in Bulgaria after the mission was established. Lynn and Beverly Nelson entered the country in February 1992, the second year after proselytizing had begun. Lynn had served as director of the Sheltered Workshop, a special education school program in Logan, Utah. The Nelsons' charge was simply to reduce the suffering of the Bulgarian children.[102]

Just as the Nelsons entered the country, a large container arrived from Deseret Industries. The staff at the Medical School in Sofia was ecstatic. To make sure the supplies reached them, they sent their own vehicle to pick up the container at the Varna seaport. The service workers spread the contents of the container on a schoolroom floor to examine what they had received. The Nelsons distributed the supplies while senior missionary Morris Mower stood at the door to ensure that everything was properly accounted for as people left.[103]

The Nelsons also visited the director of Special Schools in the Ministry of Education and asked what Bulgarian children needed. They discovered the officials wanted assistance in psychological testing and curriculum development. The Nelsons relayed these requests to officials in Salt Lake City, and specialists were contacted to donate two or more weeks in Bulgaria as needed. One of those answering the call was Cregg Ingram from Brigham Young University. Brother Ingram visited special education schools in Bulgaria for four weeks and worked closely with the school's dean to train special education teachers at the University of Sofia. He returned home and devoted six more months to develop the needed curriculum.[104]

Meanwhile, the Nelsons determined that some Bulgarian education specialists needed firsthand experience in America. They selected the headmaster of a school for the deaf and an associate professor from the University of Sofia to visit Utah in early 1993. Professor Ingram hosted them at Brigham Young University. They also visited the University of Utah and Utah State University. The foreign visitors were impressed by the respect given to the disabled and by the special education programs in the universities.[105]

The Nelsons suggested that the Bulgarians create a model classroom—a wood workshop with modern tools where disabled students could develop a skill that would provide them some measure of independence in life. The headmistress of the selected school believed so strongly in this program that she defied the old system by demanding contributions from chambers of commerce in various cities. She obtained the funds for the facility, and in May 1993 the Church gave the new classroom $8,000 worth of equipment and tools.[106] The instructor of the model workshop was devoted to the task, especially since both his father and grandfather had taught the disabled.[107]

The Nelsons found time to expand their work into other areas. They met with the head pediatrician in Bulgaria and asked what was most needed in his field. In response to a request for training, Fanny Tait, a neurologist, and Blair Bybee, an oncologist, both from the University of

Utah Medical Center, volunteered to go to Bulgaria for two weeks. Bulgarian doctors gathered from throughout the country to be instructed, and the U.S. doctors developed a warm rapport with their colleagues. During their term of service, the Nelsons arranged for six other pediatric specialists to visit and conduct more training seminars.

Through the Nelsons, the Church helped implement a project for the International Eye Institute. The Institute provided funds to purchase modern equipment, and the Church provided the doctors to train Bulgarian specialists in its use. The first volunteer was Dr. Gregory Brinton, a specialist in retina surgery. He was there for two weeks, teaching and performing surgery. Seven more specialists followed.

The Nelsons oversaw other services such as coordinating the delivery of textbooks to schools and libraries, microfilm equipment to an archive, clothing and blankets to orphanages, and braille typewriters to two schools for the blind.[108] Though they were under the direction of authorities at Church headquarters, they coordinated their efforts with President Warner, who counseled them about their efforts in Bulgaria.[109]

Inured by decades of cynicism under Communist rule, the Bulgarians were leery of accepting help without payment. Community service had always been forced in the Communist system, and they found it difficult to believe in a free offering.[110] But through the Church's efforts, they learned of the benefits that came from receiving voluntary service. The pediatricians and ophthalmologists were taught not only new techniques but also given examples of an important social ethic they could use to help build their country.[111] On May 18, 1993, Elder M. Russell Ballard of the Quorum of the Twelve observed the results of the Nelsons' work, assuring them that they had accomplished their task of blessing Bulgaria's children.[112]

The Church's service program aimed at meeting needs defined by officials from the host country. This impressed officials, one of whom commented privately to President Warner that, unlike some other religions they had dealt with, the Latter-day Saints kept their promises.[113] The labors of the humanitarian service workers also sparked the Bulgarian's interest in this new religion. Individuals often interrupted technical lectures to ask questions about the Church. Many influential people who knew of the service projects also became friendly to the Church.[114]

Distinguished Service

Although humanitarian service was rendered elsewhere in the Eastern Bloc besides the southern tier, Armenia, Romania, and Albania were exceptional because the service workers preceded or arrived concurrently with the first missionaries. More often, humanitarian service complemented the missionary program, as in Bulgaria, providing a witness of the Church's benefit for body as well as soul. The humanitarian service workers in the Eastern Bloc sacrificed their own personal comfort to aid people in need. Their exemplary lives attracted attention to their faith, the wellspring of their service. This faith provided evidence along with testimony, fruits along with words.

As an ultimate aim of the gospel, service can appropriately accompany the Church's message. Church officials continue to develop the humanitarian service program, affirming their intention to pursue it in the long term and countering the argument that their efforts were temporary only until they could send in proselytizing missionaries. If government authorities or potential converts were favorably influenced by the humanitarian service program, then it was worthwhile from the Church's perspective.

Notes

1. Matthew Brown, "LDS Relief Efforts are Expanding to Fill Global Role," *Deseret News,* April 17, 1995, A-1.

2. Leo A. Jardine and Judith C. N. Jardine, *Out of Obscurity, Out of Captivity, Out of Darkness* (Salt Lake City: L. and J. Jardine, 1998), 5.

3. Vera Merrell, telephone interview by author, February 26, 1997. Vera had volunteered at the Sort Center since 1992.

4. "Am I My Brother's Keeper?" *Church News,* published by *Deseret News,* November 29, 1997, 3, 6.

5. "Church Gives $100,000 for Relief Efforts in Quake-Stricken Armenia," *Church News,* December 17, 1988, 5.

6. "Church Will Help Armenian Homeless," *Church News,* August 19, 1989, 4; Peter R. Huntsman, talk, funeral of David Horne, January 24, 1996, Monument Park Stake, Salt Lake City.

7. Huntsman, talk.

8. David Horne, interviewed by author, May 12, 1993, Yerevan, Armenia.

9. Horne, interview, May 12, 1993.

10. Horne, interview, May 12, 1993. Except as noted, the source for the next two paragraphs as well.

11. Kahlile Mehr, journal, May 10, 1993.

12. Roger Doxey, telephone interview by author, February 8, 1996.

13. Narina Sarkissian and Susanna Sarkissian, interviewed by Matthew K. Heiss, March 23, 1995, Provo, Utah, typescript, 10, copy in possession of the interviewee, Provo, Utah.

14. Doxey, telephone interview.

15. Sarkissian and Sarkissian, interview, 10; Nara Sarkissian, talk, November 19, 1993, audio tape, in possession of author.

16. Scott Hurst, telephone interview by author, February 29, 1996; Doxey, telephone interview.

17. David Horne, interviewed by author, August 21, 1995, Salt Lake City; Doxey, telephone interview.

18. Mehr, journal, May 10, 1993. Source for the next paragraph as well.

19. Elyanor Vardanian, "Goodbye: American with an Armenian Heart," *Republic of Armenia*, April 24, 1996, typescript translation, 3–4.

20. Huntsman, talk.

21. Doxey, telephone interview.

22. Horne, interview, August 21, 1995.

23. Hurst, telephone interview.

24. "Church Sends Dry Milk to Armenia," *Church News*, December 2, 1989, 4.

25. Huntsman, talk.

26. Horne, interview, August 21, 1995.

27. Linda Thomson, "Huntsman Giving No-Interest Loan to Armenia," *Deseret News*, September 30, 1998, B-2.

28. Horne, interview, August 21, 1995.

29. Horne, interview, May 12, 1993.

30. "Two Republics in USSR Are Dedicated," *Church News*, September 28, 1991, 3; Sarkissian and Sarkissian, interview, 31; Mehr, journal, May 10, 1993.

31. Horne, interview, August 21, 1995; Mehr, journal, May 10, 1993.

32. Doxey, telephone interview.

33. Doxey, telephone interview; Hurst, telephone interview.

34. Anna Sargsian, telephone interview by author, March 14, 1996. Source for the next two paragraphs as well.

35. Hurst, telephone interview.

36. Doxey, telephone interview. Source for the next two paragraphs as well.

37. Doxey, telephone interview; Hurst, telephone interview. Sources for next paragraph as well.

38. Sarkissian and Sarkissian, interview, 2–5.

39. Sarkissian and Sarkissian, interview, 12–17.

40. Sarkissian and Sarkissian, interview, 19–21.

41. Sarkissian and Sarkissian, interview, 22–24; George Cannon, untitled manuscript dated March 25, 1995, in possession of author.

42. Sarkissian and Sarkissian, interview, 27–28.

43. Doxey, telephone interview; Sarkissian and Sarkissian, interview, 25.

44. Sarkissian and Sarkissian, interview, 25–26.

45. Sarkissian and Sarkissian, interview, 27.

46. Sargsian, telephone interview.

47. Sarkissian and Sarkissian, interview, 28.

48. Hurst, telephone interview.

49. Doxey, telephone interview; Sarkissian and Sarkissian, interview, 29.

50. Mehr, journal, May 7, 1993.

51. Hurst, telephone interview. Source for next paragraph as well.

52. Sargsian, telephone interview.

53. DeAnna Ball and Terry Ball, eds., *Each One a Miracle* (Orem, Utah: Grandin Book, 1994), 1–2.

54. "Czechoslovakia Recognizes Church; Romania and Bulgaria Are Dedicated," *Church News*, March 3, 1990, 7.

55. Thomas S. Monson, "A Little Child Shall Lead Them," *Ensign* 20 (May 1990): 54.

56. Gerry Avant, "LDS Humanitarian Relief in Romania," *Church News*, August 18, 1990, 3.

57. "Members in Netherlands Gather Food," *Church News*, March 17, 1990, 4.

58. Avant, "Relief in Romania," 3.

59. Jeanine Tew, "Romania, Land of New Light," unpublished ms., 3–10, in possession of author; Romanian Relief Project Report, August 11, 1991, in Hungary Budapest Mission, Historical Records and Minutes, 1991 report, Church Archives, The Church of Jesus Christ of Latter-day Saints, Salt Lake City. Sources for next paragraph as well.

60. Beverly Cutler, homecoming speech, March 8, 1992, Church Archives.

61. Tew, "Romania," 10.

62. Vaunene Thygerson, "Missionaries Perform Humanitarian Service," *Church News*, December 7, 1991, 10.

63. Thygerson, "Humanitarian Service," 10; Tew, "Romania," 8–9.

64. Jardine and Jardine, *Out of Obscurity*, 10–11.

65. "Y Books to Go to Literature-Starved Romania," *Church News*, March 30, 1991, 6.

66. "BYU Project Replenishes Romanian Library Shelves," *Church News*, August 17, 1991, 5; Harold Davis report, September 14, 1991, in Hungary Budapest Mission, 1991 report.

67. Tew, "Romania," 9.

68. "Concert Assists Romania," *Church News*, November 21, 1992, 7.

69. Christopher Jessop, interviewed by author, March 4, 1995, Provo, Utah, 1. Also the source for the rest of this section.

70. Albert Choules Jr., "A Child's Love Matured," *Ensign* 24 (May 1994): 13.

71. Ball and Ball, *Each One a Miracle*, 3.

72. "All of a Kind Family," *Ensign* 23 (December 1993): 57.

73. Octavian Vasilescu, interviewed by author, October 4, 1993, Salt Lake City. Also source for the next paragraph.

74. "All of a Kind Family," 57.

75. Ball and Ball, *Each One a Miracle*, 20–21, 67, 109, 113, 130–31.

76. Vasilescu, interview.

77. "All of a Kind Family," 57.

78. Cutler, homecoming speech.

79. Jessop, interview, 2.

80. Jessop, interview, 2. Unless otherwise noted, this is the source for the rest of this section.

81. Cutler, homecoming speech.

82. Vasilescu, interview.

83. Charone H. Smith, "Albania, a Labor of Love," in Susette Fletcher Green and Dawn Hall Anderson, eds., *To Rejoice as Women* (Salt Lake City: Deseret Book, 1994), 153.

84. Edwin E. Jacques, *The Albanians and Ethnic History from Prehistoric Times to the Present* (Jefferson, N.C.: McFarland, 1995), 701.

85. Kenneth Dudley Reber, interviewed by Matthew K. Heiss, 1994, Salt Lake City, typescript, 79–80, copy in possession of the interviewee, Sandy, Utah.

86. Beverly Campbell, telephone interview by author, January 30, 1997.

87. Reber, interview, 75–76.

88. Reber, interview, 77, 81.

89. Thales Smith, "A Balkan Adventure: Humanitarian Missionaries in Albania," *Journal of Collegium Aesculapium* (fall 1994): 29; Reber, interview, 82.

90. Thales Smith, "Humanitarian Missionaries," 29–32; Charone Smith, "Albania," 155–56.

91. Reber, interview, 79.

92. Reber, interview, 79, 81–82, 86. Source for next paragraph as well.

93. Reber, interview, 82–83.

94. Blendi Konkona, interviewed by Matthew K. Heiss, 1996, Provo, Utah, draft typescript, 16–20, copy in possession of the interviewee, Provo, Utah.

95. Reber, interview, 83–84, 91.

96. Reber, interview, 78, 82, 85.

97. Reber, interview, 87–88.

98. Reber, interview, 88.

99. Reber, interview, 90–91.

100. Thales Smith, "Humanitarian Missionaries," 33.

101. Charone Smith, telephone interview by author, January 9, 1997; Charone Smith, "Albania," 157.

102. Lynn Nelson, telephone interview by author, December 31, 1994. Unless otherwise noted, this is the source for the rest of the section.

103. Morris Mower, telephone interview by author, March 9, 1995.

104. Lynn Nelson, telephone interview by author, December 31, 1994.

105. Gerry Avant, "Volunteers Bring Hope to Bulgarian Children," *Church News*, June 5, 1993, 4.

106. Dale Warner, interviewed by author, December 26, 1994, Ogden, Utah.

107. Lynn Nelson, telephone interview by author, December 31, 1994. Source for the next two paragraphs as well.

108. Avant, "Volunteers Bring Hope," 4.

109. Warner, interview.

110. Timothy J. Kuta, "Apostles to the Slavs," *Latter-Day Digest* 3 (August 1994): 22.

111. Kuta, "Apostles to the Slavs," 23.

112. Avant, "Volunteers Bring Hope," 4.

113. Warner, interview.

114. Kuta, "Apostles to the Slavs," 23.

8

Outer and Inner Frontiers

1993–2002

The spiritual and social advancement of new members presented a challenge for Church leaders, as did establishing and maintaining good relations with the various governments. This effort needed continual attention, especially when representatives from traditional religions began pressuring government leaders to keep out Western churches and the populace became increasingly disenchanted with the West. Religious receptiveness declined, and missionaries encountered more difficult proselytizing circumstances. In addition, political and social freedom created a power vacuum that was quickly filled by the lawless rather than the lawful. Criminal activity, social disruption, and economic decline caused problems for members and missionaries alike.

New converts in the East began facing the trials of membership in a religion that required more than a casual commitment. The new members joined with others who had little background in the Church and its programs. The experience members of the Church had in central and eastern Europe during the 1990s was much like that of the members in America during the 1830s.[1] Socializing converts into the gospel community was not an overnight process, particularly with a sparse membership. That process was characterized by President Gary Browning in 1991:

> I think some people thought droves of persons would join the Church once the gospel became available to citizens of Russia. Yes, there will be many members someday, but as in any land, the Church grows slowly. First, a lot of people find interest in it, find the Church has some fascination for them. But when they probe into it and find out that personal discipleship of Christ is the goal, then other things often begin to take precedence for some of them. The result is that when it is all shaken out, there is a residue of beautiful people, truly the salt of the earth, who have testimonies, who know the gospel is true, who want to live it, who will do anything

righteous for it, and who know its power and impact in their lives. The gospel works here as it works anywhere else in the world: one person at a time making a covenant with the Lord to change his or her life and to progress with God.[2]

Little in the people's cultural traditions, particularly those of Russia, Belarus, and Ukraine, existed to prepare them for the distinctive practices and social community of the Church. As explained by President Howard Biddulph:

> The mode of worship, spiritual community, member participation, and lay leadership of the Latter-day Saints differed fundamentally from the liturgy, clergy, and parish life of Orthodoxy; and it also contrasted with participation in the official social organizations of Soviet Communism. . . . Only the state bureaucracy could administer aid or assistance to the needy. Only official organizations controlled by the Communist Party could engage in significant social purposes. As a consequence, Soviet society produced a people who were highly distrustful and cut off from the personal lives of one another.[3]

Having crossed the Communist frontier, Church leaders now confronted the task of building up a faithful membership in the East. The congregations faced attacks against their new faith from the public as well as from within when converts forsook their membership. At the same time, the Church rapidly advanced eastward across the expanses of the Ukraine and the vast hinterland of Siberia to the shores of the Pacific. In the period from 1987 to 2001, the eastern frontier of the Church had multiplied from the East Central Districts of the Austria Vienna Mission (illus. 8-1) with only a handful of members and uncertain prospects to nineteen missions (illus. 8-2) and a membership of approximately thirty-two thousand.[4]

Eastward Expansion

Elder Hans Ringger's service in the Europe Area Presidency lasted for eight years (1985–93). During that time, he provided continuity in the administration of the Church's eastward expansion. Elder Ringger was replaced by Elder Dennis Neuenschwander who, with fifteen years of service in the East, was well prepared for this new calling. As members of the Quorum of the Twelve, Elder Dallin H. Oaks and his 1995 successor, Elder Jeffrey R. Holland, served as the first point of contact for the Church. However, many Apostles visited eastern Europe to dedicate

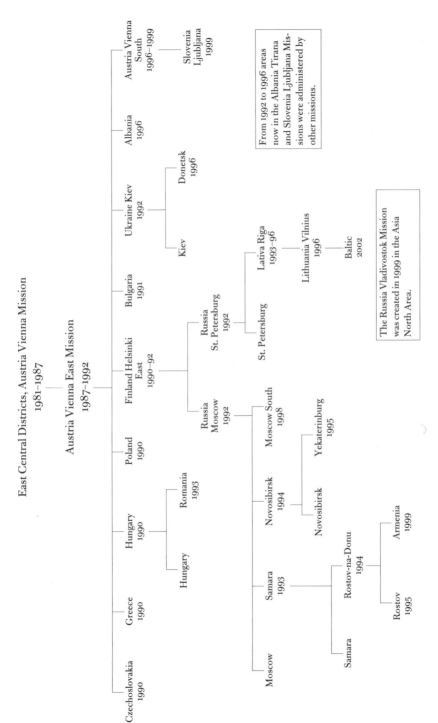

Illus. 8-1. Chart illustrating the rapid increase of missions in central and eastern Europe from 1981 to 2001. Nineteen missions grew out of the Austria Vienna East Mission. Dates of new missions and name changes are noted but are not included with the name of the parent mission after a division. Courtesy Dennis B. Neuenschwander

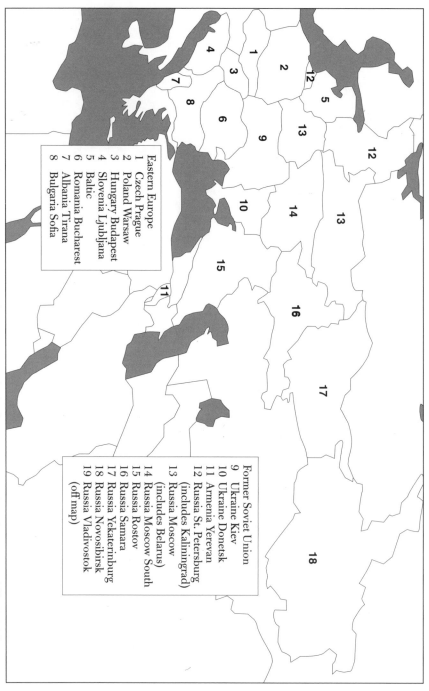

Eastern Europe

1 Czech Prague
2 Poland Warsaw
3 Hungary Budapest
4 Slovenia Ljubljana
5 Baltic
6 Romania Bucharest
7 Albania Tirana
8 Bulgaria Sofia

Former Soviet Union

9 Ukraine Kiev
10 Ukraine Donetsk
11 Armenia Yerevan
12 Russia St. Petersburg
(includes Kaliningrad)
13 Russia Moscow
(includes Belarus)
14 Russia Moscow South
15 Russia Rostov
16 Russia Samara
17 Russia Yekaterinburg
18 Russia Novosibirsk
19 Russia Vladivostok
(off map)

Illus. 8-2. Map showing the Church's missions, as of January 2002, in the former Eastern Bloc. Courtesy Kahlile B. Mehr newly opened countries for the gospel message. The Church then expanded its missionary corps in the new missions of the former Soviet realm. From the four senior couples that had served in Yugoslavia, Hungary, and Poland in 1985, the missionary force in the former Communist world grew to more than 300 by the end of 1991, doubled to 650 by the end of 1992, and rose to 1,650 by the end of 1997.[5]

As early as 1993, missionaries had entered virtually every country in central and eastern Europe that had previously been under Soviet influence. The long-awaited hour for the door to open had now arrived. The challenge of nurturing the Church's membership in the region was just as great as the process of conversion. The following section examines this process from the western to the eastern edges of the former Communist realm.

Hungary, Czechoslovakia, and Poland had once constituted the western barrier of the Communist world. By 1992 the countries had become a doorway for Western enterprise as the promises of a free market system began to be realized. The economic situation started to improve as more food products became available, imported goods appeared on shelves, and buildings underwent renovations. However, this prosperity was only for some, since many were impoverished from the turmoil of changing from command-driven to market-driven economies. In either case, baptisms leveled off after the intense growth of the first few years, a trend observed elsewhere in central and eastern Europe.

Hungary. In the early 1990s, baptismal success in Hungary (in terms of the number of converts per missionary) exceeded any other country in central and eastern Europe.[6] Reflecting on his service, President James Wilde said, "I was privileged to be part of a miracle. I have never seen better missionaries who actively loved the people they served. They were superb proselyters, and the Hungarian people were prepared to listen."[7] When President Wilde left in July 1994, three-quarters of the leadership in the branches was native born.[8] The year 1994 saw many members of a family joining those who had already converted to the new religion, a basis for building strong congregations.[9] Many new members progressed on to receiving their endowments in the Freiberg Temple, with five bus loads going there in 1995 alone (illus. 8-3). By 1995 three new chapels had been completed, more than in any other country of the former Soviet world (illus. 8-4). In November 2001, a fourth new chapel was completed in Debrecen, where János Denndörfer and Margit Toth had worshipped in isolation for decades. At the end of 2001, Hungary had about thirty-six hundred members.[10]

Illus. 8-3. Hungarian Church members traveled to the Freiberg Germany Temple, c. 1996.

Illus. 8-4. This chapel in Györ, Hungary, was dedicated on February 14, 1996.

Czechoslovakia. Annual Church growth in the Czech Republic and Slovakia averaged about 200 per year between 1991 and 1994 before tapering to 176 in 1996 and dropping to about 50 for the rest of the decade.[11] As of 2001, the Czech Republic had 1,750 members and Slovakia 100. The Church did not endure official opposition, though it did face people's reluctance to break from religious tradition.

According to one observer, active anti-Mormon opposition from other faiths discouraged many new members not well founded in their faith. The observer noted that members who had struggled through years of persecution resented what they perceived as casual attitudes toward the Church from those who joined with little struggle and seemed unappreciative of their new faith. On the other hand, the observer concluded that the Church grew stronger in the lives of those who endured. Losses in quantity were offset by gains in quality. Also auguring well for the future of the Church, sixty native Czech returned missionaries were then living in the country.[12]

The annual pilgrimage to the Karlštejn Castle continued to be faithfully observed by members and missionaries in remembrance of John A. Widtsoe's 1929 dedicatory prayer. Consisting of two disparate nationalities, Czechoslovakia quietly parted into the Czech Republic and Slovakia in 1993. Slovakia, in the eastern region, was generally less attentive to the missionaries. After one year (September 1991–92), missionaries had baptized only three people in Bratislava. These more provincial and conservative citizens, who spoke Slovak, did not want to have to read the Book of Mormon in Czech, the only published language in which they

Illus. 8-5. The mission office in Prague, Czechoslvakia, 1997.

Courtesy Walter Whipple

Illus. 8-6. Missionaries at the Missionary Training Center in Provo, Utah, preparing to serve in Poland, December 1991. Their language instructor, Elder Matthew Binns, is third from the right, wearing a white name tag.

could understand it.[13] Total membership in both the Czech Republic and Slovakia amounted to approximately nineteen hundred at the end of 2001 (illus. 8-5).[14]

Poland. In Poland, Church growth occurred even more slowly than in either Hungary or Czechoslovakia. Having been staunch Catholics, the people could not easily sever traditional ties with church and family. Many regarded conversion to the Church as a family catastrophe. Some who did join the Church eventually succumbed to their familial ties and soon became inactive or left the Church. The average for baptisms per missionary peaked in 1990. An expanded missionary force increased baptisms, but the ratio of converts per companionship diminished (illus. 8-6).[15] During the late 1990s, about eighty to a hundred Poles joined the Church each year. By the end of 2001, there were approximately twelve hundred members in Poland.[16]

The Church's Southern Tier in the Former Communist World

The southern tier of the Church in eastern Europe consists of Slovenia, Croatia, Serbia (officially Yugoslavia),[17] Albania, Romania, and Bulgaria. As in Czechoslovakia, Hungary, and Poland, the Church growth in numbers blossomed, then leveled or waned. In addition, political and social problems were more pronounced than in the north. War, government turmoil, economic woes, the unbridled voice of an irresponsible press, and internal frictions within the Church weighed down a fledgling membership that faced challenges similar to those of nineteenth-century Church members who sought refuge in the American West.

Slovenia, Croatia, Serbia. After the dissolution of Yugoslavia, the Church had a presence only in the states of Slovenia, Croatia, and Serbia (illus. 8-7). Situated in the northwest, Slovenia and Croatia were part of the Austro-Hungarian Empire until World War I and were preponderantly Roman Catholic. South and east of these two states, Serbia had been part of the Ottoman Empire for centuries, and its traditional religion was Eastern Orthodox. The Church had never thrived in these countries torn by ethnic enmity.

In April 1993, thirty-six missionaries from Croatia and Slovenia assembled at the Zagreb chapel for instruction from Elder Dallin H. Oaks and President Neuenschwander. Among other remarks, Elder Oaks discussed 1 Nephi 14:12, saying the whole earth was not going to be converted, nor whole nations. It offered a message of comfort and encouragement to the missionaries. Even though the success of the past few years among the southern Slavs had been unprecedented, the membership was still but a small sampling of the total population. Elder Oaks also called on the missionaries to continue to find those few who would respond to the gospel message.[18]

The next day, a district conference was held for the members in Croatia and Slovenia. President Kenneth Reber rented a three-hundred-seat auditorium, and he challenged the missionaries to fill it. At 10:00 A.M. many seats were still empty, so after the opening prayer and a song by the primary children, the missionaries exited to the streets. For a half hour they invited anyone who would listen to come hear an Apostle. By the time Elder Oaks spoke, the audience numbered 286 people. Eighty-seven came to a subsequent conference in Serbia later that year.[19]

The ongoing political conflict continued to present problems for the missionary program. In June 1992, the U.N. levied sanctions against Yugoslavia (now a confederation of Serbia and Montenegro), causing anti-American sentiment to increase in that country. Since communications between Budapest and Beograd were better than those between Vienna and Beograd, Serbia was temporarily transferred to the Hungary Budapest Mission in November 1993. However, in the wake of growing antagonism toward America, missionaries were soon removed and reassigned to Slovakia and the Czech Republic.[20]

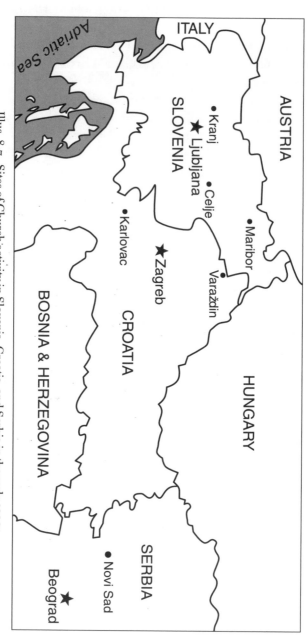

Illus. 8-7. Sites of Church activity in Slovenia, Croatia, and Serbia in the early 1990s.

Missionaries in Croatia were unexpectedly overtaken by shelling. During an investigator fireside in Karlovac on July 14, 1993, a thunderous blast shattered the air. The air raid sirens began wailing a tardy announcement of the bombardment. Some shells even landed across the street. In a panic, everyone headed for shelter. The missionaries, including two sisters, found shelter behind shelves in a shoe store. The bombardment lasted from 8:30 P.M. to 1:30 A.M. During a lull, Elder Halgren procured the missionary car, taking the missionaries home to Zagreb. The bombardment resumed a few hours later and lasted until 6:30 A.M. No one was injured, but life-threatening danger was no small matter to Church leaders. The next day, mission leaders removed the missionaries from Karlovac and reassigned them elsewhere.[21]

In summer 1994, the Beograd authorities withdrew permission for the missionaries to openly proselytize in the city. Because of international political conflict arising from the war in Bosnia, Serbia canceled the visas of all foreign missionaries and the last two elders left in September 1995.[22] For nearly a year, the Austria Vienna Mission president, Swen Swensen, visited members in Serbia monthly. During this time, the Church continued providing welfare assistance to the war-beleaguered nation. The Yugoslavia Red Cross even held a press conference to recognize the contributions, and Church representatives had a good forum to explain the worldwide humanitarian assistance program. The Minister of Religion contacted Church leaders a few weeks later, suggesting it was time to let the missionaries return. In June 1996, two missionaries resumed the work in Serbia.[23] In just over two years, the missionary force increased to fourteen—only for them to be pulled out again in October 1998 because of the Muslim-Serb conflict in the Kosovo region of southern Yugoslavia.[24]

After years of unrest, several new countries now reside in the boundaries of the former Yugoslavia. These new countries experienced great freedoms and even greater tragedies. A country born of war also dissolved in war. Holding on tenaciously for nearly a quarter of a century, the Church has attracted some members. Still, in comparison with the effort, the numbers are few. In July 1996, the Church united the former states of Yugoslavia by creating a new mission, the Austria Vienna South Mission, with Johann Wondra, a prominent Austrian, as president.[25] As the general secretary of the Vienna Court Theater in 1988, President Wondra had received the Austrian Cross of Honor First Class, the highest honor given in the Austrian Theater.[26] He was well acquainted with the area, having served as a Church regional representative for eastern Europe from 1985 to 1992.

Under President Wondra, the new mission began to progress. Twenty-five investigators came to a Church conference in Zagreb held in September 1996, fully a fourth of the ninety-five in attendance. In January 1997, two small Zagreb branches were combined to form a strong branch. After ten years of service, Ivan Valek was released as the district president and subsequently appointed president of the newly combined branch. From July 1996 to February 1997, the mission had thirty-eight baptisms, exceptional growth in comparison to the past.[27] Despite this success, the Church in Yugoslavia is still numerically small, considering that the missionaries first entered there in 1978. At the end of 2001, Croatia had about 350 members, Slovenia 250, and Serbia 200. In 1999 the headquarters was transferred from Vienna to Ljubljana, and the mission was renamed the Slovenia Ljubljana Mission. In September 2000, responsibility for Serbia was transfered to the Bulgaria Sofia Mission.[28] In December 2001, that mission was permitted to send six missionaries to Serbia, where they had not been able to serve since 1998.[29]

Krešimir Ćosić continued to serve his country, not as an athlete but as a diplomat, when he was appointed to serve as the Croatian deputy ambassador to the United States in September 1992. Brother Ćosić sought to improve relationships with the U.S. and thereby provide security and economic well-being to his country. Once a steadfast opponent of Communism yet a hero in a Communist nation, he was now a person without a political past, appointed to a high political position.[30] He was not entirely unprepared for the job. Referring to Ćosić's student days at BYU, Truman Madsen noted, "He was not just a 'jock,' he was brilliant and studied political and historical topics like he was 'on fire.'"[31]

A year after his assignment began, doctors diagnosed him with cancer. Ćosić took the news with the same good humor that had sustained him throughout his life, speaking only of how grateful he was to have more time away from work so he could be with his wife and three children. He also used the time to work on his family history, often attending the Washington D.C. Temple to do work for his ancestors. At the same time, he enjoyed the peace he found there, since he had not lived near a temple for most of his life. Brother Ćosić died May 25, 1995, at age forty-six. Ten thousand Croatians and foreign dignitaries paid their respects when he was interred among other national heroes at the national cemetery in Zagreb. His country honored him for his accomplishments in sports, while Ćosić's church recognized him as a pioneer of the gospel in the Communist realm when it was still the ideological adversary to the free world.[32]

Albania. Humanitarian service workers began serving in Albania in 1992. The government granted the Church recognition three years later. In July 1996, Church leaders established the Albania Tirana Mission. At the end of 2001, membership in Albania had grown to about one thousand.[33]

Unlike other European countries, Albanian citizens are primarily Muslim. Yet they do not adhere to the extreme religious practices found in some areas of the Middle East. A national program of atheism that arrived with the Communist dictatorship after World War II inhibited and tempered the Islamic faith in Albania. It was the first Muslim country in which the Church prospered.

Monika Kadi was a Muslim, but her faith did not adequately answer her questions about the purpose of life. When invited by a friend to attend a church service, Monika accepted and intended to go for only a few minutes, but she stayed all three hours. Baptism into the Church marked a new direction in her life. In September 1994, a year after her baptism, Sister Kadi traveled to Salt Lake City to serve as a missionary on Temple Square.[34]

As in Yugoslavia, civil conflict in Albania disrupted missionary activities. A nationwide investment fraud collapsed in early 1997, and many Albanians lost their life savings. The infuriated populace blamed the government and rejected civil authority. As the country descended into chaos, police fled their posts, and the populace looted weapons from the armories. In March missionaries were evacuated even as Albanians were shooting randomly in the streets. The missionaries returned in September 1997, only to be pulled out again temporarily in August 1998 because of anti-American threats.[35]

Romania. Humanitarian service workers initiated efforts to gain legal recognition for the Church in Romania. Short of the desired goal, they achieved recognition for the Liahona Association, an agency to conduct interactions between the government and the Church in obtaining visas and making legal purchases.[36] Taking advantage of the opportunity, leaders opened the Romania Bucharest Mission in July 1993. John Morrey, a nuclear physicist from Washington, became the president. He did not speak Romanian but, according to Elder Thomas S. Monson who issued the call, no language-qualified person could be found.[37] So President Morrey studied it alongside the young missionaries.

A variety of circumstances hindered Church activity in Romania. Other religious denominations actively used the mass media to attack the Church. In 1995, *The Godmakers,* an anti-Mormon movie, was regularly shown on television. Fortunately, the Church established a good relationship with the Minister of Religion and received his support. Internally, Church leaders struggled to retain Romanian converts. It was not difficult for members to find reasons for offense. For example, early translations of hymns were not proofed and the rendering was poor, leaving some members to conclude that Church officials were not concerned with their needs.[38]

Church opponents harassed missionaries working at street displays. Member referrals were sparse. This limited proselytizing to street contacting and knocking on doors to find interested individuals. In response to a growing anti-Western sentiment, mission leaders instructed missionaries to grow their hair longer and to remove name tags so they would be less noticeable. When it was determined that the large number of missionaries in Bucharest was attracting persecution, they spread out from the capital to other large cities in Romania, such as Braşov (Brassó) and Timişoara (Temesvár)—cities not visited since the beginning of the twentieth century. The missionaries had success, and persecution declined. Concurrently, the press in Bucharest lost interest in the Church.

Though Romania's transition from Communism ranked among the bloodiest in eastern Europe, it did not suffer continuing upheaval like Yugoslavia and Albania. Besieged by economic and social problems, the country managed to remain stable, and the Church grew steadily. In December 1998, the newly translated Romanian language Book of Mormon was released.[39] A year later, the first chapel in Romania was dedicated in Bucharest.[40] At the end of 2001, Romania had nearly two thousand members. Moldova (in the Romania Bucharest Mission) was dedicated for missionary work on May 16, 2001, and by the end of the year it had 140 members.[41]

Bulgaria. The overnight transition from totalitarianism to freedom benefited not only the Church but also all other western religions intent on introducing their beliefs. Many people listened to the religious tidings from the West out of curiosity. A few of these new faiths staged revivals and rallies, performed faith healing, and used extravagant techniques to get attention. This led some citizens to associate the Mormon missionaries, easily recognizable in their dark suits and name tags, with other evangelistic groups, making them targets when religious persecutions resumed in 1993.[42]

A Swedish evangelist held a revival in Bulgaria in 1992, and he planned to return in 1993. Posters decorated the city, and flyers filled mailboxes. When the evangelist was refused entry for allegedly profiteering, the media portrayed it as a government-initiated crackdown on all Western religions.[43]

The press indiscriminately indicted the Church along with the other religions. A flurry of negative reporting began mounting in late 1993. Articles distorted gospel beliefs about progression toward godhood, eternal marriage, and baptism for the dead. For instance, one paper reported that Latter-day Saints threw children off balconies expecting to kill them so they could go to heaven quickly.[44] When a Sofia branch clerk fell to his death from an apartment window in December 1993, the press claimed that he "fanatically hoped to become a god on another planet."[45] Although the press reported the incident as a suicide, the case was never investigated. Yet the story was televised nationally three times in a seven-day period. In another instance, the media photographed and broadcast the tithing records that were in the branch clerk's room, implying clandestine financial operations.[46]

Untutored in dealing with an irresponsible public media, Bulgarians willingly gave credence to scurrilous stories. One television program portrayed a Latter-day Saint meeting place with a background of eerie music. After missionaries visited a residence, neighbors sometimes pounded on the investigator's door or covered it with graffiti.[47] Opposition deterred the curious from seriously investigating the gospel message.[48] Although Church activity declined over all, opposition strengthened the testimonies of some members who remained firm in their faith.[49]

The harassment in Bulgaria was more severe than anywhere else in central and eastern Europe. The mission office's windows were broken regularly with rocks. At times, missionaries even became the objects of ridicule and physical violence. In addition to receiving verbal harassment, people spit on the missionaries, and in a few cases gangs attacked them with their fists or objects such as a wrench, a 2x4, or a handgun. Some missionaries suffered injuries that forced them to be hospitalized. Sister missionaries experienced sexual harassment on crowed public trams. Once the mission president and his wife, Edward and Sara Partridge, had to beat off two assailants at the mission home. In April 1997, a group of new missionaries was detained at the airport. Authorities confiscated some diet pills, and the government tried to prosecute Elder Derek Allred for bringing drugs into Bulgaria. He was detained, placed in solitary confinement, and starved, but eventually released.[50] In February 1998, the case was finally dropped.

Attempting to combat some of these problems, Church leaders hosted a delegation of prominent journalists to Utah, and, upon their return to Bulgaria, they generated substantial favorable press.[51] One of the journalists interviewed Elder Allred and wrote a very favorable article about the missionary's attitude toward the airport affair, "Young American Stays in Our Jail, and He Likes It."[52] The new mission president, Gary Stephens, started a program of meeting with civic leaders in all the communities where the missionaries worked, explaining their purpose and allaying fears.[53] The harassment of missionaries eventually dissipated. In the end, the missionary program had been hindered but not stopped.

Not all problems encountered by the Church in Bulgaria have been external. Bulgarian branches evolved from small, intensely knit groups into multiple units with many new faces. One member observed that when branches were split, old friendships were lost, and some people became inactive or persisted in attending branches to which they did not belong.[54] The excitement of conversion sometimes faded, and some individuals separated from their new religion. The chrysalis of mistrust engendered under the Communist system was not easily shed by new converts.[55] One family cheerfully accepted baptism, but, after being active for a short time, quit coming to Church. When the missionaries encouraged them to return, the mother responded that they "would rather repent once a year and go into the church, light a candle, and kiss an icon."[56] In 1996 a local Church leader apostatized. Then he sent out letters discussing various incidents in Church history that attempted to discredit the Church and its leaders.[57]

In addition to external and internal problems, the mission faced a serious economic crisis in Bulgaria during the winter of 1996–97. Hyperinflation drastically affected the quality of life. Members had rent payments larger than their incomes, and they could not pay for transportation. Church attendance and activity plummeted, making it necessary to consolidate branches. Reportedly, fifteen thousand people committed suicide in the country in 1996.[58]

In the midst of this turmoil, thirty-nine Bulgarians overcame numerous obstacles and traveled by bus to Freiberg, Germany, to receive temple ordinances for themselves and for their ancestors. More trips followed.[59] In 1999, the complete Bulgarian Book of Mormon was published.[60] In Sofia on the tenth anniversary of the mission (July 2000), Europe Area President Charles Didier dedicated the country's first chapel.[61] By 2001 the Church's membership in Bulgaria approached sixteen hundred living in twelve cities. As of September 1998, twenty-two Bulgarians had already served missions, and ten more were ready to serve.[62] Though many faltered, faithful members emerged from the most trying of circumstances and demonstrated firm commitments to their new religion (illus. 8-8).

Armenia. On the isolated and barren slopes of Armenia, on the

Courtesy Renee Warner

Illus. 8-8. These young women in Bulgaria read all the Book of Mormon selections for their personal progress award in 1993.

opposite side of the Black Sea from Bulgaria, the humanitarian service workers nurtured the Church. David Horne's original three-month missionary call lasted three years. After Elder Oaks released Brother Horne in 1992, Jon Huntsman sent David and his wife, Jeanne, back to Armenia to continue their humanitarian efforts in the country. Brother Horne continued to supervise the Church in Armenia while Sister Horne organized the Young Women's program.[63]

The Church in Armenia grew steadily. The font at the home of Roger and Jewell Doxey served as the baptismal site for 130 members before the couple's service ended.[64] Afterward, a portable font was built and used at the concrete plant. During summer 1993, the first group of five humanitarian service couples returned home, and five others arrived. To permit the development of local leadership and the integration of members, a limit was placed on baptisms in fall 1993. For a year and a half, only ten converts per month received permission to be baptized.[65] In November 1993, Armenia became part of the Bulgaria Sofia Mission, directed by Dale Warner.[66] President Warner set up a more formal church structure in Armenia, dividing member and missionary responsibilities among leaders. Brother Horne served as his chief assistant. In 1994, Armenia was transferred to the Russia Moscow Mission, presided over by Richard Chapple.[67]

The Armenian government granted the Church legal recognition on

December 22, 1994, much of it resulting from the government's long-term dealings with Brother Horne. During January young missionaries came from Moscow and, for the first time, walked the streets of Yerevan. In February 1995, the limit on baptisms increased to twenty per month. Approximately 75–80 percent of the members attended church services each month. In July 1995, President Chapple set up a district with six branches. Brother Horne served as his counselor in the mission presidency. By then, young missionaries were regularly entering and leaving the country for one- or two-month stints, supplementing the teaching efforts of the humanitarian service couples. In 1996 new couples arrived, but not to work in the concrete factory. Rather, they assisted in a variety of other humanitarian service projects.[68] At the end of 1998, responsibility for the Church was transferred to the Russia Rostov Mission. In July 1999, it was made the Armenia Yerevan Mission. As the Armenians celebrated 1,700 years of Christianity in 2001, the Armenian Book of Mormon was published.[69] And by the end of 2001, Armenia had about 850 members.

Armenia's economic situation has improved since the black days of 1992–93. By 1995 electricity had become more abundant, new goods had begun to pass over the Iranian border, and new businesses had opened. Roads were repaired, and the conflict with Azerbaijan had quieted. Armenia finally had a brighter future.[70]

On the other side of the globe in Salt Lake City, Nara Sarkissian was able to visit the building she had seen in her dream. During her first time in a temple session, Sister Sarkissian felt as if it had all happened before. Even small details seemed familiar, and she needed no assistance to complete the ceremonies.[71] While the Sarkissian family was being taught by the missionaries, Sister Sarkissian's mother had dreamed of her family dressed in white and she in a wedding dress, all standing beneath a beautiful chandelier. In March 1995, the dream became a reality when the family was sealed in the Salt Lake Temple.[72]

In early December 1997, the first temple excursion of Armenians, consisting of 32 members, made the long trip from their isolated country to the Freiberg Temple to receive temple ordinances.[73]

Tragically, Brother Horne, long-time shepherd of the Armenian Saints, was unexpectedly taken from the scene. Early one morning, he was severely burned in a propane gas explosion at his apartment. Jon Huntsman immediately had him flown home to the University of Utah Medical Center.[74] The injuries, however, proved fatal, and Brother Horne died January 21, 1996.[75] At the funeral, Brother Huntsman read a

Illus. 8-9. Fountain memorial in Armenia to David Horne.

few select letters—out of the hundreds sent by Armenians from all levels of government and society—filled with thanks and praise for Brother Horne's efforts and achievements. Armenia has a centuries-old tradition of erecting drinking fountains in honor of the deceased where one must bend over, humbling oneself in honor of the dead. In April 1996 such a fountain was erected by Armenians in Horne's memory (illus. 8-9).[76] His life, lost in the service of others, along with the exemplary lives of his fellow workers, brought lasting comfort and light to a nation in an hour of darkness.

The Church's Northern Tier in the Former Communist World

The northern tier of the Church in eastern Europe consists of the Baltic states of Estonia, Latvia, and Lithuania; Kaliningrad, a non-contiguous state of Russia along the Baltic Sea is also included. The missionaries entered much of this area after the swell of curiosity about the West had begun to subside. Communism had actually strengthened the Lutheran and Catholic traditions in these states, lessening the people's disposition to respond to a new gospel message.

Estonia. Conversions in the Baltics came relatively quickly during the early years, but then diminished. Fifty-eight members lived in Estonia at the end of 1990 and 139 at the end of 1991.[77] During the next two years, membership grew to only 170.[78] The wave of fascination with the West had passed. Economic devastation caused people to focus on temporal needs. Traditionally, the citizens had adhered to the Lutheran faith, which had served as a buttress of their nationalism, a fact that did not readily dispose them to learn about other religions. There was little Church literature available in the native tongue, forcing early converts to study gospel materials in Finnish or Russian. To the delight of the members, the Estonian Book of Mormon was published in January 2000. Still, it was not always easy to sublimate ethnic tensions among newly converted Church members. For similar reasons, the modest growth rate in Estonia was mirrored in Latvia and Lithuania.

Latvia. In March 1993, Elder James E. Faust arrived in Latvia to offer an apostolic dedication on the country. In a missionary conference, he consoled the missionaries about the paucity of native-language materials. He related his own experience preaching the gospel in Brazil years earlier with the Book of Mormon in Spanish and not Portuguese, telling how he had compensated with his own testimony and desire to build up the Church. Elder Faust emphasized that it would not halt the work, prophesying:

> In your lifetime you will see several stakes organized in the country of Latvia under the Latvian leadership. You are pioneers; you can tell your children about it. You have been hand selected. . . . I bless you that you will be wise beyond your years, that you may learn and cultivate the whisperings of the Spirit, never to be deceived by the adversary.[79]

That evening, the eve of the country's dedication, more than two hundred people attended a fireside at the University of Latvia to hear the visiting Apostle. The following day, March 17, a group of twenty-eight members, missionaries, and authorities gathered on the beach at Dzintari,

Jūrmala, northwest of Riga. Facing the nation with his back to the sea, Elder Faust pronounced a blessing on the land and its people (illus. 8-10). The first branch in Latvia was organized two months later in Riga.[80] Still, the Church grew slowly. By the end of 1993, only forty-four members had joined the twenty-eight already baptized.[81]

Lithuania. When Elder M. Russell Ballard arrived in May 1993 to dedicate Lithuania for the gospel message, he counseled the missionaries not to lose courage, that the blessing of the Lord was upon the land. The group attending the dedicatory services stood on Gedimino Hill with a panoramic vista of Vilnius at their feet (illus. 8-11). It was a clear spring day, flowers abounded, and the sun shone brightly.[82] By virtue of his apostolic authority, Elder Ballard turned the key, unlocking the door of the nation to the preaching of the gospel. He also invoked a blessing

Courtesy Boris Schiel

Illus. 8-10. Missionaries on the beach at Jūrmala after the dedication of Latvia for missionary work, March 17, 1993. *Right to left:* Elder and Sister Robert K. Dellenbach, Elder and Sister James E. Faust, Elder and Sister Boris A. Schiel, President and Sister Charles H. Creel, Elder Matthew H. Lyman, and Elder Dale Franklin. *Kneeling, right to left:* Elder Michael Van Patten and Elder Dennon Ison.

Courtesy Kahlile B. Mehr

Illus. 8-11. Dedication site for Lithuania at the top of Gedimino Hill, 1997.

on the land that there might be sufficient moisture; there had been a drought the previous year, but the rains returned during the six months following the country's dedication. Church membership grew modestly. At the end of 1993, the congregation in Vilnius consisted of twenty-one members, thirteen of whom were priesthood holders, which augured well for the future leadership of the Church.[83]

On July 11, 1993, four elders—Shane Allred, Brandon Rohrer, John Dobbs, and Jason Riggs—entered Kaunas, the second major city in Lithuania. Other missionaries came to the city, and the group gathered for a sacrament meeting in the Hotel Lietuva. They then went to the street corner by a large fountain and began singing in English. After a few songs, they announced a meeting to be held later that day. The missionaries repeated this process for an hour and a half and then held the meeting. Thirty-nine people came. It appeared auspicious, but six months passed before the first three were baptized.[84]

Latvia Riga Mission. In July 1993, the Baltic nations were divided from the Russia St. Petersburg Mission to become the Latvia Riga Mission. Robert Blair, a linguistics professor from BYU, assumed the task of directing the multilingual checkerboard of the Baltics as well as Kaliningrad (previously Königsberg, East Prussia), a piece of Russia isolated along the Baltic coast by Lithuania and Poland. A missionary couple,

Oliver and Barbara Moretti, were transferred to Riga from St. Petersburg to serve as the mission office couple.[85]

The Europe Area Presidency wanted the missionaries to learn to speak Lithuanian and Latvian as well as Estonian, which was already spoken by some. On July 2, President Blair announced to the Vilnius missionaries still struggling to learn Russian that, "Some of you in this room will be called to learn Lithuanian while maintaining your Russian, enabling you to teach in either language."[86] Later in the month, he directed Marvin Folsom, a senior missionary, to supervise Lithuanian classes for eight missionaries—four in Kaunas and four in Vilnius. Commenting on the classes, the Folsoms wrote,

> Imagine an elderly couple, not knowing the language, with no materials provided, except what grammars and dictionaries we can scrounge, having the audacity to attempt to run a crash course in Lithuanian. It's high pressure, nerve-wracking, challenging, and exciting. . . . I can testify that the gift of tongues is alive and well."[87]

On the 15th, President Blair initiated an eight-week Latvian language class in Riga for four Russian-trained elders to learn Latvian. Elders Joseph Silver, Brandon Wilding, Janis Cilderman, and Frank Roberts were taught by Elder Schiel and two local members, Viesturs Tivums and Juris Pavlovičs. President Blair provided pedagogical direction for the course. In September 1993, a second group, consisting of four Russian-trained sisters and two elders, took the course.[88]

During the Blair presidency (see chapter 6), tracting door-to-door became a regular part of the missionary routine. Tracting had not been necessary in the early years because contacts abounded. Once utilized, this proselytizing technique had some interesting effects: seeing strangers dressed in suits and knocking at doors struck fear in those who had grown up in a system where it usually meant a visit from the police. Sometimes people would not answer the door. But after hearing the missionaries converse with neighbors, they would open the door and apologize, explaining that they now realized it was not a dangerous situation.[89]

Missionaries encountered attitudes and traditions that were hard to overcome. Traditional Christianity, whether Lutheran or Catholic, was an important part of ethnic identity in the Baltics, and to give it up was considered, by many, to be treasonous. It was also difficult to comply with the Word of Wisdom. The water was often polluted and the thought of drinking it abhorrent. Juices and milk were expensive. So in some minds, if they did not drink tea or coffee, there was nothing else to drink.

Missionaries also began to face the results of anti-Mormon material being published by the media.[90]

As the gospel message spread, opposition increased. However, the media could also serve Church interests, as demonstrated by Elder Rees, who mounted an effective public relations campaign in Kaunas, Lithuania. In the first six months of 1994, he had five Church-produced programs broadcast over Lithuanian television. In addition, Elder Rees succeeded in getting newspaper as well as television and radio stations to feature material on missionary activities like teaching English, playing with children at an orphanage, and discussing gospel topics.[91]

The effort to contact and convert was only the first of two challenges, the second being to train and retain. In this regard, the Latvian experience was typical of the many newly formed congregations throughout the East. The new members were willing to assume leadership positions, but they needed time to develop skills in such activities as conducting meetings, performing ordinances, issuing calls, and sustaining those called. Of necessity, people were called as leaders and left with little guidance, especially since they did not have manuals. Teachers had to be trained to give lessons rather than simply lecturing, as had been their common experience in Soviet schools. To help remedy these situations, missionaries provided shadow leadership and let some things slip by without critique to avoid embarrassing those in charge. The sister missionaries, fewer in number than the elders, had an even larger task because of the preponderance of women, girls, and children who needed guidance in running Primary, Young Women, and Relief Society. It was hard to organize non-Sabbath branch activities, such as branch socials and home-making meetings, because members could not grasp the purpose of such meetings. Furthermore, transportation costs and distance discouraged Latvian members from doing visiting and home teaching, especially when the concept of being responsible for watching over each other was new and difficult for many to comprehend.[92]

If these challenges were not enough, two blows struck the Riga Branch in fall 1993, testing the new members' will to remain faithful. The branch president turned cynical and left the Church. Some of his friends followed. At the same time, a sister in the branch died of cancer. Members, who had been unaware of the illness, blamed the Relief Society president because nothing had been done to assist this sister prior to her death. Members demanded to know why money had not been raised to buy medicine, without understanding that it was equally important to give of one's time and love. The president did not know what to do, and she resigned her position rather than bear the criticism. As a result of these circumstances, attendance in the Riga Russian branch dropped from about 80 to 50 percent. However, the principles of compassionate service were practiced a year later when another sister became ill and the members nursed her back to health.[93]

The second blow came in October 1993 when the Church was seeking official recognition. More than a year earlier, Elder Schiel had begun the process of obtaining government recognition for the Church in Riga. During his March visit, Elder Faust had consulted with the head of the Department of Religious Affairs, Arnolds Kublinskis. On that occasion, the minister inquired whether the Church had existed in free Latvia between the two world wars—a question Elder Faust could not answer affirmatively. In October the desired recognition was postponed for a three-year waiting period since it had not existed in free Latvia before the Communist take-over. It was later learned that the deputy minister in the Department of Religious Affairs had argued against the Church as a non-Christian sect. While Church officials received assurances that missionaries could continue to work in Latvia, their ability to function freely was curtailed.[94]

Those who joined the Church in the Baltics began to give as they had received. Even as missionaries had come to the Baltics, young men and women from the Baltics began to serve missions elsewhere. In 1995, fourteen missionaries from the Baltics were serving abroad. Six returned missionaries lived in Estonia, building the Church in their own country by contributing the knowledge from their service.[95] The story of the first Estonian missionary was related in chapter 5. The first Latvian missionaries began their service abroad in early 1994, Sergej Moroz in the Samara Russia Mission and Juris Pavolovičs in the New York Rochester Mission.[96] Later that year, Marek Vasilkov became the first Lithuanian to serve a mission. He was assigned to the Utah Salt Lake City Mission. The first Lithuanian sister missionary, Ilona Mahinič, followed, serving on Temple Square.[97]

Members who had matured in the gospel qualified for temple ordinances. By 1995, Estonians had taken several temple excursions to Sweden. That year, groups went from both Latvia and Lithuania. Their experience continued to broaden the new members' spiritual world. Viesturs Tivums from Riga, who received his temple ordinances in March 1995, later wrote to the Schiels:

> It seemed that the Holy Ghost was there with us and above us. . . .
> I pondered many things and felt a great gratitude to both of you for

showing me the way to this Church. Now I cannot imagine my life without it. All of us were touched by the solemnity of the temple and that great feeling of the divine purification and cleansing prevailing there.[98]

Even though the Church operated in the Baltics, the process of receiving and maintaining legal recognition was torturous and continuous. In 1993, Estonia passed new laws requiring all churches to register with the government again. The following year, the task of gaining recognition for the Church was successfully completed, due in part to the efforts of Jussi Kemppainen and senior missionary James Ames. In 1995 the Church registered in Vilnius and Kaunas, Lithuania, just in time to avoid a visa problem. A day prior to the registration, the local government office had refused to issue temporary missionary visas. This newly acquired registration gave the Church a legal basis to obtain residence visas, obviating the need for the temporary ones.[99]

By December 1995, nearly three years had passed since the Church's effort to register in Riga, Latvia, had been rebuffed. New laws had increased the requirement from ten to twenty-five adherents signing the petition for recognition, and they had to be ethnic Latvians, not Russians. The government-appointed registration time was a dark, cold winter evening. The mission leaders were not allowed to be present, but thirty-five members braved the elements to sign the document. Still, President Blair waited in suspense until March 1996 when he received official notification that recognition in Riga had been granted.[100]

In 1996 Church officials realigned the Latvia Riga Mission's boundaries to include Belarus. Since the office was moved to the more centrally located city of Vilnius, it was renamed the Lithuania Vilnius Mission. During the three years the mission was headquartered in Latvia, Church membership grew gradually at the rate of between one hundred and two hundred baptisms each year.[101]

Membership challenges continued to arise. In 1997 the mission combined weak branches to strengthen them, ultimately providing a better impression for investigators. The two Estonian-speaking branches in Tallinn were combined in 1997. In Vilnius, Lithuania, the Lithuanian and Russian-speaking branches were combined to revitalize one of the branches that had stagnated.[102] The immediate impact was negative as many Lithuanian-speaking priesthood holders, failing to understand the principles of priesthood governance, protested the change by refusing to attend services.[103]

Kaliningrad. In 1993 missionaries from the Latvia Riga Mission entered a part of Russia along the Baltic coast that, with the collapse of Communism, was geographically orphaned from its parent country. At the beginning of October, the Blairs, the Schiels, and the missionary assistants (Elders Douglas Derrick and Todd Hale) visited the capital city of Kaliningrad. The region had a German heritage, having been part of Prussia for centuries. The Latter-day Saint delegation met the head of the Department of Religious Affairs and the mayor of the city. Later in the month, President Blair sent Elders Eric Paul, Douglas Derrick, Todd Hale, and Logan Wentz to the province. The work was grueling and baptismal success slow in coming: five months passed before two baptisms occurred.[104] However, the conversion rate soon accelerated. By the end of 1994, the country had twenty-eight members. In 1995 this province was transferred to the jurisdiction of the Russia St. Petersburg Mission to allay visa problems caused by moving between Russia and the Baltics.[105]

Baltics. The Church progressed and continued to change in the Baltics. In 1999 the first Church structure erected in the Baltics was dedicated in Tallinn, Estonia.[106] Two years later, leaders simultaneously issued translations of the Book of Mormon in Latvian and Lithuanian.[107] By the end of 2001, there were approximately six hundred members each in Estonia, Latvia, and Lithuania.[108] Responsibility for Belarus was transfered to the Russia Moscow Mission in July 2000.[109] Two years later, the mission home was moved back to Riga, Latvia, and in a departure from traditional mission nomenclature, rechristened as the Baltic Mission with no city designator.[110]

The Church on the Eastern Edge of the Former Communist World

Russia and Ukraine formed the core republics of the former Soviet Union and the heart of the Russian Empire that preceded it. In terms of population, Russia's population of 145 million is equivalent to the combined population of 145 million living in the other countries covered in this volume. Ukraine has a population of 52 million. As the dominant states in eastern Europe, Russia and Ukraine are keys to the Church's future in the region. In both countries, the Church has faced, and continues to face, unstable political and social circumstances that have threatened, and continue to threaten, its presence.

Ukraine. From 1992 to 1993, President Howard Biddulph began the process of sending missionaries to new cities in eastern Ukraine. Once the Church was established in six cities, leaders could apply for the registration of a national center, the equivalent of being recognized as a legal entity in the Ukraine. Four missionaries left for the east Ukrainian city of Donetsk in March 1992. They found early converts among members of the Donbas Ukrainian Dancers and Choir that had been to Rexburg, Idaho, performed at Ricks College, and stayed in the homes of Church members. Other missionaries soon opened the neighboring cities of Gorlovka and Makayevka. In September missionaries entered Kharkov, 150 miles northwest of Donetsk.[111]

Administering distant districts from mission headquarters posed tremendous challenges in a country where the transportation, communications, and economic infrastructure were inadequate, and the region was in political turmoil. Because the banking system could not transfer funds electronically and the supplies were not available locally, President Biddulph had to visit the newly opened cities once a month. During his visits he interviewed the missionaries, distributed proselytizing materials, and dispensed cash, medicines, and other essential supplies. One winter trip to eastern Ukraine in November 1992 was unusually difficult. A national fuel shortage grounded air traffic unexpectedly, so train tickets had to be purchased at the last minute from hawkers. Also, there was no assurance of getting tickets for the return journey, even though the president had to attend essential meetings on December 2. President Biddulph and his two assistants, Aaron Love and John Lunt, left on November 27. They locked themselves in the train compartment for most of the seventeen-hour trip. Carrying enough cash for thirty-two missionaries concerned them because of the risk of an armed robbery on the train.[112]

The next morning, they attended a public meeting to request the official registration of the Church in Donetsk. The city already had 110 members, and 85 of these were present. Following the public meeting, the president held a zone conference with the missionaries. Returning late in the evening to the dilapidated "luxury" hotel, President Biddulph found fetid water covering the floor in the bathroom. It was cold and he was tired, so he donned a sweater, overcoat, and fur cap, and shivered through a miserable night hanging off the edges of a mattress too small for his frame.

The next day, the president left without breakfast to attend Sabbath services at Gorlovka. Sixty came to the meetings, fifteen of them members. Returning to Donetsk, the van stalled short of its destination. The president then shouldered his baggage and started walking. Unfortunately, he slipped on the ice, injuring his knee. He was finally able to obtain a taxi, though he worried about the large sums of cash he still carried. President

Biddulph arrived at a scheduled baptismal service with his knee swelling and throbbing. At the train station that evening, he had to stand for two hours, in spite of his injury. The president had eaten little on Saturday, nothing all day on Sunday, and there was no food on the train to Kharkov. The throbbing knee prevented him from sleeping. He and his assistants arrived at 1:30 A.M. in Kharkov, where the temperature registered -15° Celsius. They slept briefly at a missionary apartment before attending a missionary zone conference, once again without having breakfast.

The zone conference was held in an ornate, prerevolutionary hall around a huge table. With his knee stiff and throbbing, President Biddulph felt inspired to ask for a blessing of healing. Elder Love administered, his voice quavering. The impact was immediate: the swelling and stiffness left and the throbbing ceased. It was a spiritual experience that confirmed the conference's message that miracles follow righteous desires. Following the meeting, one of the elders served the travelers a plate of spaghetti, their only meal in the previous forty-eight hours.

The three travelers succeeded in procuring train tickets for the return journey. They rode in a rickety coach filled with double-decker bunks, a moving "gulag." The men pushed through a mass of unwashed bodies and found their places on filthy mattresses. All eyes were on the Westerners.

Courtesy Kahlile B. Mehr

Illus. 8-12. The first Latter-day Saint chapel in Ukraine, located in the city of Donetsk, 2001.

The temperature was sub-zero outside and the car had no heat. The president shook from cold throughout the ten-hour night ride. Returning to Kiev, President Biddulph rejoiced, experiencing the joy that comes not from a set of pleasant circumstances but from fulfillment in the midst of great challenges.

In 1992 tremendous growth occurred in the Ukraine Kiev Mission. Almost eight hundred Ukrainians joined the Church, a baptismal rate unexcelled that year elsewhere in the East.[113] It was a propitious moment in the history of the Church's eastward expansion into the Slavic world. The old ideologies were crumbling, forcing people to look for meaning in life. Ukraine had a history of religious pluralism, and many Ukrainians had relatives in the United States, disposing them to be pro-American. Moreover, the country's intelligentsia was internationally oriented. The converts included scholars, journalists, lawyers, artists, musicians, and scientists—well-educated, discriminating individuals who joined a church that answered their deepest questions.[114]

In May 1993, missionaries began serving in two cities of southern Ukraine: Odessa, situated on the Black Sea, and Simferopol, the capital city of Crimea, a peninsula extending into the Black Sea. They also entered Dnepropetrovsk, down the Dnieper River from Kiev. In July 1993, Church officials created a new Ukrainian mission, presided over by Leo Merrill, with its headquarters in Donetsk (illus. 8-12). This new mission directed the work in eastern Ukraine.[115]

Missionary work through 1996 focused on central and eastern Ukraine, where Russian was more commonly spoken at the time. Sending missionaries into the western territory of the Ukraine was intentionally delayed so Church literature could be translated into the Ukrainian language. This was crucial since most people knew only Ukrainian. To jump-start the process, the Translation Department sent in Steven and Elgenia (Jean) Struk, Ukrainian natives who had lived in Toronto, Canada, for forty years. The Struks were two of the first Church missionaries to have translation work as their main assignment. Arriving in February 1992, they assiduously selected and assisted a group of native Ukrainians in translating basic Church texts, including the Book of Mormon.[116] Zoya Gulko, a newly baptized member who taught English at a school attended by the children of prominent Ukrainians, led the translation project. While continuing her full-time employment and serving as Young Women's District Leader, Sister Gulko completed a first draft of the translation of the Book of Mormon in nineteen months, a nearly unbelievable feat. She experienced divine assistance as words streamed to her spiritually, beyond her previous understanding and ability.[117]

In August 1994, the Ukrainian government began to refuse to issue visas to new missionaries. Despite Church officials' efforts to regain this privilege, the missionary corps began to dwindle. President Biddulph responded by calling young, single, adult Ukrainians to serve as district missionaries. They dressed and taught as missionaries and maintained the proselytizing program until April 1995 when the visa problem was solved, and new missionaries from abroad once again entered the country.[118]

With the Church now recognized in six Ukrainian cities, leaders submitted papers to achieve national recognition. Ukrainian law required that the head of the Church's national center be elected. The branch presidents elected Aleksandr Manzhos[119] to be the Church's representative to the nation. As a scientist in the Ukrainian Academy of Sciences, Manzhos was an able and influential representative. The documents were filed on April 6, 1994. Ukrainian nationalists, traditional churches, and media representatives opposed the Church's petition for recognition. Government leaders asked the President of the Ukrainian Association of Religious Studies, Anatoly M. Kolodny, to study the Church's application and make recommendations on it. Kolodny reviewed the materials objectively and supported the Church's petition. His recommendation ultimately influenced the State Council for Religious Affairs to favor the Church, granting it official recognition two years later in 1996.[120]

While the Church had expanded eastward across Ukraine from Kiev since October 1990, the first branch in western Ukraine was established in Lviv in August 1995.[121] Other cities were opened, a total of sixteen by the end of 1998, and twenty-seven by the end of 2001.[122] In 2001 membership approached eight thousand, making Ukraine one of the most successful missions, numerically, in the East.

In November 1992, twenty-two Ukrainian members undertook the first group temple excursion to Freiberg, Germany, crossing the long-impenetrable Western frontier of the former Soviet Union to receive spiritual blessings. It was the first of such excursions, and other excursions followed from the different missions in the East. Reflecting the sentiments of many, one of those in the first group described the meaning of the experience: "Until we experience and understand the temple, we are but schoolchildren in the gospel of Jesus Christ. The temple is the higher spiritual university of the gospel and the Church of Jesus Christ."[123]

On the other side of the world, in July 1998, President Gordon B. Hinckley dedicated the Monticello Utah Temple. He mentioned the new generation of smaller temples to be built in areas of sparse membership and announced the planned construction of a small temple in Kiev, Ukraine.[124] This was startling news for a country where no stake yet existed, and the first meetinghouse had only been completed a month earlier.[125] Centrally located in the former Soviet sphere, this temple was intended to serve members from Bulgaria and Romania to the west, Belarus and the Baltics to the north, and Russia to the east.[126] Though its construction had not yet started in 2002, as the most sacred structure of the Church, its announcement symbolized a long-term commitment to this region of the world.

In October 2000, Church leaders called Aleksandr Manzhos of Ukraine to be the first Area Authority Seventy from eastern Europe.[127]

Belarus. The president of the Ukraine Kiev Mission administered Church affairs in Belarus from 1993 to 1996. The Lithuania Vilnius Mission oversaw activities there until July 2000, when it was transferred to the Russia Moscow Mission. When Elder Russell M. Nelson arrived on May 10, 1993, he and President Ringger addressed a group of 450 people. The size of the group indicated the interest generated by the missionaries who had been there for only a few months. Elder Nelson concluded his talk with a testimony pronounced perfectly in Russian, manifesting his desire to communicate in a language commonly spoken in Belarus. Over two hundred people asked to be contacted later and learn more. The next morning, Elder Nelson dedicated Belarus in Yanka Kupala Park, located in central Minsk. Twenty-two members gathered in the park at 7:00 A.M. A few birds, whose song quivered through the morning air, joined the members for the special ceremony.[128]

In a short while, Minsk had four branches, all directed by local leaders. Anatoly Neverov's (biographical sketch in chapter 6) local evangelical church chastised and eventually cut him off for helping the Latter-day Saints. Assured through prayer that he was in the right, Anatoly accepted their judgment. In fall 1993, he joined the Church, which he, as a nonmember, had helped to bring into Belarus.

On January 17, 1994, Belarus registered the Church as a legal entity. Reporters interviewed Elder Dennis Neuenschwander, President Biddulph, and two branch presidents for a "prime time" television spot publicizing the event throughout the entire nation. Belarus registration permitted the Church to exist as a legal entity, but it still carried a restriction against proselytizing. The missionaries spent most of their time involved in welfare services, assisting at hospitals and orphanages.[129] Although they could not proselytize, missionaries were permitted to answer questions. Church progress was hampered by a repressive regime that curtailed many political freedoms. Still, by 2001 nearly four hundred members resided in Belarus.

Church leaders sought to improve the material situation of the country by sending in potato farmer John Hess from Idaho. In 2000 he set up a plot within feet of a government plot and with experience, work, and prayer taught them how to produce 550 sacks per hectare as compared to the historic yield of 50 sacks per hectare.[130]

Russia. Russia is the largest and most diverse of the former Soviet republics. In spite of its diminished international stature with the end of Soviet power, it is still the major player politically, economically, and socially in eastern Europe. Any reversals here could send shock waves throughout the Church in the Slavic world. Russia has been the scene of several dramatic episodes in which the fate of the Church in this area hung in the balance.

Missionary work in Russia before 1993 relied heavily on street contacting and member referrals. Being approached by missionaries on the street startled most Russians, normally uncommunicative and withdrawn in public. Still, many invited the missionaries into their homes and treated them hospitably, displaying the Russian warmth of personality known as *shirokaya dusha* (literally "broad spirit"). On occasion, Russians independently contacted the missionaries. For example, a young girl approached two missionaries sitting in a Moscow park and asked if they were Latter-day Saints. Receiving their affirmation, she said, "In California three months ago, I lived with a Mormon bishop and his family for two weeks. He said that when I returned home I would find the missionaries. I have looked for three months and here you are." Three weeks later she was baptized.[131]

At first, missionaries did not tract since they often spent ten or more hours teaching or traveling between visits each day.[132] While this was the case during winter months, summer months moved at a slower pace as Russians left the cities to spend time in the country. Since most missionaries came from America, they attracted widespread interest in the early years.[133] In time, the novelty dissipated, and contact with Westerners became more commonplace and even distasteful to those who blamed Russia's growing economic and social ills on Western influences. Beginning in 1993, missionaries did more tracting as the initial enthusiasm of a newly freed people turned to a preoccupation with surviving in a land of rampant inflation, persistent shortages, and increasing poverty.

Even before the demise of Communism, few modern conveniences existed. Consumers often waited in lines to buy food and other goods, which were costly when available. Except within the walls of one's home (usually an apartment), nothing was clean, convenient, or comfortable. As was the case elsewhere in eastern Europe, political freedom did not bring economic prosperity. The inability of Russia to compete in a free-market world soon resulted in inflation, which soared between 1990 and 1996, the exchange rate of rubles for dollars going from six for one to 5,600 for one. In January 1998, the government dropped three zeroes from the ruble. But the severe economic turmoil caused by the government's default on foreign debt in 1998 and the resulting devaluation of the new ruble made it virtually worthless again. At the same time, incomes were flat or grew slowly, and the conditions for the masses worsened.

Added to the element of a declining economy was the rise of criminal activity and a general disregard for the law. In late November 1993, the author sat in the apartment of Irina Maximova, Relief Society president for the St. Petersburg North District. Irina, a contact of Nellie Jäkkö in Finland, had been baptized three years earlier. It was early evening, and, to reduce costs, we sat in near darkness with only minimal lighting. When asked about her concern for the future, Irina responded that she feared for the children growing up in a chaotic society where laws were not observed. The fear of good people in a troubled land was very real and palpable on that occasion, yet equally tangible was the hope that buoyed this sister because of her faith.[134]

This tragic aspect of Russian life was widely publicized in both Church and national circles in 1998 by two separate events. In March two missionaries in Saratov, 450 miles southeast of Moscow along the Volga River, were kidnapped and held for a $300,000 ransom. Apparently scared by the international attention, the kidnappers reevaluated the situation and freed the hostages after four days.[135] The potential danger turned into tragedy when two other missionaries were stabbed in an unprovoked attack in Ufa, 750 miles east of Moscow, in October. Elder Jose Mackintosh from Hiko, Nevada, died of the attack. From the age of eight, he had talked to friends and family of his fascination with the Russian people and his desire to serve there. He died while fulfilling his quest. Elder Mackintosh's father, in spite of the overwhelming loss, urged that there be "no animosity and no ill feelings whatsoever for the people of Ufa—or Russia. They are our brothers and sisters."[136] The missionaries had been performing volunteer service at the local hospital prior to the incident, and the staff showed their appreciation by giving exceptional care to Elder Bradley Borden, who later recovered.[137] Neither incident dissuaded Church officials from continuing missionary work in Russia.

Beginning in 1991 and continuing through the end of the decade, the Church sent humanitarian aid to Russia to help alleviate the distress of members and of the general public. Twenty-three tons of food and vitamins in eighteen hundred packages, donated by Church members in Europe and elsewhere, arrived in Russia in February 1991. Each twenty-six-pound box was delivered individually to the appointed recipient.[138] A sixteen-ton shipment of clothing and shoes arrived in August 1993. It, too, was distributed to Church members and others as identified through contact with local government authorities. Because of limited warehouse space, members manhandled the hundred-pound bales up two stories for temporary storage in an apartment until they could be distributed.[139]

Church leaders continued to build up the missionary force in Russia. Rapid expansion with only a limited number of branches dictated a temporary policy of creating branches to spread out the missionaries. Some new branches were formed, not by splitting old branches but rather by missionaries being assigned to a geographical area with few or no members and creating a branch from the ground up. In early 1991, two branches existed in St. Petersburg, six in early 1992, and in late 1993 nine branches (presided over by missionaries) and six groups.[140] During 1991 three groups were created in Moscow with an initial membership of about three per group.[141] When the mission was split in February 1992, Moscow was divided into five branches.[142] A year later, fourteen branches were created from the initial five.[143] Although many branches had been successfully established under this policy, in February 1995 a conference of mission presidents from the countries of the former Soviet realm resolved that weak branches would be combined to create larger and stronger ones.[144]

Conversion meant more than just changing belief—it meant adopting new life principles and taking the lead in a society that stifled initiative and spawned passivity. Mission presidents taught new members to magnify their callings. Leaders learned how to follow through on interviewing, issuing calls, delegating authority to counselors, holding the prescribed leadership meetings, and spearheading such programs as home teaching and quality instruction in the meetings (illus. 8-13).[145] Effective administration played a key role in helping instill leadership in a populace raised to be submissive.

Illus. 8-13. St. Petersburg women's chorus, 1991.

Student Interns Represent the Church

The Church's presence in Russia received unanticipated nurturing from a unique language project implemented in Russia by two BYU professors. Human development professor Trevor McKee developed a system of effectively teaching foreign languages to children. He tested the program on his family, in a nursery school that he purchased and ran for this purpose, and in a nursery lab at BYU. An internship program evolved where students spent six months in a foreign country teaching English to young children. Concurrently, BYU linguistics professor Robert Blair, who later served as the mission president in Riga, attended a conference in Greece in September 1991. There he developed a strong and cordial relationship with a dean at the Moscow State University. She invited him to attend the first Russian conference on teaching English as a second language to be held at her university later that year. Through the contact with Professor Blair, Professor McKee was asked to be the keynote speaker.[146]

Deans from different parts of Russia showed immediate enthusiasm for McKee's program. The first group of students entered Moscow in January 1992 and lived with families that could support them. The interns used McKee's methods to teach English to the children. McKee insisted that all the students represent the best of American and Christian ideals. Their honest example elicited the program participants' interest in the students' background, their motivation, and eventually their faith. Though the program was conducted strictly to teach English, many became interested in the Church.

Nina Bazarskaya—native of Voronezh, a city several hundred miles south of Moscow—attended the Moscow State University conference. When the topic of religion came up in a roundtable session, Professor Blair asked the question, "What religious changes have occurred in Russia?" Silence followed. Nina feared to speak English and publicly express religious feelings, which was still unusual at the time. Overcoming her anxiety, she revealed her religious background, and expressed her gratitude for Russia's new religious freedom. When student interns taught in Voronezh during the second half of 1992, Nina regularly attended their religious services because she enjoyed the "simplicity, light, and spirit of mutual love" she felt there. After joining the Church in December 1992, she was asked to coordinate the English teaching program in Voronezh. Later, Nina assumed responsibility for the entire program in Russia.[147]

By 1996 about fifty student interns taught in St. Petersburg, Voronezh, and Perm each semester. BYU sponsored only the two semesters in 1992; thereafter, it has been run privately as the International Language Program. As with Sister Bazarskaya, many adults learned faith while witnessing the dedicated work of the interns as they taught English to the children.[148]

Missions Burgeon in Russia

Church leaders first divided Russia into two missions in 1992, each centered around one of the two principal cities of St. Petersburg in the west and Moscow in the center. By 1996 two additional missions had been created around major cities along the Volga River on its course from Moscow to the Caspian Sea, another further east in the Urals, and the last in western Siberia—a total of six missions spanning Russia from the Baltics to central Siberia. The Moscow South Mission became the seventh Russian mission in 1997. On the Pacific shore of Russia an eighth mission, the Russia Vladivostok Mission, was created in 1999.

The Russia St. Petersburg Mission (illus. 8-14) in northwestern Russia adjoined the borders of Finland and the Baltic nations. Charles Creel presided over the mission until July 1993, when he was replaced by Thomas Rogers, a BYU Professor of Russian. In a trend already observed throughout central and eastern Europe, baptismal totals peaked two or three years after initial entry, then declined to a lower rate in the years thereafter.[149]

The novelty of contact with Westerners had begun to wane, and the necessity of tending to survival in an increasingly chaotic society supplanted concerns about religion. In 2000, President Rogers conducted a survey of the mission presidents who had served in Russia during the 1990s, asking what factors affected declines in conversion or activity. The response was that the foremost factor was "encroaching materialism." Secondary factors were "poorly trained local leaders and poorly administered Church programs, and inadequate meeting facilities."[150]

The missionaries worked primarily in St. Petersburg, a city of five million, to establish a firm foundation before spreading out into other cities. The second major congregation was in Vyborg. In May 1996, the Church's first chapel in Russia was dedicated in this city. Constructed in the first city beyond the Finnish border, it symbolized the entry of the gospel into Russia from Finland. Andrei Semionov, a citizen of Vyborg and the first Russian to receive the Melchizedek Priesthood, offered the dedicatory prayer.[151]

East of St. Petersburg was the Russia Moscow Mission. Gary Browning presided there until July 1993, when he was replaced by Richard L. Chapple, a professor serving as chairman of the Department of Modern Languages and Linguistics at Florida State University prior to his presidency.

Courtesy Kahlile B. Mehr

Illus. 8-14. The mission office in St. Petersburg, Russia, was located behind the arch in the foreground in the middle of the building, 1995.

As in the St. Petersburg Mission, baptisms peaked in 1993 though the rate of conversion (number of conversions per missionary companionship) had been slowing since the previous year.[152] The gospel spread further east and south into Russia's interior. In 1992, President Browning opened three cities along the Volga: Nizhni Novgorod (Soviet name Gorky), Samara (Soviet name Kiubishev), and Saratov.[153] In 1993, President Chapple sent missionaries to open Yekaterinburg (Soviet name Sverdlovsk) in the heart of the Ural Mountains—the dividing line between Russia and Siberia—and Novosibirsk in western Siberia.[154]

Church officials established the Russia Samara Mission in July 1993. Arlo Nelson, a retired planning consultant from Farmington, Utah, was called as the first president. From 1993 to 1994 he opened additional cities: Ufa further east, Rostov on the Black Sea at the mouth of the Don River, and Volgograd on the lower reaches of the Volga River below Saratov.[155] In the Samara Mission, as elsewhere in Russia, the Church administered its program of humanitarian assistance concurrently with the missionary effort. Church members in Germany sent a large food shipment to Samara for Christmas 1993. After distributing the boxes among the members, the excess was given to Samara's senior citizens. During 1994, Church leaders shipped forty thousand English books to schools in Ufa and the surrounding area.[156]

In July 1994, Ukrainian-born Vladimir Siwachok, from Ashton, Idaho, was called to preside over the newly created Russia Rostov Mission. In late 1996, President Siwachok sent missionaries to the city of Aksai, a scene contemplated thirty-five years earlier by young Howard Biddulph from a boat on the Volga. Also in July 1994, the Russia Novosibirsk Mission was created on the western edge of Siberia. President Jerald C. Sherwood, a former assistant dean of students and international student adviser at Ricks College, was transferred from the Spain Bilbao Mission to assume leadership. Yekaterinburg, a ten-hour train ride east from Samara and a twenty-two-hour train ride west of Novosibirsk, became the headquarters of the sixth Russian mission in July 1995. Viacheslav Efimov, from St. Petersburg, was called to be its president (illus. 8-15), the first Russian to serve in this capacity.

Brother Efimov, who supervised public transportation in St. Petersburg, had been a Church member for only five years. His apprenticeship was quick but effective. He was baptized with his wife and children on June 9, 1990, the first complete family in the city to join the Church all together.[157] He soon became a branch counselor, then a branch president, and a district president. The Efimovs' membership altered everything in their family life as they began to hold a weekly family home evening and serve in Church callings.[158] By the time Brother Efimov became president, he had learned to seek and abide the influence of the Spirit. According to one of the missionaries, they all left their initial interviews with the new president saying, "Wow!"[159] Another missionary referred to him as the "Russian Brigham Young." This enthusiasm carried over into the missionary work, and 457 baptisms occurred in the mission in 1996.[160] His ability reflected the faith and commitment of many of his fellow countrymen. Tragically, he passed away unexpectedly in February 2000.[161]

Courtesy Mary Kay Stout

Illus. 8-15. Galina and Viacheslav Efimov, 1991. Brother Efimov became the first native Russian mission president in 1995. One of his missionaries called him the "Russian Brigham Young."

The Church quickly expanded throughout Russia. In February 1992, a Canadian expatriate family, Tom and Rae Lynne Barnes and children, moved to Magadan, a port city along the eastern coast of Siberia. They interested the Nechiporov family in the gospel and the parents were baptized in Alaska in late 1992. The Church was registered in Magadan in June 1993.[162]

Michael Williams, from Centerville, Utah, was sent by his company to set up a cellular phone service in Vladivostok at the southern tip of Russia's Siberian littoral in fall 1994. His family and seven children soon followed. In 1995 three humanitarian service couples arrived with the assignment to teach English. Proselytizing missionaries were then transferred from the Moscow Mission; ten served there in late 1996. A humanitarian service couple and missionaries also served in Magadan. The Church on the Pacific shore of Russia came under the direct supervision of the Asia North Area. In December 1996, Elder Joseph B. Wirthlin became the first Apostle to enter Siberia, visiting Vladivostok and addressing a congregation of seventy-six people, of which 60 percent were members.[163] In 1999 the Russia Vladivostok Mission was created in eastern Siberia. The Church now spanned the length of Russia.

In the nine years from January 1992 to December 2001, Church membership from St. Petersburg to Vladivostok grew from just 760 to over 15,000.[164] In September 2000, Church officials realigned area boundaries in Europe, creating a new area office in Moscow, Russia, something unimaginable a mere decade earlier.[165] The first generation of members included people from all walks of Russian life. With the exception of a privileged elite, Communism had leveled people across the board. Many well-educated people, humbled by their circumstances, readily listened to a message that may have gone unheeded in a more self-satisfied Western society.[166] Reflecting the Church's vision of the future, Elder Jeffrey R. Holland, addressing an audience in a twelve-hundred-seat facility in November 1995, said, "In my life time I will return to Moscow, and a hundred theaters like this will not be enough to hold the members of the Church."[167] In September 2001, St. Petersburg was preparing for the organization of the first stake in eastern Europe.[168]

Tantamount to Treason

In spite of the successes, the Church's presence in Russia was not a foregone conclusion. Along with other Western religions, Church members faced an uncertain political future in Russia where resurgent xenophobia, particularly against foreign religions, had been evident since 1993. In August of that year, the Russian parliament, packed with conservatives and former Communists, attempted to outlaw foreign-based religions. This was one of multiple issues in which the parliament opposed the pro-Western President Boris Yeltsin. A struggle for power culminated in October 1993 when the army, loyal to Yeltsin, fired tank rounds through the parliament building and regained it from legislators barricaded inside.

The sentiment against foreign religion was not just a superficial reaction to religious forays into Russia but the reflection of historic roots in Orthodoxy. Wilfried Decoo, a member in Belgium with extensive contacts in Russia, summarized what some Russians have expressed regarding foreign religion:

What they [Westerners] don't understand is the magnitude of our ancestral Orthodox faith, the deep-rooted traditions of our culture and our soul, the generations of dedicated priests who have always continued to nurture the millions, in spite of limitations or persecutions.

> ... Who can understand the tragic depth of our past decades?
> In Russia the blood of 60 million men, women, and children cries
> from the gulag soil. ... We—*we*—must sanctify our ground again;
> we must find room for reflection and the difficult meeting of each
> other, without anger, revenge, nor suspicion. ... The Baptists, the
> Mormons, the media preachers have been waiting behind the iron
> gates with the eagerness of vultures enjoying the weakening of an
> enemy they did not even have to fight. We did the battle for them,
> during decades of torment. But now that the gates are open, they
> plunge into our disarray, adding to the spiritual chaos.[169]

Russian Orthodox Church leaders argued that leaving the traditional
faith of Russia was tantamount to treason, and when converts to foreign
religions became disillusioned with those faiths they would become emo-
tionally unstable and turn to the government for social and medical assistance, further burdening Russian society.[170] While these sentiments are
as distorted as the position that the benefit of foreign religions is uni-
formly positive, they provide a sobering perspective: the opposition is
neither rash nor just a matter of ill will.

In June 1996, Alexander Lebed, cabinet minister under Yeltsin,
labeled Mormons as "mold and filth," a polite translation of the gutter
language he actually used.[171] Although he later retracted his specific
slur against Latter-day Saints, he reconfirmed his attitude that foreign
influence was not welcome in Russia. The attention his statement drew
was not necessarily negative. The Russian media publicized the words of
U.S. President Bill Clinton defending the Church. President Rogers
of the St. Petersburg Mission regarded it as one of the finest publicity
coups the Church had experienced in Russia to that date.[172]

Not only national leaders but also local leaders greatly impacted missionary activity. Even with recognition granted on the national level, a
congregation needed to be registered separately in each city so it could
issue invitations for missionaries to work there. Registration requirements varied from city to city. In the absence of registration, missionaries
could be—and often were—expelled from cities before there were sufficient members to get the Church registered. In January 1994, missionaries were temporarily expelled from Nizhni Novgorod, a major city in the
Russia Moscow Mission, until registration could be achieved.[173] In 1995
registration problems were encountered in Ufa, a large city in the Russia
Samara Mission.[174] In 1995 when they were due to be expelled from
Omsk, President Sherwood knelt in prayer with the missionaries in the
forest. The next morning the responsible official, who had been terse and
unresponsive the previous week, relented, granting a three-month

reprieve.[175] By January 1997, about a fourth of Russia's regional governments had adopted laws to regulate religious activities they deemed as illegal. These restrictions, however, did not apply to the Russian Orthodox Church.[176]

On the positive side, fortuitous circumstances attended efforts to expand. Tomsk, in western Siberia, had been restricted from foreign visitors since tsarist times because of its arms industry. The deputy major of Tomsk was appointed as the Siberian representative of the Krieble Institute, a private foundation based in Washington, D.C., established to foster democratic principles in the successor states of the Soviet Union. In 1991 the Institute sponsored Gary Lawrence and Bruce Hughes—political and business professionals, respectively, as well as Church members— to direct seminars in several Siberian cities. They became friends with the Tomsk deputy mayor and later were able to provide medical assistance for his daughter when she was injured in a car accident. Visiting the United States on several occasions, the deputy mayor stayed with his Latter-day Saint friends, becoming well acquainted with the Church's message and programs. He invited the missionaries to Tomsk and faced down opposition from the mayor and religious authorities to accomplish the task.[177]

At the national level, the matter of religious freedom came to a head in September 1997 when President Yeltsin signed a law placing limits on religious groups that could not prove they had been operating in Russia for at least fifteen years.[178] W. Cole Durham, a BYU professor and authority on religious liberty, was the principle author of two widely circulated documents relating to the law that appeared to have an impact on the version that was ultimately adopted.[179] Commenting on the bill, Elder Jeffrey R. Holland stated that Church history in Russia dated back to the beginning of the century. He cited Elder Francis M. Lyman's 1903 dedication of Russia as one instance of this activity.[180] The Church reached a resolution in May 1998 when, along with Roman Catholics, Baptists, three Pentecostal churches, and the New Apostolic Church, it won official recognition under the 1997 law.[181] But in August 1998, the Russian government required religious workers from abroad to renew their visas every three months.[182]

In early 1999 missionaries again faced anti-American sentiment in Russia because of the NATO bombing in Serbia, a fellow Slavic country. In response, Church leaders instructed missionaries to temporarily remove name tags, not put on any street displays, avoid all groups of people on the streets, and refrain from speaking English in public.[183] In

November 2000, Russian nationalists protested the construction of a Latter-day Saint chapel in Volgograd by dumping a half load of concrete on the site and setting a cross in it. A year passed before the congregation of four hundred members was able to use the facility.[184] The Church in Russia has weathered political storms for a decade, a circumstance that seems at present to be unending.

The Inner Frontier

Between 1977, when Poland recognized the Church, and 1998, when the Church received its second recognition in Russia, the gospel spread through the entire expanse of central and eastern Europe. Though there are millions that still have not been touched in this realm, many have. And, more important, some have found a new faith that satisfies their inner needs.

In Russia, Church members in Krasnoyarsk decided to celebrate the Church's pioneer sesquicentennial by reenacting the epic trek of the Mormons to the Western frontier of the United States. Two handcarts were constructed of Siberian pine and spruce. On February 22, 1997, a parade of nearly two hundred people, both members and investigators, started across Krasnoyarsk, which was the first of many cities in Russia and the Ukraine scheduled to see the event. The parade for that day concluded in a snow-covered park. Munching on Relief Society refreshments, the group sang hymns accompanied by an accordion player. The Novosibirsk Mission president, B. John Galbraith, spoke of pioneers both past and present. The group placed handmade dolls, Siberian bears, and written testimonies in the cart—the first in a collection that grew as the carts headed west.[185] Who would have imagined such a scene only two decades earlier when missionaries first entered the Communist realm?

Sisters Kristen Bowers and Angie Thomas labored in the city of Omsk during winter 1995-96. As foreigners in the provincial remoteness of Siberia, the missionaries were generally regarded with suspicion. People on the streets yelled at them, and a few even pushed the male missionaries around at times. In December the sisters met and taught a family that was "so golden, so good to meet, and so willing to learn; they asked to be baptized even before they were challenged. We would leave their home so edified, that we would gasp with happiness and jump up and down with joy in the street."[186] Who in late 1989 would have imagined young sisters dancing for happiness on a frozen street, surrounded by the stillness of the Siberian winter? Missionaries had come to Siberia not to be punished, as dreaded by Mischa Markow at the beginning of the twentieth century, but to publish tidings of the restored gospel.

Political and social forces outside the Church's control opened a door previously knocked on by President Spencer W. Kimball in the late 1970s. Missionaries took the gospel message first to countries along Communism's western border, as those political powers fissioned. The Soviet Union itself, heartland of Communism, soon succumbed to the rebellion of a long-suppressed populace, and the missionaries entered this realm as well. This transformation allowed Western religion to inundate and even surfeit seekers adrift in social and political chaos. Many found the goodness of the restored gospel and were baptized. The Church strives to embrace these converts so that they might endure any opposition.

While the Church experienced worldwide growth during its move eastward in Europe, the drama was never more suspenseful than in the former Communist world. It happened unpredictably and unexpectedly, almost overnight. The territorial frontier has given way to the frontier of the soul and a trek fraught with struggle as well as reward.

Notes

1. Spencer J. Condie, interviewed by James B. Allen, March 15–22, 1989, Provo, Utah, audio tape 3, in possession of the interviewer, Orem, Utah.

2. "Church Growth in Tour Areas," *Ensign* 21 (October 1991): 37.

3. Howard L. Biddulph, *The Morning Breaks: Stories of Conversion and Faith in the Former Soviet Union* (Salt Lake City: Deseret Book, 1996), 147–48.

4. Management Information Center, 1999 Statistics, LDS Church headquarters, March 2002.

5. "Europe Area Convert Baptisms, December 1992," typescript; Management Information Center, November 3, 1998.

6. Bruce A. Van Orden, *Building Zion: The Latter-day Saints in Europe* (Salt Lake City: Deseret Book, 1997), 280.

7. James Wilde, telephone interview by author, February 7, 1997.

8. James Wilde, interviewed by author, February 21, 1997, Provo, Utah.

9. Hungary Budapest Mission, Historical Records and Minutes, 1994 and 1995 report, Church Archives, The Church of Jesus Christ of Latter-day Saints, Salt Lake City.

10. "Elder Holland Visits Hungary, Bosnia," *Church News*, published by *Deseret News*, August 24, 1996, 6.

11. Czechoslovakia Prague Mission, Historical Records and Minutes; 1992–94, and 1996 reports, Church Archives.

12. David Stewart, "LDS in the Czech Republic: Part II," February 11, 2000, <lds-eurasia@egroups.com> (February 12, 2000).

13. Steven Layton, telephone interview by author, February 4, 1997.

14. Management Information Center.

15. Walter Whipple, interviewed by Matthew Heiss, June 23, 1994, Provo, Utah, typescript, 22, copy in possession of the interviewee, Provo, Utah; Poland Warsaw Mission, Historical Records and Minutes, 1993 report, Church Archives.

16. Management Information Center.

17. Serbia and Montenegro are still confederated in the state of Yugoslavia but I chose to use the term Serbia so as not to confuse it with the former Yugoslavia.

18. Wendy Danley, Journal, April 25, 1993.

19. Danley, Journal, April 25, 1993; Kenneth Dudley Reber, interviewed by Matthew K. Heiss, 1994, Salt Lake City, typescript, 73, copy in possession of the interviewee, Sandy, Utah.

20. Cindy Hall, interviewed by author, October 28, 1995, Sandy, Utah; Reber, interview, 1994; Kenneth Dudley Reber, interviewed by author, October 28, 1995, Sandy, Utah.

21. Danley, Journal, July 14, 1993, photocopy in possession of author; Doug Van Woerkom, interviewed by author, October 28, 1995, Sandy, Utah.

22. Leo A. Jardine and Judith C. N. Jardine, *Out of Obscurity, Out of Captivity, Out of Darkness* (Salt Lake City: By the authors, 1998), 81–82; Reber, interview, 1994; Reber, interview, October 28, 1995.

23. Jardine and Jardine, *Out of Obscurity,* 84–85; Swen Swensen, telephone interview by author, March 15, 1997.

24. "14 LDS Missionaries Pulled Out of Serbia," *Deseret News,* October 4, 1998, A-10.

25. "New Mission Presidents," *Church News,* July 27, 1996, 13.

26. "Earns Austrian Cross," *Church News,* July 16, 1988, 10.

27. Austria Vienna South Mission, Historical Records and Minutes, reports of September 1996; January and February 1997, Church Archives.

28. I. S. Makarov, "President Galbraith's Letter," October 7, 2000 <lds-eurasia@egroups.com> (October 9, 2000).

29. "Missionaries Return to Serbia," *LDS Church News,* January 26, 2002, <http://www.desnews.com/cgi-bin/libstory_church?dn02&0201280011> (March 15, 2002).

30. Carri P. Jenkins, "Kresimir Cosic Moves from Basketball to Diplomats Courts," *BYU Today* 46 (November 1992): 10–12.

31. Truman Madsen, speech, Memorial Service for Ćosić, May 31, 1995, copy in possession of Everett Smith, Providence, Utah.

32. Lee Davidson, "Cosic Was a True Man of Principle," *Deseret News,* June 3, 1995, A-9; Reber, interview, 1994; Kurt Bestor, telephone interview by author, November 20, 1995; Radmila Ranović, "Missionary Reunion," talk given at Yugoslav Mission Reunion, October 28, 1995, typescript, 9, in possession of the author.

33. Management Information Center.

34. Monika Kadi, interviewed by author, January 29, 1996, Salt Lake City.

35. "Church Reassigns Missionaries Serving in Albania," *Church News*, August 29, 1998, 5.

36. Romania Bucharest Mission, Historical Records and Minutes, 1993 report, Church Archives.

37. John Morrey, telephone interview by author, November 13, 1998.

38. Kelly Bangerter, telephone interview by author, January 19, 1997; Harvard Heath, MHA presentation, June 22, 1995, Kingston, Ontario; Romania Bucharest Mission, Historical Records and Minutes, 1995 report. Sources for the next paragraph also.

39. LaRene Porter Gaunt, "The Church in Romania," *Ensign* 31 (June 2001): 32.

40. Carey Wolfley to David Stewart, "LDS in Romania," February 17, 2000, <lds-eurasia@egroups.com> (February 20, 2000).

41. Management Information Center, October 6, 1999; "Moldova is Dedicated in Picturesque Setting," *LDS Church News*, June 9, 2001, <http://www.desnews.com/cgi-bin/libstory_church?dn01&0106110026> (November 9, 2001).

42. Dusty Kawai, interviewed by author, February 11, 1995, Draper, Utah.

43. Dale Warner, interviewed by author, December 26, 1994, Ogden, Utah; Kawai, interview.

44. Misty Whitaker Nielson, interview by author, March 17, 1997, Salt Lake City.

45. Diana Petrova, "The Sect Hides Its Address from the Authorities," *Trud*, December 8, 1993, translation by the author.

46. Warner, interview.

47. Nielson, interview.

48. Mirella Lazarova, talk, Bulgarian fireside, April 21, 1994, Salt Lake City.

49. Kawai, interview; Nielson, interview.

50. Edward Partridge, telephone interview by author, November 2, 1998; Sara Partridge, telephone interview by author, November 2, 1998; Jeremiah Fountain Syndergaard to Lee Telfer, February 13, 1996, in possession of author; Nielson, interview.

51. The author helped host the delegation of journalists and is personally aware of the favorable impact.

52. Derek Allred, telephone interview by author, April 6, 1999.

53. Gary and Annette Stephens to Friends, October 1997, photocopy in possession of author.

54. Olia Botcheva, interviewed by author, August 4, 1994, Provo, Utah.

55. Nielson, interview.

56. Christian Elggren, Missionary journal, April 12, 1991, in possession of Christian Elggren, Salt Lake City.

57. Morris Mower, telephone interview by author, January 29, 1997.

58. Morris Mower, telephone interview; Annetta Mower, interviewed by author, January 31, 1997, Salt Lake City.

59. Aunya Ivanova, interviewed by author, November 4, 1998, Salt Lake City; "History of The Church of Jesus Christ of Latter-day Saints in Bulgaria," in Bulgaria Sofia Mission, Historical Records and Minutes, 1997 report, Church Archives. The first trip was made in 1995.

60. *2001-2002 Church Almanac* (Salt Lake City: Deseret News, 2000), 590.

61. Esther McFarlane, "LDS Bulgarians Come Together for Historic Dedication," *LDS Church News,* July 8, 2000, <http://www.desnews.com/cn/view/1,1721,100000927,00.html> (July 16, 2000).

62. Zlatan Denchev to Morris and Annetta Mower, September 10, 1998, photocopy in possession of the author.

63. David Horne, interviewed by author, August 21, 1995, Salt Lake City.

64. Roger Doxey, telephone interview by author, February 8, 1996.

65. Doxey, telephone interview. David Horne, interviewed by author, July 25, 1995, Salt Lake City, Utah.

66. Bulgaria Sofia Mission, Historical Records and Minutes, 1993 report, Church Archives.

67. Horne, interview, August 21, 1995; Horne, interview, July 25, 1995. Except as otherwise cited, sources for next paragraph as well.

68. Jardine and Jardine, *Out of Obscurity,* 118, 124.

69. "97th Translation, Armenians Receive Book of Mormon," *LDS Church News,* May 5, 2001, <https://www.desnews.com/cn/view/1,1721,175001292,00.html?> (May 11, 2001).

70. Horne, interview, August 21, 1995.

71. Narina Sirkassian and Susanna Sirkassian, interviewed by Matthew K. Heiss, March 23, 1995, Provo, Utah, typescript, 35, copy in possession of interviewee.

72. Sirkassian and Sirkassian, interview, 44; untitled memorandum prepared for Salt Lake Temple History, in possession of author.

73. Russia Rostov Mission, Historical Records and Minutes, 1997 report, Church Archives.

74. Doxey, telephone interview; Joseph Bauman, "Utahn Pulls Out All the Stops to Rescue His Injured Friend," *Deseret News,* January 18, 1996, A-1.

75. "David Mack Horne," Obituary, *Deseret News,* January 23, 1996, D-6.

76. Elyanora Vardanian, "Goodbye: American with an Armenian Heart," *Republic of Armenia,* April 24, 1996, typescript translation, 2.

77. Gary Browning, *Russia and the Restored Gospel* (Salt Lake City: Deseret Book, 1997), 340.

78. "State of the Mission, January 1994" in "Latvia-Riga Mission Yearbook, 1993–1994," unpaginated manuscript, in possession of author.

79. Boris A. Schiel, "The History of the Latvia Riga Mission of The Church of Jesus Christ of Latter-day Saints, June 17, 1992–December 14, 1993," typescript, 15, in possession of author.

80. Schiel, "History," 15–17, 21.

81. "State of the Mission."

82. Robert and Ruth Rees, "Elder and Sister Rees," in "Latvia-Riga Mission Yearbook."

83. Jason Swenson to Sister Moretti, December 7, 1993, in "Latvia-Riga Mission Yearbook."

84. Shane Allred, "Kaunas, Lithuania," in "Latvia-Riga Mission Yearbook"; John F. Dobbs to unnamed person, April 24, 1994, in "Latvia-Riga Mission Yearbook."

85. "Elder and Sister Moretti" in "Latvia-Riga Mission Yearbook."

86. Dobbs to unnamed person.

87. "Excerpts from Letters of Elder and Sister Folsom" in "Latvia-Riga Mission Yearbook." Elder Folsom was a retired German professor. To prepare for his call to Lithuania, he had studied the language on his own and read the New Testament in Lithuanian. He taught the class in Kaunas with the help of Lithuanian students who knew some English. He supervised the teaching of the class in Vilnius, done by a Lithuanian. Robert Blair, interviewed by author, February 21, 1997, Provo, Utah.

88. Schiel, "History," 28, 30, 32.

89. Amy Searle and Jennifer Turner, interviewed by Matthew K. Heiss, 1996, Provo, Utah, typescript, 20–21, copy in possession of Amy Searle, Salt Lake City.

90. Latvia Riga Mission, Historical Records and Minutes, 1995 report, Church Archives; Searle and Turner, interview, 24, 27.

91. "Media Boosts Profile," *Church News,* July 9, 1994, 11.

92. Searle and Turner, interview, 10, 19, 32–33, 36.

93. Searle and Turner, interview, 29, 32–34; Schiel, "History," 31, 33.

94. Schiel, "History," 3, 5, 14, 34, 36–37.

95. Latvia Riga Mission, 1995 report.

96. Schiel, "History," 5–6.

97. Ilona Machinič, interviewed by author, January 9, 1997, Salt Lake City.

98. Schiel, "History," 43.

99. Latvia Riga Mission, 1995 report; James and Janet Ames, "Estonia," in "Latvia-Riga Mission Yearbook"; "State of the Mission"; Kemppainen, telephone interview by author, January 24, 2000.

100. Julia Blair, interviewed by author, February 21, 1997, Provo, Utah.

101. Latvia Riga Mission, Historical Records and Minutes, 1995 report; "State of the Mission."

102. Lithuania Vilnius Mission, Historical Records and Minutes, 1997 report, Church Archives.

103. Personal knowledge of the author who visited the branch the second week after it had been combined.

104. Schiel, "History," 34, 36; Logan S. Wentz, "Kaliningrad," typescript, 3, in possession of author.

105. Russia St. Petersburg Mission, Historical Record and Minutes, 1995, Church Archives.

106. Erki Kõiv, "New Meetinghouse Dedicated in Estonia," November 25, 1999, <lds-eurasia@egroups.com> (November 27, 1999).

107. *Lithuania Vilnius Mission News Page,* February 19, 2001, <http://www.mission.net/lithuania/vilnius/news.php> (March 10, 2001).

108. Lithuania Vilnius Mission Office to author, email, May 9, 2000.

109. David Stewart, "Re: Cheboksary," September 22, 2000, <lds-eurasia@egroups.com> (September 23, 2000).

110. Shaun D. Stahle, "Seven New Missions Created," *LDS Church News,* March 9, 2002, <http://www.desnews.com/cn/view/1,1721,255001086,00.html> (March 14, 2002).

111. Biddulph, *Morning Breaks,* 63–64.

112. Howard Biddulph, "Winter Mission, December 1992–January 1993," typescript, in possession of the author. Also the source for the next four paragraphs.

113. "Europe Area Convert Baptisms, December 1992."

114. Howard Biddulph, interviewed by author, February 21, 1997, Provo, Utah.

115. Biddulph, *Morning Breaks*, 64.

116. Steven Struk, interviewed by author, October 30, 1992, Kiev, Ukraine.

117. Biddulph, *Morning Breaks*, 77; the Ukrainian translation began circulating in September 1997. David Stewart, "The Church in Ukraine," <www-lds@makelist.com>, (July 5, 1998).

118. Biddulph, *Morning Breaks*, 117–18; Ukraine Kiev Mission, Historical Records and Minutes, 1995 report; Biddulph, interview.

119. Aleksandr Manzhos became the first Ukrainian to serve as a mission president when he was called to preside over the Ukraine Donetsk Mission (1996–1999).

120. Howard Biddulph to Richard Bennett, May 16, 2001, copy in author's possession; Ukraine Donetsk Mission History, <www2.et.byu.edu/~parkje/history.html> (July 22, 1997); Biddulph, interview; Biddulph, *Morning Breaks*, 44.

121. Ukraine Kiev Mission, Historical Records and Minutes, 1995 report, Church Archives.

122. David Stewart, "The LDS (Mormon) Church in Ukraine," <http://ldsmissions.net/rspm/europe/ukraine.htm> (March 18, 1999).

123. Biddulph, *Morning Breaks*, 180, 186–87.

124. David V. Tilton, "Ukraine Temple," <www-lds@makelist.com> (July 29, 1998).

125. "First Meetinghouse in Ukraine Dedicated," *Church News,* July 25, 1998, 5.

126. "A Temple in Ukraine," *Church News,* August 8, 1998, 3.

127. "Three Members of Seventy Given Emeritus Status," *Deseret News,* October 14, 2000, <http://www.desnews.com/cgi-bin/libstory_reg?dn00&0010160041> (October 27, 2000).

128. Biddulph, *Morning Breaks*, 68–70. Also a source for the next two paragraphs.

129. Ukraine Kiev Mission, Historical Records and Minutes, 1995 report.

130. Jeffrey R. Holland, "'Witnesses unto Me,'" *Ensign* 31 (May 2001): 14–16.

131. Dave Robbins, interviewed by author, February 6, 1993, Draper, Utah.

132. Matthew Riddle, interviewed by author, January 26, February 22, 1992, Draper, Utah; Robbins, interview.

133. Brigham Redd, interviewed by author, July 19, 1993, Draper, Utah.

134. Irene Maximova, interviewed by author, November 25, 1993, St. Petersburg, Russia.

135. Lois M. Collins and Lee Davidson, "Missionaries Freed; 2 Arrested," *Deseret News,* March 23, 1998, A-1.

136. "Elder's Life and His Love of Russia Recalled," *Deseret News,* October 27, 1998, A-6.

137. Dr. Douglas C. Heiner and Richard Wirthlin, "Doctor at Hospital in Ufa, Russia," found on *LDS World,* n.d., <http://ldsworld.com/gems/wws/display/0,2624,4207,00.html> (October 19, 2001).

138. "Food Shipment Eases Soviet Hunger," *Church News,* March 30, 1991, 3.

139. Mary Kay Stout, "Russian Members Distribute Bales of Clothes and Shoes among LDS, Others," *Church News,* September 4, 1993, 3.

140. Robbins, interview; Maximova, interview.

141. Redd, interview.

142. Robbins, interview.

143. Russia Moscow Mission, Historical Records and Minutes, 1993 report, Church Archives.

144. Russia Moscow Mission, Historical Records and Minutes, 1995 report.

145. Russia St. Petersburg Mission, Historical Records and Minutes, 1993 report, Church Archives.

146. Trevor McKee, telephone interview by author, March 13, 1997; Robert Blair, telephone interview by author, February 28, 1997. Sources for the next paragraph too.

147. Nina Bazarskaya, as told to Valerie Parker, "I Spoke Out for Faith," *Ensign* 26 (February 1996): 56–57.

148. McKee, telephone interview.

149. David Stewart to author, March 18, 1999. Concerns a downturn in Russian baptisms during 1994.

150. Thomas F. Rogers, "Mormonism's First Decade in the Former USSR: Patterns of Growth and Retention," paper presented at the Mormon History Association Annual Meeting, June 25–July 2, 2000, Copenhagen and Aalborg, Denmark, typescript, 6, copy in possession of author.

151. M. Keith Richardson, telephone interview by author, March 14, 1997. Supervisor of Vyborg chapel construction.

152. Russian Moscow Mission, Historical Records and Minutes, 1994 report, Church Archives.

153. Robbins, interview.

154. Russia Moscow Mission, 1993 report.

155. Hannah Clarke, "Russia Samara Mission Historical Summary, 1993–1994," typescript, 1993 report, 9, 1994 report, 6, in possession of Hannah Clarke, Salt Lake City.

156. Clarke, 1994 report, 1, 5, 7.

157. Eric Thorley to David Stewart, "Tribute to President Efimov," February 28, 2000, <lds-eurasia@egroups.com> (March 1, 2000).

158. Tamara Efimov McKane, interview by author, March 31, 1992, Mesa, Arizona.

159. Tamara Baird, interviewed by author, December 10, 1996, Bountiful, Utah.

160. Kenneth Crowther, <lds-eurasia@egroups.com> (December 15, 1999); Russian Yekaterinburg Mission, Historical Records and Minutes, 1996 report, Church Archives.

161. Kent Larson to David Stewart, "President Efimov Obituary," March 6, 2000, <lds-eurasia@egroups.com> (March 7, 2000).

162. David Stewart, "Europe East Bulletin #3," March 23, 1999. Information from Gwen and Glen Edmunds, returned missionaries from the Russian Far East.

163. John Morgan, interviewed by author, November 21, 1996, Bountiful, Utah, "Former Closed City Visited by Elder Wirthlin," *Church News,* December 7, 1996, 5.

164. Figures for 1992 are from Browning, *Russia and the Restored Gospel,* 340;

Management Information Center.

165. Scott Lloyd, "European Continent Realigned into Three New Areas," September 16, 2000, <http://www.desnews.com/cgi-bin/libstory_church?dn00& 0009180038> (March 14, 2002).

166. Riddle, interviews.

167. Russian Moscow Mission, 1995 report.

168. Yura Kondratieva to David Stewart, "Updates," September 29, 2001, <lds-eurasia@egroups.com> (October 23, 2001).

169. Wilfried Decoo, "Issues in Writing European History and in Building the Church in Europe," *Journal of Mormon History* 23 (spring 1997): 156–57.

170. Jardine and Jardine, *Out of Obscurity*, 89–90.

171. Peggy Fletcher Stack and Michael Nakoryakov, "Yeltsin Adviser Wants LDS Out of Russia," *Salt Lake Tribune,* June 28, 1996, A-1.

172. Thomas F. Rogers, homecoming speech, July 21, 1996, Bountiful, Utah, notes of the author.

173. Russia Moscow Mission, 1994 report.

174. Russia Samara Mission, Historical Records and Minutes, 1995 report, Church Archives.

175. Russia Novosibirsk Mission, Historical Records and Minutes, 1995 report, Church Archives.

176. "Religious Freedom Seems to be Strangling in Russia," *Deseret News,* January 15–16, 1997, A-4.

177. F. Enzio Busche, interviewed by author, Bountiful, Utah, April 19, 2001.

178. The limitations included bans on the right to hold public meetings, to own land or building, to actively proselytize, or to bring in foreign missionaries.

179. "W. Cole Durham, Jr.," *Brigham Young Magazine* 52 (winter 1998): 23.

180. Carrie A. Moore, "LDS Church Says Work in Russia Will Continue," *Deseret News,* September 27, 1997, A-1.

181. Peggy Fletcher Stack, "It's Now Official: Russia Recognizes Mormon Church," *Salt Lake Tribune,* May 16, 1998, A-1, A-12.

182. "Russia Adopts New Visa Regulations," *Deseret News,* August 15, 1998.

183. David Kenison <ldsworld-gems@lists.ldsworld.com> (March 29, 1999), information from Lisa Kelly, wife of Russia Moscow Mission President Michael R. Kelly.

184. Alexander Evreinov, "A Cross for the Mormons," November 14, 2000, posted by David Stewart, November 17, 2000, <lds-eurasia@egroups.com> (November 17, 2000).

185. Michael S. von Rosen, "A Demonstration of Faith," *Church News,* March 8, 1997, 8–10.

186. Kristen Bowers, telephone interview by author, March 13, 1997.

9

Eastward in Europe

The Russian and Austro-Hungarian empires of the nineteenth century mounted impenetrable barriers against the message of a gospel that had been restored in America. Mormon missionaries who entered this realm met with little success, were often arrested, and were frequently banished from various countries.

At the beginning of the twentieth century, Mischa Markow, a native son of central Europe, pierced the political barriers and established a congregation in Temesvár, Hungary. Though missionaries followed in his steps for over a decade, Church officials terminated the Hungarian effort in 1913 because of a poor response. Elder Francis M. Lyman dedicated Russia for the preaching of the gospel in 1903, but Elder Markow walked away from a chance to establish a congregation in Riga, thereby avoiding possible exile to Siberia. The First Presidency declined to follow other Western religions that pursued a chance to preach—and that met with some success—before the establishment of Communism, which in 1917 enveloped the Russian Empire in a new orthodoxy inimical to public religious worship. Deciding against fielding and committing language-qualified manpower, Church leaders focused their attention on preaching to people in other lands.

The Czechoslovak Mission, established in response to the humble entreaty of Františka Brodilová, reaffirmed the hope that central and eastern Europe would one day hear the gospel tidings. During a 1932 conference in Czechoslovakia, Elder John A. Widtsoe envisioned the day when the handful of worshipers in that region of the world would evolve into thousands. A few hundred had responded to the missionaries' message in Czechoslovakia before World War II, but the Church did not expand into the Baltic States, Hungary, Poland, Romania, or the Balkans at that time. There is no indication that Church leaders even considered this seriously, as they moved into Latin America and Asia instead.

After World War II, Soviet power sealed off central and eastern Europe behind a political, social, and cultural barrier: the Iron Curtain. Despite this obstacle, small Latter-day Saint congregations created on the western edge of the Slavic world endured for forty years. Jiří Šnederfler explains how he and others learned to cope: "We Church members who lived under Communism in constant danger ceased after a certain time to be aware of it. If one has to live in constant danger, the danger ceases to exist; it turns into normal, everyday life."[1]

Those from other religions endured likewise. The Russian Orthodox Church regained its strength when Stalin was forced to include its moral authority in behalf of the war effort during World War II. The peoples of central and eastern Europe clung to traditional religions such as Roman Catholicism and Lutheranism to retain a cultural identity separate from Soviet uniformity. Ironically, the pressure exerted by the Soviet system fostered the growth of sub-rosa Western religions: Baptists, Jehovah's Witnesses, and Seventh-Day Adventists. Religious belief became a revolt against a uniform way of thinking, a way of rebelling against a carefully conditioned public opinion.[2]

The Czechoslovak and East German experience of Church members remained marginal in the region's religious life until 1989, when Communist power fell and the Iron Curtain rose, heralding a new era of interactions between West and East.

Before the Soviet Union collapsed and its satellites in central and eastern Europe regained their independence, Church leaders began utilizing a new missionary tactic. They sent senior couples into Poland, Hungary, and Yugoslavia to visit scattered members and respond, when legally permitted, to inquiries about their faith. These couples operated in obscurity, laying a small foundation on which to build the Church later. Following the pattern established by Matthew and Marian Ciembronówicz in Poland from 1977 to 1979, the senior couples quietly sustained the few members in central and eastern Europe and occasionally added additional converts who sought them out.

Efforts to have young missionaries proselytize in Yugoslavia prior to the demise of Communism met with less success. While Krešimir Ćosić fearlessly promoted his adopted faith, much in the tradition of Mischa Markow, the response was minimal. Neither the place nor the time was yet right for the Church.

The isolation imposed by Soviet authority was counterproductive in the end. In the early 1990s, many in the East were intensely interested in what the West had to offer. Whereas the Church had voluntarily withdrawn from Hungary in the early part of the twentieth century, it had some of its greatest success there in the 1990s. To some degree, Communism destroyed old traditions, creating fallow soil for new ones. Yet it did not destroy religion. In some areas, it even enhanced faith in established religions, for instance among Catholics in Poland and Lutherans in the Baltics. Nevertheless, Communism did sever the symbiotic relationship between church and state that had stymied religious diversity in the nineteenth-century empires. The religious freedom promised by Tsar Nicholas II in 1903 was finally granted by the Communist Party General Secretary Gorbachev by century's end.

Young missionaries arrived in the various countries of the former Communist realm in quick succession. Initially they taught constantly without needing to find investigators through traditional methods such as door-to-door contacting. Though this curiosity was satisfied within a few years and the people's attention shifted to providing for daily sustenance when eastern Europe's economic system collapsed, the Church rapidly expanded into every country. Its message brought new hope and understanding to thousands, beginning the fulfillment of Elder Widtsoe's vision sixty years earlier.

Humanitarian assistance provided another method of presenting the restored gospel in deeds as well as words. Throughout central and eastern Europe but particularly evident in Romania, Albania, Yugoslavia, and Armenia, humanitarian service workers offered assistance. They distributed welfare supplies but, more significantly, they attempted to provide the means and training for people to help themselves. In southeastern Europe and Armenia, service workers preceded and prepared the way for young missionaries, but elsewhere they operated independently or concurrently with them.

Many came into contact with the Church and a few were converted, finding a new inner joy. As one new member in Russia wrote, "The joy I had inside me was like a fountain. I smiled, not knowing what for. I laughed, not knowing why. And for the first time I really felt that these people around me were indeed my brothers and sisters."[3] When asked why she was baptized, Irina Maximova's simple response is indicative of what many others in central and eastern Europe have always desired. She said, "I wanted to be a better person."[4]

Unfortunately, not all converts endured. Inactivity or disbelief claimed a large percentage of those who had joined the Church. External persecution and internal dissension exposed new members to the reality of living a different life constrained in temporal pursuits and amplified in spiritual strivings. The transition was particularly challenging in the East, where Communism's social ethic discouraged individual initiative and leadership at the local level—traits that are necessary to a religion that expects full participation from its members.

The Church reentered most of central and eastern Europe in an era of transition. An old system collapsed and a new system was not yet in place. Russia continues to reel from repeated financial crises. In 1998 the country's stock market collapsed, the government defaulted on debt, and the banking system failed. Per capita income has fallen to 4 percent of the U.S. level, whereas in 1980 it was about 38 percent.[5] A political retrenchment seems to be in progress. Russia has tried reform, but the result has been misery. When some democratic politicians demanded a legal ban of the Communist Party in Russia, one Communist leader responded, "Communism is immortal in Russia, because it is in accord with the natural way of the thinking and living of masses of the Russian people."[6] While many countries in central and eastern Europe do not share this same heritage, they nevertheless remain in the shadow of this more powerful neighbor. The political and social transition has not yet run its course, and the milieu to be faced in the twenty-first century has yet to be clearly defined.

During the late twentieth century, Church officials began committing the manpower to preach the restored gospel in central and eastern Europe. By 1999, nineteen missions had germinated from the East Central Districts (1981–87) and the lone mission of Austria Vienna East (1987–92). Thousands of missionaries now labor where only a handful served in the 1970s. More than thirty-two thousand people have been baptized into the Church—not many in comparison with the millions of inhabitants in that region of the world. Though dramatic and unexpected, the events of the last decade are but a prologue to more momentous events in the offing.

In 1843, Joseph Smith foresaw that missionary work in Russia would be connected to "some of the most important things concerning the advancement and building up of the Kingdom of God in the last days, which cannot be explained at this time."[7] The history of missionary work in central and eastern Europe illustrates that a change in the world order can be swift as well as glacial. Change occurred gradually in imperial Europe in the eighteenth and nineteenth centuries. In contrast, the bipolar reality of the post–World War II era lasted for just forty years, dissolved precipitously, and shattered into a myriad of possibilities. Perhaps the Prophet Joseph, raised before America's Industrial Revolution even began, could not explain "the most important things" to his generation because no one would have been able to imagine or comprehend them if he had. Between Ferdinand Hintze's visit in 1888 and the fall of the Berlin Wall in 1989, the Church made few advances in central and eastern Europe. In a mere decade all that changed. Moving eastward, missionaries have come into contact with an expansive group of humanity whose conversion will, in turn, help shape the future destiny of the Church. While history does not define the details of the future, it shows us that the outer frontiers that often seem impenetrable are not always so, and that in breaking through we transition to the inner frontier, where the spiritual journey begins.

Notes

1. Marvin K. Gardner, "Jiří and Olga Šnederfler: A Closer Look at Two Czech Pioneers," *Liahona* 21 (September 1997): 18.

2. Roland Gaucher, *Opposition in the U.S.S.R., 1917–1967* (New York: Funk and Wagnalls, 1969), 486.

3. Gary Browning, *Russia and the Restored Gospel* (Salt Lake City: Deseret Book, 1997), 205.

4. Kahlile Mehr, Journal, November 25, 1993.

5. Holger Jensen, "U.S. Lost Billions in Russian Reform," *Deseret News*, January 20, 1999, A-11.

6. Vladimir Soshnikov, "The Current Situation in Russia," *RAGAS Report* 4 (fall 1998): 3–4.

7. Browning, *Russia and the Restored Gospel*, 5, quoting from Joseph Smith Jr., *History of The Church of Jesus Christ of Latter-day Saints*, ed. B. H. Roberts, 2d ed., rev., 7 vols. (Salt Lake City: Deseret Book, 1971), 6:41.

LIFE AND HISTORY OF ELDER MISCHA MARKOW

Edited and annotated by
Matthew K. Heiss

"My Duty Was to Preach Every Where": The Missionary Reminiscences of Mischa Markow and the Church's Entry into Central and Eastern Europe

edited by Matthew K. Heiss
The Church of Jesus Christ of Latter-day Saints Historical Department

One of the significant events in the establishment of The Church of Jesus Christ of Latter-day Saints in central and eastern Europe was the organization of the Austria Vienna East Mission in July 1987. Mission president Dennis B. Neuenschwander was responsible for missionary work and the Church's thirty-four missionaries serving in the nations behind the Iron Curtain. In November 1989, the Berlin Wall, arguably the world's most recognized symbol of the Cold War, was breached, which seemed to unleash a series of revolutions that brought about the demise of the Eastern Bloc. Setting the Church within the context of this historic event, Elder Neuenschwander wrote,

> By the time the Berlin Wall opened in November 1989, the Church had already established a firm base in Eastern Europe. Fifty-four missionaries were laboring there and in Greece. By then, the Church had also received official recognition from Poland (May 1977), Yugoslavia (October 1985), and Hungary (June 1988). Ground had been broken for a chapel in Warsaw, and a building in Budapest had been purchased and dedicated.[1]

Prior to this time, the missionaries had been extremely limited in their missionary work. In the decade preceding the creation of the Austria Vienna East Mission, missionary couples were called as "special representatives" and instructed to make friends for the Church. In the former

Yugoslavia, young missionaries wore casual clothes ("P-day clothes") and acted as students and tourists. All that changed with the Austria Vienna East Mission.

Shortly after arriving in the mission, President Neuenschwander met with Elder Russell M. Nelson, the member of the Quorum of the Twelve Apostles responsible for Europe. While in Prague, Czechoslovakia, at a mission presidents' seminar, President Neuenschwander asked Elder Nelson if the Austria Vienna East missionaries were to proselytize. Elder Nelson replied, "The Lord is the master of the unlikely, and he expects the impossible."[2] From that point, President Neuenschwander's missionaries started to more actively seek after those who would listen to their message. People began to listen, some were converted, and the Church began to grow in countries that once seemed forever closed to the restored gospel of Jesus Christ.

However, this was not the first time missionaries of the Church had set foot in Eastern Europe. At the turn of the nineteenth century, Elder Mischa Markow made the first attempt to preach the gospel and establish the Church in many of the nations that were initially assigned to the Austria Vienna East Mission. Shortly after his baptism, Markow returned to his home in Hungary and began to teach his parents and brother. The missionary who baptized him, Ferdinand Hintze, visited the Markow home and helped teach the Markow family, who, except for Mischa, eventually rejected the teachings. Hintze invited Markow to emigrate to Utah. Markow, yearning to share his new-found faith, asked if he could engage in missionary work before emigrating. According to Markow's writings, an informal call was extended and Markow was given the freedom to travel and preach as he pleased or as he was led. On the inside of the front cover the history of his missionary experiences, which he entitled "Life + History of Elder Mischa Markow" (hereafter "Life History"), he summed up his missionary travels and the conflicts he had with local governments: "I, Mischa Markow Preach the Gospel in 8th Kingdoms."[3] While serving in Belgium, Hungary, Romania, Bulgaria, Germany, Turkey, Russia, and Serbia he was, at times, dragged before municipal magistrates, called before supreme courts, and jailed. He was eventually banished from two countries. But his fervent zeal to spread the gospel of Jesus Christ resulted in the baptisms of forty-five people, twenty-three women and twenty-two men. Indeed, Markow seemed to share in Elder Nelson's sentiment that "The Lord is the master of the unlikely, and he expects the impossible." While several articles have been published that describe Markow's missionary work, this is the first time the entire text of the

English portion of Markow's history describing his missionary labors has been printed.[4]

Biographical Sketch and Synopsis of "Life History"

Mischa Markow was born on October 21, 1854, in Serb Zernia in Hungary.[5] Little is known about his youth other than that he was born of mixed parentage. His father, who was Serbian, and his mother, a Romanian, raised Mischa in an Eastern Orthodox home. Markow's certification as a U.S. citizen describes him at the age of fifty-one as being five feet, five inches tall. He had a square face, a "full" forehead, blue eyes, a straight nose, a medium mouth, a short rounded chin, and dark hair and complexion. As a boy, he attended a Serbian school and worked with his parents on the family farm. He also served in the army for a time. That Markow had religious inclinations is shown by a pilgrimage he made in May 1886 at age thirty-two to Jerusalem, where he stayed and worshiped for about two weeks. He then went to Alexandria, Egypt, where he worked as a barber and had his own barbershop. While in Alexandria, he was, according to his history, studying the Bible and searching to find the true church. After praying, he concluded that he would travel to Constantinople, where he thought he would have access to a variety of Protestant churches that he could investigate.

At the same time, Markow writes, Jacob Spori, who was serving as president of the Turkish Mission, felt impressed to travel to Egypt. According to Markow, Spori had a vision and was told to find Markow in Alexandria. Spori, who was traveling through Palestine teaching and baptizing Germans living in the Holy Land, left Palestine and went to Egypt to find Markow. After three unsuccessful days, he boarded a steamer en route to Constantinople and found Markow as one of the passengers. While on the steamer, Spori taught Markow the gospel and prepared him for baptism. On February 1, 1887, Mischa Markow was baptized in the Black Sea by Ferdinand F. Hintze and confirmed a member of the Church by Joseph M. Tanner, both missionaries in the Turkish Mission.[6] Markow was later ordained an elder on February 26, 1888, by Hintze, who encouraged Markow to emigrate to "Zion." As previously mentioned, Markow declined the invitation. With the zeal of a new convert, he did not want to leave before preaching the gospel and baptizing those who believed and accepted his message. Markow went to Odessa, Russia, for a time, then to London. Markow does not indicate that he went to Odessa or London to preach the gospel. Rather, he alludes to the fact that he went to earn money. In the German text of his history he writes that he worked in Odessa for four months. While in London he looked for work, but because he could not speak English, he soon traveled to Belgium where he fulfilled his missionary desires. In his history, he recounts how he was led to a German family that he taught and baptized. Four years later, he had a joyous reunion with his converts at a meeting of the German Latter-day Saints in Salt Lake City, Utah.

From 1892 to 1898, Markow lived in Salt Lake City, where he worked as a barber. He married Jonetha (also known as Nettie) Hansen, who was born in Norway in 1860, in the Salt Lake Temple on May 24, 1893. According to Church membership records and Markow's obituary, the Markows were the parents of three children, one of whom died in childhood: Royal Clarence, Lucille Olga, and Florence.[7] In 1899, Markow was once again serving as a missionary. For nearly two years he labored alone trying to establish the Church in several central European nations. Markow's mission call indicates that he was assigned to serve in Europe. His letter of release denotes that at the end of his mission he was reporting to the German Mission. He began in Beograd, Serbia, where he worked for a month before being banished to Hungary. While in Hungary, he was arrested, paraded through the streets, accused of being an anarchist, and put in prison. Markow wrote that he boldly testified before judges and magistrates, much like the Apostle Paul did before King Agrippa. "The Lord was with me," he recorded, "and I did rejoice and shed Tears of joy that I was brought before the magistrate and High Court before the rulers to testify that God did spooke again from Heaven and restored his church." Nevertheless, he was banished from Hungary. Later he wrote, "The more I was persecuted, the stronger I felt."[8]

In July 1899, Markow went to Constantinople to confer with his friend Ferdinand Hintze and Turkish Mission president Philip Starkey Maycock. President Maycock told Markow he could go where he pleased since he had such extensive language abilities and a knowledge of central and eastern Europe. When Markow expressed a desire to go into Russia, he was dissuaded by Hintze, who feared for his safety. Markow then traveled to Romania and began to preach the gospel in Bucharest. He baptized nine persons in the Romanian capital before being banished. Bulgaria was his next field of labor. He arrived there in June 1900. A dream, which he recounted in his history, warned him that he would have problems in Bulgaria. Sure enough, when he arrived in Sofia, he encountered opposition. He was confronted by a Methodist pastor with anti-Mormon literature, denounced to the police, arrested, and put on trial. He appealed for permission to preach in Bulgaria but was denied and eventually left.

Markow then decided to take his chances again in Hungary. According to his writings, he was led to Temesvár, now Timişoara, Romania, by a dream. He wrote, "Then I got awake from my Sleep and that was my Dream. And I felt strong like a Lion and I bless the Name of the Lord and thank him very much that he did reveal un to me where I shall go."[9] On September 3, 1900, he arrived in Temesvár, registered as a missionary, and began to distribute tracts from house to house. From the president of the German Mission, Arnold H. Schulthess, he also requested a companion, who arrived on October 4. The new missionary was Hyrum Moroni Lau, who had been working in Germany. Together they had success, eventually baptizing thirty-one people. However, on April 1, 1901, he and Lau were ordered to leave Temesvár by the local government. They traveled to Austria where they met President Schulthess, who sent Lau to Hamburg and Markow to preside over the branch in Munich, Germany, where he spent the final three months of his mission. According to Markow's own records, he had spent twenty-six months and fourteen days on his mission.[10]

A little over two years later, Markow was called to serve another mission in Europe. While Markow was assigned to the Turkish Mission, he was inclined, once again, to establish the Church in Russia. In 1903, European Mission president Francis M. Lyman appointed him to initiate missionary work in the Russian Empire. However, Lyman warned him that if he began to face opposition, he was to leave Russia, fearing that Markow would be sent to Siberia. In August 1903, Markow traveled from Zürich, Switzerland, to Budapest, Hungary, and from there to Warsaw, Poland, which at that time was part of the Russian Empire. After only one day in Warsaw, he was impressed to leave. On October 9, 1903, he arrived in Riga, which was also part of the Russian Empire at that time. Riga, which had traded hands many times over the years, had a sizable German population. Markow had Church literature in German, and he began to preach there among the Germans. Experience had taught him to register himself as a missionary of "The Church of Jesus Christ" and not to mention anything about Mormonism to the city officials and police. This he did in Riga. But after twenty-eight days, he was summoned to appear in court. He tried to obtain legal permission to preach in the city, but the lawyer he hired, upon finding out Markow was a Mormon, declined to take the case. Heeding the warning Apostle Lyman had given him, he left Russia on November 5, 1903.

Shortly after leaving Russia, Markow was assigned to labor in Turkey. His mission president, Joseph W. Booth, gave Markow the option of preaching wherever he wanted. He selected Alexandretta, a port city in southern Turkey now known as Iskenderun. Booth warned him that Alexandretta was "the worst place in Turkey. Many Elders were banished out and put in jail."[11] Undeterred, and perhaps used to such treatment, Markow went to Alexandretta anyway and began to work among the Greeks and Armenians. While in Turkey, he had several brushes with the law and found himself once again declaring his faith to police officers and judges. On November 5, 1905, Markow was released from his mission, and he arrived in Salt Lake City on December 9, which is about where the English text ends. The final page and a half of the account contain Markow's observations on religious intolerance in Russia and the penalties for preaching against the Russian Orthodox religion.

After his mission, Markow settled in Salt Lake City. For a time he worked as a barber with Anthon Olson at a shop located at 321 South State Street. In 1908, Markow was living in the Salt Lake Fifteenth Ward and, according to the city directory, had his barber shop in his home located at 773 West 200 South. He remained there until his death on January 18, 1934.[12] One of Markow's patriarchal blessings describes him as a "tried servant and a valiant standard bearer in the cause of the Master."[13] This unique personality in Church history, a polyglot of languages, was a visionary man, a courageous man, a man of great faith and missionary zeal.

About the Manuscripts

Documents pertaining to Mischa Markow in the Church Archives are cataloged as "Reminiscences" and "Papers." The "Reminiscences" is a single volume containing "Life +. History of Elder Mischa Markow" ("Life History"). This document, probably written after 1917,[14] focuses primarily on his missionary experiences and contains lists of priesthood ordinances he performed, a page and a half of self-improvement ideas, a yearly synopsis of tithing he paid from 1892 to 1932, and birth and baptismal information pertaining to his two children, Roy Clarence and Lucille O. Markow. The "Life History" was written in two parts. The first portion of the text, pages 1–49, is in German.[15] The second portion of the text, pages 50–86, is written in English. The edited transcript below is of the English text only.

Markow's "Papers" consist of two folders. The first folder contains thirteen documents belonging to Markow and includes his 1894 Elder's

Certificate, an affidavit confirming his ordination to the Melchizedek Priesthood signed by Ferdinand F. Hintze in 1893, Certificate of U.S. Citizenship dated 1898, Seventy's License and Missionary Certificate dated 1899, 1901 letter and certificate of release from missionary service, 1903 missionary call to Hungary, 1903 Missionary Certificate and letter of release dated 1905, a document certifying that Markow is a U.S. citizen and is to be accorded safe passage out of Turkey dated 1905, High Priest certificate dated 1919, and 1924 Certificate of Release as a missionary in the Salt Lake Stake. The second folder of the "Papers" contains eight documents including copies of Markow's patriarchal blessing given on April 12, 1894—written in both German and English—two other patriarchal blessings given in 1914 and 1917, and copies of missionary blessings received in 1899 and 1903.

Description of the Transcription

The following text is a transcription of the English portion of the "Life History." Beginning page numbers are given in brackets so that this typescript can be easily compared with the original text. Markow's phonetic sometimes creative and often inconsistent spelling is maintained so that the reader can "hear" Markow's Eastern European accent. Punctuation has been omitted or inserted and paragraph breaks have been included to aid modern readers. Clarifications and corrections have been added in brackets (for example, [ ]). As is the practice in Europe, Markow placed periods after most of the numbers in the text. The periods after numbers do not signify the beginning of new sentences. Words that appear in carets (for example, < >) are insertions in the text. Strikeouts in Markow's writing are rendered as strikeouts (for example, ~~strikeouts~~) in the transcription.

Special thanks goes to Hyrum Mack Patten, a Church service missionary working in the Historical Department, for help creating and proofreading the transcription to ensure the accuracy of the transcribed text. I must also acknowledge the assistance of Alexander E. Schmalz who together with Mack Patten created the transcription of the German portion of the "Life History," which is not published in this book but is available in the Church Archives.

Notes

1. Dennis B. Neuenschwander, "Reflections on Establishing the Gospel in Eastern Europe," *Liahona* (October 1998): 45, 46.

2. Neuenschwander, "Reflections," 44.

3. Mischa Markow, Reminiscences [n.d.], Church Archives, The Church of Jesus Christ of Latter-day Saints, Salt Lake City. Punctuation throughout is supplied by the editor to quotations of Markow's writing.

4. Four published articles describe portions of Markow's missionary work. Richard O. Cowan, "Mischa Markow: Mormon Missionary to the Balkans," *BYU Studies* 11 (autumn 1970): 92–99, contains brief biographical background and excerpts from Markow's letters that were published in the *Latter-day Saints' Millennial Star* and the *Deseret Evening News*. William H. Kehr wrote three pieces about Markow: "Missionary to the Balkans: Mischa Markow," *Ensign* 10 (June 1980): 29–32, which is a synopsis of Markow's missionary experiences and contains quotations from Markow's autobiographical writings. Kahlile Mehr wrote two other articles on Markow pertaining specifically to the establishment of the Church in Hungary and containing passing references to Markow's conversion and early efforts to preach in Hungary: "The Gospel in Hungary Then and Now," *Ensign* 20 (June 1990): 8–14; and "The Eastern Edge: LDS Missionary Work in Hungarian Lands," *Dialogue: A Journal of Mormon Thought* 24 (summer 1991): 27–45.

There is also mention of Markow's conversion in Rao H. Lindsay, "A History of Missionary Activities of The Church of Jesus Christ of Latter-day Saints in the Near East, 1884–1929" (master's thesis, Brigham Young University, 1958), 21–22.

5. The present-day location and name of this town is Srpska Crnja, which is located in Vojvodina, Yugoslavia, near the Romanian border.

6. While on his mission, Spori kept fairly detailed journals, which are found in the Church Archives, of his experiences. Unfortunately, there is a gap in his journals for the period of Markow's conversion. Volume seven of Spori's journals ends on September 28, 1886, and volume eight begins on February 10, 1887. However, Hintze's journals from that time contain information about Markow's arrival in Constantinople and his baptism. These passages are cited in note 6 in the following facsimile typescript.

7. Church membership and census records, as well as the obituaries printed in the local Salt Lake City papers and Markow's own records have variant spellings for the children. See Record of Members, Fifteenth Ward, Salt Lake Stake, Church Archives; Obituary, *Salt Lake Tribune*, January 19, 1934. In the German text of Markow's "Life History," pages 15–16, Markow wrote briefly about his marriage and his three children. Marriage date is confirmed in the Ancestral File, Family History Library, Salt Lake City.

8. Markow, "Reminiscences," 60–61.

9. Markow, "Reminiscences," 77.

10. German text of "Life History," in Markow, "Reminiscences," 32, translated by Matthew Heiss.

11. Markow, "Reminiscences," 84.

12. The cause of death listed on his membership record was "Sinility Myocardi-tis." See Record of Members, Fifteenth Ward, Salt Lake Stake, Church Archives. Residency information taken from *Salt Lake City Directory* (Salt Lake City: R. L. Polk, 1905–11).

13. Markow, Papers, Church Archives.

14. Three loose pages found in the back of the book contains much of the same information found on pages 83 through 85 of the bound text. The loose pages contain this line, which helps to date when it was written: "Of course now at the present time under the Administration of the Soviet Bolsheviky Laws and rules it is Diferent and I believe it is more Liberty and the Gospel can be preach it to the Russian People now."

15. The German text of Markow's history contains much the same information as the English text. Excerpts of the German text that elucidate passages in the English text are included in the notes. The final portion of the German text contains more detail about Markow's experiences in Turkey after leaving the Russian Empire in November 1903.

Life and History of Mischa Markow

Edited and annotated by Matthew K. Heiss

[page 50]

I was born in October 21.st 1854, in Serb-zernia Torontal Comitat, Hungary [present-day Srpska Crnja, Vojvodina, Yugoslavia], in the Ortodax Church which is Greek Katholic church. My Father was a Serbien and my Mother was a Romanien by birth.[1] I Graduated in Serbien School. I was very much religious inclined and I have had a Great desire to go to Jerusalem. and when I was 32. years of age I was in Bulgaria in the City of Warna [Varna] and in <January> 1886. I went to Konstantinople and then I went to Jerusalem. and I came to Jerusalem in May 1886. and I became a Pilgrim in the Ortodox Church and I got my Pilgrim certificate from Patriarch.

after in June 1886. I left Jerusalem and went to Egipt and I come to Alexandria, a City of 300,000. Population, and start to work on my Barber trade & after Eight months while I was reading & Study the Bible [it] come to my min<e>d that my church is not the ~~truth ch~~ true church and I pray the Lord to show to me where can I find the true church. then I come to a conclussion to go to Konstantinople and visit all the Protestant churches and which I like the best I will join to that, in asmuch in Konstantinople have all kinds of churches of all creeds & Denominations. but the Lord God was with me in all my ways and he did hear my Prayers. and he revealt to his Servant in Jerusalem, Jakob Spory, a Mormon Elder.[2] at the same time Brother J. Spory had a vission and he saw me in the vission and he was told in the vission that he shall go right away to Egipt in the City of Alexandria and look for me becaus I want to join to the true church. then Brother Spory start right away for Egipt and I was in a hury.

350

I sold my Barber Shop and bought a Ticket on the Arabik Steamer to sail for Konstantinople and by that time Brother Spory arived to Alexandria and he look for me Three Days, ~~by~~ but Alexandria is a Big City and he could [page 51] not find me. than he bought a Ticket for Konstantinople on the Arabik Steamer and that was in January 1887. and when I come on the Steamer, Brother Spory was allready on the Steamer and when he saw me he look at me and ask me where was I from. I told him I am from Hungary and he ask me what is my Religion. I told him I belong to the Ortodox church and I am a Serbien by birth. and he Speak to me in German Language. than he said to me, "I did not find you, but you found me. "then he said to me that the Lord did revealeth to him in a Vission and he was told to go to Egipt to Alexandria and look for me, and he said to me, "I look for you Three Days in Alexandria and I co<u>ld not find you and now you found me."

and Brother Spory, he start to Preach the Gospel to me and I tought he was an Angel so did appear to me. then I told him I want to be Baptised riht away because I believed every word what he Said to me. then he said to me, "when we come to Konstantinople, then I shall be Baptised <you>." and in about five Days we arived in Konstantinople and he told me there are Other two Missionarys in Konstantinople and he wants to see them first. then we went to Hotel. and he left his Trunk and other things what belongs to him in my Care and he went to see Brother F. F. Hintze[3] and Br. J. M. Tanner.[4] and he was away Two Days & two nights and I was afraid that he was lost. and I start to Pray to the Lord and I said, "O Lord, thy Servant whom thow has send to me got Lost and now who shall Baptise me that I may receive the Holy Ghost?" and at the same time he cames and he introduse me to Brother Hintze and Br. Tanner and they give me more instruction about the Gospel nevertheless. we went all Four to the Black Sea and Br. Hintze Baptised me & Br. Tanner Confirmed. and the Brothern want me to stay with them and help them to Preach the Gospel because I Speak many Languages. then I said to them I am not a Preacher, but I thank the Lord and the Brothern that I was received in the [page 52] church of Jesus Christ of Latter day Saints.[5] and the Brothern blesed me and they said, "God will be with you."

so I was Baptised February 1.st 1887.[6] then I went to Romania and in January 1888. I left Romania and went to Hungary to vissit my Parents in asmuch I was not Home for Seven years. then I start to Preach the Gospel to my Parents. now my Father & Mother and my Brother they want to be Baptised. and I was only a member in the Church so I can not Baptise them. then I (vired) Telegraphet to Konstantinople to Br. Hintze that he shall come and Baptise them. but the Lord revealeth to me that my Parents will reject the Gospel and they did reject.

now Br. Hintze came to my Father House February 25.1888. first thing he said to me, "Br. Markow, the Lord did revealeth to me I shall ordain you to be a Elder in the church of Jesus Christ of Latter Day Saints. will you accept it?" I said yes. I was ordained February 26. 1888. by Br. F. F. Hintze.[7] and next Day all Day long the House was filled with the People. Br. Hintze and my self Preach the Gospel to them, and next Day again.

Three Police men with the Guns were send by <the> Priests to bring us before the Courth. and the judge told Br. Hintze in 48 hours he mus Leave Hungary and he registered his Passeport to be sure and Leave Hungary. then Br. Hintze he wants to go right away.[8] but I told him, "you have 48. hours time so I want you to teach me what shall I do and how shall I Preach the Gospel." then Br. Hintze told me, "now Br. Markow, you are an Elder in the church of Jesus Christ and you have Authority to Baptise and to Lay Hands for the recception of Holy Ghost and you shall Preach the Gospel where ever you have oportunity. and I am going back to Konstantinople." then I ~~tould~~ told him, "it is not Liberty in Hungary and how shall I Preach?" then he said to me, "Br. Markow, how long will it take to make $.80.^{00}?" I told him I can safe $80.^{00} in about a year. then he said to me, "you can send the money to me to Konstantinople and I will safe for you and by that time I will be [page 53] released and then you can go with me to Zion." then I told him, "Br. Hintze, now you ordainet me to be an Elder in the church to Preach the Gospel. and now I shall not go to Zion until I Baptise some." then he look it at me and said, "Br. Markow, you have a Strong faith but that dont go so easy." then I said to him again, "I shall not go to Zion until I Baptise some." and when I said that I felt like I must do it or othervise I could never go to Zion. so where ever I went I Preach the Gospel.

now I did not know where they are which I shall Baptise, but the Lord God he knows it, but my Duty was to Preach every where, where ever I have oportunity as Br. Hintze told me, and I did so. then Br Hintze and I, we went both to Romania in the City of Bucarest and I remain in Bucarest and Br. Hintze went to Konstantinople. after I went to Russia in the City of Odessa and from Odesa I went to England London.

I came in London in August 1888.[9] and I could not get any work because I cant speak English. then I went to Austro Hungary Konsul and I told him I want to be Transported to Romania and he said to me I shall go to Hungarian relief society and they will give me the free pass. then I went to Hungarian Relief sociaty in London. now Konsul gave me 2. Shillings and Relief Society gave me 5. Shillings and they told me that they can only give me free Pass to Belgien Antwerben [Antwerp, Belgium]. <and then they> ~~but they~~ give me a Letter and they told me to go to shore and Board the Hungarien Shipp. the Name of the Shipp was Count Osterhasy & had a Hungarian flag. and I w~~h~~ent there and give my Letter to the Captain of the Ship and when he read that Letter, he gave me 5. Franks money. then I got my free pass to Antwerben Belgien.

Antwerben is about 200,000. Population. they speak Franch and Flamish, but very little German. I come to Antwerben in September 1888. I went to German Club and start to Preach the Gospel to them, but they did not lessen to me because I did look so simple to them.[10] and I Pray [page 54] the Lord to reveal~~eth~~ to me if it was any in that City who will receive the Gospel. and the Lord revealeth to me that are some who will receive the Gospel. and he also revealeth to me that I am the first to Open the Mission in Belgien. and I Pray again to the Lord he shall show me where are they who will receive the Gospel. then I went in a Park Walking towards East and at once the Spirit of the Lord rest upon me in a Great messure and I start to call in a Loud voice and said, "O Lord, where are they whom I shall Baptise and make a Start and how shall I find them?" and right then I turned (or) (swinget) <towards> South by the Power of that spirit which did rest upon me and walkt about 60. feet and I saw a Bench. then I set on that Bench and while I start to thing [think] how I did turned South and then I lookt to ward North. then I saw a men walk quick to wards me and Look sharp in my face and Salute me and said, "Hello Country men," and then he set down by me. then he said, "I see you are a Stranger. where are you from?" I said to him I am from Hungary, a Serbien by Birth. and he said to me, "are you a Katholik?" I said, "no, I am a Elder of the Church of Jesus Christ of Latter day saints." then he said to me, "I have investigated many Churches but I never heard of a church by that name." and I start to Preach the Gospel to him. and he was very interested so that his eyes were full with Tears. and it was in evening start to be Dark. then he said to me, "it is late but I invite you to come to my place to morrow noon at Dinner. my Wife is very Relgious and we want to investigate." and he gave me his address.

and in that Night Sister Eselman,[11] she saw me in the Dream that I come to her and ~~told her~~ stratch my right arm to wards Heaven and told her I am the servant of God. then I went at noon to vissit Sister Eselman. [page 55] I dont remember the street but they did live on the 3rd floor. and I stod on the Street and lookt at that Building and Sister Eselman looketh trough the window and saw me and she said to her Daughter Matilda, "go down on the Street and call that Gentlemen in. that is the men who is invited to us." and when she start to go down stairs she saw a men in white apearal having a light Burning in his right hand. then she went back and told her mother, "mama, I can not go down stairs. it is a men there cloathed in white and he has a burning light in his right hand." and when Mother went to see, she cant see nobody and so Matilda come down and she said to me, "sir you are ivited to us. come with me."

and when I come to sister Eselman, they were all filled with joy and the Spirit of the Lord rest upon us and sister Eselman Start right ~~awgy~~ away to speak and said, "I have seen this Gentlemen in a Vission last Night. and when I saw him on the street I know that it was him and now I believe that he is a servant of God." and they got the Dinner ready and invite me I shall eat with them, but I said to them, "no. I shall first deliver to you my message." and I took the Bible in my hands and start to preach the Gospel to them and they all rejoice and sister Eselman got up and said, "Mr Markow, I believe every word you said and now you shall not leave us and not go away from us. we will keep you and give you what you need.[12] because we all will receive the Gospel and we will join to the church of Jesus Christ Latter day Saints." then we start to Eat our Dinner.

now I like to relate Sister Eselmans Situation. no doubt she was a good Lady, very Religious and Strong faith and the Lord did work trough her as a instrument to ~~spead~~ spread the Gospel in Belgien. now her real Name was Henriete Eselman. then she married Mr. Pieper and she have Four Children with ~~him~~ her First Husband. and the way she told me that her Husband did not treat <her> ~~it~~ right. <then> ~~so~~ she left him [page 56] without being Divorced and took her Four little children with her and then she got in love with Mr Karol Beckhaus. then they left Germany and went to Belgien in the City of Antwerben and she have Three Children with Mr. Karol Beckhaus, but she ~~never~~ was <not> married to him. but they have lived to gather as men and Wife. then I told them that they can not live to gather that way because they live in Adultery and if they should be Baptised, they can not live togather accept the[y] Marry.

I start to Preach the Gospel to them. they all Believe and they want to be Baptised. but inesmuch the Devil he knows that the Lord God will use me as a instrument in his Hands to make a first opening in Belgien, so the Satan start to work on Karol Beckhaus to persecute me that I may leave Belgien and not Start. then he said to me, "Mr. Markow, I believe the church you advocate is the true church, but at the present time I dont want to be Baptised, but my Wife she is free. she can be Baptised if she want to." now Mr Beckhaus try it in every way to persecute me and Stop me that I shall not Baptise any, but Mrs Eselman told me that I should not leave Antwerben if the Police men or any from the City Authority should come and try to drive me out from her place. then she said, "I will rent a Room for you and send my Girl to bring some food for you and I will give you every thing you need so you dont need to go away." but Mr Beckhaus was very bitter against me. he went to <the> Pastor of the Protestant chuch and complain against me that I was a Mormon Elder and preach Poligamy. then the Pastor told him that he has no right to interfere because in Belgien is Religious Liberty for all creeds. then he ~~wen~~ went to Police Headquarter and complain about me. and they ~~toul~~ told him the same ~~way~~ thing that in Belgien is Religious Liberty. then he came Home and was very angry against me, so angry that if he could he would [page 57] tear me up to pieces. and I felt miserable. I felt just like I was in the fire. them [then] Mr Beckhaus said, "now I comend you to go out from my place. this is my Family, my children, and now go out from here. I have right to put you out from my place. I am the head of my Family." and I look at him and told him, "I shall not go out from here. I have a big work to perform and the Lord send me here, but if you tuch me and push me out, then I go." then he come close to me but, he felt feeble and timid and I felt strong and I tought he will melt away. then he said, "I can not tuch you. I can not tuch you because I invite you to come to my place."

after that I spoke to Mrs Eselman privately. I said to her, "what use is it for me to stay here? I am in Agony and misery. it will be better if I write to President ~~s~~ Stucky[13] in Swizerland and he will send Elders and they will Baptise you and your Children." then Mrs Eselman got up and said to me in a loud voice, "Mr Markow, the Lord revealth to me that you are his servant, and my children and I did Believe that you are send from God and we all repant and are ready to be Baptised. and now if you dont Babpise me and my children, my blood and my sinns and my children's Blood and their sinns be on your Head." when I heart those words I was astonishet. then I took courage and felt strong in the Lord and told her I will do as the Lord comendet me. "I will Baptise you and your children and make a Start in Belgien." and then sister Eselman and her son and myself we went to the Sea Lake and I Baptised Sister Eselman first, and told her, "now remember you are the first one Baptised in the Kingdom of Belgien on the Belgien Soil." and then I Baptise her Son and told him, "you are the Second Baptised in the Kingdom of Belgien on the Belgien Soil." then I told to Sister Eselman, "now you will be a instrument in the Hands of the Lord and you shall spread the Gospel in the Kingodom of Belgien." and she Start right away to write Letters to her

Friends [page 58] and where ever she went she preach the Gospel. and after I Baptised Sister Eselmans Three Daugthers. you will find their Names on Page 175.

and inesmuch Mr Karol Beckhaus could not live with Sister Eselman togather after she was Baptised. then Mr K. Beckhaus Start to Repant and said to me, "Mr Markow, I know that I did comit a big Sinn against God and you. I know that you are the Servant of God and yet I did Persecute you and try to stop the work of the Lord, and I know the Gospel is true and the church you advocate is only the Church of Christ, but the Devil deceived me. and now I pray you ~~from all~~ to vorgive me and I repant from all my Heart and Please forgive me." then I went and Baptised Brother Karol Beckhaus who was a Bitter Enemy against me, but never the les God did Extend Mercy to him and he Repantet and then I join them to gather and Performed the Marriage ceremony for this Life as a Elder of the Church of Jesus Christ of Latter day Saints. so I Baptise Six Persons in Antwerben and I was two months in Belgien.

then I wrote to President Stucky in Bern, Swizerland, to send some Missionary in Antwerben, Belgien, but Sister Eselman and her Children and Brother Beckhaus, they want me I shall stay with them and they will soport me because the[re] will be many who will receive the Gospel and is nobody there to Baptise them. and I said to them, "after I leave here they will many come to Belgien." and I bless them and Kiss them all and they all whip [weep] like Little Children. when I left Antwerben then Sister Eselman ask me, "Brother Markow, when shall we meet again?" I told her we will meet in Zion. and Four years after we surely mett in Salt Lake in Social Hall in German Metting in October 1892. they were all in German Metting and they come to me and Kiss me and told me that my word is fullfilled as I told them that will meet [page 59] in Zion. and Sister Eselman told me that after I left Antwerben that Br Tailor, Br Brandly, and Br. J. Grimm[14] came to Antwerben and in Two Months 80. Persons were Baptised in to the Church of Christ, and when I left Antwerben, Belgien, I was perfectly sadisfied and felt Easy and rejoice in the Lord that I did with the help of the Lord fulfilled my promise to the Lord [and] that what I said to Br. Hintze, "I shall not go to Zion until I Baptise some." then I went to Romania[15] to work and make some Money to go to Zion and the Lord bless me and I came to Salt Lake in October 1892.[16] Mischa Markow

In Dezember 1898. I was Called to go on a Mission to Europe in Diferent Places, to Serbien [and] Bulgarien and Romania and Hungary to make a Start in those Countries. and inesmuch I Speak those Languages

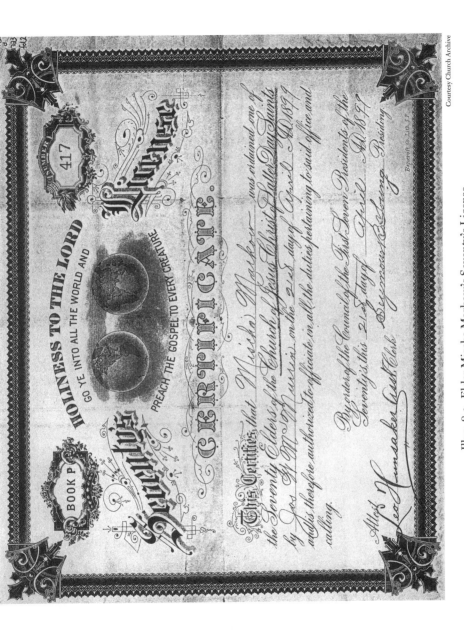

Illus. 8-1. Elder Mischa Markow's Seventy's License.

I was send to open those Countries and Kingdoms. and on 22.nd Day of April 1899. I started on my Mission from Salt Lake and I came to Liverppol. then I bought a Ticker for Serbien and I arive in the City of Belgrad, Capitol of Serbien, in May 1899. and start to preach the Gospel among the Serbiens. and many did Believe on my words and were glad to hear me. and one officer came to me and he spoke brocken English and we have had a Long conversation togather and he said to me,"when ever you will make some Converts to Establish a Branch in Serbien, I will be one of the of the first to Eccept it and be Baptised and I will help you that you can remain here." but many of the Serbien were against me.

and some of the Protestants came to me to hear me. and one of the Protestants went to the Authority and accuse me and they put the guard to prevent the People not to come to me. but People want to hear me and they did come anyway. and that Night I was up to about two ocklock in the Night. and some of the Ortodox Priests came to Listen to me, and they told me, "we know that our church is not like it was in time of Christ, but we can not changch it now. we are brought up in our church [page 60] and we do not believe to join to another church."

and in the morning I was brough before the <distric> Court. an[d] from there they send me to the High Court and I did speak nice to them. and that officer who told me that he wants to be Baptised, he was there too. he plead for me that I shall not be banish from Serbien, but they did not listen to him. and they were Engry at me and the judge told me that Banishment is to good for me. I should be throw in Danube <river> to drown. and the Police men went and bought me a Ticket and put me on the Train, and in that way I was banish out from Serbia to Hungaria in June 1899.[17] but the Lord was with me and I did rejoice and shed Tears of joy that I was brought before the magistrate and High Court before the rulers to testify that God did spooke again from Heaven and restored his church. then

I went to the City of Great Bechkeret, Torontal Comitat, Hungaria [Nagy Becskerek, Hungary].

in Great Bechkeret there are Serbiens, Romanies and Germans, but few Hungariens. and I start to Preach the Gospel to them and distribute some tracts and Books and I gain some friends, and many did Listen to my teaching. and when I have ben there about Forty Days one men went to the City mayor and accuse me that I was a Ana<r>chist. then the City mayor took with him two Police men and my accuser, and came to my place. and the mayor he had a cane in his hand and he lift up his Cane and wants to beat me over the Head. and I told him that I am American sitisen[18] and I did not do anything wrong. and then Two policemen put their hands on me and search my Pockets and took everything I got and comend me to go forwards and they drive me trough the Main Street. one Policemen to my right side and one to my left side and the mayor and my accuser behind me. and we walk on Main Street and I walk between two Police men and the mayor walk ~~bet bek~~ behind me and call in a lout voice, "Anarchist." and the People and some of my friends look at me and they tought that I was in reality a big Criminal.

and then I was [page 61] brought before court and the judge ask me what I am doing here. I told him that I was send from the church of Christ to Preach the Gospel and that God have spooken again from Heaven and restored his church to the Earth and I preach repantance. then the Mayor said, "this men is not with the right mind. he speak that Engel appear to Joseph Smith and God have spoke again from Heaven. he is a fool." and he said, "what do you listen to him? put him in the jail." then another men said, "no, he is not a fool. he dont speak ~~like~~ like a fool men." and they put me in a Dark room and give me a Bottle of water and no Bed. and they could not read my Passeport and my Missionary Certificate. and they call one big Merchant. he speaks broken English and he read my Passeport and my ~~G~~ Certificate. then he said to them, "that men is a Priest and he is a Gentlemen. he has his Missionary Certificate and he is authorised to Preach, and you shall not put him in the ~~a~~ Dark room in jail." and then they let me out and give me a nice room. and One of my friends come to see me and brought me something to Eat, and he said to me, "I will go and speak to the Mayor that he shall let you out because you havnt don any wrong." but that did not help anything.

and the Mayor send a Spy to me to catch me in the politics. and at the same time the Spirit of the Lord whispers in my right Ear, "this is a Spy. do not speak politic. preach the Gospel." and he said to me, "why Mr Markow, I am a Serbien and you are a Serbien, so you are my friend. and what do you Drink, a ~~Glass~~ of Beer or Wine? I want to treat you." I said to him, "I dont Drink." then he start to talk to me politic and I preach the Gospel to him so he could not find anything against me. then he left me.

and the Police men went and bought me a Ticket and put me on the Train. and so I was banish out from Great Bechkeret, Torontal Comitat, Hungary. and I thank to my Heavenly Father for his kindness towards me. then the more I was persecuted, the stronger I felt. and I was [page 62] perfectly sadisfied and shed tears of joy.

Then I went to ~~Br. Hintze~~ Konstantinople to see Br. Hintze and ask him for some advice. I came to Konstantinople in July 1899. I was very glad to meet Br. Hintze and ask him for advice. Br. Maycock[19] was President over Turkish Mission and we meet to gather to keep Council where I shall go to preach the Gospel. then Br. Maycock said, "Br. Markow, you know all this countries, so you are free to choose for you selfs and go where ever you feel like." then I said, "I will go to Russia to preach the Gospel." then Br. Hintze said, "I am not for Br. Markow to go to Russia. there is no Liberty in Russia. and they will send him to Siberia and you will never come back from there."

I stay one Week in Konstantinople and then I desidet to go to Romania. I came to Romania in july 1899. in the city of Konstanza [Constanța, Romania] and I Baptised one in the Black Sea. then I went to Bucarest, Kapitol of Romania. I arive in the City of Bucarest in August 1899. and start to Preach the Gospel Among the Romanien People. and I gain some friends while I labored Six months in Bucarest and I Baptised only One.

and then I pray to the Lord to shaw me where are those who shall receive the Gospel. and on the 10.th of Dezember 1899. I had a Dream. I Dream that I prepair my self to go to vissit a Family. and I took some Tracts with me, and my room was crowd it with People, and they start to prevent me that I shall not go to visit that Family. and while I start to go, they attack me and take ~~hohold~~ hold of my Coat and pull me back, but I felt very strong and push them all away and open the Door and went out. then I went to that family and knock on the Door. an the Door got Open and I saw a old Lady set by a Little ~~Table~~ sqyuare Table lean her Elbow on the Table, and I walk in to that Lady. then I look back and I saw a young Lady. she closed the Door and look ~~me~~ at me and smiles a little. and I ask the old Lady [page 63] if she have a Bible. and she said yes and she comend that young Lady to bring the Bible, and that young Lady brought the Bible. and she give me and I open the Bible and start to preach to them, and they were Exceedingly glad and we all rejoice. then I got awake. now that was my Dream and I praise the Lord that he did revealet to me who will receive the Gospel.

then I got up and wants to see if my Dream was true. I took some tracts with me and went right away to that family and I knock on the Door, and the Door Opens. then I look in the room and I saw that old Lady set by a Little square Table lean her Elbow on the Table. I walk in to the Lady, then I look back and I saw a young Lady. she close the Door and look at me and smiles a Little. and I gave the trakts to that old Lady and I start to preach to her Repantance & Baptism. and she said to me, "I am a Baptist and I am Baptised." then I told her that, "the Priest who Baptised you, he is not authorised from God to Baptise you." and then she said to me, "how can you prove that?" and I said to her, "do you have a Bible here?" she said yes. then she call that young Lady and said, "go bring the Bible to this Gentle men." and the young Lady Brought me the Bible. and I open it and start to preach to them and we all did rejoice. then I saw that my Dream was fullfileth.

that young Lady, she was the Daughter to that Old Lady. and they both said to me that they will receive the Gospel. and they invited me to come on Sunday to Dinner. and that old Lady, she has Three Daughters, and they wants all to hear me. and on Sunday I went to them, and the old Lady introdused me to her Three Daughters. and I start to preach the Gospel to them, and they all wants to be Baptised. and then the Old Lady said to me, "Mr Markow, will you please vorgive me?" and I said, "what shall I vorgive you? you did not do anything wrong to me." then she said, "I read a Book about Brigham Young, that he has 17. Wifes and that Mormons Live inimoral lifes. and I said, 'the first Mormon who Comes to my House, I will throw him out.' and now you are a Mormon and will you [page 64] please vorgive me because I said so." then I said, "yes, I vorgive you."

and then her Oldes Girl said, "Mama, Mr Markow is not One of those Mormons." then I said yes. and she said to me, "do you realy believe in Poligamy?" I said yes. then she said to me, "can you prove it in the Bible?" I said yes. and she said to me, "what ever you can prove in the Bible we believe." and I did prove in the Bible and they did Believe. then I said to them, "I dont preach Poligamy and we dont practise Poligamy." and one of the Girls said, "even if they practise Poligamy, I believe thats right." ~~and~~ and after two Months they were Baptised all four, the Old Lady and her Three Daughters. and I kept meeting every Sunday in their House.

and when I went to Baptise them it was in Winder — bad weather — and I was afraid that the Police shall not find out where I shall Baptise them and went to Bathing House and hired a private Pool for 4. Four franks or 80.¢ in Amerikan Money. and [it] took us about half hour to walk to the place of Baptism. and when we start to walk, I felt that I have a Companion with me, but I can not see him. then I look ahead of me and I saw a men ahead of me or in the frant on me about 40. forty feet apart Distance, and he walk ahead of me up to the place of Baptism and then he Disapearet. he was Dress it in Summer cloaths. the color of his Cloaths was tan or cream color. he was about five 5. feet and 11. inches Tall and I look how he walk. he make big staps. his Hair was cut round even with the Ears and he had a full Beard. and the Spirit of the Lord whispers to me, "that is the Engel of God. fear not." and I felt strong and rejoice and I remember that the Lord promiss to his Servants that the Engels shall be around them D. & C. Section 84. vers 88.[20] then I Baptised Nine 9. Persons in Bucarest Romania. you find the Names on [page 65] Page 175. & 176. and I ordaint Argir Dimitrow a Teacher February 12. 1900.[21]

and the Gospel was spraid in Bucarest so that many of the Romanien People did come & visit the Metting on Sunday. and Argir Dimitrow, he was very active in Preaching the Gospel. and we preach in the Metting on Sunday in Four Languages — Romanien, Bulgarian, Germans, and Greeks. we have Five Bibles — Romanien, Bulgarien, German, Greeks & Serbien. but some of the Romanien were my Enemys. and the[re] were other Two who wants to be Baptised. and One of the Detective secret Police, he came to my place and he said to me, "Mr. Markow, I come to investigate the Gospel." and I preach to him the Gospel. then he said to me, "I believe every word what you said to me and I repent and I want to be Baptised." then he said to me, "I heard that you wants next Sunday night to go to River (Gurla) and Baptise Two more, and I want to be Baptise too." then I told him, "I canot Baptise you so quick. you must investigate longer until you are convinced that this church is the true church." and I did not know that he was a Secret Police (or) a Spy – my Enemy.

now on Sunday morning I went earlier to Metting to give more instruction to them who wants to be Baptised, and instead to start Metting in Ten Ocklock, I start Nine Oklock. and when I start the Metting, House was filled with People. and many Romanien did come to hear me. and one of the Romanien said to me, "where did you got the Authority to hold Mettings and Deceive the Romanie People?" I told him that I was authorised to Preach the Gospel. then he went right away to the Police Station and accused me. and then chief of Police came with Two Policemen in the Metting and he Speaks friendly to me and he said, "Mr. Markow, somebody did accuse you and you are unter arest. we must take you before the Distric Court." and at the same time that secret Police came. and he said to the chief of Police, "why did you take him away? I prepair [page 66] my self with Four men to go in the night with him to the Place where he will Baptise <the> Two men, and when he comes out of the water wet, then we will beat him in the Darkness and run away Disapear, and he will not know who beat him." but the Lord did not let me in their hands to beat me.

and the Chief of Police with 2. Police men took all My Books away. and some of the Members must go to to the Distric Court. and them 2. Persons who were prepairt to be Baptised, they took them to the Court also. and when I apeared before the Judge, he ask me what do I preach. I told him I preach the Gospel of Jesus Christ. and he said, "we have the Gospel." then I told him that it was universal Apostasy of the Church of Jesus Christ, and now the Church of Christ is Reorganised and God have spoke again from Heaven. then he said to me, "I can not leave you. you must go to the High Court."

and then 2. Police men took me and braught me before the High Court. and the members of the church were send away. and them Two which were prepaired to be Baptised, they vorbid them to be Baptised and they send them away to. now I was left alone in the Court. it was a Big Room about 30. feet high sealing and it was round. and there were Benches all round. and all Editors of the News Papers did Came in in the Court. and many Others High men and Merchants did Come to hear me. and the room was filled. and I stood in <the> midst of them befor the Judge and I give to some of the High men their own Bible and the New Testament to prove that what I will speak to them. and the Judge ask me, "what do you preach to the People?" and when I start to talk (or) speak to the Judge, I saw in the front of my Head a Person stood in the air above my Head clothet in white like the Temple Cloaths, and that did strenghten me and I felt strong [page 67] and the spirit of the Lord rest upon me and I start to Preach to the Judge first principles of the Gospel and then Apostasy of the church of Jesus Christ and restoration of the Gospel and that God have spook again from Heaven. and some of them High men got up in the Court and said, "that is very true what Mr. Markow Preach. our church is not the true church and he proves in our own Bible" and then many Others got up and start to Argue and qyarrel. then I was send to another room.

there was the Highiest Judge which is called Perfect.[22] and the Perfect said to me, "why do you deceive our People? are we not christians?" "yes," I said, "Ortodox church is knowen by that name, but it was universal Apostasy and now the church of Christ is Reorganised with Authority." then he said, "do not our Priests have authority?" and I said no. then he got very Engry and right away he called a Soldier and put me in the Jail where the Kriminals are. and the Soldier was on the guard with a Bayonet on the gun and all night stod guard by my Bed. and in the Day time he walk in the Loby (or) Hall [and] pass by the Door, and in the Night he come again by my Bed [and] watch me all Night.

and it was a Russian Spy in the Jail and he ask me why did they put me in jail. I told him because I preach the Gospel and I start to Preach the Gospel to to him to. then he said to me, "now you claim you are the Servant of God, now I will see if that God whom you serve will Deliver you out of this jail because who comes here, that is the last. it is very seldom who comes out from here." then I told him, "My God whom I serve, he will Deliver me and very soon too." and they gave me half Pound of Bread and One quart Bottle of water Daily.

Second day they call me again to Explain to them how is the church of Jesus Christ of Latter Day Saints Organised. and a clark was called and he start to write down. then I told him the Name of the Prophet, Two Councils, Twelve Apostels, High Priests, Seventies, Elders, Priest, [page 68] Teachers, and Deakons in Unite States in Utah. so that did take me about One hour to Explain to them.

and they told me, "we will Send this Petition to our Mitropolit. he is the Highiest Priest in Romania, and if he say you can stay here and Preach, then you are at Liberty. but if he forbid, then you must be Banish out of Romania." and then I Sign the Petition and the[y] send to Mitropolit, but Mitropolit did not accep it. he forbids. and then they want to Banish me out of Romania, and they ask me where I wants to go. I told them I wants to go to Bulgarien. and they told me that they want to pay my way to Bulgaria. then I ask them in which way they want to Banish me. and they told me I will be acompanied by a Soldier and my Passaport and Missionary Certificate shall be given to Bulgarien Authority. then I told them that I don want to be Banish in that way, then Bulgarien Authority will not receive me. and they told me that is the Law in Romania. then I told them I am Amerikan Sitisen and I want to see the American Konsulat first.

and nobody was allowed to come and see me in the jail and I can not write any Letter because everything was taken away from me. but some Members of the Church which I Baptised went to the Unite Statee Konsulate and Complain about me. then Konsul Telephone to the Judge that he shall let me out because Konsul wants to speak to me. then they let me out and I Come to my Konsulate. I told him I dont want to be Banish out of Romania and to be acompanied by a Soldier. then Konsulate said to me, "I can not do much in the Religion way, but they dont have right to banish you." then Konsul Telephone again to the Judge that they have no right to Banish me, but the Judge said that is their Law and I shall [page 69] be Banished. then Konsul said to the Judge, "then I will Telephone to the King." so I was not Banished then, but I can not stay in Romania.

and then they put my Name in the News Papers. they are Four News Papers in Bukarest. this are the names of the Papers—Universal, Gazeta, Patrioty, and Adiverul, which means the Truth. in One Paper they put My Name "an Engel or a fool." and in One Paper they put "Priest from America." and Patrioty News Paper did speak nice about me, that every thing what I said was the truth, and they wish to meet me. again my Name was Honored in Patrioty News Paper. and then they did put Buletin on the Corners of the Streets and on Big Trees about me. and my Name was on the Buletin. then I ask the Chief of the Police to allow me Two Weeks time to colect my Tracts and Books and to prepair my self for Bulgaria. and the Chief of Police did allow, but he ~~put~~ he notify the secret Police Detectives to watch me not to preach the Gospel. and some of the Romanien did seek me to hear me Preaching and some did seek me to Beat me. One of the Sister whom I Baptised wrote to me a Letter and told me, "Brother Markow, dont go nowhere in Evening. stay Home because they look for you to beat you." I was invited to a Priest to go to Explain to him the Gospel, but I was afraid so I did not go. then I went to Bulgarien Konsulate and registered my Passport for Bulgaria. then I went to the chief Police and shaw him that I go to Bulgaria. I start for Bulgaria June 3.rd 1900.

in June 2.nd 1900. I Dreamed that I went from Bucarest, Romania, to Bulgaria. and when I cross the water Danube, I come to Bulgarien Boarder (or) limit and it was a big wall about 30. feet high and I can not go to Bulgaria. and I walk along that wall that I may find some opening, and while I walk I saw 3. men. then I ask them how can I inter in Bulgaria, and they told me I shall walk East along that wall and, "then you will see a Big Gate, then you walk through [page 70] that Gate." then I walk a Distance and I saw a Big Gate then I tuch the Gate and the Gate opens. then I walk in and it was a narrow Road about 10. feet broad, and on both side of the road was mountains and it was Dark just like moonlight but foggy. and I walk a long Distance and I saw a fance [fence] in my Road, and I did not know how to pass that fance because it was very high and I felt sorry that I can not go further. but when I came near to that fance, I saw in the middle of the fence was a little Door, and the Door got open and a men stand by the Door and he had a sword. then he pull of his sword and was Engry, and he said to me, "what do you want here?" I told him I want to Preach the Gospel to the Bulgarien People. and he said, "this People belongs to me and I am a Preacher Myself." and I got awake and felt very sorry and I know that I will not have much success in Bulgaria.

then I took with me Michael Dimitrov, he was a Bulgar, to help me in Preaching the Gospel.[23] he was Baptised in Bukarest, Romania, and on June 3.rd 1900 we went to Bulgaria and I remain in Ruschuk [Ruse, Bulgaria], a City of about 30000 Population Located by the Water Danube, and I send Brothe Dimitrov to Sofia to make a Preparation for me. Sofia is the Kapitol of Bulgaria. and I labor in Ruschuk about 20. Days, and there are many Methodists and Baptists. and I had conversation with the Methodist Pastor, and he said to me that he knows all about the Mormons. and he show to me a Book in Bulgarien Caracter and in Bulgarien Language.[24] it was about John Lee masacre and Brigham ꝑ Young, how many Wifes he had and how the Mormons Live immoral life. that Book was about 300. Pages and about 8. inches wide and 14. inches Long. and I was surprised when I start to read that Book. I told him that that Book was Printed by our Enemies and nothing is [page 71] true what is in that Book. and he said that Book was Printed by our own People. I said, "yes, those who where cut of[f] from the Church and they became our Enemies, then they will speak all kinds of lie aganst the Saints."

after while I received a Letter from M. Dimitrov. he want me I shall come to Sofia. I arrive in Sofia about June 25. 1900. but it was very hard for me to make a Start in Sofia because I did not have any Tracts in Bulgarien Language. then I went to the Police Station and registered my Name as a Missionar of the Church of Jesus Christ. and the Chief Police tought that I was a Protestant, and it was all right. then I took Br. Dimitrow with me and we went to Methodist chuch in Evening Meeting, and I went to the Pastor and present myself as a American Missionar, and I ask of th him permission to Preach in the Methodist church. he was very friendly with me. then he ask me to which church do I belong. and I told him to the Church of Jesus Christ of Latter Day Saints. then he said to me, "I never heard of that church." and he speaks English to[o]. then he said to me, "I can not alow you to speak, but after Metting I like too investigate."

and so I speak to many Bulgarien too that after metting they shall meet with me togather. and after metting the Pastor invitet us in his room, and about 8. Bulgarien were with us, and we have had Conversation about 4. hours. we stay to Half pass twelve in the night. and I give my Address to them who were with us, and then they start to Come to my Place and I Preach the Gospel to them.

and next Sunday Br. Dimitrov and I, we whent to the Baptist church and I present myself there as a American Missionar and ask them if I can preach in their Metting. and they ask me to which church I belong. I told to the Pastor I belong to the church of Jesus Christ of Latter Day Saints. and they told me that after metting they wants to investigate. so after Metting many Bulgars did not go Home, but they wants to hear me. and we have had a conversation [page 72] from 12. Ocklock to 3.30. afternoon, and I gave them my address. so I gain many Friends.

after while One Gentlemen came to my Place and he speaks good English, and he had a Tract in his hand. it was I believe Milenial Star. and he knows much about the Mormons. he was in England a Baptist Preacher, and he have a Brother in Utah. his Name was Yosuf and he was very bitter against the Mormons. he was Jenator in Prespetarian Church and in 1898. when I was called to go on a mission, he read in the News Paper about me. then he came to me and said, "Mr. Markow, your Name was in the Paper and I hear you wants to go to My Native Country, to Bulgaria. you better not go there to Delude my People. I have a Brother in Sofia, and he is a Baptist Preacher, and I will write to him a Letter about you. and when you come to Bulgaria, he will wait for you and he will prevent you (or) accuse and persecute so that you can not stay there." and I said to him, "I am not afraid of that. I will go anyway."

now that Gentlemen who came to me, he was a Brother to Mr. Josuf, and he ask me to which church I belong. then I said I belong the church of Jesus Christ of Latter day Saints. then he said to me, "you are a Mormon." then he ~~sart~~ start to talk to me in English Language, and said to me, "you believe that Adam is your God." I said to him, "no I dont. we dont worship Adam. we worship God." then he said to me, "here, read this Book. Brigham Young said that Adam is God." and he was very Engry. and I speak polite to him. then I ask him, "what is your Name?" then he said to me, "I am not a Police men. you dont need to know my Name." and I said to him, "you have a Brother in Salt Lake City, Utah, in America. his Name is Yosuf." then he said, "yes, and he told me all about you." then he said to me, "I will prevent you and persecute. you cannot stay here." and he got so Engry. then he [page 73] whent and when he open the Door I call him back and said to him, "now before you go, shake hands with me as a friend and dont be so Engry. and if God permit you to put something in my way, do it. go and do it right now." then he went.

and after few Days many Bulgars start to Come to my Place to investigate all Day long and late in Evening [to] 10. Ocklock in the Night. and I was full of joy Preaching the Gospel to them. and High men and Merchants and Officers from the Army Come to hear me and they Speak to gather, "how is it this is Diferent what we have heard and read?" and they ask me so much about Poligamy. and some of the Ortodox Priests came to hear me. and it was about 6. Days My room was full with People so that I went to the Neighbors and borrow some chairs. then I ask the People, "how is it ~~that~~ that you find my Place?" then they told me that Three Days ago my Name was in the News Paper. then I send Br. Dimitrov to buy that Paper. and Mr Yosuf advertised my Name in the Paper: "A Mormon Missionar is all ready in Sofia, Kapitol of Bulgaria. he Preach that Mormon Church is only the True Church Organiset with Apostels, Prophets, High

Priests, Seventies. and and further more all Priests, Kindgoms, Nations must be subject to that church (or) Prophet. and every Mormon have more then One Wife. and we ask the Authority of this City and the Bulgarien S Citisens to vorbid that Mormon Missionar that he may not Delude our People and Spraid Delution among our People. and we ask also to warning our People. and this is his Address: Mr. Mischa Markow, N⁰ 48. Koslodui Street. Sofia." and it was lots more then this.

and after few Days I met Mr Yosuf on the Street and I shake hands with him. and I told him, "I thank you very much for advertising My Name in the News Paper. you was a Instrument in the Hands of God to Open my way for the Gospel. I am very Sadisfied that them Big men and officers of the Army Came to me to investigate the Gospel, mormonisum." and he [page 74] was Engry and he said to me, "did you Baptised any?" and I said not yet. and all Baptist Church arouse and said to Mr Yosuf, "you did Open the Way for him and now all our People goes to him."

and then One Russian, A member of the Baptist Church, went to the chief of Police and accused me. then I was Called to the Police Station and the Chief of Police, he said to me, "you transgress our laws when you registered your Name. you did not say that you are a Mormon." I said to him, "I registered My Name as a Missionar of the church of Jesus Christ. the Church of Jesus Christ is not called by that Name. that is a neck name, so I can not registered my Name as a Mormon." well he said, "you are accused from the Baptists and you must appear before the High Court." then I was acompanied by a Police men, and then they Call me in the Court room. they were two officers in the room and they ask me what is mormonisum, and I start to talk to them abaut restoration of the Gospel. and I had some tracts in my Pocket. and I ask them, "do you Speak franch?" then One said to me, "I speak and read Franch." and the Other said, "I speak and read German." and then I give to one two Franch Tracts, and to the other, two German Tracts. it was Apostasy and Restoration of the Gospel. and they took the Tracts and told me I shall come tomorrow.

Next Day I came to the Court and I ask them if they did read my Tracts. they told me they did and they unterstud very well, and I ask them if they Believe that is the truth. then G I said to them, "do you know that you Persecute the servant of God who brings to you Salvation? and you will be responsible for it." then he look at me and said in a Humble voice, "if I had the Power, I would let you at Liberty to Preach, but we are Comendet from the Supream Court Judge [page 75] to stop you. and if we dont stop you, then we will lose our office and Panished too." and so they want me that I shall go right away out from Bulgarien, but I did not know where to go. I was Banished from Serbia, Romania, [and] Hungary. so I need more time to think over where shall I go. I did not tell them that I was Banished. but I told them, "I can not go right away out from Bulgaria. I must wait about Three Weeks for Money from Amerika." and then they told me, "you go to the English Konsulate and he will give you the Money. and when your Money comes, then he will keep it your money." I said, "no, I will not do that." and so they let me wait until my Money come, but they put a Police by the Gate to watch that no body shall come and have convesation with me. but some Ortodox Priests did come any way in the Night, and I had a long conversation with them, and One of them said to me, "I am against the Baptists because they dont have the Truth. but the church which Mr Markow Preach is the thrue church." and he said to me, "I will go with you to the (ministerium) (or) Supream Judge and I will plead for you that he may give you Liberty." then we went both to Supream Judge, but it was all in vain.

then I spooke to One Bulgarien Lawer how can I get Permission to Preach the Gospel in Bulgarien. he told me he believe that Liberty can be Granted to me, but it will take Six 6. months. he said that in Three Months they will call a Mass Metting, and the Lawer will speak about the organisation of the Church. and if they dont give Liberty in 3. months, then after Three months they will call another Mass Metting and then how they deside. and he said to me, "that is the Law in Bulgaria, and so have the Baptists and Metodist got their Liberty by the Law." then I ask him if he knows for sure that I will get Liberty. he said he dont know for sure. but that is the way to find out.

then I went to English Consulate and told him that I am American Citisen and show to him my Passeport and my Missionary Certifacate. and [page 76] I told him that City Authority forbids me to Preach the Gospel. then he said to me that he dont have right to interfier much in the Religion matter. and I had some English Tracts with me and I said to him, "you can read some of our tracts and then you will know that we are real Christians." and he said, "no no. I dont want to read Mormons tracts." and then he said, "why did you come here? we are all Christians in Bulgarien." then then I said to him that Church of Jesus Christ is Reorganised. and I said, "you are my Defender and you shall go to the Authority and speak for me." then he said, "no no. but if they hurt you or do some hurm to you then I will Defend you."

so Twenty 20. Days did pass since I was forbiden to Preach. then I got my money and One Lady told me that I shall not go out from Bulgarien until I Baptise her. and I promiss her that I will Baptise her. she did investigate the Gospel about Two Months, and before I left Sofia I baptised her. and then I left Sofia Bulgaria August 31. 1900 and start again for Hugary. and after Three Days the Police in Sofia found out that I Baptised One Lady after I was forbiden to Preach. and then they ask that Lady which I Baptised — her Name was Anna Kiru — they ask her where I went and she did not want to tell them. she said, "I dont know." and then they look in cloaths closset and unter <the> Bed and in every corner in her House. and then they Telegraphet in every Direction to catch me, but they could not find me. Sister Anna Kiru, she wrote to me a Letter and told me all abaut.

When I left Bulgaria I did not know where to go, but my toughts were allways to go again to Hungary, although I was Banished out from Hungary. but the Lord was with me. in Hungary there are many Provinces (or) States. so I desidet to go in another State. then I come to a Conclusion to go to Orshova [Orşova, Romania] which is Located on the Romania [page 77] Borders. and in Orshova there are Three class of People: Romaniens, Germans, and few Serbiens. and if I shall be Banished from Orshova, then I will go back again to Romania. nevertheles I was afraid becaus I was Banished from Romania. then I took the Ship on the Danube River from Bulgaria to sail to Hungary, Orshova, but I Pray to the Lord constantly to reveal to me where shall I go and what shall I do. and while I was on the Ship I had a Dream that I was in the City of Temesvár [Timişoara, Romania] and I saw the People in the Group assembled in many Places. and they were all Bare Heads and it was foggy and cloudy in that Place; so to say they were in Darkness, yet I can see their Faces just Like in the night when little moonshine. and I was about 100. feet apart from them. and I look at them and they all Pray to the Lord and Sigh. and I heard those words from them, "O, when shall the Servant of the Lord Come to us? we want to be Baptised in the Name of Jesus Christ." and when they have said that, the sun rises from the East and Reach to the Heaven just like a Big Mountain. and the Ray of the Sun apear to them and Iluminate them, and I was in their middst. and we all rejo[i]ce. then I got awake from my Sleep and that was my Dream. and I felt strong like a Lion and I bless the Name of the Lord and thank him very much that he did reveal un to me where I shall go.

then I come to Orshova, but I did not stay in Orshova. I took the Train and whent right away to Temesvár. and I arrive in Temesvár September, 3.rd 1900. then I went to the Court and Registered my Name as a Missionar of the church of Jesus Christ. then I start right away to Preach the Gospel and Distribute the tracts from House to House among the Kathololiks. and many of Katholics told me, "thank God that he send you to us because we want to be Baptise and be a member of the Church of Jesus Christ of Latter day Saints."

and in asmuch I did work all alone for 19. months so I wrote to Br. Shulthess,[25] President of the German [page 78] mission to send me a Companion. and Br. Shulthess, he send me Br. H. M. Lau[26] from Germany to help me Preaching the Gospel. Br. Lau came October 4.th. then I whent with him to the Court and he registered his Name as a Missionar. and I give some tracts to the City mayor and inesmuch we gain many friends and Converts and some of the Katholics Priests read our Tracts too. and they were Bitter Enemys to us and they start to Persecute us. and the Katholik Pishoph accuse us. and on October 10.th we were ~~brou~~ Summond to apear in the Magistrate in the High ~~Cor~~ Court and the Judge ask us what ~~w~~ we do in the City. I told him we Preach the Gospel and Distribute tracts to the People, make them knowen about Restoration of the Church of Jesus Christ. and the Judge took from us 4. Tracts and our Passeports and my missionary Certificate. and then he told us he will send that to the Supreme Court in BudaPest, Kapitol of Hungary, to investigate and find out if we can have Liberty in Temesvár, but the Judge did not vorbid us. and on Dezember 5th we received our Passeports, but my Missionary Certificate did not come back from BudaPest. and on January 24th 1901 we Baptised 9. (Nine) Persons.

and on February 5th we went to Mayor and ask him to give us Permission to hold Mettings. but he told us he can not give us permit until the[y] gat answer from Supreme Court from BudaPest. and on February 16. we were again Summoned to the High Court and judge ~~v~~ forbid us to Preach the Gospel and to Distribute the Tracts. then I said to Br. Lau we will not go away from Temesvár, but we will work on ~~Sly Sly~~ Sly. then I send Br. Lau to BudaPest, Kapitol of Hungary, to Supreme Court to find out if we can get Liberty to Preach the Gospel in Hungary. and Br Lau, he went to Amerikan Consulate and to Supreme Judge, but it was all in vain. they did not gave us Liberty. then we work on Sly so that Police can not find out what [page 79] we do. and we kept Mettings Three times a week in Diferent Places to the Members of the Church. and Sundays we Admister the Sacrament. and most [meetings were] in the Night. and the Lord God was with us. and on March 8th we Baptised again 10. Ten Persons, and so we have allready 19. Members, and we have many friends and many who wants to be Baptised.

and on March 28. we were Summoned again to apear in the Magistrate in the High Court before the Judge. and the Judge gave me my missionary Certificate and told us we received A Letter from BudaPest from the Supreme Court that, "you shall Absolute Leave Hungary (or) you will be Banished out." then I start to taulk nice to the Judge and told him we need at Leas five Days time to gather our Tracts and Books. then he said, "I give you 24. hours." then I said to him we can not gat ready in 24. hours. then he gave us Three Days. and then we Sign our Names that in Three Days we will leave Hungary. and on March, 30. we went in the Night and Baptised again 12. so that we Baptised alltogather 31. Persons in Temesvár. we Baptised 22. after we were forbiden. this was the first Opening in Hungary. and I ordaint Two Elders to Preside over the Branch in Temesvár and to Teach the Saints and watch over them. and on March 31.st it was Sunday, and we invited all our Friends and the Members of the Church, and we kept a Big Metting before we left Hungary. and the Members of the Church, they felt very sorry that we must Depart from them and they weep like Little Children. and when we Start to Shake Hands with them we could not keep our Tears back, and we weep too. then we Bless them and Depart from them.

and on April 1.st we left Hungary and went to Austria in to Oderberg, Shlesien Located by the Germany Borders [more than likely Neu Oderberg, presently Novy Bohumin, Czech Republic, six miles north-northeast of Ostrava]. then Br Shulthess and Br McMurin,[27] they came to see us and we were very glad to meet with them. and Br Shulthess apointed me to Munik [Munich] in Bavaria, Germany [page 80] to Preside over the Munik Branch and Br Lau was apointed to go to Hamburg. and I Baptised 4. Four Persons in Munik. I arrived in Munik April 6th 1901[28] and on July 15 I went to Stuttgart Conference. then I was Releaset in July 27. 1901. and I arrived to Salt Lake August 28. 1901.

On my 2.nd Mission I start on my Second Mission on August 3.rd 1903. and went to Liverpool. and Apostel Lyman[29] Preside over the European Mission, and he Apointed me to go to Russia to find out if I can Open that field. and Apostel Lyman told me that in Russia is Danger and he told me, "if you see that they are after you, Leave Russia and then you can go back again. I dont want that you shall be put in jail. be very careful and Pray the Lord and he will prapare the way for you before you come there." and at the same time Br Lyman Apointed me to Labor unter the German Mission, and the Headquarter of the German and Swis Mission was in Zürich, Br H. J. Cannon[30] Presidet.

and in August 26. I arrived in Zürich, Svizerland, and from there I went to Budapest, Kapitol of Hungary. and on August 31.st I left BudaPest and went to Transilvania, City of Kronstatd (or) Brosso, Hungary [Kronstadt

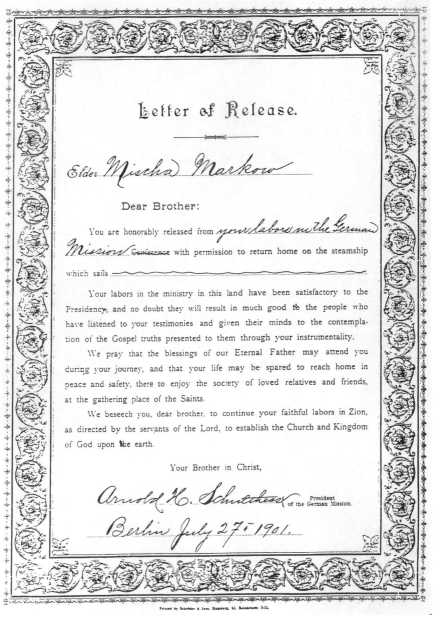

Illus. 8-2. Mischa Markow's 1901 missionary release.

was named Brassó when it was part of Hungary. In 1950 it was renamed Stalin or Orasul Stalin. Presently it is Braşov, Romania]. and then I went to the City Mayor and he give me Permission for 5. weeks to Preach the Gospel. then I could not stay any longer because I was knowen in Hungary and I was banished twice. then I left Hungary and went to Russia.

I came to Warshau [Warsaw] and I was only One Day in Warshau and I notice that there was so many Polish jew. then I did not feel to stay there.[31] then I went to City of Riga, and on October 9.th 1903. I arived in Riga. Riga has 200000. Population and are many Germans, and I had 150. German Tracts with me. and I start to work among [page 81] the Germans inesmuch we do not have Tracts in Russian Language. and the Law in Russia is that any Stranger in 48. hours must Registered his Name in the District Court. so I did not want to go Myself because they will ask me many quastions, but I send the Lady with my Passeport to Register My Name. and the Lady where I did Lodge, she went to the Court, but they did not want to Register My Name. they want me I shall come Myself, so I went. then they ask me what I am doing in the City. I told them that I was a Preacher, and they ask me to which church I belong. I told them the Church of Jesus Christ of Latter Day Saints. and he said to me, "that is a very long Name. I dont have <so> much space in the Book." then he said to me, "dont that church has another Name?" I said, "yes, the Church of Jesus Christ." then he put "Church of Christ," and then he Registered My Name as a Missionar of Church of Crist, but they did not know that I was a Mormon.

and I start right away to work among the Germans, and they were Baptists. and I had Germans Tracts with me. and the Lord was with me and I was blessed and I distributed about 150. Tracts among the German People. and I have had many conversation with Russians so that 3. Germans Family ask for Baptism. and I Preach to the Russian People and I told them that their Priests did not have Authority from God because the Gospel was taken from the Earth, and now in our Days the Gospel is Restored Again. then One German Lady said to me, "Sir, you dont need to tell that Russian Priests dont have Authority. if ~~they~~ you tell them that, they will surely take you from the Streets and send you to Siberia in such a way that no body will know it. look out and be careful what you say to them." and at the same time a German Lady invite me to Dinner. they were Baptists and they did read my Tracts, and they want to be [page 82] Baptised ~~and they invite~~ and they invite Baptist Minister to[o] (Pastor) because he read my Tracts to[o], and he want to see me. and then after we had Dinner, we start to talk about the Church of Christ. then he said to me, "I never tought that Mormon were Christians and have such Perfect Church Organisation." and the Lady who invite me to Dinner said, "I believe that the Church which Mr Markow advocate is the True Church." and when the Pastor hear that, he did not like it. than he start to speak about Poligamy and I felt that he was My Enemy. I dont know for sure, but I believe that the Chief of Police have heard about Poligamy trough Baptist Minister.

I was 28. Days in Riga.[32] then I was Summon to go to Court. and when I appeared in the Court, Chief of Police was very Angry with me, and he introduse Me to City mayor and ask me what I am I doing in the City. I told him I want to find out if I can get Permission to Preach the Gospel and make the People aquanted with church of Jesus Christ, and the Chief of Police said to me, "you are a Mormon and you Preach Poligamy. and why didnt you say when you registered your Name that you was a Mormon?" than I said to him that Mormon is not the Real Name, but that was a Nick Name. the Real Name is Church of Jesus Christ of Latter day Saints. and the Judge comend me to go to the High Court. and right away he call a Soldier with a gun and Bayonet on the Gun to acompany me to the High Court. and when I appeared in the High Court before the Judge, they all come to Look see at me, to see a Mormon. and the Judge was very kind to me and he speak nice to me. he ask me what am I doing in the city. I told him I wants to find out if I can get a Permission to Preach the gospel and make the People aquanted with the Church of Jesus Christ. then he said, "you must go to a Lawyer as and ask him to make a Petition to the Governor. and then if you [page 83] get a Permit from the Governor then you can stay here, otherwise you canot Promulgate Mormon Doctorine."

then I left the Court and I went to a Lawyer and I told him about it. "yes," he said, "but I must know the Name of your church." I told him the Church of Jesus Christ of Latter day Saints. then he ask me if that church has another Name, becouse he said, "I must know all the Principals and Organisation of that church." then I said to him, "the world commonly call us Mormons." and when I said that, he was scared and he said to me, "and you are a mormon?" I said yes. then he said, "I canot take your Case. it will be danger for me to Defend the Mormons." and he said to me, "how did you alow to come to Russia to Preach Mormonisum? dont you know that they will take you Privately and send you to Siberia and nobody will know it?" then I told him again, "I can Explain to you the Doctrine of the Church of Christ from the Bible and New Testament." and he said to me, "you may go to another Lawyer and they may take your case up, but I dont think that you will get Liberty. but I admonish you to be very careful."

before Leaving the City, I went again to visit my German friends and told them that I must go out of Russia because I cant get any Permit to Preach the Gospel. but they told me diferent. they said they can make a Petition to the Governor and all them who read my Tracts, they will sign their Names that I shall remain and Preach the Gospel only among the Protestants and Roman Katholiks, and not Preach to the Russian People. and they told me in that way the Governor will (grant) or give me Permission to stay. and they told me they know that that can be done. but inesmuch Apostol Lyman told me, "if you see that you are in Danger, you must Leave Russia, and after you can go back again." so I did not Know what to do, aldough I was afraid. then I left Russia Novembe. 5th 1903. [page 84] and went to Austria. I arived in Oderberg, Shlesien, Nov. 9th.

then I wrote a Letter to Apostel Lyman all about Russia. and on Dezember 17. 1903. I received a answer and he appointed me to go and Labor in Turkey. and I arived in the City of Aintab, Syria, Turkey [Gaziantep, Turkey, located 115 miles east northeast from Adana], January 8. 1904. Brother Booth,[33] Presidet over the Turkish Mission, and he said to me, "Bro. Markow, I am very glad to see you becouse you was in Turkey before and you know the Country & Citys. and in which part of Turkey would you like to Labor?" I told him I would like to Labor in Alexandrette [Iskenderun, Turkey]. then he said to me, "that is the worst place in Turkey. many Elders were banished out and put in jail. but if you want to go there, you can go." I told him, "I go there. and if I can not stay there then I will go to Konstantinople." then I went to Alexandrette and I start to Distribute some Tracts among the Armenians and Greeks. and One of the Armeniens said to me, "give me a Tract to." and I give him a Tract and after while he came to my ~~p~~ Place and he said he wats to be Baptised, but I ~~toulo~~ told him he must investigate ~~more~~ <longer>. then I give him other Tracts, and after while he came again to me and ask to be Baptised, and I had a Long conversation with him. then we went to Mediterranean Sea in the Night and I Baptised him. and when we Come out of the Water, he kneel down and I lay my Hands upon his head and confirmed him a Member in the Church of Jesus Christ of Latter Day Saints and to receive the Holy Ghost. then he ~~got~~ got up and Bowed his head to the ground before me and took my right Hand and kiss it. then I told him, "dont kiss my Hand. I am not Katholik Priest, but thank God and give glory to him because he revealet to you the True church." then ~~s~~ he start to tell me about his afair. he said to me that he fast it Eleven Days and

Eleven Nights vith out Eating or drinking, and he [page 85] Pray it to the Lord. he wants to know how is his standing before the Lord. and his great Desire was to have comunication with Angels. and in all that time he had a Dream that Four (4). of the ancients Apostels came to him and told him, "the Lord God will send to you a Preacher, and he will tell you what you shall do." and then he told me that I was that Preacher whom the Lord shall send to him, and he became a good member in the Church and paid his full Tithing, and he keep the Sabath Day Holy and he attend it to all his dyuty. his name was Gevorg Dunavetian.

I labor in Turkey up to October 26. 1905. then I went <to> Athen (Attina) Greek [Athens, Greece]. I stay in Athen 5. Days and on November 5.th 1905. I was Released. and on Dezember 9.th I arived in to Salt Lake City.

Now I write here about Laws and rules of Ortodox Church in Russia. in Russia have many Secterians: Baptists, Methodist, Roman Katholiks, Protestants, and many others, but the[y] can not make converts with Russian People who belong to Ortodox Church. they can make converts among them selfs, but not tuch the Russian who belong to Ortodox Church. for instance, if a Missionar (or) Pastor (or) Priest Speaks against the Ortodox Church that they dont have Authority and that it is wrong to worship images, and if some make Complain to their Priests, and the Priest will right away accuse that Minister who Preach it against the ortodox Chuch. the Penalty will be Two years in Siberia Hard Labor. and if a Missionar (or) Pastor Convert and Baptised a Russian Male or Female, and he or she leave the Ortodox Church and belong to Other church, the Penalty is the Minister who convert that Russian to his church, he will get 12. years in Siberia. and that Russian male or Female, Poor or Rich, who leave Russian Church will be Expelt or banished out from Russia. they will give him sertan time to sell his Property, and then he will [page 86] be Banished out of Russia. and he can never return back again to Russia. that was the Penalty of the Russia People, and that law was made in the Holy Sinod by the Russian Priests. and when they send them to Siberia, they are very few who comes back. they keep them there for life. that was the Law in 1903. under the administration of Zar.

Notes

1. Page 1 of the German text contains a few more details about Markow's parentage that shed light on his interest in establishing the Church in Russia: "meine Muter war Eine Echte Romänin und mein Vater stamt von Die Serben, und Die

Serben Die stamen von Rusland. Die komen von Stadt oder Gowern Sorbi von Rusland." Translation: "My mother was a real Romanian and my father comes from the Serbs, and the Serbs, they are from Russia. They come from the city or *Gowern Sorbi* from Russia." All German to English translations done by Matthew Heiss.

2. Jacob Spori was born in Oberwil, Switzerland, in 1847. He was baptized in May 1877 and labored as a missionary in Switzerland in 1879. He emigrated to Utah in July 1879. He filled a mission to Switzerland and Palestine from 1884 to 1887. He was called to serve as president of the Turkish Mission in 1885. He died in 1903. Andrew Jenson, *Latter-day Saint Biographical Encyclopedia: A Compilation of Biographical Sketches of Prominent Men and Women in The Church of Jesus Christ of Latter-day Saints,* 4 vols. (Salt Lake City: Andrew Jenson History, 1901–36), 4:391.

3. Ferdinand Friis Hintze was born in 1854 in Roskilde, Denmark. He was baptized in 1862 and emigrated to Utah in 1864. He served several missions for the Church. His first two were in the Northern States Mission from 1877 to 1878 and from 1879 to 1880. He then served in Scandinavia from 1884 to 1886. He served as president in the Turkish Mission from 1887 to 1889 and 1899 to 1900. He died in 1928. Jenson, *LDS Biographical Encyclopedia,* 4:390–91.

4. Joseph Marion Tanner was born in 1859 in Payson, Utah. He was a member of the Brigham Young Academy's first graduating class in 1878. In 1884 he was called to serve a mission in Germany. In 1885 he was transferred to Turkey to help open the mission there. He returned to Utah in 1887. In 1888 he was elected president of Brigham Young College in Logan, Utah. He later studied law at Harvard University. In 1896 he was elected president of the Agricultural College in Logan, as well as becoming the first Utah Supreme Court reporter. In 1901 he was chosen as second assistant superintendent of the Sunday School. He died in 1927. Jenson, *LDS Biographical Encyclopedia,* 1:709–11.

5. Pages 3 and 4 of the German text contain a bit more detail that shows how Markow viewed himself at this time: "Die Brüder wolten aber das ich mit ihnen weiter verbleiben soll, um das Evangelium zu verbreiten, aber ich bin nicht so beredet und kan nicht so gut Spröchen. und so habe ich mich Entschuldigt den ich Dachte ich tauge nicht zu predigen. und die Brüdern haben mich gesegnet und Gott der Herr war mit mir." Translation: "The brethren wanted me to remain with them to preach the gospel, but I am not eloquent and cannot speak so good. So I excused myself because I thought I was not worthy to preach. And the brethren blessed me and the Lord God was with me."

6. Concerning this event, Ferdinand Hintze wrote: "Feb. 1st 1887. . . . Yesterday Bro. Jacob Spori arrived from Palestine where he has been laboring for some time. He has met with some success among the German colonies in the Holy Land, where he has baptized 3 persons. He has also had the good fortune by following the influence of the spirit of bringing over an honest soul on the way from Alexandria, Egypt, to this city, a Servian. He will be baptized to night all being well. . . . This evening by request of the brethren I baptized the gentleman that Bro. Spori got acquainted with. He is a Serb, but is an Astria Hungarian subject, and is somewhat educated. His name is Micha Markow, and is about years old. [Ed. note: Hintze left a blank in his journal implying that he did not know Markow's age.] If it please the

Lord we intend to use him as a help to get before this people with the gospel as he has some knowledge of the Turkish language. He was confirmed by Elder Tanner." Ferdinand Friis Hintze, Papers, Diaries, 1882–1916, Church Archives, The Church of Jesus Christ of Latter-day Saints, Salt Lake City.

7. In the Markow Papers appears an affidavit written on stationary of the Presiding Bishopric that reads: "Salt Lake City, Utah, March 6th 93 This is to certify that Brother Mischa Markow, born Oct. 21st 1854, at S. Zernia, Torantal Co Hungaria, was ordained an Elder on or about Feb. 26th 1888, at S. zernia, Torantal Co Hungaria, by Elder F. F. Hintze." It is signed by Hintze.

8. Concerning this event, Ferdinand Hintze wrote: "March 10th 1888. The past 6 weeks has been spent in the usual way, reading and studying the Turkish language. Last month I had a letter from Bro. Markow at Serb Czernia, Hungaria, stating his father and mother and 2 more wished baptizm. After some correspondence I started out on the trip." Hintze gives a detailed account of his trip to visit Markow, after which he describes his experiences in the Markow home: "I found Bro. M. and family after but little searching, but was astonished that they were not ready for baptism. We conversed that day upon religious matters and between 100 to 200 people assembled upon hearing the stranger had arrived. Owing to the son not being home we could not perform the rite of baptism. So the 3rd day having arrived the police put in this appearance and I was marched off to the Magistrate and the priest and I was interogated about my business, but as I was no regular missionary to that country I could truthfully state I was only making a visit. This I did, and I got along very well. I was ordered out though just the same after being abused by the priest by being called a beggar and the like. This prevented baptism and perhaps it is just as well as the people were country people that wanted much teaching from all appearance. However I feel well my duty is done and I have seen the people and the country and will be able to give a report about that part of the world in due time. I returned home to Constantinople at once and arrived here March the first."

9. While in London, Markow spent six nights living on the streets because he had no money for lodging. On page 7 of the German text Markow wrote, "Wie Ich in London angekomen bin, Ich konte kein Arbeit bekomen, den ich konte nicht Englisch Sprächen. kein Geld hate Ich auch nicht gehabt. Ich hate in London 6. sex Nächte Darausen geschlafen. Den ich hatte kein Geld Quartier zu zahlen." Translation: "When I arrived in London I could not find any work because I could not speak English. I also had no money. I spent six nights in London sleeping outside because I had no money and could not pay for lodging."

10. On page 9 of the German text, Markow described his appearance, which explains his self-conscious feelings: "Ich war aber sehr schlecht gekleidet so das ich mich schenirt habe ihm zu besuchen, aber den noch bin ich hingegangen. ich habe nur ein Rock gehabt und meine Schuhe waren so schlecht das ich mit schnur verbunden habe so das Sie haben nicht wollen glauben das ich Ein Eldester der Kirche Jesu Christi bin, den ich habe wirklich ausgeschaut wi ein Handwerks borsch." Translation: "However, I was very poorly dressed so that I was embarrassed to visit him, but I went anyway. I only had a coat, and my shoes were in such bad condition that I kept them together with a string, so that they would not believe

that I was an elder in the Church of Jesus Christ, because I really looked like a working-class boy."

11. Henrietta Conradine Esselmann was born on May 26, 1849, in Werther, Westphalia, Germany. She married Friedrich Gottfried Pieper and had six children with him. She was living with Carl (or possibly his name was Rudolph) Beckhaus when she first met Markow. She had three children with Beckhaus. She immigrated to Salt Lake City with seven of her children in 1892. Her husband, a seaman, did not follow her to America. She was endowed in the Salt Lake Temple on December 1, 1893. She was a member of the Twentieth Ward in Salt Lake City. An entry dated July 9, 1897, from the Twentieth Ward Teachers' meeting minutes reads: "Bro. [William] Service reported that Sister Essellman was very sick and wished the prayers of the brethren in her behalf." Twentieth Ward, General Minutes, Church Archives. She died in Salt Lake City, Utah, on July 20, 1897. Her obituary, which appeared on page 2 of the *Deseret Evening News* on July 21, 1897, reads: "Esselman – July 20th 1897, at the Holy Cross hospital, Salt Lake City, through cancer of the bowels. . . . she was operated upon twice for this desease [*sic*]." Bobette Mitchell Beck, Esselmann's great-granddaughter, told the editor that Beckhaus was a seaman and did not emigrate with Esselmann. Bobette Mitchell Beck to Matthew Heiss, March 2, 2000, in possession of author.

12. Markow lived with and was supported by this family. On page 11 of the German text he wrote, "und Ich blieb bei Dieser familien zwei monate lang." Translation: "And I stayed with this family for two months."

13. John Ulrich Stucki was born in 1837 in Ober-Neunforn, Switzerland. He was baptized in 1856. He emigrated to the United States in 1852. He was in Williamsburg, New York, from 1852 to 1860, after which he moved to Utah. He was president of the Swiss, German, and Italian Mission from 1874 to 1876. He returned to Europe to serve as president of the Swiss and German Mission in 1888–90. He died in 1918. Jenson, *LDS Biographical Encyclopedia*, 2:29–30.

14. In the 1880s and 1890s, Belgium was part of the North German Conference of the Swiss and German Mission. Jacob Grimm, a traveling elder, was in Belgium at the end of 1891. See Swiss and German Mission, Manuscript History, December 31, 1891, Church Archives. The Brandley referred to in this passage was likely Theodore Brandley, who served as president of the Swiss and German Mission from 1889 to 1890. His journals contain references to his visiting the Latter-day Saints in Belgium. See Theodore Brandley, Journals, November 25–27, 1890, Church Archives. See also Jenson, *LDS Biographical Encyclopedia*, 1:387–88. Further information about the Elder Tailor (or Taylor) mentioned by Markow is not available.

15. It took Markow, who was traveling without purse or scrip, two months to travel from Belgium to Romania. On pages 12 to 14 of the German text, he described in greater detail his travels to Romania. Portions of his narrative are quoted here: "dan wolte ich nach Deutschland Reisen in dem ich aber nur 3. frangen Franken Geld gehabt habe, so bin ich zum östereichische Konsulat gegangen um ein wenig unterstützt zu werden. Der Konsulat gibt mir 2. frangen und er fragte mir ich soll für die 2. frangen bilet kaufen und nach Brüssel zu fahren. Ich aber damit ich die

2. frangen ersparen soll, so bin ich zu fuß gereist. und bin über die Nacht daraus geschlafen, wi wohl ich schon mehr Nächte daraus geschlafen habe. so gar in der Regen und auch in der Schne, in grosse kälten wi ich in anderen Tag nach Brüssel (Bruxel) angekomen bin." Translation: "I wanted to travel to Germany, but since I only had three francs, I went to the Austrian consulate to get a bit of support. The consul gave me two francs and told me I should buy a two franc ticket and ride to Brussels. But to save the two francs, I walked. I slept outside, as I have done on many a night, in fact in the rain and also in the snow, in great cold, as I arrived in Brussels." Markow visited foreign consuls seeking travel funds. To save money, he often walked, as noted in this brief passage, "und so bin ich zu fuß durch ganz Deutschland gereist 28. Tage bis ich auf die Böhmische gränze angekomen bin in die Stadt Egert [Markow probably means Eger, presently located in northern Hungary twenty-four miles from Miskolc, which at the time had the German name Erlau]." Translation: "And so I walked through Germany in twenty-eight days until I reached the Bohemian border and arrived at the city Egert." At this town he attempted to get a free train ride to Hungary, but only got as far as Vienna. From Vienna, he walked to Romania: "so bin ich zu fuß gereist von Wien bis nach Romänien. zwei 2. volle Monate bin ich gereist oder hat die reise gedauert bis ich nach Romänien angekomen bin." Translation: "So I walked from Vienna to Romania. Two full months I was underway or it took to travel until I arrived in Romania."

16. On page 15 of the German text, Markow wrote a more detailed description of his journey to Utah: "in 6. Oktober in Jahre 1891. bin ich nach Newjork angekomen. ich arbeitete in Newjork zwei 2. Monate und dan reiste ich nach Chikago. Ich arbeitete in Chicago neun 9. Monate dan Reiste ich nach Utah Salz See Stadt. ich kam in Salz See Stadt im October 1892." Translation: "I arrived in New York on 6 October 1891. I worked in New York for two months then traveled to Chicago. I worked in Chicago nine months then traveled to Salt Lake City, Utah. I arrived in Salt Lake City in October 1892." A brief article appeared on page 8 in the *Deseret Evening News* on October 17, 1892, announcing the arrival of Mischa Markow under the title of "An Arrival from the Orient": "Mr. Mischa Markow, a native of Servia, favored us with a call this morning. He embraced the Gospel in Constantinople in 1887. Some time afterwards he left the orient and has now been in the United States about a year. He arrived in Salt Lake City yesterday. Like most of the sons of the East, he is a polyglot, speaking fluently half a dozen different languages. He says he feels well and is glad to see our fair Territory, of which he has heard so much."

17. On page 17 of the German text, Markow wrote that after being banished from Serbia, he returned to his home and preached the gospel for two weeks: "Der Polizist bekleidete [begleitete] mich bis nach Eisenbahn bis ich in die wagon Eingestiegen bin. und so haben Sie mich nach Ungarn Expedirt. Ich ging gleich zu meinen Eltern wo ich geboren war und brachte dort 2. zwei Wochen an in Predigen das Evangelium." Translation: "The policeman accompanied me to the train until I got in the car, and so he banished me to Hungary. I went right to my parents where I was born and spent two weeks preaching the gospel."

18. Markow was granted American citizenship on September 12, 1898. His Certificate of Citizenship is in his Papers.

19. Philip Starkey Maycock was born in 1872 in Salt Lake City. He served as president of the Turkish Mission from 1897 to 1899. He died in Salt Lake City in 1907. Jenson, *LDS Biographical Encyclopedia*, 4:243, 391.

20. Doctrine and Covenants 84:88 reads: "And whoso receiveth you, there I will be also, for I will go before your face. I will be on your right hand and on your left, and my Spirit shall be in your hearts, and mine angels round about you, to bear you up."

21. Little is known about Argir Dimitrow. The German Mission, Record of Members, in the Church Archives lists the following information: Argir Dimitrow was forty-six and single when he was baptized by Markow on July 3, 1899, in the Black Sea. He was living in Bucharest. He was born in Stanimaka, Bulgaria, which in 1934 had its name changed to Asenovgrad.

22. "Perfect"—Markow no doubt meant *prefect.*

23. Little is known about Michael Dimitrow. The German Mission, Record of Members, in the Church Archives includes the following information: "Michail Dimitrow" living in Bucharest when he was baptized by Markow on April 15, 1900. He was born in 1879 in Malkara or Malgara, Turkey, which is on the Europe side of Turkey.

24. The book that Markow saw was probably John Hanson Beadle's *The History of Mormonism. Life in Utah; or The mysteries and crimes of Mormonism. Being an exposé of the secret rites and ceremonies of the Latter-day Saints, with a full and authentic history of polygamy and the Mormon sect from its origin to the present time,* which was translated into Russian and published in St. Petersburg, Russia, in 1872. This was one of the few anti-Mormon texts published in the Cyrillic alphabet, which Markow mistakenly calls "Bulgarien Caracter and in Bulgarien Language." See Chad J. Flake, *A Mormon Bibliography, 1830–1930* (Salt Lake City: University of Utah Press, 1978), entry number 358.

25. Arnold Henry Schulthess was born in 1865 in Neukirch, Switzerland. He was baptized in 1882. In 1898 he was called to preside over the German Mission. He returned to Utah in 1901 and died in 1924. Jenson, *LDS Biographical Encyclopedia,* 1:598–99.

26. Hyrum Moroni Lau was born in Providence, Utah, in 1870. He served a mission in Germany from 1899 to 1901. He later served as bishop of the Soda Springs Ward, Idaho Stake. He died in 1927. Jenson, *LDS Biographical Encyclopedia,* 4:492.

27. James Leaing McMurrin (1864–1902) served as first counselor to Francis M. Lyman, president of European Mission. Concerning this meeting, McMurrin wrote in his journal under April 2, 1901: "We took the train to Breslau, seperated here from the rest of the party and Pres. Schulthess and I went to Oderburg to meet Elders Markow and Lau who were recently banished from Temesvár, Hungary. They have done a fine work there, 31 having been baptized in five months, all Catholics but one. The priests were at the bottom of the banishment. Two local brethren were ordained Elders however and will continue the work. A fine lot of people have been found in this field. We met our Brethren and had a Joyful time. It was decided to send one of them to Hamburg and the other to Munich. . . . We took a long walk by moonlight on a nice road and had an interesting time with the brethren." James Leaing McMurrin, Journal, 1899–1901, Church Archives.

28. On pages 31 and 32 of the German text Markow wrote additional details about his stay in Munich: "Die Gemeinde war 104. Mitglieder und ich taufte am 9. Mai noch 2. zwei Personen. so ging es mir sehr gut und am 15. Mai segnete ich 2. Kinder. aber in München haben wir keine freiheit. und wir hielten versamlungen in verschidene Plaze, bei die Mitglieder in geheimen das die Polizei uns nicht erwischen soll, und wir haten viele feinde und durch unsere feinde sind wir auf einmal angezeigt worden. und am 24. Juni 1901. in einen Sontag wehrend wir versamlung abhielten komt ein komissar mit 3. drei Polizisten in der versamlung. es war ungefehr 50. Personen. und Sie haben uns alle die Namen aufgeschrieben. dan haben sie uns eine Wahrnung (Note) geschikt. das wen wir uns noch einmal wieder versameln werden, dan werden sie Mitglieder bestrafen mit 20. Mark und die Missionare ausweisen. ich ordinierte am 29. Juni Br. Wishen ein Deakon in die Kirche Jesu Christi zu sein. und am 11. Juli taufte ich noch 2. zwei Personen. am 13. und 14. Juli nahm ich abschid von die Heilige zu München." Translation: "The branch had 104 members, and I baptized two persons on 9 May. Things went well for me. On 15 May I blessed two children. However, in Munich we had no freedom. We held our meetings in different places in the homes of the members in secret so the police could not discover us. We had many enemies. Through our enemies we were all of a sudden discovered. On 24 June 1901, on a Sunday as we were having our meeting, the commissioner and three police officers came to the meeting. There were approximately fifty people. They wrote down all the names. They sent us a warning that if we were caught meeting again the members would be fined twenty Marks, and the missionaries would be kicked out. I ordained Brother Wishen a deacon in the Church of Jesus Christ on 29 June. On 11 July I baptized two more people. And on 13 and 14 July I departed from the Saints in Munich."

29. Francis Marion Lyman was born in 1840 in Illinois, the eldest son of Amasa M. Lyman. He arrived in the Great Salt Lake Valley in 1848. He was ordained an Apostle on October 27, 1880, by John Taylor. He died as President of the Quorum of the Twelve Apostles in 1916. Of particular interest to the Markow journal is that Lyman served as president of European Mission from 1901 to 1904. Also, Lyman dedicated Russia for missionary work in 1903. Jenson, *LDS Biographical Encyclopedia*, 1:136–41. See also Gary L. Browning, "Out of Obscurity: The Emergence of The Church of Jesus Christ of Latter-day Saints in 'That Vast Empire' of Russia," *BYU Studies* 33, no. 4 (1993): 674–88, and Kahlile Mehr, "The 1903 Dedication of Russia for Missionary Work," *Journal of Mormon History* 13 (1986–87): 111–23.

30. Hugh Jenne Cannon was born in 1870 in Salt Lake City, the son of George Q. Cannon. He served as a missionary in Germany from 1901 to 1905 and was chosen to be mission president while on his mission. He later served as president of the Liberty Stake in Salt Lake City from 1905 to 1923. He again presided over the Swiss-German Mission from 1925 to 1928. He also served as a member of the General Board of the YMMIA and the Sunday School Board. He died in 1931. Jenson, *LDS Biographical Encyclopedia*, 4:233, 507.

31. On pages 34 and 35 of the German text Markow wrote about additional reasons for his not staying in Warsaw: "Ich kam nach Warschau Russisch Pol. und wi ich die stadt angesehen hatte da sprächen sehr wenig Russisch. man Sprächt

bei nahe überall Polnisch. und sind auch viele Polische juden in die Stadt. und ich fühlte mich so das ich dort nichtz machen kan. in dem aber ich gehört habe das in Riga viele Deutsche sind, so bin ich nach Riga abgereißt." Translation: "I arrived in Warsaw, Russian Poland, and as I toured the city there were few who spoke Russian. Nearly everyone spoke Polish. And there were many Polish Jews in the city. I felt I could not accomplish anything there. But I had heard that there were many Germans in Riga, so I left for Riga."

32. Warsaw and Riga were part of the Russian Empire in 1903. "In 1709–10 the Russians took Riga, and Sweden formally ceded the city by the Treaty of Nystad in 1721. By 1914 Riga was the third largest city of Russia." *The New Encyclopedia Britannica,* 29 vols. (Chicago: Encyclopedia Britannica, 1994), 10:66. Russian influence in Warsaw culminated in the Russo-Polish War of 1831, which began thirty years of military rule. A revolt broke out in 1863, which was suppressed a year later. "Warsaw became a provincial city of the Russian Empire's 'Vistula Land.' A period of Russification was launched. . . . After World War I the city regained its status as the national capital." *New Encyclopedia Britannica,* 29:698.

33. Joseph Wilford Booth was born in Alpine, Utah, in 1866. He served as president of the Turkish Mission from 1904 to 1909 and 1921 to 1924. He then became president of the Armenian Mission in 1924 and served in that capacity until his death in 1928, which occurred while he was still in the mission field. He is buried in Aleppo, Syria. Jenson, *LDS Biographical Encyclopedia,* 4:305. A typescript of Booth's diary is in the Church Archives and contains a reference that the Booths and Markow traveled to the mission field together in August 1903. It contains several other references to Markow's missionary assignments and his association with President Booth. For more information on Booth's first mission to Turkey (1898–1902), see David P. Charles, "The Day the 'Brave Sons of Mohamed' Saved a Group of Mormons," *BYU Studies* 40, no. 4 (2001): 237–50.

Index

Numbers in italics indicate illustrations.

About the Authors and Artist

Kahlile B. Mehr holds an MA in family and local history as well as a master's in library science from Brigham Young University. He works at the Family History Library in Salt Lake City, where he helps develop the collections of eastern Europe, the Iberian Peninsula, and the Pacific Islands. He also is a retired lieutenant colonel in the U.S. Army Reserve. He has received the Mormon History Association's T. Edgar Lyon Award three times, once for best article of the year and twice for excellence. He co-authored the widely circulated *Hearts Turned to the Fathers: A History of the Genealogical Society of Utah* published by BYU Studies in 1995.

Matthew K. Heiss received a bachelor's degree at Brigham Young University in humanities. He earned a master's degree from the University of Virginia in history of religion. In 1987 he began working at Church Archives, where he is responsible for documenting Church history in Europe and Africa.

Ljiljana Crnogaj Fuleep, a graduate of the Zagrab School of Art, painted the scene that is detailed on the cover. Entitled *Missionaries*, this work is oil on glass, and it features her ancestral village in the former Yugoslavia. In 1987 she and her family converted to the Church; two years later, she became a Relief Society president in Croatia. The Museum of Church History and Art in Salt Lake City commissioned Sister Fuleep to create this painting in 1990.